To Ch[...]ham

b[...]

Candan Pearson

Mar. 1992

Children of Glasnost

Children of Glasnost
Growing Up Soviet

Landon Pearson

LESTER
&ORPEN
DENNYS
PUBLISHERS

Canadian Cataloguing in Publication Data

Pearson, Landon
　Children of glasnost

Includes bibliographical references.

ISBN 0-88619-249-8

1. Children - Soviet Union.　2. Education - Soviet
Union.　3. Politics and education - Soviet Union.
4. Education of children.　I. Title.

LA832.P43　1990　　　370'.947　　　C90-094432-3

Jacket design by Avril Orloff

Printed and bound in Canada

Lester & Orpen Dennys Limited
Toronto, Canada

To my husband who took me there
To my children who taught me what to look for
To my grandchildren for whom it all matters

Contents

Preface

Writing about any aspect of a society that is as deep in the throes of social and political change as the Soviet Union today is a daunting task. But there is a genre, which scholars describe as "the history of the present", and to which I believe this book belongs, that accepts such an undertaking as legitimate as long as the current scene is shown as integrated in historical continuity. With this in mind, I have given an historical dimension to every chapter; without it, what I have to say about the making of this generation of Soviet children would not be very meaningful. Most of the events now taking place in the Soviet Union have roots in the Revolution of 1917, or in the early years of the Soviet state. The formative years of a nation born in revolution can be just as important for its future development as the formative years of those who will grow up to be its future citizens. This is especially likely when, as in the Soviet Union, institutions were deliberately designed to shape a new kind of person.

Mikhail Gorbachev and others now refer to the current period of Soviet history as a second revolution. This means that the USSR is passing through a second formative stage, and what is happening in Soviet children's lives becomes exceptionally important for the future. In writing this book, I have tried to capture the general direction of the changes that are taking place in Soviet society and to suggest what influence these changes are likely to have on Soviet children now in their formative years.

This book has taken me a long time to write. It was conceived while my husband and I were still living in Moscow, and since we left the USSR in the autumn of 1983, I have returned five times in order to keep abreast of changes. (My last visit was in the spring of 1989, just after elections to the new Congress of People's Deputies.) The subject is large and complex, and I have been challenged by the task of organizing the material I gathered so that it would reflect, as accurately as possible, the distinctive patterns of culture that embraced the vast majority of children who grew up in the Soviet Union during the 1980s. To grasp these patterns, which are themselves in the process of change, I immersed myself for several years in Soviet studies, acquiring along the way the rudiments of not just one but two new languages—Russian, and the rhetoric of Soviet ideology. Studying the rhetoric has no more made me a Marxist-Leninist than speaking the language has made me a Russian, but knowledge of both has been essential to my understanding of the historical and political context of Soviet childhood, past and present.

In particular, it was important for me to gain some understanding of what Soviet authorities and Communist Party members actually meant during the 1980s when they referred to communism. Here is an official definition that dates from 1982: communism is a "social and economic formation…based on public ownership of the means of production". Socialism is the lowest level of communism, which, when it finally comes into existence, will be "a highly organized society of free, socially conscious working people in which public self-government will be established [and] labour for the good of society will become the prime vital requirement of everyone". No one now denies the many evils that have been committed in the name of communism, yet its central vision remains one of economic and social justice. I have no doubt from what he says that Gorbachev continues to believe in this vision and so I expect that Soviet children will continue to be taught that a collective society, in which everyone is prepared to pull his or her weight for the good of the whole, is what they should aim for. I will spell out, where appropriate, other messages about communism that the Soviet children of the 1980s were exposed to as they were growing up, but it is important to keep in mind the basic proposition from which these messages derived.

Understanding the ideological context of Soviet childhood was only half the battle. The other half was applying to this understanding my knowledge of children and of child development. To this task I came better equipped. Raising five lively children in the enriching but disruptive conditions of foreign-service life gave me a good deal of practical experience. So did the years I spent working in schools, as a professional and as a parent-volunteer. Along the way, I earned a graduate degree in educational psychology and added an understanding of how cultural differences are shaped in childhood by working with local children in the various countries to which we were posted—France, Mexico, and India.

I spent 1979 as the vice-chairperson of the Canadian Commission for the International Year of the Child. This responsibility introduced me to a whole range of children's policy issues and opened doors for me in the Soviet Union that might have remained closed to an ambassador's wife; being an ambassador's wife opened others, particularly outside of Moscow. After my return to Canada, I became president of the Canadian Council on Children and Youth and continued to work with a children's mental-health program in the elementary school. These activities provided me with an ongoing basis for comparing the conditions of North American and Soviet childhoods throughout the entire decade of the 1980s. While this book is an examination of a specific society in the process of change, and is not intended as a comparative study, I believe it is useful to reflect on how children are growing up within our own borders and learn what we can from the Soviet example.

Ottawa, May, 1990

Acknowledgements

Writing this book has brought me two unexpected pleasures; the first has been the new friends and acquaintances I have made along the way, and the second, the support and practical assistance of so many of my old friends and relatives. I am indebted to each and every one of them because, without them, I would undoubtedly have given up once I discovered how difficult the task I had undertaken was turning out to be. I would like to thank Katherine Beaton, John Flood, Nancy and Charles Gordon, William Kilbourn, Jane Legg, Dr. Monique Lussier, Jacqueline Neatby, Calvin Rand, Dr. Anna Sharpe, Susan Thomas, Dr. Bea Wickett-Nesbit, and Claire Ziegler, all of whom took time to read and comment on several chapters, or helped me in some other way. I would especially like to thank Paul and Judy Meyer, Elizabeth Robinson, and Dr. Lloyd Strickland, who read the entire text with care and made invaluable suggestions. Members of my family, particularly my children, my brother Hugh Mackenzie, and my sisters-in-law Dorothy Mackenzie and Patricia Hannah, were also very helpful. I only regret that my mother, who was at least able to read every chapter in manuscript, did not live long enough to see the book in print.

Then there are the specialists who have added immeasurably to the content by their comments on individual chapters: Dr. Urie Bronfenbrenner ("Vospitanie"); Dr. Alex Kozulin, Dr. Michael Cole, and Dr. Jaan Valsiner ("Growing Up Human"); Dr. Yury Luryi and the Hon. Gordon Fairweather ("Child Welfare and Juvenile Justice"); Dr. Terry Laughlin, Dr. Andrew Sutton, Michael Lambert ("Special Schools"); Dr. Norman Schniedmann and Dr. Jim Riordan ("Games"); Joan Askwith ("Books"); Dr. Geoffrey Robinson and Shirley Post ("Health"); Dr. John Dunstan, Jeanne Sutherland and other members of the U.K. Soviet Education Study Group (all the chapters related to education); Walter Slipchenko and John Hannigan ("Unity in Diversity", with special reference to native peoples); Dr. Eric Chivian and the late King Gordon ("War and Peace"). I am grateful to all of them for their thoughtful comments and hold none of them responsible for my conclusions.

On the Soviet side, I would like to thank the Canadian Embassy in Moscow, the Ministry of Foreign Affairs of the USSR, Freda Lurie of the Soviet Writers' Union, members of the Soviet Women's Committee, and all the other individuals who, out of their care and concern for children, met and talked to me so freely everywhere I went. In particular, I would like to thank Dr. Igor Kon, Dr. Vladimir Lubovsky, Dr. Viktor Perevedentsev, and Simon Soloveychik for their extraordinary insights and advice. And a special thanks to Nina Ryan for helping me in so many ways—translating, commenting, and showing me the reality of motherhood in the Soviet Union. I would also like to express my gratitude to our successors at the Embassy, Peter and Glenna Roberts and Vernon and Beryl Turner, for their hospitality and support, and to Ann and Christopher Young for welcoming me to their apartment on two of my return visits.

I have enjoyed working with everyone at Lester & Orpen Dennys, and it is hard to single anyone out. However, I am grateful to Beverley Beetham Endersby for her careful editing, and I would particularly like to commend Kirsten Hanson for shepherding the book through the production process.

Finally, there are seven people without whom this book would never have seen the light of day; my daughter Hilary who patiently read first drafts, second drafts, fifth drafts, and final drafts of every chapter, editing me tactfully for both sense and structure; my friend Ronald Bryden who with equal patience and tact edited me for content and style; Victoria Ivanova, my Soviet research assistant who organized my visits and interviews in Moscow with admirable persistence and endless telephone calls, translating and interpreting when necessary and keeping me fully supplied with the information I needed; Eugenia Lockwood, my indispensable research assistant in Ottawa, who read and commented on the stacks of Russian-language materials I kept bringing back from the USSR, translated the extracts I needed, and took responsibility for all transliterations; Heather Morrison who typed and retyped my manuscript more times than either of us cares to remember and did so with a skilfulness I would not have believed possible, as well as cheerfulness and interest; Louise Dennys, my editor, who never flagged in her encouragement as the years went on and whose comments were always sensitive and apt; and finally, my husband, Geoffrey, who put up with the prolonged disruption of our domestic environment with humour and always made me feel that I was engaged in a true endeavour. My heartfelt thanks to them all.

Notes to the Reader

Transliteration

To preserve consistency in transliterating Russian personal and place names, as well as various terms and idioms quoted in Russian, the MLA System I of Transliteration of Modern Russian into English (J. Thomas Shaw, *The Transliteration of Modern Russian for English-Language Publications* [New York: The Modern Language Association of America, 1979]) is used throughout the text with the exception of those well-known proper names and terms that have become familiar to an English-speaking reader in a different transliteration: e.g., Lake Baikal, Tchaikovsky, Izvestia, perestroika, etc.

School Grading System

Because the school reform, adding an extra year at the bottom end of the system, will not be completed until the 1990s I have used the old grade numbers throughout the text. As the children who entered grade one at the age of six in 1985 move up the ladder the grades will change with them and eventually what is now known as grade ten will become grade eleven.

Introduction

The Canadian Embassy stands on a quiet street in the old Arbat, a pleasant residential quarter of Moscow, not far from the Kremlin Wall. Facing the Embassy gates, in a decaying four-storey building of indeterminate age, is School no. 59. When my husband and I arrived in Moscow at the beginning of October 1980, the school year was already well under way. From the windows of our official Residence, a large apartment on the Embassy's second floor, we soon began to take note of the daily comings and goings of the students. We peered regularly into their busy classrooms, down at the machine shop in the basement or up at what appeared to be a chemistry lab on the top floor. Every day, through the great arched window directly across from us, we stared at the back of an outsized bust of Lenin brooding over the assembly hall. Until the snow came, the children played noisily under the trees in the packed-earth schoolyard. In winter, they set out for the nearby Garden Boulevard, carrying cross-country skis. In April, on Lenin's birthday, they swept away the debris from the playground and tidied up the front of the school. Then, in May, exams over, they streamed away, laughing and joking, swinging their empty satchels.

Over the summer, the dust settled and greenery sprouted from the plaster moulding above the school's heavy central door. Only in late August were there new signs of activity. Solid Soviet ladies in paint-spattered coveralls and white head scarves arrived with buckets of peach-coloured wash, which they spread on the outside wall with long-handled mops. Some reedy young men wiped the windows and repaired the battered wooden desks. One day, a new spray of plastic carnations garnished the small plaque to the left of the entrance that commemorated an event in the Great Patriotic War.

On September 1, we awoke to a tremendous chattering outside the Embassy. Rushing to the window, we looked out on a delightful sight—little children on their way to school for the very first time. Arriving in their brand-new uniforms, boys in blue-grey, girls in dark brown serge with white pinafores and huge bows in their hair, they were all carrying, in the hand that was not clutching tightly the reassuring one of mother or father, a bouquet of fresh flowers. The children and their parents went into the school, presumably to register. When they came out again, each small subdued child was entrusted to an older one standing lined up on the sidewalk. Every little separation was a personal event to those of us who were watching. The child was embraced, the small hand released and pressed into the hand of the senior student, and then the two of them waited, close together, for the signal to enter the school building. Parents and relatives milled about in the street, talking and laughing and taking photographs. Monitors marched back and forth, shouting through miniature megaphones to produce a semblance of order. The little children looked about them at the crowd and then up into the faces of their new protectors. Then off they all moved in uneven procession, waving their red gladioli, their yellow and white asters, their pink and purple phlox.

It was obvious to me as I watched the door shutting behind the last of them that an extraordinary effort was being made to allay the apprehension of all those uncertain seven-year-olds who were about to enter the formal school system. And they had every right to feel nervous. Most of them had already been to kindergarten, probably to nursery school. But kindergarten in the Soviet Union is, for the most part, a comfortable and undemanding place, where the emphasis is on health and play, on team games, dancing, singing, and other forms of group activity suitable to the youngest citizens of a collective society. Now the children were going to have to learn to read and write and do arithmetic as well as study, each and every one of them, the documents of the XXVI Congress of the Communist Party of the Soviet Union.

This scene made a powerful impression on me. I liked the warmth and colour of it, the ceremony, the sense of family and community support. I liked the fact that it was the littlest pupils who were the focus of attention, that the relationship between the older and younger children spoke of trust and responsibility, that going to school was held in such high esteem. I was less certain about some of the ideas I knew the children would be encountering once they passed through the school door. It was clear, however, that none of the parents and relatives, neighbours and friends who had come to school with the children had the slightest intention of abandoning them outright to the tutelage of the State. On the contrary, there was every indication they intended to remain important agents in their children's lives. As I reflected on the ritual of the first day of school, I realized that what I had just witnessed was a special manifestation of that collective concern for children that has long been such a significant feature of Soviet life.

It is now nine years since those seven-year-olds entered the doors of School no. 59. For them childhood is nearly over. For almost a decade, the schools and other child-related institutions in the Soviet Union have been preparing them and their friends to carry the "historic destiny of their nation" into the twenty-first century. But the nation in which they are coming of age is in the process of radical change. Under Gorbachev, the political system is being restructured in ways that would have been unimaginable in 1981. The transformation of cultural life is just as dramatic. Social and economic conditions are changing more slowly, much too slowly for some, but the changes are real.

As a result of these changes, the book I started is not the book that I have completed. I started out to write about Soviet childhood as a way of understanding Soviet society. If I could learn enough about the system that turned Soviet children into Soviet citizens, then perhaps I could discover why the Soviet society I encountered in the early 1980s was in many ways so strange and contradictory. But, as soon as I began to investigate the subject, I discovered that the system of childhood socialization that I wanted to focus on—the making of the so-called new Soviet man (or woman)—was already changing. In spite of what seemed at the time total stagnation, a great deal of constructive activity was going on under the surface; a coral reef was being built in the sea, ready to emerge into the air as soon as the climate changed. For everywhere I went in the USSR during Brezhnev's last days, I would meet parents and grandparents, teachers and school administrators, psychologists and doctors, artists and writers, and a host of other people (including Party officials) who cared so deeply about children as individuals and about childhood as promise that each one of them was doing what he or she could to create a more open and humane society for the children of the future. This is what makes this generation of children so interesting and so exciting to write about.

The children I watched entering school in 1981 are members of a generation that is unique in Soviet history. Not only are they the first to be growing up in the ferment of *glasnost, perestroika,* and what Gorbachev has been calling "new thinking" about international affairs but they are doing so on the shoulders, so to speak, of adults who cared enough about them to make a difference. These children are still stamped with the Soviet hallmark but they are different from their predecessors. And, if some of them become Communist Party members, as some of them still may, they will be communists in Gorbachev's mould, not Stalin's.

There is already evidence that this generation is more optimistic and forward-looking than the one before it, a generation blunted by stagnation and scarred by Afghanistan. This is good news for Gorbachev because it is the children of *glasnost* who will provide his successors with the human resources of knowledge, imagination, energy, and commitment that the Soviet Union must have if it is to survive its first hundred years as a state.

This is good news for the rest of us as well. For we are moving into a new era. The cold war has come to an end, and beyond the issues of war and peace that have separated us for so long, it is now possible to see the global problems that we share: the degradation of the environment, the unequal balance between North and South, the human limits to growth. As the century turns, our children and grandchildren will almost certainly have to co-operate with this new Soviet generation if the human race is to continue.

So what are they like, the members of this generation, the children of *glasnost*? In order to describe them I have organized my book in the following manner. The first chapter focuses on the Kremlin as a way of introducing the historical, political, and ideological context of contemporary Soviet children's lives. What is going on there now is very important for this generation of children. But so is what went on there in the past, for the Soviet children of the 1980s will always be distinguished from children who grew up in other countries during the same decade by the uniqueness of Soviet history, and by the force, even as it dissipates, of communist ideology.

The next five chapters are devoted to the formative years of Soviet children and to the quality of their daily lives. Child-rearing practices in the family and the social upbringing that continues to be advocated by the State set the tone for a child's life at home and at school. In the Soviet family and the Soviet school the atmosphere is changing, but slowly. In fact, the major difference over the decade was probably the greater openness with which problems were discussed and the wider variety of acceptable solutions. Children's daily lives are affected, and not only in the Soviet Union, by the sex roles that they are taught. So Chapter 5 is about boys and girls together. The quality of a child's life is also influenced by the stage he or she is at, so the subject of Chapter 6 is child development according to Soviet psychology.

The next section of the book, "The Best Interests of the Child", focuses on the provisions the Soviet state makes for children with special needs: the handicapped (and the gifted); the orphaned, abandoned, and poor; the delinquent; the sick. Chapters 7, 8, and

9 are devoted to special-education provisions; the child-welfare and juvenile-justice systems; and the child-health system. These systems, with all their flaws, reflect the Soviet state's long-standing commitment to its children.

Chapters 10, 11, and 12 concentrate on the cultivation of children's bodies through physical culture, sports, and recreation, and on the nurture of children's souls through art and literature. Art for children and children's literature, particularly the latter, have probably had more to do with conserving the magic of childhood in the Soviet Union during the darkest periods of that country's history than anything else. The innovative artistic programs that have been introduced into the schools during the 1980s should be of particular interest for the future.

The last three chapters of the book describe the education of the young Soviet citizen. Educating its young to be devoted workers, socialist internationalists, and patriots committed to the virtues of communism is a task that has preoccupied the Soviet state since the time of Lenin. It has never been easy. Over and over again the heavy hand of ideology has quashed better intentions. The generation of students who left school in the 1970s and early 1980s was better educated than any of its predecessors, yet it may turn out to be the least public-spirited one that the Soviet Union has ever produced, so completely was it alienated by the empty rhetoric and the hypocrisy of the so-called period of stagnation. The children of *glasnost,* however, will be different. They are spending their formative years in a changing climate where they are experiencing more openness and freedom of choice as well as more uncertainty than has any preceding generation. The book concludes with a study of the collected wishes of some younger children in the Soviet Union as a way of testing how the wind is blowing.

There are two threads that link each chapter to all the others: the first is the process of growing up human, which is universal; the second is the process of growing up Soviet, which is not. Every day thousands of babies are born in the Soviet Union. In Moscow and Kiev, Tashkent and Magadan, bundles of human possibility snuggle in their mothers' arms. Each one can expect to make a personal journey shaped by universal human experiences. But each one will also make a social journey according to a Soviet road-map. How these two journeys are joined is what will shape the behaviour of the adult Soviet citizen, behaviour that may not be what the State nor, indeed, the child's parents had in mind.

The human journey is primary. How it starts and what happens along the way during the formative years is what conditions a child's response to everything else that may occur during the course of a lifetime. Was the child cherished and respected and nurtured with care? Or mistreated and neglected? These questions are so basic to the human condition that they can be asked about children growing up anywhere in the world. And the answers that are forthcoming help to explain how any individual child will interact with the emotionally charged webs of culture that all societies spin around their young.

Studying these two linked processes, the process of growing up human and the process of growing up Soviet, has thrown light on them both. As I investigated the social forces shaping children in the Soviet Union, I noted that some were more effective than others and came to respect more than ever the capacity some children have to shape their own destinies, a capacity all children must be encouraged to develop. This is what is now slowly beginning to happen in the USSR.

Predictions are risky in an area that is as complex as the making of a generation, but my final conclusion is one of cautious optimism. It is true that Gorbachev and his colleagues are faced with massive problems: an economy that scarcely functions, an empire in dissolution, an entrenched bureaucracy, a dissaffected population. And yet new civil structures are beginning to emerge and youngsters are showing signs of taking charge of their own lives. The long-term future looks bright and this generation should be much better equipped to take advantage of openings than its immediate predecessors. So, barring an unforeseeable castastrophe, I am hopeful that the children of *glasnost* will carry *perestroika* and "new thinking" forward into the next century with energy and conviction.

In the spring of 1989, I returned to School no. 59 to talk with some of the seven-year-olds I had watched from my window in

1981. They were now fifteen, a remarkably attractive and fresh-faced group of youngsters, still uniformed and still respectful, but considerably more relaxed than the fifteen-year-olds I had spoken with in 1982 and 1983. And it had been much easier for me to gain access to them than in the past because school directors are now able to act on their own authority. Even the school had been refurbished. It is now painted pale green, the colour of new beginnings.

The director had warned the class to expect a visitor but had not told them who I was or what I wanted to talk to them about. Indeed, she had not known herself until we met in her office before she took me to the classroom. Once there she introduced me simply as a Canadian educator and left me to conduct the session as I wished.

"Think about the year 2000," I said to the students, "and then tell me how you see yourselves there, how you see your country, how you see the world." At first the responses came slowly because, as the director told me later, young people in the Soviet Union, no longer surrounded by the rhetoric of "the radiant future", have to think for themselves. After some hesitation, they began to talk about what they expected to do with their lives. Katya saw herself as a teacher in an institute; Yulya, as a doctor; Yasha would be a musician; Alyosha, an army officer. Kostya saw himself working in industry but, when I asked him if he was interested in business, he wasn't sure what I meant; for him industry was a place to work as a chemist, which is what he wants to be.

And what about their family lives? Did they expect to be married? All the girls said yes, and then they laughed when some of the boys said no. The boys and girls were quite comfortable with one another because most of them had been together since the age of seven. "How many children?" I asked. "Two," they answered promptly, one girl adding wistfully that it had not been much fun being an only child. "And if you are able to make a choice between staying at home with your children and going to work"—I turned to the girls—"what will you do?" "Stay at home," they replied unanimously. "It's too difficult to do both."

None of the students wanted to go into politics but at least they believed that, once they were adults, they would have a say in the way their country was governed. "In the year 2000 life will be much more interesting in the Soviet Union," claimed Kolya. "And easier," added Sveta. "The borders will be open and we will be able to go where we want." "Once we learn how to manage our bureaucrats," said a boy whose name I did not catch. "Tell us how do you deal with them in Canada." So I tried to explain how checks and balances come with political pluralism, and the boys, in particular, listened intently.

Then we began to speculate about the future of the world. Katya expected that the human race would have learned by the end of the century how to avert environmental catastrophes (when you are only fifteen, ten years seems like time enough). Sveta and Maxim dreamed of the elimination of nuclear weapons. Yelena wondered whether robots might not be able to solve our problems. Tanya talked about Nicaragua and hoped that people in the poorest countries would find their lot improved. Andryusha found it difficult to imagine what the world would be like in the year 2000. But, of one thing he was certain, he wanted to be there. And so do I.

"The Rising Generation"

CHAPTER ONE

"The Rising Generation"

On our first night in Moscow we went down to Red Square. Filling my mind's eye as we drove through the dim city was a vast space massed with marching soldiers and bristling with armaments. It was still the Brezhnev era and for years Red Square had meant nothing to me but military parades and newspaper photographs of old men in fur hats standing on Lenin's squat tomb, their backs to the Kremlin wall. So I was not prepared for what I saw when I looked up from the shadowy river bank where we had parked the car. Suddenly I was back in my childhood, reading *Old Peter's Russian Tales*; for directly above me, freshly painted for the 1980 Olympics in the brightest of primary colours, rose the floodlit cathedral of St. Basil the Blessed, built by Ivan the Terrible and named for a Holy Fool. From a gaily decorated jumble of arches and apses, stairways and galleries, cones and pyramids, my eyes lifted in delight to nine magical multicoloured domes. Onion and acorn squash, pine-cone and pineapple, striped, swirled, and studded, they jostled and bobbed in the warm yellow light.

Beyond St. Basil's, Red Square lay in darkness, but a light shone on the Kremlin wall and a ruby star burned on the clock-faced tower gate. I gazed at it and then past it, and saw for the first time the delicate soaring crosses and the glorious golden domes of the

13

shimmering white Kremlin churches. Later, there would be days when Red Square matched my old sombre vision and I would be painfully reminded that Russian fairy-tales are charged with dark forces, but on that first night of my stay in the Soviet Union I could respond only with wonder to the unexpected sight.

For most people in the West, the Kremlin is a metaphor for Soviet power, a metaphor that over the years became loaded with the darkness of what that power was doing. Soviet children have also always associated the Kremlin with power, but the emotions it evokes in them are less likely to be fear and dismay than reverence and awe—the same emotions that almost overwhelmed me when, as a young woman of twenty, after a childhood spent in London, Ontario, I crossed the Atlantic to visit the "real" London. Born in 1930, I, too, grew up in an imperial world and I will never forget the feelings with which I first laid eyes on Buckingham Palace, Westminster Abbey, and the mother of parliaments.

The word "Kremlin" comes from the Old Russian word *kreml,* meaning a fortified city wall. In the West, we used to see that wall as a barrier, intended to keep the rest of us out, but Soviet children have long seen it differently. For them it was, and for most of them, still is, the safeguard of their national pride. At least, this is what they have been taught. From the time of the Revolution, the State has used every means at its disposal to attach a child's natural feeling for his or her native soil to the image of the Kremlin. On the first day of school, small children in Odessa open their readers and see a brightly coloured picture of boys and girls just like them holding up their flowers in front of the Kremlin's Spassky Gate. Other children, standing at their desks in distant Siberia, recite from memory poems about the Kremlin Towers. A third set of children in the city of Murmansk, north of the Arctic Circle, dip their paintbrushes in pots of gold to reproduce the burst of fireworks over Red Square they have so often seen on television. Bit by bit, a positive image of the Kremlin, and all it stands for, is built up in these children's minds and hearts.

From its earliest years, the Soviet state has tried to fill every Soviet child with respect for the unifying power that is symbolized by the Kremlin, and to instil in him or her an unshakeable loyalty to the Communist Party as it guides the national destiny. Gradually, children in school discover that the Kremlin is more than a symbol, that it is a real place within whose halls and meeting rooms decisions are taken and orders issued that alter the course of history. Decrees emanating from the Kremlin have never been the only forces, of course, shaping the lives of children in the Soviet Union but, since the time of Lenin, policy decisions made there have been responsible more than anything else for causing children in the USSR to grow up "Soviet".

The territory of the Kremlin is roughly triangular in shape. Its three sides are bordered, respectively, by Red Square, the Alexandrovsky gardens, and the Moscow River. Behind the massive wall that separates the Kremlin from Red Square are the buildings in which the highest levels of Party and State hold their regular meetings. On the side nearest the Alexandrovsky Gardens stands the huge Palace of Congresses, completed in 1962 for the vast Party meetings that have been held there every five years to set the national agenda. It is now also used for the Congress of People's Deputies, the new legislative body that emerged from political reforms initiated at the XIX Party Conference in June 1988. Dominating the river on the third side of the territory is the Grand Kremlin Palace, constructed in the middle of the last century for Tsar Nicholas I. For seventy years, its spacious halls witnessed the token meetings of the Supreme Soviet, the former rubber-stamp parliament of the USSR. A new Supreme Soviet elected by the Congress now sits there, much smaller in size but with real power at last.

The Grand Kremlin Palace surrounds Soviet power with the aura of the vanished tsars. The symbols of the Soviet state, the hammer and sickle, have been worked in white stucco and added to its yellow façade without in the least spoiling the classical elegance of the rows of arched and pedimented windows. In the same way nineteenth-century architects seamlessly incorporated two older palaces already on the site. The fifteenth-century Palace of Facets has an unusual vaulted ceiling supported by a single interior pillar. State banquets are still held there—the Reagans attended one in June 1988—as they have been for hundreds of years. The seventeenth-century Terem Palace, once a royal residence and now a museum, has richly decorated blood-red walls redolent of ancient power.

On the second floor of the Grand Kremlin Palace there is a resplendent hall named for St. George, the patron saint of Moscow. Designed to commemorate every Russian military victory from the fifteenth century onwards, it is now used for only the most important of State occasions. In November 1982, Yury Andropov stood under its crystal chandeliers to receive the formal condolences of foreign dignitaries on the passing of Leonid Brezhnev. Fifteen months later, it was the turn of Konstantin Chernenko. Then Chernenko died, and in March 1985, a much younger man stood on the gleaming parquet floor vigorously shaking the hands of world leaders. Within days, this man, Mikhail Sergeevich Gorbachev, became General Secretary of the Communist Party and the effective leader of the Soviet Union. He quickly disassociated himself from his predecessors, especially Stalin, and turned to the founder of the Soviet state for his inspiration. Lenin had wanted to build a new society and now Gorbachev intended to try again. What the old leader knew and the new one understands is that the building and rebuilding of nations cannot be done without the active participation of the young.

Lenin's Testament to Youth

During the course of my husband's term as ambassador to the Soviet Union, I climbed the long, red-carpeted staircase to the second floor of the Grand Kremlin Palace on several formal occasions. Each time, I paused for a moment to study the huge painting that hangs on the landing. It depicts Lenin standing on a stage under a red banner. We see him from the perspective of the wings, stage right. His coat-tails flare and his right fist is upraised. A crowd of young people, their faces alight, lean forward from the audience to hear what he has to say. It is October 2, 1920, the date of the Third All-Russia Congress of the Komsomol (Young Communist League) and Lenin is urging the youthful delegates to devote all their strength and energy to the building of communism. The fact that this painting hangs where it does, and that thousands of deputies, officials, and senior

Party members see it regularly as they attend important sessions and meetings affecting the governance of the Soviet Union, is an indication of the special significance that the younger generation has for rulers of the Soviet state, past and present.

Lenin knew that the attitudes and actions of Komsomol members would be crucial for the success of his political vision, and this painting captures him in the act of making his testament to Soviet youth. What Lenin said that day about communist ethics still informs the Soviet approach to policies with respect to children and youth, for the moral quality of what Soviet authorities like to call "the rising generation" remains a concern of first priority for leaders in the Kremlin. It is this fact that has long made the experience of growing up in the Soviet Union different from that of growing up in the West. Unlike the governments of Western countries, the Soviet state takes responsibility not only for educating its future citizens in all the usual ways but also for directing their moral upbringing. A close reading of Lenin's speech to this special group of young activists, all of whom had been deeply involved in the struggle to overthrow the old regime and establish the power of the Bolsheviks, will show the direction he set for his young "builders of communism", a moral compass that Gorbachev would like to reset.

Like all great leaders, Lenin was both a visionary and a man of action. He knew where he wanted to go, and he also knew that getting there would place extraordinary demands on the people to whom the task of building his new society would be entrusted. It was this knowledge that was at the origin of the concept of communist ethics that Lenin introduced in this frequently quoted speech to the members of the Komsomol. Dismissing his own generation as "wearied", he told the young people that it was they, not their elders, who would be able to build communism, who would live in a land that was fair and comradely without class oppression and without State control. Everything they did to realize this dream of "truth and justice" would be moral and right. Everything that they or others did to delay its coming into being would be immoral and wrong. Because they were young, Lenin said, they had not been "deformed" by working under capitalism. Because they were "starting to work under the new conditions in which relations based on the exploitation of man by man no longer exist", they would be better able than their elders to build the new world. He told them that they would have to use their brains as well as their hands for this task. "Study, study, study!" he urged them, explaining that the world out there was knowable and that, when the laws governing its evolution were understood correctly, communism would be revealed to everyone as the logical and scientific outcome of the whole of human history. If they studied, understood, and were prepared to work hard, together with their comrades, then "those who are now fifteen will see a communist society and will themselves build that society". His speech was received with "stormy applause".

It is one thing to read Lenin's words today and quite another to get inside the heads of his young listeners to comprehend how those words were able to stir them to action. Fortunately, during the first summer I lived in Moscow, I was given an opportunity to enter the revolutionary context in which this speech was given through the medium of works of art created during the early years of the new Soviet state. This experience enabled me to empathize, to some extent, with the emotional receptivity of his hearers.

From June to September 1981, the second floor of the Pushkin Museum of Western Art in central Moscow was taken over by an exhibition called "Paris–Moscow 1900–1930". If I had been surprised by my first sight of Red Square, I was even more astonished by what I saw in this show. I had often admired works by the brilliant Russian-born painters Wassily Kandinsky and Marc Chagall in European and North American galleries. Some of the other pre-revolutionary painters on exhibit were also familiar. But most of the gifted and original artists who worked in Russia after the Revolution were quite new to me. I was fascinated by their works. And I was not alone. During four bright summer months, hundreds of thousands of Soviet citizens crowded into the museum, and I am sure that what they found there was as much a revelation to most of them as it had been to me. Until I saw this exhibition, I had not thought very much about what life had been like in the 1920s for the workers and peasants for whom the Revolution had ostensibly been fought, nor for the artists and intellectuals who had sympathized with them. But, in 1981, the force of their post-revolutionary energy pulsed unabated across the second floor of the museum. Paintings and sculptures, architectural designs, sets and costumes, posters, clothing, even household articles, all were informed with verve and excitement. More than six decades after these works had been created, I could still sense the electricity, feel the shock of the new.

Studying these works of art I learned that in the early post-revolutionary years, the years when Lenin was still alive and active, the working poor and the poor young, people who had never felt valued by society before, were being told by artists and intellectuals as well as by Party activists that the success of the new society depended upon them, that the old order had changed and the keys to the future were now in their hands, no longer in those of the tsar or the church. In this new world ordinary people were treated as heroes and heroines. Painters designed posters and made banners for them. Writers composed plays for them that actors performed in public squares, on special trains, or on showboats cruising the Volga. Designers created strikingly original clothes for them to wear on the factory floor. Vladimir Mayakovsky, the poet of the Revolution, the people's poet, sang songs of glory to "the land of spring".

A year or so later, I was able to share in the mood of Lenin's young audience in the very same hall, now known as the Lenin Komsomol Theatre, where he actually gave his speech. In 1982, I saw a play there, *Revolutionary Etude—Blue Horses on Red Grass*, by Mikhail Shatrov, a popular contemporary playwright who writes thought-provoking works about Lenin. This particular play ends as Lenin begins his address to the Komsomol; it was mesmerizing to relive, as a member of an audience, the same exciting atmosphere I had discovered at the Pushkin Museum. Shatrov's play, which he describes as "an experiment in publicistic drama", explores the burning issues of 1920 as seen through the eyes of the present. The play begins with an ominous early-morning discussion between Lenin and his doctor, and takes him through meetings with peasants, workers, and soldiers, to tea-time with his wife and his women friends. These events are interrupted by lively public debates on the topics of art, literature, and sex, as they might have been conducted at the time. The theatre is hung with posters and draped with banners bearing slogans. Throughout the play reference is made to a young artist wounded in the Civil War who is trying to finish a painting that will depict in symbolic form the future Lenin has promised. Towards the end of the play, news arrives that the artist has died without completing his painting. Then the actor playing Lenin walks to the front of the stage and stands under a red banner. His coat-tails flare slightly as he raises his right fist. He smiles and says, "Greetings to all of you! Today I would like to speak to you about the goals of the Young Communist League." As he extends his hand to the audience the curtain falls.

The Moral Code of the Builders of Communism

Shatrov's play suggests that Lenin was aware that he might die before the task of building communism could be accomplished. He knew that a whole generation would have to be educated in a new way before a communist society could be created. This is why he put so much energy into his speech to the Komsomol. He warned them that getting rid of the tsar, the landowners, and the capitalists had been easy compared with the task of changing the mentality of the vast population that remained, particularly the peasants, who were so set in their ways. He told his young listeners to be clear in their convictions or they would never be able to convince anyone else. They had to be able to prove that, by sharing the ownership of the means of production, a better life could be achieved for all. Under the old regime no one had thought of anyone but himself, Lenin reminded them, but under the new, the good of society would come first.

"There is no such thing as a morality that stands outside human society," said Lenin, explaining that morality is about human relations and economic justice. Divine guidance is a delusion, he went on, but that does not mean that communists are immoral; quite the contrary. But communist ethics are defined by the goal of building a communist society, and so the virtues of a young communist must be the personal qualities that will enable him or her to work towards that end. Lenin did not actually spell out a moral code of behaviour for his young listeners. He left that for others. Yet, almost all the morality that has been preached to Soviet children for more than seven decades is implicit in what he said that day.

"The Party holds that the moral code of the builder of communism includes...devotion to the cause of communism...conscientious labour for the good of society...a high sense of public duty...collectivism...moral purity...concern for the upbringing of children...an uncompromising attitude to injustice, parasitism, dishonesty, careerism and money-grubbing" and "solidarity with the working peoples of all countries". That is what Nikita Khrushchev said forty years later in his speech to the XXII Congress of the Communist Party when he confirmed the Party's return to Lenin's ethical principles after the death of Stalin.

Khrushchev was convinced of the inherent superiority of the Soviet system and was certain that the virtues of the Soviet people would surface once they had shaken free of Stalinism. Yet, the years that followed his departure from the political scene, the years during which his successor, Leonid Brezhnev, was in power, were characterized by increasing social and economic stagnation and, worse, by moral corruption at various levels of society. So, in the early 1980s, sixty years after Lenin's speech to the Komsomol and twenty years after Khrushchev's, a new version of the moral code of communism appeared. It was contained in official guidelines for the reform of the Soviet school system. The preamble to the decree on school reform issued on April 4, 1984, states: "The immense tasks posed by the final years of this century and the early years of the next one will be accomplished by those who are sitting at school desks today. They will have to continue the cause of Great October, and they will bear the responsibility for the country's historical destiny, and for the all-round progress of society and its successful advance along the path of communist construction."

Although the advent of Gorbachev has softened the rhetoric and changed some of its terms, the State continues to preach most of the virtues espoused by Lenin and Khrushchev and to try to instil them in today's children. This means that, no matter what happens in the future, members of this current generation will carry elements of the moral code of communism with them to their graves just as I carry, at some profound level of my being, the messages of the ten commandments of Moses memorized in childhood.

So, what are the virtues that the Soviet system of public upbringing has been designed to inculcate in young children? Among the most important, from the Kremlin's point of view, is commitment to a communist world-view. A world-view is a way of looking at the world as it is, rather than a vision of what the world should be like and the communist world-view uses dialectical materialism, a method created by Marx, to interpret things and events. Children at Soviet schools are taught that the natural world is the only one that exists and that science, not religion, is the route to understanding. Everything in the universe has a material base, there is no ghost in the machine; there are no solutions but human ones. The world is objective, out there, waiting to be transformed by the activity of men and women (and children, too). But it is not static, for, according to the communist world-view, nothing ever stays still. There is a constant dynamic interaction going on between human beings and the world they live in during the course of which both get transformed. This is known as the dialectical process.

What makes this world-view *communist* is that, when students apply dialectical materialism to the study of history, they are supposed to discover, according to Marxism-Leninism, that one type of society invariably gives rise to another in a historical movement that should eventually lead to the communist society of Lenin's vision. One of the axioms of this world-view is that societies are defined by those who own the means by which material goods are produced. Once everyone owns these means, there will be no ruling class and that will be the best kind of human society, superior to any other that has ever existed. It will be a society in which Peace, Work, Equality, Freedom, Brotherhood, and Happiness will exist, or so states the social-studies textbook that has been required reading for senior high-school students for years. Acting according to the moral code of communism will hasten the process by which this utopia comes into being.

Commitment to a communist world-view, however, entails more than using dialectical materialism to understand the world and the course of human history. It also demands a certain type of political consciousness, one that looks to the Communist Party for leadership. Soviet children's organizations, such as the Pioneers, have long been geared to developing this consciousness. Change is now in the wind, but many generations of Soviet children, including those who grew up in the 1980s, will have had full exposure to this influence.

Another virtue, as high on the list of the rulers in the Kremlin today as it was on Lenin's, is studiousness. Gorbachev's vision of the future places great emphasis on the role of science and technology. Soviet young people are urged to study hard so that they will acquire the sophisticated knowledge and the technical skills that will turn the USSR into an advanced industrial society, once it has solved its current economic ills.

In addition to having a communist world-view and superior knowledge and technical skills, contemporary Soviet youth are still expected to be "collectivists", fully committed to socially useful activity. They are exhorted to look at events in terms of their impact on society first, and only then to weigh them from self-interest. The idea of the collective is firmly rooted in Russian as well as Soviet history and is one of the most important means by which children are socialized in the Soviet Union. A collective is more than just a group. It is an organic entity, a living whole, woven from the intentions, actions, and emotions of its members, and from the ties they create among themselves. A collective expects from its members those virtues that are most familiar to us in the West. In the introduction to the 1984 decree on educational reform, they are listed: "honesty, truthfulness, kindness, devotion to principle, steadfastness and courage of character", as well as (less familiar to us, at least as a virtue) "exactingness towards one another".

The moral code also emphasizes attitudes to work. According to Lenin, work is what gives meaning and justification to life; those who can work but do not are parasites on the body politic. The changes that Gorbachev is bringing about in the economy will require some adjustments to this concept, but a positive attitude to work will remain an important part of the moral code for the foreseeable future.

Other personal traits Soviet authorities consider important include self-discipline and a trained will, a love of beauty and high standards for its appreciation, a love of nature and a willingness to care for the environment, a commitment to physical fitness, patriotism, and a feeling of friendship for all the nationalities of the Union, as well as a sense of commitment to socialist internationalism. Socially useful activity (social learning through practice) is particularly emphasized in contemporary statements of the moral code, and student self-government has acquired new prominence. Under the influence of the principal Soviet institutions, organizations and cultural forces that affect them directly, Soviet children have been, and to a lesser extent still are, expected by state authorities to develop harmoniously integrated personalities marked by an inner need to act according to the principles of communist morality and, when they are adults, to have all the characteristics I have cited and more.

It is worthwhile pausing for a moment to consider what has been left off this list. Not long ago, I spent two days with a group of elementary-school teachers, child-care workers, public-health nurses, and other people concerned with children, most of whom were parents as well. We had been brought together by the Ontario Ministry of Education as part of a study on early childhood education. One of our tasks was to draw up a list of the characteristics we would like to see in young people emerging from the Ontario school system. I found it fascinating to compare our list with the Soviet one. Some desirable characteristics were common to both, although the priority accorded to them was different. The Canadian list ranked patriotism and socially useful activity rather lower than independence, self-reliance, and initiative. We also put a good deal of emphasis on imagination, creativity, and problem-solving skills. Flexibility of mind and tolerance of spirit were high on our list, as were self-knowledge and self-acceptance. We said that we would like to encourage spontaneity, curiosity, and a continuing sense of wonder. Finally, we wanted our new graduates to be compassionate and humorous. (This last characteristic does not figure on official Soviet lists but I found it be very common among the people we met throughout the USSR.) Political consciousness was scarcely mentioned in our group, and capitalism, not once. We agreed without hesitation that children should learn to listen to one another and to work in groups. Furthermore, and we decided that this was very important, children should acquire the skills as well as the intention to resolve conflicts without violence.

In recent years, the formal version of the moral code of communism became an increasingly heavy weight for young people to carry. No wonder so many of them shook it off during the 1970s and the early 1980s, when they sensed, as children invariably do, the hypocrisy with which it was being preached. Unlike the young people who had listened to Lenin, these young people could not be energized by a message that had lost its vitality. Cynicism in their generation is causing genuine distress to many of their elders who still care passionately about morality, and they are hoping that a better job can be done with the children who are now at school. Since the advent of *glasnost* I have read numerous letters and articles in the Soviet press about how to rekindle the moral energy stifled for so long by the formalism of the school system and how to realign students with at least some of the ethical principles that Lenin put forward in his speech to the Komsomol.

Lenin turned to the young with hope because they had not been "deformed" by working under the old system. Gorbachev is doing the same. In his book, *Perestroika and the New Thinking,* he echoes his predecessor when he writes, "Many of us were born, formed as individuals, and lived in conditions when the old order existed…many decades of being mesmerized by dogma, by a rule-book approach have had their effect." Turning to his own "rising generation", Gorbachev is prepared to rally the resources of the State to its support. He confirmed this intention in a message he sent to the founding meeting of the V.I. Lenin Soviet Children's Fund in October 1987 in the course of which he restated once more the Kremlin's aims with respect to Soviet children. He called upon the "kind and energetic people" who had initiated the fund to work "together with the organs of the state to protect children and help them become genuine human beings, ideologically convinced, work-loving, educated, worthy citizens of their great motherland".

Social Policy for Children

To nurture a specific moral code in the hearts and minds of young children an institutional structure has to be created. When Lenin urged the Komsomol to "Study, study, study!" he made a commitment on behalf of the new Soviet state to an enormous investment in education. He knew, however, that on its own the educational system would not be able to ensure that Soviet children grew up as builders of communism. Many other forces would also have to be deployed. There would have to be legal protections for children, good health care, and nurseries and kindergartens as well as schools. Furthermore, the family, as the fundamental unit of Soviet society, would have to be aided in its task of raising committed Soviet citizens by teachers, artists and intellectuals, ordinary workers, peasants and soldiers. No influence that shapes the character of children could be left out of the calculus. With this in mind, more than three hundred decrees relating to children were issued from the Kremlin during the first five years after the Revolution. Major decisions about state policy with respect to children have been made there ever since.

The moral code of communism is primarily a Party matter. Revisions to it have normally been made by the Central Committee of the CPSU or by the Politburo, and moved in and out of the Kremlin along Party channels. Legislation concerning children, including statutes regulating the school system, the health system, and the child-care system, has followed government pathways. When policy is made to link ideology with institutions, then both Party and government have been involved. Until the CPSU abandons its "guiding" role in the affairs of the nation, this will continue to be the case.

During the 1980s, social policy with respect to children was frequently initiated by the standing commissions of the Supreme Soviet, especially the commissions for "work and welfare of women, protection of motherhood and childhood" established in 1976. Each of the two chambers of the old Supreme Soviet had its own commission but they worked together to influence State policy through the ordering of budget priorities. These standing commissions have been reconstituted as committees in the new Supreme Soviet and now have legislative as well as budgetary responsibilities. In 1984, to learn how children's issues were addressed by these commissions, I met with Lidiya Lykova, then chairperson of the standing commission on women and children in the Soviet of Nationalities. The Soviet of Nationalities represents, in both the old and the new Supreme Soviet, the multinational character of the Soviet Union. The other chamber, the Soviet of the Union, represents Soviet citizens in constituencies of equal size, regardless of nationality.

At the time of our meeting, Lidiya Lykova was one of the most experienced women in the Soviet government. Not only was she a deputy to the Soviet of Nationalities but she was also the vice-chairperson of the Council of Ministers of the Russian Federation, the largest of the Union republics, encompassing Moscow and Leningrad as well as Siberia, a land mass equal in size to all of Canada.

We met inside the Kremlin in a room with a spectacular view of the crosses and domes of the ancient churches. Lykova, whom I had met before in a different capacity, cheerfully greeted me and we sat down across from each other at a long table. Given her rank, she had been supplied with a brief, from which she read out, her eyes twinkling, that two other events of great importance had already taken place that week. Soviet cosmonauts had landed safely after a record 237 days in space, and the last spike joining the two ends of the Baikal-Amur railway (BAM) had been driven in. (The BAM is a second trans-Siberian railway running north of Lake Baikal and east to the Amur River. It has been built to provide access to the great natural resources of northeastern Siberia.) During railway construction, more than sixty thousand children had been born to young BAM construction workers. Towns had sprung up along the new rail line, and many of the young builders had decided to stay on in Siberia to help develop them into stable communities. When the babies arrived, all the institutions representing the State's concern for its new citizens followed: well-baby clinics, child-care centres, kindergartens, schools, libraries, sports facilities, Pioneer palaces—the whole network, in fact, of interlocking children's services that Lenin and his colleagues had planned at the beginning of Soviet power in order to create builders of communism.

A task of Lykova's commission, and of the committee that has replaced it, was and is to monitor the institutions in this network, which are so important for the upbringing of Soviet children. Another is to study the impact of the world of work on women and children and recommend policies to alleviate negative effects. A third is to channel concerns to the senior levels of government raised by similar commissions or committees at regional, district, and local levels. As we spoke, Lykova's commission was in the process of responding to a request from a commission in Turkmenia to examine the problems of working women in that republic who, generally speaking, have much larger families to contend with than women anywhere else in the USSR. Other standing commisions of the Supreme Soviet helping to formulate and push forward policies concerned with children during the 1980s were those responsible for public education, health, and youth affairs, most of which have also been reconstituted as committees.

Describing her commission's work, Lykova warmed to her subject. She and her colleagues at the table obviously enjoyed discussing the machinery of government. They argued with one another about facts and figures but they were confident that children would remain high on the national agenda. They were as frank as I think they knew how to be, but I am not sure that they were aware then of some of the problems concerning children that have since come to light in the Soviet press. In the days before *glasnost,* even the best-intentioned of decision-makers worked in the dark.

Now, however, the situation is different. While the Congress of People's Deputies, and the smaller Supreme Soviet it has elected, has real power, the situation concerning children in the Soviet Union has in some ways deteriorated, owing to the stress created by social and political transformation. Should a committee for the "work and welfare of women, protection of motherhood and childhood" with its broad mandate, remain the principal focus for children's issues in the Kremlin? A new public organization thinks not. The time has come, says the V.I. Lenin Soviet Children's Fund, to establish a special standing committee entirely devoted to the welfare of children.

The Soviet Children's Fund is an important new player in the process of formulating social policy for children in the Soviet Union. This organization, which came into existence in 1987, is one of a number of recently established public voluntary organizations that represent essential first steps towards the creation of a civil society in the Soviet Union. For the first time, voluntary organizations that are legally independent of the government, and can raise money from the public at large, are being encouraged to exert *real* influence on the conduct of public affairs. For Soviet children (and for the population as a whole), this is a promising change.

In March 1988, I went to see Gennady Savinov, the energetic deputy-director of the Soviet Children's Fund, in a tiny temporary office in the Yunost (Youth) Hotel. He told me that he hoped the fund would continue to occupy modest premises to prevent it from becoming bureaucratized or overcentralized. He also hoped that autonomous branches would evolve in each of the Union republics to deal with local issues because local initiatives and local responses were what was needed to address the problems with which the fund is most concerned. The Soviet Children's Fund receives public donations from all over the USSR, a portion of which it redistributes to its branches for local use.

Savinov drew diagrams all over his desk pad to show me how the fund was going to function. This circle—he pointed— represented a council focusing on children in institutional care (it was the deplorable condition of Soviet orphanages that first motivated the founder and now chairman of the Children's Fund, the writer Albert Likhanov, to agitate for its creation). The next circle represented a family council that had just been established to examine the problems of contemporary families in the Soviet Union. He drew yet another circle, this one to represent a council for encouraging creativity in children, made up of artists and intellectuals and including intermediaries prepared to take the ideas of the former to ministries and government bodies. Savinov added that a number of other tasks had been mandated by the fund's founding conference and written into its statute, but, as the fund had just got going, it would take a while before these other tasks could be addressed.

When I returned to Moscow a year later, Savinov had lost none of his initial enthusiasm. He welcomed me to a new office in an old building donated by the city of Moscow. The building had been derelict and the Children's Fund was restoring it with money raised by its profitable co-operative business ventures, among them a highly successful newspaper called *Semya* (Family). Savinov was eager to tell me what the fund had accomplished since I had seen him, including the contributions it had made to the health and welfare of children affected by the earthquake in Armenia. But most of all he was excited by the election of the new Congress of People's Deputies. The Soviet Children's Fund was one of the public organizations allotted seats in the Congress, five in total. But twenty-two of the other new deputies were also members of the fund, some of whom were subsequently elected to the Supreme Soviet. As a result, according to Savinov, children will have a stronger voice speaking for them inside the Kremlin than they have had since the time of Lenin.

Savinov is clearly an able man, keen and intelligent. The first time I met him, I asked him where he had come from and why he was working for the fund. He replied that he had grown up in a town on the Volga in a poor family of ten children. There was not enough money to go around, so he had to go to work and finish his education by correspondence. He taught for a couple of years and then became a full-time Komsomol worker. After joining the Communist Party, he came to Moscow to work for the Central Committee. The Party then assigned him to this job (the legal independence of the fund has not led to the board hiring its own executive director) and Savinov was eager to pursue it. He cared about children, he said, and believed his personal experience qualified him to understand the problems of contemporary Soviet youngsters. Besides, he considered that the resolution of children's issues was absolutely vital for the future of the USSR. I looked at him and thought of Lenin's Testament to Youth. Seventy years later, here was a young man still prepared to take up Lenin's challenge.

Soviet children are taught that Lenin loved children; at the very least, he understood their importance for the survival of his political vision. Gorbachev appears to be equally committed to the young. He, too, needs their energy and skills. As General Secretary of the Communist Party and now as President of the Soviet Union, Gorbachev is still trying to build a society not unlike the one Lenin dreamed of. In his report to the Party Conference in June 1988, he described that society "as a system of genuine and real humanism, as a system of effective and dynamic economy, as a system of social fairness, lofty morality and culture and genuine people's government". Communists believe that history has a forward movement and so, like Lenin, Gorbachev has his eye on the future. As a result, he and his supporters in the Kremlin will continue to be concerned about the moral values of the rising generation.

Under *glasnost*, however, the State has admitted at long last that it is not the perfect guardian of Soviet children that it claimed to be for so long and that there are serious problems concerning children that it is not constituted to solve, problems that owe more to disruptions in family life, and to the fact that parents are often too busy and too preoccupied to pay attention to their children, than they do to capitalism or socialism as economic systems. So now the State is prepared to share responsibility for children's issues with non-governmental organizations such as the Soviet Children's Fund; in this way it can tap the energy and experience of people who work directly with children. Nevertheless, the Soviet state, under the guidance of the CPSU, reserves the right to define the moral code of communism and to determine the overall direction of social policy regarding the upbringing of children.

On my frequent walks from the Embassy to the Kremlin, I would usually spend a few minutes in the Alexandrovsky Gardens, watching little children at play. Outside the Kremlin walls, children jump and shout. Inside, however, they walk quietly and are hardly heard at all. Inside they are documented and labelled, discussed and planned for—they are even eulogized. In flesh and blood, however, they are still welcome only under controlled conditions.

Every year hundreds of thousands of children come to visit the Kremlin with their parents. Even more come on school excursions. Considering how they have been taught to feel about the Kremlin, they are bound to be excited. Once they enter the Kremlin gates, however, they must restrain their enthusiasm and behave with decorum. Occasionally, children are invited to special events inside the Palace of Congresses. During the time I lived in Moscow, I witnessed two such occasions exposing public and official attitudes to children so deep-rooted that I almost despair of change. Yet I was also present at a third that showed what can happen when Soviet children are respected as individuals and encouraged to play roles that truly suit them.

The first event was the ceremonial concert in 1982 that commemorated the sixtieth anniversary of the formation of the Union of Soviet Socialist Republics. This form of ritual celebration still accompanies virtually every state event of any importance in the Soviet Union. It follows a regular pattern: a "pas de deux" from a classical ballet, an operatic solo or two, a couple of patriotic choruses, a piano excerpt (usually Tchaikovsky), and an item showing children as adults would like to see them. Children dressed in colourful national costumes sang and danced to sanitized folk music with remarkable force and precision. Georgian boys went up on their toes, and Ukrainian lads kicked out their legs. Little girls flirted and twirled. Sighs went up from the audience. Later, another regular concert feature: little children ran up the aisles of the auditorium, girls in ultra-short flaring skirts and huge taffeta bows, and boys in short pants, their red Pioneer ties flying, to present flowers to members of the Politburo.

A second Kremlin event I witnessed was the traditional New Year's party for schoolchildren, held in the vast lobby of the Palace of Congresses. A New Year's tree (*Yolka*), resplendent with tinsel and lights, stretched upwards almost out of sight. Grandfather Frost (*Ded Moroz*) in a long white beard and a red and white coat arrived in a sleigh, carrying bags of presents. He was accompanied by his granddaughter, the Snow Maiden (*Snegurochka*), in a silver-spangled blue hooded cloak. A mass of little children in starched finery solemnly watched the distribution of gifts. A little girl I know was chosen to be one of the four representatives from her school to go to this annual party. She returned home disappointed. It was too big, she said, too impersonal, too crowded, the gifts were meagre, and the Snow Maiden wore too much make-up.

The third event was quite different. I had come to watch the young students of the Bolshoi Ballet School give their year-end concert, a presentation of the ballet *Coppelia*. It was a Saturday evening in late spring when daylight in Moscow lingers until past ten o'clock. Tender green leaves trembled outside the streaked plate-glass windows of the Palace of Congresses, the descending sun illumined the golden domes, and the air was fragrant with the scent of lilac. I entered a lobby full of cheerful children running about and eating ice cream, and I sat in an audience of families. The performance was enchanting, the sets and costumes, fresh and delightful. The youngest students occasionally stumbled, and the flat-chested beginning ballerinas quivered on their pointes. But the seventeen-year-olds, in their first solo roles, were full of grace. The children in the audience and the children on the stage were all caught up in the same magic. Then, for a little while, in that huge auditorium within the Kremlin walls, at the very heart of the Soviet Union, not far from the painting of Lenin lecturing the young Komsomol, there was a suspension of disbelief, a moment of beauty and truth.

The Formative Years

CHAPTER TWO

"Vospitanie": Soviet Upbringing

It can be very hot in Moscow in August. The asphalt goes soft in the streets of the city. In dooryards and empty lots, the leaves of shade trees hang dusty and limp. Scattered patches of dry grass and unnameable weeds crunch under foot. At the end of each stifling day my husband and I would go out from the Embassy to get some air on Gogol's Garden Boulevard, the nearest green space. Once there we would stroll from the Kropotkinskaya Metro station at one end to the pigeon-stained statue of Gogol at the other, and then back again. The thick poplars that arch over the boulevard muffle the sound of the passing traffic, and it would usually be so quiet under the trees that we could hear the soft click of dominoes as we walked along.

Every summer morning, almost before the dew has gone, pensioners bring their game-boards to Gogol's Garden Boulevard and insert them carefully through the slatted backs of the white park benches that line the central pathway. Then they settle down to play away the day. Friends and onlookers hang over them, leaning down from time to time to place a bet. Near the exit from the Metro station, busy men pause for a moment to read the daily papers pasted up on the free-standing display boards: *Pravda* (Truth), *Trud* (Labour), and especially *Sovetsky Sport*. When it is particularly warm the nearby drink machine is crowded. People wait until someone puts down a glass, then grab it, rinse it over a jet of water, and fill it with cool lemon fizz at three kopeks a shot. Lovers buy an ice-cream bar at a kiosk and go off to share it beyond the bushes. Old women gossip, bulging shopping bags nestled at their feet. Younger women hurry by in both directions. But where are the children? During the rest of the year, they are all over the boulevard, swinging and sliding and playing on the hard-packed earth. In the winter, they bring skis or tumble in the snow. But in August, they are gone, gone from the dusty city, gone to the country, gone to the sea.

One weekend in early August, we, too, decided to fly away from the city, down to the Black Sea coast. We boarded a brand-new Ilyushin airbus at Vnukovo Airport, left our luggage in its hold, and mounted to the cabin. As soon as we sat down, we found ourselves surrounded by chattering children. It was turn-over time at the summer camps in the south, and a new contingent of young Pioneers was on its way to the sea. During the short flight to Simferopol, the public-address system assaulted our ears with cassettes of adventure tales, all played at cartoon speed. I plugged my ears and longed, as I never dreamed I would, for the soothing comfort of Muzak. The children paid no attention at all.

When the plane landed, the stewardess insisted that my husband and I be the first to disembark. But as soon as we reached the terminal gate, I turned around to watch the children pour out of the open hatch. They clattered down the steps and ran gaily across the tarmac. Then they climbed up into a line of waiting buses. As soon as they were all safely stowed, the bus doors closed and the caravan moved off. With red flags aflutter and led by a *militsia* car, the buses drove slowly down the highway to the sea. As we followed in our Intourist car, the children waved at us. Before very long the caravan turned in to the gates of one of the innumerable Pioneer camps along the Crimean coast. We went on to Yalta. When we arrived at the huge hotel above the town where we were to stay, however, we discovered that not every Soviet child was in a summer camp. With the exception of ourselves, some East Germans, and the ubiquitous Finns, the hotel was packed with Soviet families on holiday. And so was the rest of Yalta. Everywhere we went during the next three days we found ourselves in the midst of family groups. We sunned with them on boards laid across the pebbly beach. We swam with them among the tiny jellyfish. We walked with them along the sea-wall and around the crowded port. Even as we wandered through the mountain gardens, full of cyprus and pine, and old, forgotten plants, we were never alone. Families filled the launch that toured us across the harbour and along the rocky coast. They joined us to inspect the Palace of Livadia built for a vacationing tsar of limited taste and used by Stalin, Churchill, and Roosevelt to settle the post-war fate of Europe. They came with us to the gates of Chekhov's charming cottage, where, in 1900, he wrote *The Three Sisters* and longed for Moscow. Had we gone to Yalta for peace and quiet we would have been frustrated, but we hadn't; we had gone chiefly to escape the city and to swim in the sea. The presence of parents relaxing with their children was a welcome bonus.

The seaside is an ideal place to observe child-rearing practices in a natural setting, for parental attitudes are continually tested by the surroundings. How parents treat their children by the sea will not only tell you quite a bit about the way they parent but will also hint at the kind of people their children are likely to become. Even the calmest sea will bring out parental anxiety and, thus, attitudes about control and independence, about holding back and letting go. How well I remember. My son crawled into the sea in Brittany before he could walk, while I sat nervously on my towel waiting for the waves to tell him when to stop. Off the west coast of Mexico, keeping a sharp look-out for sharks, I let the children ride the surf on rubber rings. In Malaysia, as I stared at the sand-filled water flooding up the beach, every floating twig looking like a poisonous snake; I watched on full alert but I held my tongue. I worried about breakers and sun-stroke on the beautiful white beaches of Goa and about undertow in the red sand-filled waters off Prince Edward Island. Over and over, watching the children slide in and out with the waves, rolling and tumbling in water and sand and pebbles, I would count the five bobbing heads. But I let them go until they could swim like seals and play like porpoises, turning brown and golden in the sun.

On the Black Sea shore, however, I saw Soviet parents holding their children back. The little ones went hand-held into the sea, their soft feet shod in plastic shoes to protect them against bruising by the small, round stones. The older ones were allowed to swim out from the pier, but not alone, and never very far before they were called back. I looked for the cuts and scratches that usually covered my children's bare brown legs at the end of a seaside holiday, but saw very few. Most of the parents appeared affectionate, and their children were amiably obedient. When they were summoned to return, there was little resistance. I never saw a child struck.

A holiday by the seaside also tests the degree to which parents are indulgent. Soft drinks and ice cream and other good things are available to tempt a child whose parents are close at hand to be cajoled. Indulgence is not quite the same thing as permissiveness. The former, however misguided, usually arises out of a positive attitude to children and childhood. The latter may be a function of laziness or, worse, of indifference. It was my observation that the parents of young children in the Soviet Union are more indulgent than they are permissive. Memories of the Second World War and of personal deprivation still persist and may explain, in part, why they are particularly indulgent with respect to food. I was surprised, now that I could see them without their outer clothing, at how many boys and girls were overweight.

Sitting beside a pudgy eight-year-old at lunch on the boardwalk, I watched with astonishment as the great pile of food disappeared from in front of him and his mother heaped his plate with more. Was she spoiling him? It would be difficult to say. He did not seem whining or petulant. Most likely he was her only child, and perhaps she had just picked him up from summer camp and was indulging her pleasure at having him close to her again. Looking at him, I wondered how the children I had seen on the airplane were enjoying their shared lunches by the sea. I knew from visits to Pioneer camps that their food would be ample if unexciting and that the children would be expected to serve it and to clean up afterwards. The atmosphere of a camp is public and collective, that of a family holiday, private and individual. Every summer millions of Soviet children split their time between the two; it is part of growing up Soviet.

Soviet psychologists lay great stress on the role that the social worlds of the child (both the private environment of the family and the public environment of the school and the camp) play in his or her overall development. My weekend in Yalta, during which I had glimpses of both, made me think about these two social worlds—the affectionate, indulgent, yet somewhat constricting world of the Soviet family and the carefully planned collective world of the Soviet school, the children's organizations, and the summer camp—and about how the interaction between these two worlds is integrated into the character of the maturing child to render him or her recognizably "Soviet".

National Character

The "new Soviet man" was intended to be a healthy, hard-working, happy collectivist, unselfishly devoted to the motherland and to the building of communism. Visitors to the Soviet Union, however, have long encountered a national character quite different from this picture: richer, more expansive, and much more contradictory than the model held up by the State. According to one English observer, "The Russians themselves speak of their broad nature...their dreamy emotionalism." Not for them the stiff upper lip and the repressed feelings usually associated with the British. Indeed, emotionalism is highly valued in Soviet society, both by the family and by the State (as long as it is channelled into proper conduits). There are, of course, many continuities between the Russians of the Old Regime and their descendants today. It would be astonishing if there were not. It would be a mistake, however, to underestimate the shaping influence of seventy years of Soviet upbringing, or *vospitanie*, as it is called.

Each generation of children in the USSR has grown up slightly more "Soviet" than the generation before it. This has not been a process of total homogenization, nor obviously, has it meant that Soviet children today are markedly less Russian, Georgian, Latvian, or whatever than their parents. The State-directed process

of social upbringing in the Soviet Union was not, and certainly
is not, intended to obliterate *all* ethnic differences. Nevertheless,
"Sovietness" has become a real and distinct part of the personality
of the majority of Soviet citizens alive today. Canadians may be
able to understand this overlay of national character on ethnic
identity better than Americans. Canada has two founding nations,
many of whose cultural characteristics have been preserved, more
or less well, by means of language guarantees and other formulas
that are enshrined in legislation and embodied in institutions.
However, the process of mutual adaptation that has taken place
over the more than a century since Canada became a state
finds itself reflected in the character of contemporary Canadians,
producing certain common qualities that many of us recognize
only when we go abroad. Then we realize that, nowadays,
French-speaking and English-speaking Canadians are more like
one another than like the citizens of any other country.

Foreigners living in the USSR note that most Soviet citizens
share a number of what might be called "all-Union" characteristics
superimposed on the ethnic ones that serve to identify them as
natives of this or that Union republic. These traits are easier to
recognize than to describe, but they clearly exist, the product of
successful interaction between State-sponsored public upbringing
and private, family-centred child-rearing practices.

One factor in the progressive "Sovietization" of children in
the USSR is a common feature of all industrialized societies.
Large-scale industrialization disrupts traditional family structures,
and new parents find themselves on their own, away from their
extended families. As a result, they turn more and more to
outside sources for advice about bringing up their children. As
they consult professionals and look to books and magazines
for advice on child-rearing, they tend to discard narrow cultural
traditions that seem to them outdated and unscientific. When the
process of industrialization has been completed, the child-rearing
practices of most families in the newly industrialized society
will be seen as having converged on a national model. Where
these practices mesh more or less smoothly with methods of
social upbringing institutionalized by the State, then individuals,
although they come from different ethnic backgrounds and are

separated by thousands of kilometres, may grow up sharing certain characteristics that are easy for others to spot.

Another factor that has to be taken into account when examining the process by which "national character" is formed is who is the principal child-rearer. In a Soviet family, that person is most commonly the mother, and so her attitudes, emotions, and values matter a great deal. Perhaps this will be clearer if I use an example from my own life. When my children were small, North American society also assumed that child-rearing during the first years of a child's life was primarily the responsibility of the mother. This made the quality of my interaction with my children a more important factor in their development than it might have been in another culture or at another time. I am a worrier, like so many of the Soviet mothers I observed. However, I tried to curb my protective impulses so that my children would develop the outgoing independence that is so cherished in North America. But, in Soviet society, the type of individualistic independence that I wanted for my own children is not highly valued. Had I been a Soviet mother, I am sure I would have acted differently towards my children as they played in the sea, and they would not, I think, have turned out to be quite as independent as they now are.

Child-rearing Practices in the Family

Family child-rearing practices consist of those techniques that parents employ to train a small child to conform with the habits and customs of the family and the surrounding culture. It is surprising how these differ from country to country. All normal children, for example, will eventually gain control of their bodily functions, but customs relating to the taking in of food and the elimination of waste will vary enormously, even among highly civilized peoples. One might think that such things would not really matter to the State as much as they do to the family and the child but, because they have to do with power and control, they do. The aim of parents is to transfer the control of their child's behaviour from themselves to the child so that the child can be trusted to do what is expected of him or her without being reminded. The interest of society is to ensure that the child grows up to behave in a socially acceptable manner. The interest of the

State, and particularly the Soviet state, is more specific. It wants children to be reared so that as adult citizens and as workers their behaviour will serve to promote its long-term goals.

In nineteenth-century Russia, child-rearing methods tended to be punitive. In an essay entitled "That Enemy is the Baby—Childhood in Imperial Russia", Patrick Dunn marshalls persuasive evidence drawn from memoirs and other written documents that life for most children in nineteenth-century Russia, including some from the upper classes, was much more perilous and miserable than in other European countries at the same time. With a few exceptions, including the family of Lenin, parents were, more frequently than not, detached, cold, even hostile towards their own and other children.

Maxim Gorky, a writer who was enormously influential during the first years of the Soviet state, writes about the situation of poor children just prior to the Revolution in his autobiographical novel, *My Childhood*. After his father's death, when he was five, he was brought to live in his grandfather's house, a house filled with a "choking fog of mutual hostility" that poisoned the adults and infected the children. He was preserved by a most remarkable grandmother (the book is worth reading just to meet her) and writes that it was her "unselfish love of the world that enriched me and nourished me with the strength I would need for the hard life that lay ahead".

Gorky's description of a boyhood that was not untypical for his time played a part in the revulsion against corporal punishment that led authorities in the young Soviet state to abolish the practice from the classroom. It has never returned. His tales of childhood beatings awoke a response in many of the revolutionaries who had also known them. In tsarist times, the great mass of peasant children had very little childhood at all. One learns, however, from the memoirs of such writers as Vladimir Nabokov, that children in upper-class Russian families in the years just before the Revolution were brought up in much the same way as the other children of privilege throughout Europe, with governesses and tutors and trips to the sea. Children growing up in the Soviet Union today are frequently reminded of the gross disparities that once existed between rich children and poor children and how the Revolution changed all that.

For the Revolution certainly did. In 1955, Margaret Mead commented in an essay on the Soviet Union that in countries that have known revolutions, child-rearing becomes one of the instruments by which the regime sets out to build a new society. Since 1917 an earnest effort has been made by the Soviet state to abolish child-rearing methods considered unsuitable and to encourage the use of more appropriate ones expressly designed to prepare children for the assimilation of communist values. In a large, and far from homogeneous, population, it has not been easy to change traditional practices perceived as contrary to the interests of the State—those that invoke religious authority, for example—and the process has been a slow and interrupted one. However, if not by the time that Mead wrote her essay, then certainly by the late 1960s when Dr. Urie Bronfenbrenner visited the Soviet Union to gather material for his book *Two Worlds of Childhood: US and USSR,* Soviet society had stabilized enough to exhibit characteristic patterns of child-rearing in the family that, by and large, complemented the carefully designed patterns of Soviet social upbringing.

In approaching the question about how children should be reared, Soviet experts make a clear distinction among three different concepts: temperament, personality, and character. *Temperament* is considered to be in-born, a property of the nervous system leading to a disposition to act in a certain way. There, as here, a child may be described as "highly strung", quick to react (often negatively), or placid and slow to respond (but easier to manage). This has to do with genetic endowment. *Personality* is not in-born but develops as the child becomes the subject of actions rather than the object, self-consciously aware of himself or herself, a *persona,* an "I", a product of all the attitudes towards himself or herself that he or she has encountered.

Character, in the Soviet view, is a construct of acquired habits and modes of dealing with the world that can be built into a person by outside forces interacting in a dynamic fashion with temperament and personality. A person's character will possess qualities that are shared with others from whom he or she may differ greatly in temperament and personality. Child-rearing practices can modify the excesses of temperament and can directly influence the growth of the personality, but it is what such practices contribute to the building of character that is important to the State. That is why the Soviet state is interested in toilet-training, for example, and why it has tried for so long to keep an eye on child-rearing in the family.

Probably the best-known of all Russian child-rearing methods is the practice of infant-swaddling. There are those who have speculated that the degree to which Russians appear to be willing to submit to their fate has been determined by the firm conditioning of early swaddling. A Western observer has even ascribed the remarkable expressiveness of Slavic eyes to the restrictions swaddling places on infants' limbs as a mode of expression. I would hardly go so far, nor am I sure how widespread the practice is among the non-Slavs who inhabit the Soviet Union. That it has had such a long history in the Russian population is not surprising given the cold winters. Enlightened commentators have often criticized the practice. In 1783, one of them pleaded that not only did swaddling deform the body but "it even has an influence on the morals of the child since his first impression of himself proceeds from the feeling of illness or suffering which joined to the feeling of obstruction of his movements sows in him the seeds of anger". Almost a century later, Tolstoy claims that his very "first recollection was that of the frightening constrictions of swathing bands in which Russian children are bound in their cots".

Yet Russian babies are still wrapped up. One of the first theatrical events we attended in Moscow was a production of *Porgy and Bess*, sung in Russian and played in blackface. The performers had beautiful voices but were obviously incapable of imagining themselves black in the southern United States, relaxing outside on a hot night in a state of fluid indolence. When I heard "Summertime" being crooned to what looked like a small white watermelon, it was hard not to giggle. Yet, after I had lived in Moscow for several months, I suddenly realized that every Russian baby I saw taking the air looked like a wrapped watermelon, and that the production designer had probably never thought of babies in any other way.

The persistence of the custom of swaddling is partly a question of tradition. But other pre-revolutionary traditions have been abandoned. There are two factors, I think, that have led to the practice being repeated generation after generation in spite of a growing body of expert medical advice to the contrary. The first is the degree to which swaddling represents the constricting affection with which so many Soviet parents still treat their children. Urie Bronfenbrenner noted this in his *Two Worlds of Childhood.* "On the one hand," he observed, making comparisons with American babies, "the Russian child receives considerably more hugging, kissing, and cuddling. On the other, the infant is held more tightly and given little opportunity for freedom of movement initiative." The second factor, I believe, is the degree to which the practice of swaddling reflects the Soviet state's historic attempts to keep the population "under wraps". The fact that the practice is now being slowly modified augurs well for the health of both child and State.

Progress, however, is slow, and not only babies but toddlers as well are still heavily swaddled. In the winter, rosy-cheeked children as round as balls made me think of the tinkling fat dolls my children played with, which when pushed over, rolled right back up. These toddlers would wear at least four sweaters under their little fur coats, wool bonnets topped by fur hats, flaps down, scarves wound several times around, double mittens, leggings, thick felt boots. You would wonder how they could possibly move. Finally, in 1983 (the last winter I spent in Moscow) I saw some children wearing North American-style snowsuits. That was the moment when I began to believe that little Soviet children were finally going to be able to breathe.

Bronfenbrenner quotes extensively from the manuals on child-rearing that were available at the time he wrote his book. There have been many new ones since he published *Two Worlds of Childhood* and they have improved in tone and in sophistication. A comprehensive series, *Mir Detstva* (The World of Childhood), has appeared under the sponsorship of the Academy of Pedagogical Sciences, aimed at parents and others directly involved in caring for children. Handsomely printed in an imaginative format, its four volumes (on the pre-schooler, the young schoolchild, the adolescent, and the youth) have been written by teams of experts from the Academy's various research institutes. The books are inexpensive, and will, I expect, be widely used because they are full of information and practical advice covering *all* aspects of children's lives.

The Canadian government publishes two manuals, *The Canadian Mother and Child* and *Up the Years from One to Six*, that present sound basic information in an unexciting format. Although the scope of these books is more limited than the Soviet series, I decided to look up "toilet-training", a prime example of social attitudes to control, in both series in order to compare nationally approved approaches to the subject. The Canadian manual deals with the subject briefly: "There is no advantage in trying to train your child to be dry before he is old enough to understand what he is doing.... By the age of three he will usually keep his clothes and bed dry." I can't say that I ever found it quite that simple. However, the manual goes on to issue a warning: "A child whose mother begins training too early or eagerly may develop a stubborn, hostile attitude which can become a permanent part of his personality." Such an outcome does not occur to the Soviets. They believe in getting them early. "At four months the child can be supported on the potty.... If you catch the moment that corresponds to his need the habit of cleanliness will gradually be formed...at eight months he can sit on his own." At a year, the child is expected to be clean and, soon after that, to be dry. The basic message is clear: parents must be prepared to train their children gently but firmly so that they acquire habits of cleanliness and bodily self-control as soon as possible; otherwise, neither the child nor, indeed, the parent will be socially acceptable.

Discussions of discipline in Soviet texts are very revealing. Since corporal punishment is unacceptable, Soviet experts recommend that it be replaced by a family environment so carefully structured that the child will internalize the norms of acceptable social behaviour without a fuss. Early on in his *Book about Bringing up Children*, Yury Azarov, a noted Soviet pedagogue, has a section entitled "The Child as Creator of His Own Upbringing". Starting from the Marxist tenet that it is man's activity (labour) that constructs the environment that, in turn, shapes him, Azarov emphasizes the child's need to acquire a certain amount of self-mastery as soon as possible so that he or she can be active in his or her own development. Internalizing social norms is considered an active process, not a passive one. It will not be successful unless the child makes it happen. This view accounts, in part, for the early toilet-training and the emphasis on self-reliance in such bodily matters as eating, dressing, brushing teeth, and so on. Such achievements are seen less as the growth of genuine independence than as the outcome of a successful management of the transfer of control in these matters from the parent to the child.

Parents are urged to be patient with their children, and to explain carefully the reasons for the activity or habit they wish their child to acquire. In simple matters the norms are quite clear. No one will dispute that it is good to be able to dress oneself, brush one's teeth regularly, feed oneself without making a mess, and so on, but the Soviets go on to assume that the smooth acquisition of physical habits of self-control will facilitate the acquisition of other good habits and attitudes.

Azarov also urges parents to be good examples to their children in the matter of self-control, which is easier said than done. Often power itself becomes the issue, displacing the desirable objective. To take a crude example that is not uncommon in our society: a father doesn't want his children to smoke, but is so authoritarian in his approach that his children take up the habit single-mindedly. This example represents an obvious failure to transfer control from an increasingly angry father to an increasingly rebellious child, with respect to an objective that both of them, in calm moments, can accept as desirable.

Most experts in the Soviet Union condemn authoritarian methods of child discipline while recognizing that they continue to be practised. But Azarov offers alternatives. He presents his reader with a typical daily event, such as getting up on a work-day morning, and outlines three scenarios of what might take place in the family apartment. The "ideal" scenario has the schoolchild getting himself up, preparing breakfast for the others, setting off for school after kissing his mother good-bye and offering to do some errands for his grandmother. The "average" scenario has the child getting up at the last possible moment, gulping down his breakfast, and running out the door, ducking his head to avoid his mother's embrace. The "scandalous" scenario has everyone yelling, and the child, who has had no breakfast, pushing away his grandmother in frustration, then dashing off much too late to get to school on time.

Azarov then offers twenty-one loosely connected versions of how to change the "scandalous" scenario into the "ideal" one, proposing that the reader "choose those which best suit your child, his age, and his individual traits". The first version he calls "the mechanism of joy". Put the child to bed the night before, he suggests, with the prospect of something really pleasurable before him the next day, for example, the excitement of having solved a difficult problem that he can demonstrate to his teacher or the promise of a visit to friends. The second version is entitled "Do not expect drastic changes!"; the sixth, "Do not ignore trifles!" By this last one he means that a parent should try to look at things through the eyes of the child. Tying a shoelace may seem trivial to father, but it is anything but that for his little son. Another version is called "Do not be afraid to caress the child". In the thirteenth version, "Fear no conflicts with children", he discusses the positive dynamic of confrontation in the development of a relationship. This version is followed by the sensible advice "avoid conflicts in the morning". The nineteenth version is called "When you resort to shouting you destroy all the results of your upbringing practice".

Among Azarov's versions is a modern form of the withdrawal of love that was much more crudely recommended in the texts that Bronfenbrenner consulted twenty years earlier. Concerned about the behaviour of the child to the grandmother in the scandalous version, Azarov recommends that the parent work with the child's need for human association. The alienation of the child from the family that is described in this scenario reflects attitudes that the author says have been unconsciously formed in the child by his parents, attitudes that they must now *consciously* try to reverse. Azarov believes that "moral behaviour is always connected with making a choice, with pangs of conscience and if you like, with moral suffering". Therefore, "you have to consciously lead a child to a suffering of his conscience." Specifically, he recommends that "immediately after his misbehaviour you should become somewhat distant. But let him see your disappointed face". One can easily see what he is driving at, but it is a tricky method, easy to abuse.

Outside observers have often commented on the technique of the withdrawal of affection in Soviet family interaction. In her 1954 essay, Margaret Mead observes, with repulsion, that the withholding of love is explicitly recommended in many of the Soviet child-rearing texts of the 1940s and 1950s. She goes on to quote from the case of an exemplary mother who is disciplining her son for the use of bad language: "And if I hear them [those words] again I will not love you." Of course, the little boy repents and reforms. Or at least so the Soviet pedagogue telling the story says. To be frank, I never saw this particular technique in use, although Soviet friends assure me that it is quite common. Given the highly emotional quality of family relations that I did observe, however, I can well believe that it is used.

I will leave the last word on the Soviet approach to family discipline to Anton Makarenko because I believe that what he said on the subject in a lecture for parents broadcast on Radio Moscow in 1937 still lies at the core of Soviet writings on the subject. He stressed that if family life is well structured there will not, in fact, be any need for punishment. "In well-adjusted families punishments are not used and this is the best, most correct path for child care in the family." For, according to this respected Soviet pedagogue, as the child grows and becomes an adult citizen he will be "expected not only to appreciate to what end and why it is necessary to carry out this or that command but also actively to endeavour to carry it out to the very best of his ability". If this happens, then the locus of control for the maintenance of Soviet values will have shifted completely from the surrounding adults to the child who has come of age.

The Fundamentals of a Collectivist Upbringing

The life of the growing child expands beyond the family hearth very early in the Soviet Union. Then the family child-rearing practices, to which he or she has been subject since infancy, begin to interact with forces of social upbringing in the outside world. Soviet parents may have varied objectives or none at all, as they take care of their children, but upbringing methods to which Soviet children are exposed in the world outside the family have been consciously devised for a clearly defined objective: the creation of a model Soviet citizen.

Actually, everybody gets involved in upbringing "work", as the Soviets call it. In the 1960s, Bronfenbrenner noted that *vospitanie* was virtually a national hobby in the USSR. It still is. There are many busy-body *babushkas* whose day is highlighted by opportunities to scold a thoughtless mother for failing to wrap up her child. People volunteer time to guide or teach children other than their own. Artists, writers, educators, sportsmen—one is not surprised to find them with groups of children. But tractor drivers? Army officers? Gold-miners? Everyone is expected to help in raising the nation's children.

The scolding *babushkas* may have no clear idea of what they are doing beyond their firm conviction that it is their traditional right to interfere, a right now sanctioned by the State. Most other people, however, are bound to be aware of the goals of their efforts. They are certainly reminded often enough. Some of them work with children on their own—a man I know teaches script-writing to adolescent film buffs in his apartment block once a week. Others work with factory colleagues to help children put on a play in a Pioneer palace. These volunteers may be recognized with special awards for making their individual contribution to the development of an educated and balanced person "who loves his socialist homeland, is loyal to communist ideals", and so on.

It should be clear by now that the focus of *vospitanie* is really *character* moulding, the development of both the disposition and the will to act in accordance with the values of the State. Since one of the highest values of the Soviet state is collectivism,

State authorities have directed the schools and the children's organizations to involve children repeatedly in children's collectives. The feeling for the collective—that is, for the emotional unity that is generated by communal life in any group endowed with a shared purpose and mutual trust—is traditional in Russian society. The specific notion of a children's collective, however, arose from Anton Makarenko's experiences with a colony of juvenile offenders in the Ukraine immediately after the Revolution. He and his small group of helpers had a difficult time with these wild youngsters and no theory to turn to as they tried to rehabilitate them. Makarenko vividly describes the situation, and how he was able to reform his delinquents, in his autobiographical novel *The Road to Life*. He was obviously a personality of sufficient strength, energy, and determination to gain the respect of his motley assortment of "insolent and cynical" young criminals and then to organize them into a functioning group. Through trial and error (but inspired by the socialist principles of the new Soviet state, "according to which the prosperity of each member was directly dependent on the prosperity of all members"), he formed his charges into a working collective where the youngsters took responsibility for their physical environment, for what the colony produced in terms of goods and services, for the allocation of income, and for order and discipline. They became not just a collection of individuals but an integrated social unit to which everyone was glad and proud to belong. In the evenings, they sat around while he read to them from the works of Maxim Gorky, particularly *My Childhood* and its sequel, *My Apprenticeship,* in which Gorky describes his adolescent years. The colony was named after Gorky.

No doubt it was Makarenko's leadership that made his ideas so successful when put in action. Not everyone is a Makarenko, but the idea of the children's collective was both so attractive and so ideologically sound that it became an established feature of the Soviet upbringing system. The collective is seen as a concrete example of the socialist way of life that helps its members become aware that the interests of society are identical with the interests of the individual. As a result children are expected to become involved in collectives as young as possible.

From the State's point of view, it would be ideal if the family would act as the child's first, and later as his or her most enduring, collective. Families are regularly exhorted and even cajoled to fulfil this role. However, the objective difficulties of daily living, the unresolved dilemmas of male-female relationships, and the lack of true dedication have so far made this the exception rather than the rule.

The school environment is much easier for the State to control. For this reason the true beginning of collective life usually takes place when the child leaves the family setting on a daily basis for some sort of institutional experience. Margaret Mead writes about "such definitely ideological measures as feeding two babies with alternate spoonfuls or hanging two babies up in a sort of net together as a learning experience in collective behaviour". Such measures supposedly were in use right after the Revolution, but I am sure they were soon seen as too complicated, if not too downright silly, to be continued. The collective experience for infants and small children that Bronfenbrenner describes in his book, however, I have verified from my own experience. In a *yasli* (nursery-school), infants are placed in group playpens and are encouraged to share the toys that they are given to play with. Small children are reminded constantly about common ownership. Collective activities of all kinds are emphasized: cleaning up the playroom, digging in the garden, group games, playing with toys that require co-operation to make them work, singing and dancing when every child has a chance to perform and no one stars. Visitors have a lot of pleasurable exposure to these activities everywhere they go in the Soviet Union. On arrival at a *yasli,* I was often greeted by a flood of little children, each one carrying a single flower that all together made my bouquet.

In the *yasli* and in the first years of the *detsky sad* (kindergarten), the group experiences organized for children are essentially preparatory to the formation of true children's collectives. These activities are invariably directed by adults, but as they grow older and more self-reliant, children are encouraged to generate collective activities on their own. It is then, returning to the idea of the "child as the creator of his own upbringing", that the children's collective begins to exercise its greatest influence. After a certain age, every Soviet child belongs to at least one and usually several collectives. The most important ones are formed in the school environment, centred either on academic work or on the socially useful activities sponsored by the various levels of the Communist youth movement: Octobrist, Pioneer, or Komsomol.

There are out-of-school collectives, too, formed around sports or other interests and hobbies. There are even spontaneous ones that spring up where children live, although whether these last ones can be called true collectives is a matter of debate. Nevertheless, they are important in children's lives, and the Soviet authorities are not likely to ignore anything that might have an influence. A collective is, by its very definition, a desirable component of Soviet society, and it is the definable, ideologically acceptable, socially useful objective of the collective that makes it beneficial to its individual members. If its objective is not socially useful then a collective is only a group. The dynamics of a group are quite different from those of a collective. They are not necessarily harmful but they will do nothing positive to make the children more collectivist-minded. While in the past children have been discouraged from joining informal groups, experts now recognize that adolescents, in particular, have needs that the collective is too structured to meet.

I encountered one children's collective in Moscow that struck me as nearly ideal. Called the "Circle of Young Patriots", it meets twice a week in a large room in the splendid new Pioneer palace in the Lenin Hills that houses not only the obligatory Lenin display to be found in any Pioneer palace but also a museum of war heroes. This little museum has been built up over the years by successive circles of Young Patriots, each one consisting of a dozen or so children, twelve or thirteen years of age. The leader of the collective is a spry retired teacher who has been involved as a volunteer in this activity for a long time. Her only concern is that one day she will have to relinquish her role because of age.

I visited the group in spring when their project for the year was near completion. The youngsters were seated at a large table, drawing a map with great care. At the beginning of each year the leader hands the newly formed collective (all of whom are members by choice) the name of someone who fought in the

Great Patriotic War. The children are also given the person's rank and military unit, date of birth and, sometimes, date of death. The collective's common task is to find out everything possible about this person and to create a documented display for the museum. With such a vast number of war dead as well as so many surviving veterans there is no lack of appropriate subjects. With the leader's help, the youngsters plan their initial strategy. They figure out how to learn more about the war itself, how to discover where this person had served, how to find out whether or not he or she was injured or killed, and how to determine whether there are any surviving relatives or close friends. Some go to the Ministry of Defence for interviews; others write letters and track down people who have been involved in military campaigns with their subject. Gradually a portrait is pieced together. One group even located the grave of their chosen hero, to the heart-felt gratitude of the family who had not known where it was.

The children I met that day found their task both challenging and enormously interesting. The old teacher, who had built up a store of experience over the years, had given them the kind of help they needed to surmount any obstacles encountered on the way. Soon they would be adding a new figure to the pantheon of existing heroes, along with the various mementoes, photographs, and letters that they had been able to unearth. Their hero would be unveiled in a solemn little ceremony. The children were eager to show me the letters they had received and other material they had gathered, and they would have kept me all afternoon to tell me about this brave soldier whom they had come to know if I had had the time to stay. These young Soviets certainly felt that they had accomplished something of national importance and had learned a great deal about collective, co-operative work in the process.

As a method of social upbringing, what kind of long-term effect does the children's collective have? This question is very difficult to answer. Productivity figures over the years suggest that large-scale central planning does not encourage the survival of collectives with the qualities I have listed. However, my own experience with an adult Soviet "work collective" was so striking in comparison with similar experiences that I have had in other countries that I offer it as an example.

I have worked with a domestic staff in four different cultures. What foreign-service people call the "representational" side of diplomatic life is almost impossible to handle on one's own, particularly if one has small children. Nowadays, spouses of Canadian foreign-service officers are permitted to opt out of these duties and responsibilities if they want to, but not in my time. A successful diplomatic social event that serves the interests of your country requires considerable planning and management. In France, it was difficult to get my strong-minded helpers to work together. In Mexico, they could agree about what needed to be done but became touchy about sharing responsibility. India was easier. Each member of the staff belonged to a different caste and knew exactly what he could or could not do, according to caste rules. There was no juggling for position and relationships were cordial and functional. As long as the complement was full, everything would go on without a hitch, and even the largest dinner party was a breeze. Problems only arose when one of them was away on holiday. The work would not be done, however, unless a person from his own caste could be found to replace him.

My Moscow staff did not know one another before they began to work for me, but they soon became a genuine collective. There was a lot of work to be done: an embassy residence is public property and must be well maintained for the representational events which follow one right after the other. There was never any problem. If I told Tamara, the cook, at 11:00 a.m. that there would be six guests for lunch she would say "*Nichego* (It doesn't matter), Madame. Just tell me what you want and it will be ready." And so it was, right on time, with everyone doing his or her share. I am sure that their experience of upbringing in a variety of children's collectives contributed to their disposition to co-operate with one another and their ability to plan how best to share the tasks. They enjoyed the challenge of the National Day reception to which we invited seven hundred people, and they made some decisions on their own about who was to do what, where, and when. However, they always depended on me, not only for overall direction, but for precise details with respect to menus and schedules.

I usually spent a couple of hours a day with them, particularly with Tamara, the cook, translating recipes and describing Canadian customs in food and food presentation, discussing primarily work-related subjects. If I was busy and unable to make the time, her cooking seemed to fall off. Makarenko said that a collective would go stale if there was no process and, indeed, that was what happened when he left his colony of youngsters for any length of time. All of which suggests to me that the personal nature of the collective, and the expectation that it will be partly structured by someone from outside with a real interest, is one of the things that threatens its long-term stability. If it is not worked at, it will fall apart, like any other personal relationship. I like the idea of the children's collective. But I suspect that, as an experience of social upbringing, it raises emotional expectations that the nature of the Soviet work-place consistently disappoints, leading to disaffection and to a turning away from the factory or office to private (although not necessarily individual) activities for personal satisfaction. Whether Gorbachev can build on the positive experiences that the children of *glasnost* will sometimes have had with children's collectives remains an open question. Success depends on sensitive leadership at all levels.

Upbringing "Models"

I have left to the last a major component of Soviet upbringing theory (and practice): the role of parents and others as models of authority and behaviour. Anton Makarenko, certainly an admirable model from the Soviet point of view (in retrospect at least), makes an interesting distinction between various forms of "false" authority within the family and the positive influence of a good parental model. He says that the imposition of authority through "oppression, arrogance, distance, pedantry, didactics, emotional manipulation, bribery" (the list goes on) is bound to have a negative influence on the child. "The main foundation for parental authority can only be the life and work of the parents, their social role, their behaviour."

This theme is elaborated with extraordinary sensitivity by a contemporary writer and thinker about children Simon Soloveychik. In a book published in 1988, Soloveychik discusses the three models of upbringing most familiar to parents in the Soviet Union (and not only there). He calls them the "street-traffic" model, the "vegetable garden", and the "carrot and stick". The first teaches right and wrong like traffic rules, and expects that children will behave properly once they know what the rules are. The second model envisions the child's soul as a plot that needs weeding; but according to Soloveychik, this leads parents and teachers to focus too much on a child's shortcomings (weeds). The third model runs the risk of implanting in a child's consciousness the idea that since you are rewarded for good behaviour the inevitable calamities of life must be a punishment for misbehaviour. The ultimate effectiveness of these child-rearing practices is further undermined for Soloveychik by the fact that the controlling adults are not asked to pay attention to their own moral behaviour.

Soloveychik then goes beyond these conventional upbringing models to seek the actual origins of good and evil in the soul of the child. These he finds in the failure of adults to establish emotional and spiritual "communion" with the child, a communion that will depend as much on an adult's personal qualities as on the child's receptivity. "Difficult children," he writes, "are those who have no emotional and spiritual contacts with adults" and "difficult parents are those who are unable and unwilling to establish such contacts, who are incensed by the very idea of treating children as equals from whom they might actually learn."

Because Marxism-Leninism emphasizes the importance of the social environment for child development, Soviet authorities surround children with "ideal" models. They are to be found in every school text, in popular children's books, on television, in films, and any other place a child might look. Lenin, of course, represents the "highest" ideal; however, as a person, he is remote from the daily lives of children. The members of a child's own family, however, are always on view. We in the West may be faulted for not loving our children enough but Soviet parents will be accused of setting a bad example.

"It is the unfavourable relations within the family and the bad example of hypocritical, rude, or dishonest parents that create an inauspicious micro-environment, one of the most important causes for the appearance of difficult teenagers," says one well-known Soviet expert on adolescence.

The ability of children to distinguish between true and false behaviour runs like a strong current through the best Soviet writing about children. For Soviet psychologists, there is no such thing as a born liar. Lying is learned behaviour, and a child who is in constant contact with people who lie or who act hypocritically will learn the worst.

I saw a revealing play one autumn afternoon at the Youth Theatre in Leningrad. The director sent his young actors into homes and schools and then into the streets of the city to observe how adults actually behave with children. Afterwards he asked them to improvise short skits based on what they had seen. The result was a highly entertaining performance, which had the entire audience of parents and teachers, adolescents, and me, rolling in the aisles. We always laugh when we see the disparities between what people do and what they think or pretend they are doing. Such is the healing power of social comedy. This production, which was called *Open Lesson,* involved a series of vignettes in which the same actors would play now an adult, now a child. One sketch focused on a family party where the birthday child was left standing at the door, his arms full of unsuitable presents, while the adults squabbled. Another re-created a school concert containing the ridiculous items most of us remember performing. Adults were shown up as being as foolish, self-important, insensitive, and self-righteous as many of us often are, and the audience watched with laughter and pain as the "children" gradually lost their innocence and integrity.

What Soviet Children Have to Say about Adults

Lada Aidarova is one adult who needs no lessons. She is a Soviet psychologist who urges parents to listen to what their children have to say, to learn from them how they perceive the world and themselves in it, and to adjust their own behaviour accordingly. She has spent years talking to children and collecting essays and drawings. In one of her books she quotes from children in the primary grades, seven- to ten-year-olds who have written about their teachers, their mothers and fathers, their friends, what makes them happy or sad, and about the future.

A seven-year-old writes about his teacher: "Anatoly Borisovich is a good instructor in gym. We all love him. Anatoly Borisovich is jolly in class. We went to the zoo with him and there Anatoly Borisovich fed a camel. We went to the forest together with him. We coasted on sleds with Anatoly Borisovich. When he was ill we were all very sorry."

Here are some reflections on parents: "Father loves Mother very much…. They get on well together and go to the theatre"; "Father beats her sometimes and we defend. And when Father flew away, Mother felt bad, asked for a mustard plaster and fell asleep"; "He is very reserved. When Mother shouts, Father speaks calmly. He used to have many shortcomings. Now he has almost none of them, because he has so much will-power. That's my father"; "Mother helps Father study French"; "I hardly ever see her. My mother often goes to the theatre and Father and I collect stamps"; "My family likes Father. Father also has a big daughter of 22".

About happiness little Tanya writes: "To my mind it isn't those who have two cars, two summer houses and a nice flat and eat four ice-cream cones a day that are the happiest but my mother and I. Mother and I have one room. I study English and teach it to my mother while she reads me books. We have everything one needs. Mother loves me and I love her. How can we be unhappy? Yes, we are the happiest."

Finally here is his future as envisioned by an eight-year-old: "If I were grown up I would be an architect and build houses. I would only paint them all in different colours and decorate them with all sorts of flowers, butterflies, and bugs. I would also paint in all sorts of ways all the restaurant windows so that meals were more enjoyable. Then I would write books of stories and fairy-tales for children. I would make up lots of things especially in fairy-tales. I make up lots of things in my drawings so I would illustrate my books myself. But I am not grown up yet." And when he is, what then? Will the way in which his family has reared him mesh with his experiences in school collectives to make him a productive member of the Union of Soviet Architects? Will I one day eat in one of his restaurants? The odds are improving.

On our way back to the airport after our weekend in Yalta, our driver slowed down to point out the site of Artek, the most famous of all Soviet Pioneer camps for children, spread out over several square kilometres of rocky terrain between the Crimean mountains and the Black Sea. The most promising Pioneers are sent there from all over the USSR, elected first by their fellow Pioneers and then approved by a local Party committee. The process of selection is by no means foolproof and there have been many complaints about the pulling of strings and the application of pressure. Nevertheless, most of those who get to Artek are model children, the better to greet the young visitors who come there every summer from countries all over the world. I was sometimes asked why I didn't visit Artek. I would make some excuse, but to tell the truth, I was intimidated by the prospect of 4,500 ideal children all in one showcase.

International festivals are often held at Artek. In 1977, a small group of American children attended accompanied by Dr. Benjamin Spock. Dr. Spock is popular in the USSR; his famous *Common Sense Book of Baby and Child Care* has been published there. Yury Azarov had some long conversations with Dr. Spock and wrote about them in his own child-rearing book. Azarov is a compassionate man and an experienced teacher, and his book is almost as full of good advice as is Dr. Spock's (for whose comforting advice to a nervous young mother I remain eternally grateful).

Both child experts agreed unequivocally on the importance of a child's early life, concluding that "all the basic traits of one's character are formed during one's first years, traits which later develop into associations with one's peers, with one's teachers, with the world of inner values, and with culture". But Azarov then adds a comment more Soviet than American: "A direct dependence can be drawn between the way the mother brings up her child and the structure of society, its values and means of asserting them." Thank goodness Dr. Spock never laid that kind of responsibility on my shoulders. However, there is much truth in what Azarov and many of his fellow Soviet experts say about the interconnections between how a child is reared and the future of society, a truth that should be pondered by parents and politicans alike.

"A capable child is not a gift of Nature" is a saying that is often quoted by educators in the Soviet Union because it implies that there have to be interventions in children's lives both at home and at school if they are to grow up as good human beings and model Soviet citizens. Children in the USSR are generally well loved and protected, and if their lives are not carefully structured at home, then they certainly are at school. Children are taught to draw emotional sustenance and satisfaction from their collective life. They are provided with models to emulate and goals to attain.

But the genuine excitement about creating a new kind of person that was so marked at the beginning of the Soviet state evaporated after Stalin came to power, and then for many years neither parents nor the State dared to sit back and let something unexpected, something unplanned for, happen. Although Marxist theory affirms that humankind has unlimited potential, for a long time Soviet practice did not encourage it. One of the traits of the Soviet "national character" that is most visible today is its cautious conservatism. This trait has its roots in the peasant society of pre-revolutionary Russia and the enthusiasms of the post-revolutionary period were too short-lived and not sufficiently widespread to change it. Since then it has been reinforced by historical events and by the Soviet child-rearing practices I have just described, combined with the highly controlled social upbringing of the school and the children's organizations.

This trait may change as Soviet society opens up under Gorbachev and change it must if the Soviet Union is to be able to rise to the challenges that threaten its very survival. There is another national characteristic, however, that is likely to persist—the emotionalism that is highly valued by both the family and the State. Emotionalism has always been associated with Slavic peoples, and it is reinforced in the Soviet population today by the intensity of family interaction in early childhood and by the use of the collective in the schools and in the children's organizations. It is depth of feeling, however, that is more valued than extravagant display of emotion. As we travelled around the country, we found that the non-Slavic nationalities appeared to value emotionalism just as much as the Russians, and the Georgians even added a little southern spice to it. It is a characteristic that many Westerners, especially young people, find particularly attractive.

A further quality that impressed me greatly when I was there, and that permeates all the literature I have quoted both on child care in the family and on social upbringing, is the highly developed moral sensibility of the "national character". This is another characteristic that I expect will endure. By this I mean that most Soviet people look at the world in moral categories. They are brought up very early to think about things in terms of right and wrong, to suffer the "pangs of conscience", as Azarov said. Most of the "right" qualities that both families and authorities want children to develop are encompassed by the Boy Scout's Code of Honour and are desirable in all human beings: trustworthiness, loyalty, courage, courtesy, and so on. The morality of contemporary Soviets is most apparent in their personal and private lives, which is where their emotions and their personal identities are engaged, and which accounts for their generosity and reliability in friendship and for their intense personal patriotism, which is informed by an almost visceral love of the motherland. In situations where relationships are less personal, where objectives are abstract and out of reach, and where there is any hint of hypocrisy, Soviet morality loses its binding force. Extending the personal morality of Soviet citizens to their place of work is one of Mikhail Gorbachev's greatest challenges.

Of course, improved morality in the work-place will not be sufficient on its own to spark the economic renewal Gorbachev seeks. It will have to be accompanied by a certain amount of entrepreneurship. This is where the interaction between child-rearing practices and social upbringing has not yet produced the right mix. I believe, from what I have observed, that the average Soviet child growing up today is more a collectivist than an individualist, and that means that he or she is better adapted to functioning inside than outside of a group. But is anything wrong with collective entrepreneurship? Soviet authorities are clearly willing to give the idea a try. The problem is that most Soviet families continue to be overprotective, and their child-rearing practices, constricting. Children who are allowed to be adventurous can quite easily find excitement in working with other children in a true collective where everyone pulls his or her own weight. In the right circumstances, these children could become enormously productive adults. In our society, because of our "national character", individual enterprise in a relatively free-market situation appears to be what works best for our economy. However, this may not be the answer for a society that is less individualistic, where people are more willing to take chances when they are supported by the collective.

A "national character" is by no means set in stone. It is printed on human beings and, as soon as enough individuals in a population change, so will the national character—more slowly, of course, but just as surely. If Gorbachev and his supporters want a dynamic future for the Soviet Union, as they claim they do, then the Soviet national character will have to display more adventurousness and less cautious reserve. For this to happen, there will have to be a better balance between holding back and letting go than appears to be the case at the moment either in the family or at school. More parents will have to unwrap their babies, teachers will have to let students experiment with both ideas and behaviour, and the State will have to be as truthful with children as it promises to be with adults. Since these things are now beginning to happen, it is the children of the 1980s who may turn the tide.

CHAPTER THREE

Family Life

Sunday is family day in Moscow. As we walked around the city on weekdays, we would occasionally meet young mothers on maternity leave, wheeling their cocooned babies along the busy sidewalk, or toddlers in the park with their grandmothers, but the older children were out of sight. Pre-schoolers were in day-care, and all the others were at school. The school day is quite short in the Soviet Union, but after-school activities keep senior pupils busy and the extended-day program looks after younger ones. The work week for most adults is five days and the school week is normally six, so on Saturday parents are free to go about their own business. On Sunday, however, families come together and, winter or summer, weather permitting, set off into the public places to enjoy themselves.

During the years we lived in Moscow, we would often join family groups relaxing on Sundays in the great green stretches of the city—Gorky Park, the Lenin Hills, the Botanical Gardens, Serebryany Bor (Silver Woods)—all the unclipped, shaggy commons of Moscow where fairy-tale figures of rough-chiselled wood stand guard over children's well-used playgrounds, and, on white slatted park benches, the old folk sit and watch. Out of cramped apartments and bleak high-rises, families pour onto the erstwhile playgrounds of princes—Sokolniki, Izmailovo, Tsaritsyn, Kuskovo—wide wooded parks eaily accessible by bus or Metro, ideal for picnicking in the summer or cross-country skiing in winter. Some parks have simple amusement sections, bandshells, open-air theatres. Others are small and have room only for the traditional European sand-piles, slides, and climbers that enlivened outings with our own children when we lived in Paris in 1950s. During the week, children study under the watchful eye of the State, and their parents are engaged in "social production", as the Soviets describe even the most boring of jobs. But Sunday belongs to the family.

We had a favourite excursion, to Kolomenskoye. Now well within the southern limits of the city, this was once a royal village, the site of a vast wooden palace built for Tsar Alexey Mikhailovich, the father of Peter the Great. The park lands of Kolomenskoye rise gently from apple orchards on one side to a bluff overlooking the Moscow River on the other. From this height the tsars had a fine view of the golden domes of the Kremlin churches. They still glow faintly through the obscuring smoke of factory stacks and the general haze of dusty city suburbs. The rambling wooden palace is gone now, reduced to a miniature model on display in a room of the old stone gate-house, but two historic churches remain. For over four centuries, the white Church of the Ascension, with its strange conical spire, has dominated the river and, since the seventeenth century, the star-spangled midnight-blue onion domes of Our Lady of Kazan have stood out against the sky.

The park is large. There is plenty of room for the thousands of families that come there every Sunday. This makes it an excellent place to observe the cycle of life through all its stages. We used to drive there from the Embassy in my sky-blue Zhiguli and park outside the gates. On one typical Sunday morning in June, as we walked up the path towards Our Lady of Kazan, we saw a line of baby carriages parked under the porch—red, green, yellow, and blue, a dozen at least. Babies were inside the church being baptized. Outside, in the shadow of the church wall, a young man snatched a dandelion crown from his girlfriend's fingers and set it on her hair. Approaching the cliff above the river, we came upon excited children taking turns straddling the cannon that had been placed there at the time of Napoleon's invasion of Russia. Nearby, a father was tossing a ball to his son, while his wife and daughter laid out their picnic.

We descended to the river. On either side of the sloping path, families had spread blankets in the long grass and the adults lay in the sun exposing their pale winter flesh. It was unusually warm for the time of year, and some young boys, quite undeterred by what the river had accumulated on its passage through the city, were swimming in its murky water. A few rough-cut steps brought us back up into a corner of the park that is now a museum of wooden architecture. A pair of youngsters were climbing up into the watchtower that had been transported there from a Siberian outpost, and several families were visiting the hunting lodge of Peter the Great, brought down from the shores of the White Sea. Small children poked at the hand-forged utensils in the kitchen alcove and gawked at the size of Peter's boots. Close by, seated across from each other on a vast stump amid the eight-hundred-year-old oak trees, two old women were playing cards.

On summer Sundays, scenes like these are enacted all over the city of Moscow and, indeed, throughout the Soviet Union. For this is the day when ordinary families shelve the problems of daily living, escape the confines of their small apartments, and go out among the remnants and reminders of their history and culture to have a good time.

When Tolstoy opened *Anna Karenina* with the words "All happy families are alike. Every unhappy family is miserable in its own way", he was saying that the happy family is an ideal that unhappy families fall short of in almost as many ways as there are human beings. And it is true that, as I have travelled around the world, I have found people's miseries more varied than their joys. Happy families are loving and communicative, and their children thrive, even in hardship. But unhappy families wound their offspring, each in its own special way. Like every other country, the Soviet Union has its share of both. That is why, to offset the familiar image of grumpy weekday crowds battling their way home from work against the driving snow, I offer my snapshots of good-humoured, affectionate families relaxing in the summer sun.

No modern state, not even the USSR, has been able to dislodge the family as the earliest and most important influence in the life of the young child. It is now more than seventy years since the coming of Soviet power and, during all that period, there has been a fascinating interaction going on between the Soviet state, with its well-defined long-term social goals, and the Soviet family. The family in the USSR has changed greatly as a result of processes that were set in motion at the time of the Revolution. Some of these processes, such as wide-scale industrialization, the mechanization of labour, and the movement of people from the country to the city, are inevitable when nations modernize. It can be assumed that Soviet families have been affected by them in ways that parallel the experiences of Western Europe and North America. Other processes and events, however, that have profoundly marked Soviet families are quite specific to Soviet history. The forced collectivization of agriculture in the early years of the Soviet state, the brutal and dehumanizing nature of ideological control under Stalin, and the enormous casualties of the Second World War have all weighed heavily on vast numbers of individual families and affected them deeply. These events have tended to make families more protective and tightly knit, more inward-looking, more self-contained, more resistant to state intervention. They have not, however, rendered Soviet marriages more stable. Stress and separation have taken their toll.

The Soviet family has also been markedly influenced by changes in the status of women. Similar changes have accompanied industrialization in many other parts of the world but they occurred earlier in the Soviet Union and have been more widespread. The percentage of women in the work-force is still much higher in the USSR than it is in the United States or Canada. This has been true, and intentionally so, since the beginning of the Soviet state.

The Soviet state has, in turn, been considerably influenced by the family, by its fertility, its growing instability, and its relative autonomy. The number of children in a family, whether or not partners stay together, how strongly the children are influenced by family traditions, all are factors of concern to a state that wants to shape its "rising generation". The climate of the school can be regulated relatively easily but the more than seventy-two million individual families living in the Soviet Union are not so accessible to State control. The conditions in which most of them live, however, and which often contribute to the happiness or unhappiness of any particular household, are very much a function of State policy and are as crucial an element in the formation of today's generation as they were at any time in the past.

The Ideal Soviet Family

The "ideal family" of the Soviet state is not exactly what Tolstoy had in mind. We met an examplar when we accompanied Eugene Whelan, then Canada's Minister of Agriculture, on a visit to a state farm in the Crimea. We were shown the best of everything. Every cow, every potato, every apple was perfect. The minister, who had once been a farmer, had rubber boots for tramping around dung-filled barnyards, but the dung had miraculously vanished. We were taken to a "typical" farm-worker's apartment, and when the door opened we stepped into an unshadowed and persuasive worker's paradise.

The apartment was rather small, four rooms including the kitchen, but it had been freshly painted and, possibly, newly furnished with shiny veneered furniture and factory-made carpets. The young father who greeted us was unbelievably handsome, blond and muscular, easy to imagine driving his tractor into the sunset. His wife was tall and slender, as blonde as her husband and dressed in a long flowered wrapper. A pretty little girl of about eight and her rather delicate six-year-old brother stood beside them. The children were shy but the parents were not and immediately offered us tea and biscuits followed by a glass of good Crimean wine. We were told that the young man was a fine worker, a leader of his work brigade, and that his wife was a teacher in a local school. They were both extensively involved in the political and social activities of the farm (which was actually a large and successful agro-industrial complex), but we were assured that they took good care of their children as well, assiduously attending parent-education classes in order to learn how to be good "upbringers". They heard themselves being talked about in another language and smiled. They offered a toast to peace and friendship and to all the children of the world. A "happy family", one that the Soviet authorities would certainly like to see replicated all over the USSR: unified, industrious, dutiful, and involved in socially useful activities, both inside and outside the family. In only one respect were they less than ideal: Soviet population experts would prefer that they had another child.

As they closed the door after us the four members of the "ideal family" had every reason to feel pleased. They had responded well to the challenge of entertaining our rather odd group and had succeeded in making us feel at home. They probably washed up the plates and the empty glasses with satisfaction, commented with bemusement on the bright green felt stetson hat that our agriculture minister was wearing, and said how kind one of his aides had been to bring toys to the children. Then, no doubt, they changed back into their work clothes and went about their normal business. They had given no hint at all that they had any reservations about their command performance.

Even when a family in the Soviet Union adopts the model of what constitutes the "ideal", it continues to exercise considerable personal autonomy. Personal decisions are involved in its very formation, just as they are in most of the Western world. The choice of the marriage partner is relatively unconstrained by family or custom except in parts of Central Asia and the Caucasus. Personal choices certainly determine family size, even more so than in the West, since abortion is universally available and the use of contraception is encouraged. If either partner decides that he or she has had enough, it is personal choice that brings the marriage to an end.

The Soviet state has legally guaranteed freedom to men and women with respect to marriage, pregnancy, and divorce. In recent times, it has also reiterated that the family is the basic unit of socialist society responsible for reproducing the population, for raising children as good citizens, and for providing for the emotional and expressive needs of family members. Therefore, the State finds itself obliged to come to terms with the outcomes of the personal choices it has left up to the family. The coercive techniques of the Stalin years backfired. The bullying of a later period was not much more successful. So, for the last decade or so, the Soviet state has introduced some quite extraordinary measures of family support, both economic and moral, in order to influence the family to make the choices the State prefers, thereby becoming more stable, having more children, and bringing them up better.

The Family and Soviet History

After the Revolution, there were many among the Bolsheviks who expected that the family would vanish under true communism, withering away as the State was supposed to. Sex would be freed from marriage, and society would bring up the children. This view was not widely popular. And indeed, for those who embraced it, it was more a reaction against the constrictions and controls exercised by pre-revolutionary families than a new vision of what the family might be.

Lenin did not think that the family as an institution should be abolished. He agreed with the position of Marx and Engels that the family in capitalist society was patriarchal and property-oriented and that women were treated as chattels to be disposed of through marriage. But this meant only that the "bourgeois" form of marriage was unfair and had to be changed. It did not mean that marriage or the family should be discarded. Since he was genuinely committed to equality for women, he envisioned that, in his new Soviet state, the union of men and women would be freed from all materialistic considerations and based, instead, on true love and mutual respect; it was to be terminated when either partner felt that these conditions had ceased to exist. The new socialist family would have the potential for encouraging the equal growth and development of *both* husband and wife.

It remained for a woman—Alexandra Kollontai—to focus on the children. "Let the working mothers be reassured," she insisted in 1918, "the Communist society is not intending to take the children away from the parents.... The Society of the workers...hails the arrival of every new-born child in the world."

It will ensure that the child "will be fed, it will be brought up, it will be educated". For this to happen, she went on to say, "the worker's state has need of a new form of relation between the sexes", one in which father and mother share equally in the rights and responsibilities of child-rearing. She also called for a change in the relationship between mother and children. "The narrow and exclusive affection of the mother for her own children must expand until it embraces all the children." Kollontai was the People's Commissar for Social Security and her position no doubt contributed to the rapidity with which the new family relations were embodied in legislation first enacted in 1917 and then in 1923 incorporated into the Code of Civil Law. No longer was anyone going to "own" anyone else. Divorce became a simple procedure, all children were to have equal rights under the law, and husband and wife acquired equal rights with respect to children.

When Kollontai made her assurances to working women, her instincts were right. During the early 1920s, some sporadic attempts continued to be made to discredit the family as a vestige of bourgeois life, and children were occasionally encouraged to denounce "old-fashioned" parents, but the Soviet people, as a whole, resisted such wholesale change. This resistance was strengthened when, by the middle of the decade, it became evident that the abrupt transformation of family relationships encouraged by the early legislation had led to some unhappy consequences. For example, citing the notion that women were supposed to be able to support themselves, many husbands abandoned both wives and children. Times were too hard, though, for the State to provide support, so this action only augmented the number of unsupervised and unhappy children and adolescents who roamed the cities and drifted about the countryside during this period. By 1926 there was no more talk of abolishing the family and taking over its functions. Instead, stricter legislation (the 1926 Code of Common Law) laid a multitude of obligations upon husband and wife when "the child truly created the family". State policy focused on the provision of economic and social support and the supremely important task of engaging the family in the joint endeavour of forming "little builders of communism".

In the early 1930s, Stalin drastically reduced freedom of choice in the family as he did in every other aspect of Soviet life. With the aim of reinforcing and controlling the family as the basic unit of society, divorce was made much more difficult and abortion forbidden except to women whose lives were in danger. Motherhood was glorified to augment the population. A loyal, obedient, and united family was the ideal for Stalin, but if there was any conflict between the family and the State, then an individual's first loyalty was owed to the latter. Stalin had no intention of abolishing the family as long as he found it useful. Rather he tried to bend it to the will of the State, to *his* will.

It is impossible to quantify the emotional toll on families of those terrible years, which extended beyond the Second World War. Nadezhda Mandelstam, the wife and later the grieving widow of the great Russian poet Osip Mandelstam, is, in my view, the best available observer from inside the Soviet Union to bear witness to the subtle psychological impact of despotism on the individual in society. In the second of her two remarkable auto-biographical books, *Hope Against Hope* and *Hope Abandoned,* she describes "the atrophy of true personality" that happened to so many members of her generation and ascribes it to "the severing of all social bonds" that occurred during the 1930s and the post-war period. "All social links such as the family, one's circle of friends, class, society itself, each abruptly disappeared leaving every one of us to stand alone before the mysterious force embodied in the State with its power of life and death." At the end of her book, Nadezhda (which means "hope" in Russian) worries that "we have muddied the waters for many generations to come and may never find our way back to their true source".

After Stalin's death, coercive measures to maintain family stability were gradually abandoned. Divorce became easier, and abortion was once again a matter of social choice. The dilemma for Soviet family policy became, and remains, the simultaneous need to keep women in the work-force and to encourage the family to stay together, reproduce, and bring up the children properly.

Currently, "the demographic policy of the Soviet state is geared to creating a favourable social climate around the medium-size family with three or four children." Some progress towards the resolution of practical family difficulties has been made through economic measures directed principally to the mother. However, the rate of family break-up remains a cause for State concern as does the growing phenomenon of parental irresponsibility. A great deal of thought is now being devoted to these issues by people in positions of authority. However, the State is aware of the limits on its ability to address family problems and so it has thrown its resources behind the creation of public organizations such as the Soviet Children's Fund. The weekly newspaper, *Semya* (Family), published by the Fund, is able to discuss family matters including sex in a way that would be unthinkable for a State publicaton. Established in 1988, it had four million subscribers by the end of 1989 and its circulation growth is limited only by the availability of newsprint.

The Soviet Family Today

The life of any one family is the stuff of novelists and film-makers. It is when all the choices that individual families make are added together that family life becomes material for social scientists, policy planners, analysts, and commentators. In the Soviet Union today, the challenge is not only to collect and sort data with respect to families but also to interpret that information correctly. For years these data have not been readily available and few sociologists and other scholars have been capable of analysing them. Since the advent of Gorbachev, the situation has improved considerably; authorities have accepted the reminder that half-truths are worse than lies and that the practical realization of change requires the open disclosure of all relevant information.

With respect to data specifically concerning the Soviet family, Soviet demographer Viktor Perevedentsev provides the greatest insights. I began to read his articles in 1982 and have followed his work ever since. I met him in 1986 and found him an open-minded man with an incredible head for figures. More importantly, although he is an economist by training, he interprets the demographic data he collects from a depth of understanding of human relations that I found quite exceptional. I have made considerable use of his material in what follows.

The press is another invaluable source of information about the Soviet family today because popular interest in the topic is immense. This was as true before *glasnost* as it is now. An article would appear on difficult marriages and immediately become the centre of a heated debate among people of all ages. If it was in a national newspaper, letters would pour in from every corner of the country, representing points of view from the deeply conservative to the decidedly liberal. Letter-writing, whether to an individual author or to the editor, is a well-established tradition in the USSR. When a subject of particular human interest is raised, such as babies conceived outside marriage, thousands of unsolicited letters arrive in the editorial room. Written responses are sought from experts to enlighten the debate and editorial comments are frequent. All newspapers have a department whose job it is to analyse the mail received, a practice that used to be, and still is, encouraged as a means of assessing and possibly directing public opinion.

The result of all this official, scholarly, and popular interest in the family is a growing body of information available to anyone who cares to look. To make sense of it, however, if one is not a Soviet citizen, requires some exercise of the imagination. In what follows I have tried to describe the conditions of family life in the Soviet Union today wherever possible from the point of view of the children in the family.

Getting Married

In Moscow and in most other parts of the country, Sunday may be the day for families, but Saturday is the day for weddings, the beginning of family life. Whenever we drove up to the Lenin Hills for a Saturday-afternoon stroll, we would meet carload after carload of bridal parties converging there from several directions. From the terrace on the ridge there is a splendid panoramic view of the city. All seven of Stalin's ostentatious "wedding-cake" buildings are visible. Looking out over the city, it is possible to see two ministries, two hotels, and two apartment blocks. Turning around, there is the sight of Moscow State University at the end of a long row of playing fountains.

Newly married couples come to the Lenin Hills to have their photographs taken against the vista of the ornamented vertical towers that Stalin built to diminish the effect of Moscow's golden domes. The bridal party lines up at the red marble balustrade, the bride in white, clutching her gladioli and holding on to her floppy hat; the groom in a borrowed black suit, a little tight through the shoulders or, perhaps, too short in the leg. They are flanked by their two best friends, each of whom wears a red sash looped over the shoulder and tied at the waist. (As witnesses, they are both liable to fines if the marriage breaks up within three months.) The champagne cork pops, the glasses are filled and lifted, the photographs snapped, and then they all pile back into the waiting cars, sometimes a big lumbering Chaika, sometimes a more modest Volga, in either case rented for the occasion and decorated with linked golden wedding bands on the roof and fertility symbols on the radiator, a plastic doll and a teddy-bear entangled in crêpe-paper streamers.

The cars take them down to the Tomb of the Unknown Soldier, where the brides leave their bouquets in a symbolic gesture of respect for the defenders of the motherland, a gesture that has become customary throughout the Soviet Union. We saw bridal couples and bridal bouquets at nearly every cenotaph we visited. In Leningrad, as a variant, brides leave flowers at the feet of Peter the Great. After bowing their heads before the eternal flame, a newly married pair sometimes joins the patient crowds waiting to visit Lenin's tomb. Since this is their special day, they are allowed in at the top of the line, and everyone smiles. In the evening there will be a jolly, noisy party at a local restaurant, many toasts and cries of "*Gorko! Gorko!*" (Bitter! Bitter!) until the bride and groom make everything sweet with a kiss.

According to statistics, the average bride, marrying for the first time in the Soviet Union today, is twenty-three and her groom twenty-five. There is a tendency towards earlier marriages and, taking into account the need for population growth, "an increase in early marriages is undoubtedly a socially useful phenomenon". Most young people say that they are marrying for love, but, since one in three marriages now ends in divorce (one in two in the big cities), either love is not enough or it may be a cover for other motives. A study of sixty couples in Moscow who were contemplating divorce and had been referred to marriage-consultation centres revealed that almost half had married for reasons that had nothing to do with the intention to found a family. They wanted to escape from their parents, for example, or get a residential permit to live in Moscow. The others married for "love", but were unable to resolve conflicts that arose during the early period of mutual adaptation.

Mobility is also a major factor in marriage failure in the Soviet Union partly because young people now meet their partners in a different way than in the past. In villages and stable communities, future spouses usually know each other for a long time before they marry, and see each other in a variety of situations. However, between three and four million people move from the country to the city every year, most of whom are young. Couples now meet during "entertainments"—at parties, on holidays, at a club— all of which are artificial rather than natural situations leading, according to Soviet observers, to unrealistic expectations.

After the wedding party, where do young couples usually go? Probably home to mother. A majority of young childless couples live with their parents during the early years of marriage and about half of them depend upon them financially. Twenty per cent do so as a matter of choice. Most would like to live separately, but still in the same apartment block or neighbourhood, close enough to be in constant contact but far enough away to avoid conflicts and hurt feelings and to be out from under direct parental supervision and control. I noticed a very strong attachment to parents, notably to mothers, among my women friends, and my male acquaintances too, an attachment remarkable for the degree of respect with which the older person was regarded. Nowadays, when the first child is born, the new parents may already be in a new flat (the government has promised to provide separate flats for every family as soon as possible, although the probability is that this will not happen before the end of the century). However, even if on their own, the young family will spend a good deal of time visiting relatives, taking the baby with them.

Most children soon become attached to family members other than their own parents and learn to call regular family friends *Tyotya* and *Dyadya* (Aunt and Uncle).

The famous *babushka* (grandmother) is becoming less of a fixture in children's lives, particularly in the cities in the European section of the country. Many are still young, pursuing their own careers. However, their influence remains strong. The availability of a grandmother to help is one of the reasons many women decide to have a child. One young woman I know told me that she was reluctant to have a second child because her *own* grandmother was now too old to look after her baby! In the Caucasus and in Central Asia the extended family is particularly influential in the lives of children.

Living Standards

Housing has been a problem since the coming of Soviet power, even more so after the enormous destruction of the Second World War. Every mayor we called upon, from the northern city of Pskov to Dushanbe, the capital of Tadzhikistan, opened our meeting by telling us about his town's housing difficulties and the plans he and the city executive had to eliminate inadequacies. In Dushanbe, plans included keeping up with the baby boom, a problem envied by the mayors of towns and cities in the European half of the Soviet Union.

Soviet apartments seem unbearably cramped to Western visitors, but then they are extremely cheap. In 1987, only 2.5 per cent of the average houshold budget was spent on housing, utilities, and services. Rural families pay slightly more than do urban ones to live in an apartment. State and collective farms once provided apartment living for their workers, but the trend now is towards constructing separate or semi-detached housing in order to encourage young families to stay on the farm. Most city dwellers also have access to the land. From 60 to 70 per cent have cottages (*dachas*), garden plots, or an allotted segment of communal land for gardening.

Although almost all housing is inadequate by North American standards, there are differing degrees of inadequacy. The worst situation for young families is hostel living. Because of its ageing population, Moscow has allowed some factories to bring in workers from outside without a residence permit and to house them in hostels. These people are known as *limitchiks*, and their situation is very difficult. The girls become pregnant and sometimes marry, and the "families" thus created still have to live in hostels. Perevedentsev strongly urges the lifting of residence permits with respect to such cities as Moscow and Leningrad. In his view, the resulting increased mobility would rejuvenate the cities because older people would be less reluctant to give up their apartments and retire to the country if they weren't so afraid of losing their residence permits.

A much better situation for young families can be found in those cities that encourage youth housing projects. In the city of Sverdlovsk in the Central Urals, as an experiment, young workers were given the necessary funds by their factories and a twelve-month leave of absence from their work to build their own housing, which they were urged to design to accommodate the needs of children. The experiment was so successful that it has been taken up in other parts of the country, but not yet widely enough.

Children experience living in communal apartments somewhat differently from their parents. A number of childhood memoirs describe with real pleasure the various people who lived in "our" house: *Dyadya* Vanya, the retired sailor who showed his navigation maps to a wide-eyed little boy, *Tyotya* Evdokia who sighed over the tattered photographs of her last love. Some of my friends, having grown up in full households, have actually turned down opportunities to move into separate apartments for fear of being lonely.

Of course, if their parents are made restive by their inadequate housing, then the children will suffer, and many parents must be unhappy because, for a substantial minority of Soviet families, housing is still inadequate by any standards. Construction is poor, the corridors smell of garbage, and the space is restricted. Lack of space is not, however, what interferes most with a child's ability to study; it is bickering parents and carping neighbours.

What the relationship of housing is to fertility rates throughout the Soviet Union is not at all clear, although housing difficulties, along with insufficient income, are usually listed among the main reasons for small families. The degree to which a woman wants to pursue a career or to continue her education is probably a more important factor influencing her decision to have a child than the housing situation, which may nevertheless be used as a justification for her choice.

If his or her standard of living is measured by family possessions, then a Soviet child might well seem deprived, although not in comparison with the children among whom I worked in India. Almost every Soviet family has a television set, for example, and most Soviet children I know spend a certain amount of time watching it, although usually not to excess. In 1988, there were ninety million television sets in the Soviet Union, of which sixty-five million were colour. The average Soviet television is on about three hours a day (closer to four on the weekends). There are also a growing number of video-cassette recorders, approximately two million in 1986. Almost every family has a radio, but telephones are in short supply. In 1988, just 30 per cent of Soviet urban families and 10 per cent of rural ones had telephones. We are so used to having a telephone in the house, and complaining that our children keep it tied up, that it is hard to imagine how families get along without one (most Soviet children communicate with their friends outside of home, either at school or in other communal places.)

In 1979, only 24 per cent of Soviet families owned cars but, in spite of the high cost of automobiles and the long wait to obtain them, that figure is steadily growing. Parents and their married children often combine resources to purchase one. In parking areas all around the city, cars spend the winter dormant in cocoons of milky plastic. But, come the spring, they emerge onto the roads to provide freedom of movement to families who take off in every direction.

Most households are now equipped with domestic appliances, such as refrigerators and washing-machines, although these are often of dubious quality. In fact, sensible women recommend going to the communal laundry where one can read a book or chat while the washing is being done rather than waste time wrestling with a semi-automatic machine of uncertain power.

Children go along with their mothers to help carry the baskets and fold the sheets. Thirty years ago the Soviet Union was still 60 per cent rural, and the atmosphere in the communal laundries I've seen in Moscow more closely resembles that created by a group of country women washing clothes in a river than the pristine isolation of the laundry room in a North American apartment building.

Families also buy record-players, tape-recorders, books, and sports equipment in considerable quantity. They would cetainly buy more if better-quality goods were available. Soviet children are not trained to be consumers by advertising, as ours are, but I have noticed as I have travelled around the world that consumerism is a habit rapidly acquired. People I met in the Soviet Union habitually showed disdain for "conspicuous consumption", although they cherished their few family heirlooms. That attitude is bound to change, however, as consumer goods become more available. Nevertheless, there are many Soviet commentators who hope that people can rise to a decent standard of living in normal market conditions without succumbing to greed for more.

Domestic Chores, Shopping, and Cooking

Children in the Soviet Union are supposed to help with household tasks. In its efforts to educate parents to educate their children, the government has issued manuals stating that children should not only learn to do their proper share of family chores but should also "love" doing them. There is not much evidence, however, that this is happening. I never saw children make food purchases except for ice cream and Pepsi at the kiosks, or bread at the bake-shops where the lines are rarely long. Most food shoppers I observed were middle-aged or elderly women or, less often, men of all ages. Muscovites told me that the shops are crowded by the people, two million of them, who come into the city every day from outside, where food supplies are even less adequate. Many of the city's inhabitants order their food through their place of work or shop very early in the morning rather than do battle with the outsiders. People also share shopping tasks with friends or relatives. When oranges were on sale, we saw men and women buying five or six dozen at a time and carrying them off in the string bag that people keep with them at all times, "just in case".

I did most of my own shopping. Once I felt reasonably comfortable in the language, I bought something almost every day from the shops around the Embassy and went twice a week to the open farmers' market, where I felt like a real customer, although I refused to buy a Georgian tomato in the middle of winter for the exorbitant price that some Muscovites were prepared to pay. I enjoyed shopping because it was an opportunity to mix with local people engaged in ordinary pursuits, something difficult to do in the regular run of diplomatic life. But I could well understand that the experience would not hold the same interest for a harried Muscovite. Choice was limited, quality questionable, and packaging execrable. According to surveys, women spend an average of six hours a week shopping and another twenty-four on other types of domestic work, not an excessive amount of time if they did not also have full-time jobs and other responsibilities or if they were sharing the tasks with their husbands. The upshot is that, when they are at home, mothers have little energy and patience to involve children in housework, and most often find it easier to do it themselves. In one urban poll, 53 per cent of parents admitted that they do not assign regular domestic responsibilities to their children.

The domestic "arts" in the Soviet Union were devalued by the Bolsheviks and further undermined by the changes in the status of women brought about by the Revolution. Later on, the absolute deprivations of the war, when sheer survival was the only thing that mattered, stripped domestic life to the bone. According to Lenin (who, no doubt, never did any, relying on his wife, Krupskaya, and her mother), household chores are "barbarously unproductive". The Revolutionaries thought in terms of domestic slavery, but now home-making is regaining a certain legitimacy. Books and magazines are available to demonstrate how houseplants and folk art can be used to decorate a home, and children, particularly girls, are encouraged, both in school and out, to learn about interior design.

Cookbooks are also becoming easier to find, and learning to cook is a popular after-school activity. The Soviet people are exceptionally hospitable. They love to entertain one another—and foreigners, too, now that it is permissible. While the new cookbooks may lead to a wider variety of dishes being offered to guests, what is really important is the talk. From my own experience, children are usually included in the long sessions at the table but sent to bed before the washing up.

Families That Play Together, Stay Together

The average Soviet worker now has a great deal more leisure time than before. During the week, parents are often too tired to go out with their children, and, in any event, theatres and movie houses are closed to children on school nights. So, family time is most commonly shared around the table or in front of the television set. On weekends, however, families go out together to movies or the theatre, to the circus (which is popular with young and old), to museums and art galleries, or into the parks. They also watch sports competitions, hockey and soccer drawing the largest crowds. Many families go out into the country, too, on family hikes, to the *dacha*, or mushroom-picking in season.

Until a decade or so ago, it was quite usual in the Soviet Union for families to take separate vacations, husbands and wives going at different times to factory rest homes while the children were away at camp. Some families still separate at vacation time, but the trend is towards joint family holidays, and the State is developing facilities to encourage this. Additional family rest homes are being constructed, where domestic tasks are taken over by the staff, allowing the family to relax—within the limits set by the rest-home routine. Most of these stays are partially paid for by the trade union of the enterprise that employs one or the other of the parents. Some families rent private accommodation in a *dacha* or in a house in the country. Hotels by the sea are particularly sought-after. The summer months have traditionally been popular with holiday-makers but a second vacation season is now evolving focused on winter sports. The conditions for cross-country skiing are excellent in the European sector of the country and downhill-skiing facilities are now available in the

Caucasus, in parts of Siberia, and in the mountains of Central Asia; the high Pamirs and the glorious range of the Tien Shan on the Chinese border. As it opens up, foreign travel will become increasingly attractive to those who can afford it.

Families in Trouble

In the days before *glasnost,* Soviet publications tended to gloss over the difficulties of Soviet family life and focus on the ideal "happy family". Nowadays, revelations about family problems flood the press, to the dismay of some members of the population who are unused to the public display of dirty linen. Tolstoy notwithstanding, I find that the tales of unhappy families have a depressingly familiar ring. One out of seven families in the Soviet Union is now headed by a divorced, separated, widowed, or never-married female; 20 per cent of children are being brought up in single-parent families. The reasons for divorce most often cited are: "lack of common views and interests, incompatability of character, infidelity, lack of or falling out of love, parental interference, difficult living conditions and infertility". Based on the cases they handle in court (only cases involving children have to go to court) lawyers also cite alcoholism (in almost 50 per cent of cases) and prolonged separation (read: "desertion"). Disputes about money matters are not often cited in the literature. It appears that power struggles within marriages in the Soviet Union are more likely to be over moral and psychological control than over economics, except in cases where there is simply not enough money to go around, no matter who earns it.

The fact that an increasingly well-educated and career-minded female population is still having to shoulder an inordinate share of the day-to-day responsibility for family life is one of the major causes of family unhappiness in the Soviet Union today. When it leads to marriage break-up, as it often does (most divorces are initiated by women), it contributes to the phenomenon of "fatherlessness". Fatherlessness was common after the war, of course, because so many young fathers were killed. Today the phenomenon is different because the children's fathers are still alive but have either abandoned them or become separated from them through divorce. Unfortunately, day-care and school systems provide few male models for fatherless children.

In response to the growing evidence of families in trouble, Soviet family policy has developed three main thrusts. The first thrust consists of legal and economic measures that are supposed to guarantee income support and appropriate working conditions for families. The second is made up of psychological and social support services that are provided to parents to encourage them to stay together and have larger families. And the third thrust comes from the educational programs the State has developed to provide current and future parents with the knowledge and understanding that will enable them to forge a strong family unit and bring up their children successfully.

Legal and economic measures are easy to devise, if not always to implement, but social and psychological support services are relatively new to the Soviet Union. Although one-third of divorces take place in the earliest stages of marriage, when the children, if there are any, are babies, studies indicate that the majority of Soviet marriages fall apart after eight to ten years, a critical time when the breach between parents has a profound psychological effect on the children. For this reason, as well as for others that are demographic (more children) or ideological (better Soviet citizens) in nature, the State is establishing more and better social services for the family. Most of them, including hospitals and schools, are administered and co-ordinated by city governments.

In 1979, the city of Moscow established a department of marriage and the family to formulate specific policies, set up new services and co-ordinate existing ones, all with the intention of strengthening the family and increasing its size. Consultation centres for family counselling based on models that have been successful elsewhere, particularly in the Baltic republics, were set up throughout the city and couples or parents concerned about their children were invited to come to them for advice. Centres providing clinical assistance to couples with sexual difficulties and fertility problems were also established. The demand proved so enormous that family services have had to expand, and more clinicians are being trained to staff them.

In 1981, the city created a phone-in distress centre. Called *Telefon Doveriya* (Telephone Confidential), it provides twenty-four-hour assistance to people with urgent problems. It is staffed by trained psychologists who are expected to have had some experience of life and the skills to talk to people in emergency situations. In the few years that it has existed, hundreds of thousands of Muscovites in crisis (there are now between five hundred and seven hundred calls a day) have used the service, bringing to the patient listeners family conflicts, loneliness, despair. In 1988, a separate help-line was opened for troubled adolescents engaged in self-destructive behaviour: attempted suicide, alcoholism, drug abuse, and so on.

The city also provides both economic assistance and legal advice to families in difficulty. It allocates special privileges to families with three or more children, which include priority status for shopping and for access to child-care facilities. But are all these initiatives bringing any results? The all-out efforts to strengthen the family and increase the population supported by the XXVI Party Congress in 1981, and reinforced by the XXVII in 1986, have only had a few years to prove themselves. At first, it appeared that the extended maternity leave, the increased number of days off to be with sick children, the additional days of annual leave for mothers of young families, the priorities in housing, the provision of more child-care facilities, had combined with the other services to increase the birth rate (from 18.5 per 1,000 in 1981 to 19.6 in 1986). To be sure, more babies were being born, but in reality the rising number of births only reflected an increase in the number of mothers in their prime child-bearing years, not an increase in family size. By 1988, the population wave had crested and the actual number of babies born that year declined. There is some evidence, however, from cities where marital counselling has been available, that the number of divorces has fallen. While that is good news, it does not, in itself, guarantee more babies. Because, where there is choice, Soviet women will restrict their child-bearing until their husbands are prepared to make the same commitment to material and moral support that the State says it is, or until both the State and their partners are prepared to lower the expectations that exhaust young mothers.

The educational measures that comprise the third thrust of Soviet family policy are primarily preventive and pro-active in nature. The Soviet Union has a strong tradition of public education and many organizations to assist the process. Through trade unions, houses of culture, societies of knowledge, and people's universities, a variety of courses are now offered to new and prospective parents. Furthermore, a new school program on the ethics and psychology of family life, has become compulsory for teenagers. Experts in the Soviet Union are only too aware that although child-birth is a natural human experience, parenting skills do not automatically arrive with a new baby. Most parenting courses are quite straightforward, covering various aspects of child development and how to deal with day-to-day problems. Unfortunately, the quality of the courses varies enormously and many parents drop out. Nevertheless, such courses, being a part of overall policy, will continue to be offered and should improve as more lecturers and trainers are qualified. The challenge there, as here, will then be to attract the parents who most need to improve their parenting skills.

The "Soviet Family" in a Multinational State

Although most of the statistics I have used in discussing the Soviet family today are derived from data collected from the entire country and although the family-policy thrusts I have described are supposed to be directed to all regions it is obvious that the multinational character of the USSR is a complicating factor. How can State authorities speak about and plan for the "Soviet family" as if an urban intellectual couple with one child in Tallinn, the capital of Estonia, is somehow interchangeable with a large patriarchal family tending camels in Turkmenia? For there are vast differences in tradition and life-style among the many ethnic groups that make up the Soviet Union. In Central Asia and the Caucasus, for example, ingrained patriarchal attitudes with respect to sex roles and family responsibility for children have persisted strongly in spite of all the messages that Moscow sends. In 1987, forty girls burned themselves to death in Tadzhikistan because they were being treated like chattels. Serious quarrels over *kalym* (bride-price) continue to be reported from Turkmenia. As long as the traditional subjugation of women persists, the economic and legal freedoms guaranteed to them by the Soviet constitution are bound to create conflict. This is a unique challenge for the State's family-support services.

Another challenge is unquestionably demographics. The birth rate in Central Asia is much higher than it is in the European regions, and if the pro-natalist policies designed for Moscow and Leningrad do not have a significant effect, this differential may increase. There is even a risk that the extra benefits accruing to large families in Central Asia may offset the trend towards smaller families that had begun to be established there.

It is hard to know how long major regional differences in family behaviour will persist. I look at my own vast country, made up of so many different peoples, and see a convergence on a common model that could be described as the North American post-industrial family. The same convergence is possible in the Soviet Union owing to the mobility created by industrialization. Besides, intermarriages among different nationalities are now increasing. But Canada is a nation of immigrants who came to our country by choice whereas most of the nationalities in the USSR are part of the Union through circumstances that were often coercive in nature. As a result, some family traditions that might otherwise disappear may well survive as a form of national protest. Besides, it would be a great loss if all local or ethnic family traditions ever vanished entirely. What should be hoped for is that the best of them, those that weave the young couple into the social fabric of the community in which they happen to live and help to support them through the difficult early days of marriage, will endure.

To return to Tolstoy, is there anything about Soviet families that makes their unhappiness different from that of families in some other part of the world? One thing we know is that history has been hard on the Soviet Union. Who would not weep with Nadezhda Mandelstam, writing to her husband in 1938, unaware that he was dying in a transit camp on the way to Northeastern Siberia? "Life can last so long. How hard and long for each of us to die alone…. I could never tell you how much I love you. I cannot tell you even now…I who was such a wild and angry one and never learned to weep simple tears—now I weep and weep and weep. It's me: Nadia. Where are you?" Who would not be moved by the "Requiem" that the great Russian poet Anna Akhmatova wrote for those other mothers with whom she waited daily outside the prison gates in Leningrad in 1939 and 1941, fruitlessly hoping to get news of her son.

> I pray, not for myself alone, my cry
> Goes up for all those with me there: for all
> In heart of winter, heat-wave of July
> Who stood beneath that blind deep crimson wall.

The tragedies experienced by families under Stalinism, witnessed by Mandelstam and Akhmatova, are now a thing of the past, but the State in its blindness creates new sorrows. The echoes of pain roll down through the generations, just as Nadezhda Mandelstam predicted they would. For the time being the family is still on its guard. The marriage bond may be fragile but family networks are strong. In spite of the fact that the Soviet state has taken over most of its economic functions (except for consumption), the family, patently, has *not* been "nationalized" and, has become, instead, an indispensable resource for the satisfaction of emotional needs and, consequently, the most powerful influence shaping the personality of the child. Recognizing this, the State is now supporting the family's nurturing function rather than continuing earlier attempts to take it over.

Over the years, the mutual adaptation of family and State has had some remarkable consequences. The State may have unwittingly enriched the family by forcing it to turn on itself to protect its members, and ironically, as the last refuge of personal choice, the family has forced the State to come to terms with it. With Soviet society opening up under Gorbachev the family may lose some of its cohesiveness as its members move away to the world of work or increasingly look outside for diversions. This development will have profound implications, not all of them happy.

Anyone I know who has lived for some time in the Soviet Union cherishes his or her memories of evenings spent with Soviet families in their small, crowded flats. There is no sitting around the living-room, drinking before dinner. Instead everyone moves directly to the food-laden table. Family members have secured delicacies from who-knows-where and the table is covered with platters of good things to eat. After *zakuski* (appetizers) of smoked fish, sausage, salad, and occasionally, as a special treat, red or black caviare, there will be *borshch* or *shchi* (beet or cabbage soup), then a meat dish—strips of beef, pork, or chicken cutlets—and home-fried potatoes. There will be mineral water and fruit juice, wine and vodka (more than one bottle in the days before Gorbachev). Afterwards the plates will be cleared away and the electric samovar brought out so that tea can be drunk with *sushki* (crusty rings) dipped in jam. And the talk will go on and on. There may be a cat curled up on the sofa-bed or a dog on the carpet. A child may leave the table and watch television. But everyone else—mother, father, grandmother, uncle, half-sister, step-son, mother's first husband's cousin—will sit around and talk. In many cases, divorces and remarriages result in an expanded rather than a broken family. Surviving years of external upheaval, State control, and internal stress, the Soviet family is a rich, complex, intimate structure that almost invariably provides Soviet children with their most fundamental sense of personal identity.

CHAPTER FOUR

School Days

Every weekday morning, from September to June, within the circle of rumbling traffic that flows endlessly around the outer ring road, the city of Moscow awakes and sends its children off to school. Apartment doors burst open, and a million and more youngsters clatter down staircases and out onto city streets. The littlest ones reach up for the hand of the parent or relative who will accompany them to the nursery or kindergarten, the older ones hitch their school-bags onto their shoulders and set off for the nearest general school.

Most students walk to class. A certain number travel long distances by Metro and bus to reach one of the many schools that specialize in foreign languages or in maths and sciences. Others go outside their catchment areas for vocational training. A few leave home on Monday morning to spend the whole week as boarders in one of the special schools that the State provides for exceptional children, those who are either handicapped or unusually gifted. Some children do not live with their families at all but in a hospital, a sanatorium, or in one of Moscow's thirteen children's homes. No matter where they spend their nights, however, the children of Moscow, like all the other children in the Soviet Union, are expected to fill their days with the serious business of learning. So, six days a week, nine months of the year, the early-morning streets are crowded with children of all ages making their way to school.

Once they arrive at their various schools, they push their way in through the front gates in twos and chattering threes. At 8:30, the first bell rings and the outside doors close. By the time the second bell rings, all pupils should be sitting quietly at their desks ready for lessons to begin. Often the desks are double ones designed to encourage sharing, a girl beside a boy to "civilize" him. As the teacher comes into the classroom, all the children rise and say "Good Morning!" to her (it is usually a "her"—there are many more women than men in the teaching profession), addressing her respectfully by name and patronymic. The only opening "exercises" will be a few gymnastic stretches before the children settle down to learn. One day the subject-matter of the first lesson will be mathematics, another day, Russian. Each day the order varies but each week it is the same. For decades there has been so little flexibility that Moscow's time-tables are replicated in schools all across the country.

All Soviet students study the same material, use essentially the same texts (although increasing allowances are being made for differences in language and culture in the various Union republics, each of which has its own ministry of education), and follow the same schedule with respect to the number of minutes allotted per class and the numbers of hours per subject per year. It used to be possible, I was told, for a youngster to close his geography book in Moscow one morning, fly the long distance to Novosibirsk that afternoon for an extended visit to his grandfather, go to school next day and find his new class studying the same page he had left the day before. This will become less likely in the 1990s as educational responsibilities are decentralized, but that will not happen overnight.

This is not to say that all Soviet schools are identical, far from it. The director (as a school principal is called) sets the tone of the school as much in the Soviet Union as he or she does in the West. One will be rigid and authoritarian; another, while still firmly in charge, quite flexible and open to experimentation. And teachers, of course, will vary as well. Some schools are better equipped with language labs, computers, and sports facilities than others because there has never been enough money to build and equip all schools at a uniform rate. Nevertheless, since educational plans for the whole of the USSR are made in Moscow, and educational research is centred there, all Soviet schools have come to resemble one another in certain fundamental ways. This is particularly true with respect to the ways in which they attempt to socialize the students who attend them by structuring their behaviour and shaping their attitudes.

Education in the Soviet Union is free and universal, open to all "regardless of race and nationality, sex, religion, property and social status", co-educational, and compulsory until the age of seventeen. It is also supposed to be scientific in character and closely tied with "life", which means that students must be taught the attitudes and skills necessary to prepare them for their working lives as Soviet citizens. Furthermore, while the content of education is expected to be "secular...excluding the influence of religion", it is also expected to be "humanistic and highly moral".

Lenin called the kindergartens established after the Revolution "nurseries for the shoots of communism". And while the Soviet school also educates its pupils in the narrower sense—giving them the fundamentals of mathematics, history, and so on—the inculcation of communist values is still a primary goal. Over the years, not much in a typical Soviet school has been left to chance. The moral climate has been carefully regulated so that respect for authority in general, and for the Communist Party in particular, could grow along with patriotism and the collective spirit. Authorities in the Soviet state understand very well that the school is the most important social institution that exists outside the family for shaping the social and moral development of children.

The Pre-schooler's Day—The Yasli and the Detsky Sad

As I looked out my drawing-room windows in the early morning I would often catch a glimpse of a young mother hurrying out of the apartment building next door, a baby bundled in her arms, on her way to the state-run *yasli* (nursery) at the end of the street or to a nursery run by the factory where she worked. Nurseries in the Soviet Union are equipped to take babies as young as two months, although many parents say that they would prefer to look after their infants at home until they are eighteen months old, at least. In 1981, the State extended maternity leave to a year and a half (it is now three years) to make this possible.

The provision of day-care is not itself at issue. Both the general population and the authorities of the State act on the assumption that child-care for all who need it is not only necessary but desirable, serving the interests of State and parents alike and also, after a certain age, the best interests of the child. Despite justifiable concern about the risk of infection in day-care centres and about how well they are managed, few Soviet women want to stay out of the work-force for very long. (The common idiom for a woman who is not working outside the home is a pejorative one, *ona sidit doma*—she *sits* at home). The question is not whether but when a new mother should return to work or to full-time studies.

Since the time of the Revolution, the Soviet day-care system has been the means by which the State shares with a working mother the task of bringing up her child. If a woman wishes to work (and her labour is always needed), then the State tries to ensure, through the day-care system, that her baby is well looked after. A woman with small children, however, is not required by law to work, as a childless woman is, and so the spaces in day-care that are set aside for infants often go begging until the mother feels her child is physically ready.

In day-care, a baby will be surrounded by warmth and affection. That was amply evident in the nurseries I visited. The littlest babies would usually be sleeping in their cots but the older ones, who were able to sit, would be placed two or three together in large raised playpens. They smiled readily, but they did not seem very active. If one cried, a plump, friendly nanny would immediately pick him up and comfort him with pats and coos; no child was left alone or isolated. But I missed the sense of adventurous energy that had reconciled me to pots and pans pulled out all over the kitchen floor and to endless washings and mendings of little overalls soiled by exploration. The hands that change the diapers in a Soviet *yasli* may be warm but I was often concerned about the quality of the psychological interaction between the child-care worker and the infant. It appeared to be neither as stimulating nor as expert as it should be.

Child-care workers in Soviet day-care centres are all women. Their jobs have the same low status and pay that they do in North America, resulting in chronic staff shortages and frequent turn-overs. Furthermore, the preparation of workers for their care-giving role has not in the past been adequate for their important task. Under reforms to the system, workers will now be better trained, but if the status and pay do not improve it will remain difficult to attract the best young women to the job and almost impossible to attract a man. As a result, Soviet parents will be wise to continue to keep very young children at home.

Once a child is eighteen months to two years old, however, the social experience of the pre-school institution becomes desirable, particularly for only children who live in apartments, a situation that is more the norm than the exception, at least in Moscow. By the age of three, the majority of Soviet children leave home every morning to go to a *detsky sad* (kindergarten). Before the end of the century there may be enough kindergarten spaces in the Soviet Union for all who want them, and then the collective upbringing that is institutionalized there will become virtually universal.

While the smaller children in the *yasli* have their day structured primarily around their physical and social needs—food, sleep, fresh air, exercise, and play—the children in the *detsky sad* encounter a daily educational and upbringing program whose rules and regulations were first formulated by Lenin's wife, Nadezhda Krupskaya. When the extensive network of pre-school institutions promised at the time of the Revolution was finally established during the 1930s, Krupskaya was Deputy-Commissar of Education, a position allowed her by Stalin, who did not like her but did not dare exclude her totally from public life. This is what Krupskaya wrote then about the *detsky sad* : "Kindergarten is a state institution of social pre-school education; its goal is to provide children with opportunities for wholesome development and upbringing; a kindergarten enables mothers to participate in the production process, in the government as well as in cultural and social-political life."

Other paragraphs of her kindergarten document specify the main tasks of educational work with children: to look after the children's health and general physical development, to ensure harmonious development of all their abilities, to encourage mutual assistance and friendship among children of different ethnic origins, and to work with children in their mother tongue. These tasks remain the principal objectives of all the kindergartens in the Soviet Union although the program developed to achieve these goals has undergone considerable refinement since Krupskaya's day and has become more child-centred.

I visited a *detsky sad* in Nurek, a little town below the world's largest earth-filled dam in the mountains of Tadzhikistan. I visited another in Kishinev, the capital of Moldavia; a third in Irkutsk, near Lake Baikal; and a fourth on a collective farm in the Crimea. Each of these kindergartens was separated from the others by an enormous distance, yet they resembled one another in every essential aspect. The buildings were similar, conforming to a central master plan sent out from Moscow. The furniture was the same: the same little wooden chairs in the classrooms, standard-issue tables in the dining-room, identical metal cots with side bars in the sleeping area, each one with a large square pillow plumped up and positioned neatly in the corner and a blanket turned down just so. The very same dolls were seated along the wall and always included one dark one. There were the same "all-Union" plastic blocks, tea-sets, trucks. It was always a relief to see that the children did not all look alike.

Most children arrive at a *yasli* or *detsky sad* between eight and nine in the morning although the doors are usually open at seven. In Irkutsk, the combined nursery and kindergarten has a small dormitory to keep children overnight. "Sometimes," the director explained to me, "parents are sick or studying for an exam or have a meeting to go to. We are happy to keep the children with us for a night or two." Not all pre-school institutions are so accommodating, but the State is making a special effort to encourage young people to come to Siberia and have many children.

Let's follow two little children, Olya and Misha, through their day. Arriving at school they take off their outside clothing by themselves and hang their coats and hats on low hooks that they have learned to recognize as their own; Olya by a painted daisy, Misha by a bear. For the first hour they stay in the classroom with their *vospitatel* (teacher-upbringer) who has planned the day's activities in units of time that correspond with their limited ability to concentrate. The whole class sings for fifteen minutes, and then Olya feeds the goldfish and Misha waters the plants. Older children spend their time playing language games to prepare them for reading and writing. At ten, all the children have a snack, hot milk with a little tea in it, perhaps, or even a little coffee, and a sweet bun. Then they go outside to play.

When Olya and Misha come back in with their playmates, it is time for dinner, which is eaten formally at small tables. The older children have tablecloths and napkins, proof that they know how to eat properly. Children are taught table manners from a very early age as a form of consideration for others. The quality of the cooking varies, of course, but there is usually plenty of food, and the children are hungry. Olya and Misha's parents are relieved to know they are eating substantially at midday and will require only a light supper.

After dinner, the children listen to a story and then take a nap. The older ones do not have to rest as long, so they have more time for educational activities: artistic ones, such as drawing and painting or modelling in plasticine, or "upbringing" ones such as didactic games. There is one more snack around four and then Olya and Misha play outside with their little friends until their parents come to collect them.

There will, of course, be variants in this routine, depending on the time of year; in the Soviet Union the calendar is punctuated with ceremonial days celebrating the ideology of the State, each of which will be the focus of school activities for a certain length of time. Also, there will be special excursions—to the local factory, to the nearest Lenin museum, to the Zoo—all carefully designed to contribute to the overall aims of the kindergarten program as first set down by Krupskaya.

Soviet experts believe that the kindergarten child learns best through play, so it is through the medium of games that many of Krupskaya's moral concepts are taught. For example, one didactic game called "Letters from a Kind-Hearted Story-teller" is recommended for use in every kindergarten in the USSR. The object of the game is to convey the meaning of the words *nelzya* (should not), *mozhno* (may), and *nado* (must) so that children learn what is "good" and what is "bad". Children are expected to pay close attention to the teacher as she explains the game (thus improving their comprehension skills), listen to the "letters" as they are read out (thus improving their listening skills), and give examples from their own lives (thus working on their skills of self-analysis). All the teacher needs is a box of brightly coloured envelopes and little booklets. She sets the scene by telling the boys and girls about Dima and his grandmother, who is always saying *nelzya* to him. Dima is troubled by this, and a kind-hearted story-teller, hearing about him, decides to write letters to all the children in all the kindergartens of the Soviet Union to help them understand the real meaning of the word *nelzya*.

The teacher shows the coloured envelopes to her pupils and asks "What do you think is in them?" A child chooses one and the teacher opens it and reads it aloud. The first letter contains a story about an old man who is shuffling down a village street leaning on a cane. Several boys follow behind and mimic his movements. The teacher asks the children what they have to say about these boys, and the children, of course, cry out, "*Nelzya*, it is wrong to make fun of old people." After some discussion of this situation, another child chooses a letter. This one tells a story in which Dima wants to continue playing when his Granny tells him to go to bed. The children are expected to say, "*Nelzya*, you shouldn't argue with people older than yourself", and agree that it is wrong for Dima to *want* to do other than his grandmother's bidding. This little story (if it can be called that—I think the teacher is supposed to embroider a bit) contains two moral messages that are typically Soviet: respect for authority (and deference to anyone older) is good, and wanting things one should not want is bad.

The religious concept of sin has no place in communist ethics, but conscience certainly does—and heavy dollops of guilt. Listen to the next "letter". Klava is cranky and starts to cry when Papa and Mama go out. Granny is very hurt. The teacher asks the children if Klava is right and the children all call out, "No! No! There is no use crying. Klava must stay with Granny, who will look after her!" But the kind-hearted story-teller wants the children to think about the situation in a more positive way. His answer is "*Nelzya*, a child should not desert an older person. Klava should remember that she is her grandmother's joy and should try to make her happy, sing her a song or play a game with her."

After reading out a couple of other "letters" and discussing the moral situations the stories present, the teacher brings the game to an end. "You see," she says to the children, "*nelzya* is a wise word. It forbids and warns. It teaches you how to act. Let us put *nelzya* into our piggy bank and tomorrow we will find out what *mozhno* means."

I always came away with mixed emotions from one of my visits to a *yasli* or a *detsky sad*. The best part had been the children in their varicoloured outfits, healthy-looking, responsive, and generally interested. I liked the warm, emotional atmosphere and bright, secure environments. Mealtimes were fun, combining table talk with ample food and conveying the message that meals are social rituals that reinforce the community feeling of any group that breaks bread together. I enjoyed the singing and dancing, even when it was a special show, because the children were so delighted to be part of it. I loved watching the babies being exercised and the older children throwing their balls and rolling their bright plastic hoops, although I found the outdoor playgrounds unadventurous. I was entertained by some of the more imaginative didactic games.

However, I was disappointed by the children's conventional artwork. And I was unhappy with the excessive neatness maintained in the classrooms. While I believe that a certain order in the physical environment is conducive to disciplined habits of thought and thus facilitates systematic learning, I also believe that it is a mistake to teach children that there is only one way of ordering the universe: that apples must always be round and red and that if blocks spend a night on the floor the kindergarten world will collapse. Under such circumstances, children lose confidence in their inner visions and suppress the spontaneity that is so essential to the development of new ways of looking at things.

The teachers and upbringers I observed during my visits to pre-school institutions were kindly people, but I found them conventional in their attitudes and lacking in imagination. Undoubtedly they were fond of children, but they were most comfortable when everything was under control and the children were engaged in useful collective activities, such as showing off to visitors or tidying up the schoolyard. While it is true that North American children often seem out of control and frenetic, the energy level of the average Soviet kindergarten is low, suggesting that the children are understimulated. Leaving a *detsky sad* after a special performance of five- and six-year-olds singing folk songs from other lands including Canada, I could not help but remember the anecdote about the old-fashioned kindergarten teacher who claimed to love her children so much that every time she saw a spark of creativity in one of them, she watered it.

Primary School Children: Open Lesson No. 1

To see how young children spend their days once they graduate from kindergarten and enter the general school, and what the upbringing atmosphere of these schools is like, come with me across the street from the Embassy to School no. 59 for an *otkryty urok* , an "open lesson". In the Soviet Union, educational authorities enter schools regularly to observe classrooms in session. If the children have learned in advance that they are going to be part of one of these open lessons, they are a little apprehensive; but if they like their teacher, they will do their best to show her off to advantage. The main purpose of an official open lesson is to inspect the interaction between the teacher and her class, to observe her teaching methods, and to check on the classroom atmosphere. Our purpose is to look for the real messages that are being exchanged between adults and school-aged children.

Although I visited many schools in various parts of the Soviet Union, I have chosen School no. 59 for my first open lesson because daily observation over three years made me so familiar with it. Besides, the rules, regulations, and routines that structure the moral-upbringing atmosphere of Soviet schools, vary little from school to school, much less, in fact, than do the buildings and the teachers.

Moscow has more than a thousand general schools. They are dotted all over the city, the newest ones in the middle of massive apartment blocks on the outskirts, the oldest ones in residential areas close to the Kremlin. The Canadian Embassy is in this long-settled part of the city on a street called Starokonyushenny Pereulok (Old Horsestable Lane). Across from it, in a building about the same age as the nineteenth-century mansion occupied by the Embassy, is School no. 59.

Built originally as a private school for the sons of the rich merchants of the Arbat, the building had changed so little when I visited it in October 1984 that I could easily envisage those boys attending prayers in the assembly hall and then ascending the wide stairs to class. Today, it is a general-education school with an enrolment of nine hundred pupils from six to seventeen years of age. Most of the children in the primary section of the school (grades one to three) whose classes end at 12:30, stay on through the afternoon since School no. 59 has an extended-day program. This program was first introduced in the 1960s as a "new public service for working mothers", a way of keeping an eye on younger school children while parents were away at work. Before it existed there were many latchkey children who had to spend nervous afternoons in empty apartments. The program, however, is intended not only as a service to parents but also as an extension of the institutionalized socialization that begins in the pre-school establishments, the *yasli* and the *detsky sad* .

The program is expanding rapidly, despite its costs to the State. By the mid-1980s, more than thirteen million children throughout the USSR were enrolled. It is not obligatory (parents have to pay a small fee) but it is popular because fewer and fewer families have grandmothers or other relatives to turn to for after-school care. Initially, the program was criticized for being only a boring extension of the ordinary school day. But considerable effort has been expended to make it more interesting. A typical program includes periods of supervised homework and extra coaching for those who need it, extracurricular interest groups, hobby circles, and sports. The personnel are not ordinary classroom teachers but specially trained "upbringers".

At the end of morning classes, primary-school children, if they participate in the extended-day program, go for lunch in the school cafeteria and then have a rest. Older children finish class at 2:30 p.m. and may then join the younger ones. Not very many do, though, because children who have reached the Pioneer age (ten to fifteen) usually have many other choices of what to do with their after-school hours.

Entering School no. 59 to conduct my special open lesson that September afternoon, I was greeted by the school director, an attractive woman in her early fifties. She appeared comfortable in her position of authority and at ease with the children, with whom she had a great deal of contact. Soviet school directors, unlike most school principals in Canada, are expected to teach as well as to administrate, even though most of them are responsible for schools that now have eleven grades.

After exchanging the short, formal pleasantries that are a ritual in the Soviet Union before an open lesson, the director took me to the music room to inspect an interest group of young singers. We sat down to listen while an unusually competent chorus of children belted out one or two well-rehearsed songs, accompanied by their enthusiastic music teacher on a bright blue upright piano. It was quite clear that we had been expected, but the children, who would not have had much choice in the matter, did not at all mind showing off to a visitor. After their little concert, they presented me with toy xylophones to take back to children in Canada.

Next I "inspected" a group of children who were involved in a local-history project and were studying the nearby streets and lanes, tracing the origin of their names and finding out who had lived on them. Did they know anything about the houses? I asked. Well, yes. They knew that Pushkin used to visit a house around the corner. But what about the building across the street? Did the children know anything of its history? They stared at me, and the teacher looked slightly embarrassed. "Well, we know that it was built at the end of the nineteenth century," she said. The Canadian flag has a bright red maple leaf that no child can possibly ignore, but obviously it was not being allowed a place in *local* history.

Then we went downstairs, past a small gym where some young adolescents were playing ping-pong, through the high-ceilinged elegant assembly hall, vacant now except for the outsized bust of Lenin, and up another flight of stairs to the crafts' room. Four little girls were doing macramé with the special concentration of the young. They looked up with a start when we appeared at the door but then eagerly showed us their work. Across the hall, some older girls were meeting with a teacher to read and study English. Too abashed to reply to my questions, they held out the books that they were reading, *Tom Sawyer* and *Alice in Wonderland*. Yes, of course they liked them, particularly *Alice*, who is a great favourite throughout the Soviet Union.

We left the shy girls, turned a corner, and I stopped short in surprise. It was as if I had walked through Alice's looking-glass into the garden of the Red Queen. The director was pleased by my reaction and explained that her biology teacher was an amateur painter. She had encouraged him, she said, to paint the walls of the anteroom to his laboratory with all the flowers and plants that Dr. Aibolit, a popular character from Soviet children's literature, would have seen when he travelled to Africa to cure the animals. The work was anything but amateur, and the total effect was delightful. Brightly coloured vegetation sprouted from the doors and luxuriated over every inch of wall and ceiling; spontaneous, magical growth, glowing with heat and enchantment, a special treat for the children of the cold North passing through it on their way to class.

Back downstairs, we spent a moment in the small library, where we found several teenagers reading science fiction. A tall, glass-fronted bookcase full of tattered leather-bound books stood against one wall. It contained volumes of Russian and French classics that had survived from the early days of the school, books by Tolstoy and Alexandre Dumas, as popular with today's students as they had been with young boys when the school was new. Then we climbed the main staircase once again to talk to some children busy with their homework. Daylight had begun to fade as we reached the top floor and started to stroll along the wide gallery that led from the front to the back of the old, rambling building. A variety of spiky green plants and trailing ferns had been set on the window-ledge to catch the natural light. Since my mind was back at the turn of the century, reflecting on the old books in the library, I naturally assumed, when I noticed a little marble figure on a pedestal surrounded by greenery that it, too, had been left over from the early days of the school. The director followed my glance and smiled. "Ah," she said, "that's the baby Lenin!"

When the children we have just met entered first grade at School no. 59, they most likely had already had three if not four years of collective institutional experience, structured, yes, but not overly demanding or particularly exciting. The extended-day program fits more or less into the same pattern, although the staff are better trained and better paid. However, children are also in school to be educated, and so it is now time to look at how children in the primary grades spend their mornings.

According to Soviet psychologists, systematic learning replaces play as the leading activity by which children of six or seven develop their higher mental functions, so the primary school is structured to encourage formal learning. Its teaching personnel have higher qualifications than those in the kindergarten, and the expectations placed on children are greater. It is normal for children of this age to *want* to learn to read, to write, to do sums. This is the age when nothing exceeds the pleasure of writing your name on the first page of a new exercise book with a freshly sharpened pencil, or solving a simple problem in arithmetic, or, best of all, cracking the code of the printed page. Soviet experts contend that, if this enthusiasm can be caught and sustained for long enough, if the child does not encounter devastating failure in his or her eagerness to learn, then he or she will grow up to be a lifelong learner.

In theory, the Soviet school system is set up to prevent early school failures; help is made available for those who are faltering, including an extensive use of "stronger" students to tutor "weaker" ones on a one-to-one basis. In practice, the sparks of enthusiasm are often doused by unimaginative teaching and too much rote learning. The curriculum for the primary grades is heavy and difficult to adapt to individual differences. As a result, many Soviet children lose their original keenness and grow to rely on outside pressures such as teacher control, rather than on their own initiative, to get them through their schoolwork.

Until very recently, most Soviet children entered the general school at the age of seven. Then a growing number of schools began experimenting with lowering the age of entry. In 1981, slightly more than 17 per cent of six-year-olds were being taught in the general school, and by 1987, nearly 70 per cent. When I lived in Moscow, I often heard heated debates on this subject, which surprised me, accustomed as I have always been to six as the normal age for starting school. Then I discovered how demanding and formally structured the first grade of a Soviet school is and could understand why many people, pre-school experts and parents alike, "accused those in favour of reducing the school starting age, of wanting to shorten childhood".

The debate has gone against those who wanted to keep six-year-olds in the freer, less constrained atmosphere of the kindergarten, but it is not entirely closed in that some children have been permitted to remain in the *detsky sad* for grade one. However, it is now state policy that, during the twelfth five-year plan (1986-91), "the instruction of children in eleven-year schools will begin at the age of six...as the necessary conditions are created".

I have some sympathy for both sides of this debate. Soviet six-year-olds are unquestionably ready for more stimulation than they have been getting up to now in the senior year of kindergarten. Yet the transition will not be easy. Teachers will need to respond in new ways to the challenge presented by six-year-olds, in part by allowing them to be playful for a bit longer while still encouraging their desire to learn in a structured way. In turn, the six-year-olds may help to modify the school atmosphere by making teachers more responsive to individual children.

This change is unlikely to increase individualism at the cost of collectivism as some authorities fear. Soviet children are too eager to be part of the group and to please any adult around. Such feelings, which are common to children of the same age all over the world, are carefully nurtured in a Soviet school by the class collectives, which generally remain intact throughout the early school years and are taught by the same teacher.

In September 1987, I returned to School no. 59 to visit the new grade-one classes. The building had been renovated since I had visited it in 1984; a sleeping room and more classrooms had been added to accommodate the six-year-olds who were now attending. Their first-grade classroom, however, looked just like others I had seen in previous years. Double desks stood in neat rows facing the front. Each child was working from an arithmetic textbook supported on a wire stand. There was little evidence of play. The teacher was young and remarkably attractive. In the short time she had been teaching them, she had not only established a sense of connection between herself and each child but had also fostered connections among the children who were thus in the first stages of forming a new class collective. The children were cheerful, looked well cared for, and appeared eager and attentive. Can their teacher keep them that way for four years? She was optimistic and I wished her luck.

Secondary-School Children: Open Lesson No. 2

School no. 73, the site of my second open lesson, is one of the fifteen schools in Moscow that specialize in teaching French as a second language. It is located in the Krasnopresnensky District of Moscow and serves a mixed socio-economic population. The block-long four-storey apartment buildings, from which most of the students come, were built well before the last war, in an architectural style I think of as "early to mid-Stalin". I assume that the school dates from about the same period, which would account for the wave of nostalgia that hit me as we came in through the main doors. Except for the glossy veneer in the director's office, and the inevitable portrait of Lenin, I could have been back in London South Collegiate Institute, the public high school from which I graduated in 1948. I recognized many elements at once: the rectangular alignment of classroom and hall; the big windows; the chemistry lab with its stained sinks, cracked rubber tubing, Bunsen burners, and glass beakers; the faint but pervasive smell of chalk; the occasional sound of a felt eraser on a dusty blackboard. These physical impressions were reinforced by what I could detect about the social atmosphere of the place. I found it, like my old collegiate, structured, predictable, unsophisticated, respectful, and friendly. When the director told us that his major discipline problem was smoking in the washrooms, I was not at all surprised. During my time at school, our principal had similar illusions.

On the day of my visit, I was accompanied by a close friend of long standing, a psychology professor from the University of Ottawa, a French-speaking woman of elegance and wit. The director beamed with pleasure when he saw her. He took us to his office to tell us about his school and then sent us off to observe some language classes. Both of us were impressed by the way in which the language was being taught and by the language skills of both teachers and students. The children in the lower grades, particularly the girls, were eager to show off what they had learned; the students in upper grades, less so. I am sure that the little ones had heard that one of us, at least, was a native French speaker, for they could not resist twisting around at their desks to see if we approved. My friend commented later that it had been a long time since she had observed French being taught with such precision. The older students had a good conversational grasp of the language and showed some understanding of French culture, talking to us about books they had read and paintings they liked.

In a school with a special language program, language classes are small, no more than ten to fifteen students in each one, although pupils spend the rest of the day in classes of thirty to forty or more. Small classes are expensive and so are the extra years of training given to foreign-language teachers, but the combination of these two factors makes the program very successful. Most of the language teachers I met in school no. 73 and elsewhere were quite young, in their twenties or thirties. They are paid a cash bonus for their qualifications, but perhaps a more attractive bonus is the opportunity given to some of them to spend a few months studying in France, England, or one of the other countries whose language they teach—perhaps the only chance that, even today, most of them will ever have to travel abroad. At the very least, they may get to accompany a group of senior students on a European bus tour. We spoke with some of the young people in School no. 73 who had been to France for a three-week tour the previous summer. In front of the director they gave appropriate responses in competent French, but when he turned away for a moment they looked up at us and their eyes gleamed.

We were shown a number of other classrooms—science, mathematics, and so on—where the students immediately leapt to their feet to greet us and then turned back to their work. The last classroom we were taken to was another throw-back. It reminded me not so much of my own early schooling as of my children's years in an Ottawa elementary school during one of our home postings. In their day, which was at the end of the 1960s, "domestic science" was for girls, and boys had "shop". The director of School no. 73 was very proud of the sewing machines and all the cooking facilities that this room provided for his female students. When I asked him if boys were encouraged to learn how to cook as well, he looked astonished. The younger women teachers who were accompanying us on our tour smiled at us ruefully. We dropped the subject, however, because some young girls were waiting for us beside a table they had prepared in the middle of the room. They had covered it with a white tablecloth and set it with pretty china and silver that had surely been brought from someone's home. We sat down, and the girls in their flowered aprons brought us steaming bowls of wild mushroom soup. It was delicious.

We left the girls washing up and returned to the office. On our way down the stairs, we passed a rush of students returning from their brief lunch break. They greeted the director respectfully by name and patronymic and then stood aside to let us pass. The director stopped in front of two boys, asked them a question, and then nodded with satisfaction at their reply. A good commander, I thought, in touch with his troops. All the school directors whom I met, male and female, conveyed a sense of their own authority in a way that suggested to me that, on the whole, they knew what they were doing and liked doing it. Soviet schools give the impression of being well managed, much better, for example, than the hotels and department stores that continue to cause such frustrations. A well-managed school does not guarantee a good education, but it does create a structure in which it is easier for all children to learn.

Overall, the "tone" of School no. 73, as well as that of all other Soviet schools I visited, was distinctly "old-fashioned", which is how contemporary young North Americans would describe the high schools my friends and I attended more than forty years ago during and just after the Second World War. At that time, there was a widespread assumption that schools should have high moral standards so that their graduates would do justice to their education and to their native land. As I remember, the many rules and regulations were generally obeyed by both students and staff without too much complaint. Teachers were formal and predictable, moral exhortations were frequent, discipline was a minor problem, and school spirit was high. It was as if there existed an unspoken contract between us adolescents and the society in which we were growing up. We were important to each other. The atmosphere of the Soviet schools I visited in the 1980s conveyed the same message.

In most respects, the pupils of Soviet schools, particularly those in their early to mid-teens, appear much younger than their North American contemporaries. Certain elements in the structure of Soviet schools encourage the prolongation of childhood. Children of all ages study together within the same building, so the artifical separation of age groups that reinforces the notion of adolescence as a distinct period of life, possessing its own norms and culture, is absent, and Soviet children are not hurtled towards adulthood with the same heedless speed as they are in North America.

Another practice that slows down the process of growing up is the common European custom of wearing a school uniform. From my brief passage through a boarding-school when I was a young teenager, I recall that certain glamorous older girls were somehow able to make our plain tunics look sexy. Nevertheless, most Soviet girls appear innocent and immature in the brown serge dresses and black pinafores that they wear until the last years of high school when (since the early 1980s) they are allowed to change into a navy blue jacket and skirt. For special days they exchange the black apron for a white one and wear a lace collar and cuffs, but no make-up is permitted in school, nor is jewellery, except small earrings. In fact, the only acceptable decoration for girls in school, or during any of the State-sponsored activities that occupy much of their time after school, is the stiff taffeta hairbow that enhances their childlike appearance. Boys wear short greyish blue jackets that button to the neck, long pants of the same colour, and white shirts that they sometimes protect in class by using sleeve guards. Out of school, and with their friends and families, children and teenagers are much more colourfully dressed; jeans and other outward manifestations of the international youth culture are on display for all to see. However, even then, there is a marked absence of that individual stylishness and sophisticated dressing that comes from hours of practice in front of the mirror and the opportunity to make daily comparisons with photos in fashion magazines as well as with one's peers.

Another factor that prolongs the childhood of the Soviet school population is the obligatory and universal nature of the curriculum combined with the continuity of the class collective. Many Soviet children can expect to graduate with the same classmates with whom they started school. This may still be the case in certain European countries but is increasingly unlikely in North America. These students will have shared with one another not only all the same teachers but also all the same subjects. Students do not have individual schedules in high school, as they do in North America, because there are few optional subjects (although the number is now increasing). Except for lab classes and two hours a week of gym, they often stay in one classroom and teachers come to them. For most of this time, they also retain the same class supervisor, or home-room teacher, who gets to know each one of them well. It is he or she who checks the daybook that students carry with them containing the timetable for each day, the homework assigned, the marks, and the daily comments from the teachers of each subject. Once a week, the class supervisor adds his or her remarks about the student's behaviour and signs it, verifying later whether or not the student's parents have countersigned.

Finally, a respectful and, indeed, slightly fearful attitude to adult authority is inculcated into Soviet children from the moment they set foot in an educational establishment. The degree of respect (and fear) increases with the age and status of the older person. The littlest pupils are taught to defer to *anyone* older than themselves, including students in the class above them. Educational authorities maintain this attitude by a strict code of conduct. Students must get up when an adult enters the room. They must hold their arm in a characteristic way on the desk with only the forearm raised when they are seated and preparing to ask a question. They must stand up to answer the teacher. It was a relief to see that the code of conduct does not seem to include silence in the halls during recess or unusually controlled behaviour on the playground, where the normal energies of childhood are often (although not always) allowed full rein. But then the object of the code is the inculcation of an *inner attitude*, not the regimentation of external behaviour. I did not see a great deal of strict regimentation, with all that that word implies of precision and imposed formal order, either inside or outside of Soviet schools, except, of course, during the parades of young soldiers and of young Pioneers. Soviet ideology expects each person to bring his or her own individuality into the collective and exercise it there for the good of all rather than lose it to regimentation. The code of conduct described above is considered reasonable behaviour, and learning it is as important for the formation of good social habits as learning the multiplication tables is for the ability to do arithmetic.

It is hard to know how long this old-fashioned school atmosphere can or indeed should be maintained. Recent reports suggest that things have already changed. Drug use has spread in recent years and there has been a marked increase in adolescent sexual activity. Social control by rules of behaviour and moral admonition is becoming increasingly difficult as adolescents gain greater access to tapes, videos, and other elements of the international youth culture. Yet, I do not expect the social climate of Soviet schools to change totally because there is another, specifically Soviet way in which the behaviour of Soviet students is influenced from the time they enter school, a way that is so effective that it will provide continuity even as the schools become more open, flexible, and sophisticated. This is the regular involvement of all school children in what is known as "socially useful activity".

"Socially Useful Activity": the Pioneer Movement in the School

"Socially useful activity" as an experience for schoolchildren is vital to the kind of socialist society that the Soviet Union has not yet given up trying to create. Krupskaya said, "It is really socially useful activity that particularly distinguishes our schools from their bourgeois counterparts since the former not only prepares the child to be a useful member of society at some time in the future but actually makes him so at the present time." The purpose of "socially useful activity" as an influence on young people is to strengthen their attachment to the collective and their sense of its social role, and to provide them with behaviour models.

In Soviet schools, most socially useful activities are carried out under the influence of the communist youth movement, which has three sections for different age groups. Almost all children between the ages of seven and ten are Octobrists, a name that links them to the October Revolution. Most children then join the Pioneer organization and are members of it from the age ten to fifteen. Then they may be invited to become Komsomol members, and many do, although far fewer than before. They can remain in that organization until the age of twenty-five. Then, and only then, will a selected few be invited to join the Communist Party. It is the Pioneer movement, however, that dominates the social life of the school, because it focuses the energies of the very age group that is keenest to be involved in group undertakings.

The organization of the Octobrists is rather loose, and most children belong simply by virtue of being part of a class. Each class will have three or four groups of Octobrists to which the children are assigned according to where they sit or by the roll-call. These groups of eight or ten are called *zvyozdochki* (starlets), and the children in them select (no doubt with the help of the teacher) a commander (male) and a nurse (female). Their socially useful activity consists of responsibility for the class newspaper and any other social task that requires co-operation, such as organizing the spring clean-up in the schoolyard. In group meetings, Octobrists are supposed to "discuss their comrades' attitude towards learning and any incorrect behaviour". Before the school year ends, Octobrists are given tasks by Pioneers in the classes above them that they are expected to perform over the summer. When they return in the fall, they will report to their group on the useful work they have done. "Pupils are supposed to live according to the Octobrist rule, 'Only those who love work are called Octobrists'." The focus of the Octobrist movement is on creating proper attitudes to study and learning and on preparing and encouraging children to become Pioneers.

"I, a young Pioneer of the Soviet Union, in the presence of my comrades do solemnly promise to love my Soviet motherland passionately and to live, learn and struggle as the great Lenin bade us and as the Communist Party teaches us." With this promise at the age of nine or ten, children are formally admitted into the Pioneer organization and receive the characteristic red necktie and the badge that says *Vsegda Gotov!* (Always Ready!). It is an important ceremony and a solemn one.

Although interesting extra-curricular activities, and the fact that everyone else belongs, may be what attract most children to the movement, it is the upbringing effect that interests State authorities. The Komsomol considers the main directions of Pioneer work to be: first, social and political activity; then, work activity; then, activities encouraging conscientious attitudes to study and learning; and, last, sports and recreation, nature appreciation, and aesthetic education.

Every class with students of Pioneer age has a unit called an *otryad* (detachment), which is further divided into *zvenya* (links). All the classroom detachments together form the school brigade, the *druzhina* (a word taken from old Russian times, when it denoted the military retinue of a prince). The *sovet* (council) of the *druzhina* is elected by all the Pioneers in the school. It co-ordinates Pioneer activities with the professional assistance of a young adult Pioneer leader assigned to the school by the district Komsomol committee. Each class will also have a class monitor called a *starosta* (another Old Russian word, meaning "village elder") to keep an eye on attendance and academic performance. The *starosta* and the chairperson of the *otryad* are both freely elected by the children in the class from among several candidates, and they usually work closely together on class activities.

Class detachments are constantly in competition with one another with respect to behaviour and socially useful activity. Each *otryad* earns points for such activities as working in the schoolyard, collecting scrap metal and paper, organizing an amateur concert for the whole school (that is, showing group initiative), or standing on duty in the halls. Points will be lost if any member of the *otryad* has to be disciplined for being involved in a fight or for other social misbehaviour. At the end of each term, the points are totalled up by the *sovet* of the *druzhina*, and the winning *otryad* is given the school *druzhina* flag and a diploma during a school assembly. Diplomas and other awards are displayed in the Pioneer room for all to see. Every school has a Pioneer room where the Pioneer council meets at regular intervals and where the "mystique" of the school *druzhina* is enshrined. This type of organization can be unusually effective in maintaining the collective spirit in the classroom. Peer sanctions for misbehaviour are keenly felt by children of this age, and ostracism by the *otryad* is much more to be dreaded than any teacher-imposed punishment, which might serve, as it often does in North America, to make a student more popular rather than less.

It may seem as if the children spend their whole day in Pioneer activities but, of course, this is not the case. There is the school curriculum to get through from 8:30 a.m. to 2:30 p.m., and it is a demanding one. History (the Soviet version) is introduced in the fourth grade, geography the following year, along with biology, physics, and other sciences. The school day lengthens. The load of homework becomes heavier. In the upper grades, social studies and a course in the fundamentals of Soviet state and law are obligatory. It is tiring but there are periods between classes for letting off steam and a rather brief lunch break when students can dash down to the cafeteria in the basement for a hot meal. Nevertheless, even if students are not physically involved in Pioneer activities during much of the school day, the school remains permeated by the collective spirit fostered by the Pioneer movement, and it is a rare child who can escape it.

The same general social and moral climate of the school extends upwards to the last two grades of the general school although the students are now at a different life stage. The active Pioneer, absorbed by his or her relationships in the class collective, has become a young person who is beginning to think about the future. After the age of fifteen, Soviet students focus more and more on what they are going to do when they leave school. An increasing amount of in-school time will be devoted to their future careers. Those students who want to go on to higher education will have to concentrate on their studies and on preparing for the entrance exams to a university or to one of the specialized institutes. Others will shift to another school to pursue technical education. The boys will be involved in preparatory military training. Being an eager and active member of the Komsomol at this stage also used to be a vocational choice, taking one in the direction of political power. Now there are other paths, but no matter what the future holds the first challenge is to pass the final exams.

As the working day draws to a close, the lights in Moscow's apartments come on, one by one. Mothers and fathers return from their jobs, occasionally stopping by to pick up a child from a *detsky sad* or an extended-day program. The older children trail home from their after-school activities: the organized ones such as sports, interest "circles", Pioneer or Komsomol meetings; and the unorganized ones, a game of pick-up hockey, perhaps, a visit to a friend's apartment, and informal group get-togethers, or a game with the neighbourhood kids in the courtyard. After supper, the older ones will have more homework to do even if they have already done some in school; they are often expected to spend up to five hours a night on their assignments. The little ones will relax and probably watch television and will go to bed when they have seen "Spokoynoy Nochi, Malyshi" ("Good Night, Little Ones"). The lights go out slowly. Sometimes the last person in the family to go to bed will not be an adult but a senior student working late on a physics problem or preparing a theme paper on

Crime and Punishment. But even he has to give up eventually. Then Moscow sleeps.

"Not Enough Wild Time"

In the Soviet Union, education is valued by both the State and the people. There is a shared belief that a good education will make a difference in life. Children passing through the system are made to feel that what they are doing there is important to society. Of course, some of their classes are boring, the hours that they have to spend doing homework are often excessive, and until recently many of their textbooks have been dull and pedantic. The new texts are bound to be an improvement, and student-teacher relations will probably relax, but the solid academic core of the general school is likely to remain. I do not foresee radical changes in the structure of the Soviet school day or in the social and emotional atmosphere, at least not for the time being.

Louis Menashe, a professor of history at the Polytechnical Institute of New York, wrote an article for *The New York Times* in 1985 about the Soviet-educated students, the children of *émigrés,* that he had come to know in recent years in his classes on Soviet history. He had learned that although "they are victims and critics of Soviet society they are…its representatives and beneficiaries as well. Their educational background, if tendentious, is solid. They are keen on political and social analysis and have a taste for culture; they are uncommonly well read." He and some of his professional colleagues had been struck by their verve and energy, not to say raucousness. They also noted that although the students from Soviet *émigré* families reveal considerable psychological insight into individual fictional characters during literature classes, there is an unnerving certainty in their general approach to right and wrong. They are very judgemental.

In a study of the children of Soviet *émigrés* in Toronto, Roberta Markus echoes Menashe's perception. She interviewed children between the ages of twelve and twenty who had arrived in Canada with their families during the period 1972-1978, when many Soviet Jews immigrated there from the USSR. She also interviewed some of their parents, many of their local peers, and a number of teachers in the schools they attended. Some teachers had reported that several of the Soviet immigrant children were having emotional, behavioural, and learning problems, and they and others wanted to know more about the cultural baggage that the children were carrying with them. Like Menashe and his colleagues, these teachers saw the Soviet-educated students as energetic, ambitious, aggressive, and opinionated but they were unable to judge the educational level of the students because of severe language problems.

The children were having a difficult time. They had left a secure and orderly school environment in which they had felt valued and had formed very strong peer relationships that they thought would be life-long friendships. Often they had not been told that they were departing forever until the very last moment. Arriving in Canada, they encountered indifference and even hostility from their new schoolmates. More than two-thirds of the local students sampled by Dr. Markus expressed negative opinions about the Soviet newcomers, and very few of the latter had been able to make Canadian friends, at least in school. Given the supportive collective school environment from which they had come, these Soviet children must have felt their isolation with a special keenness.

What the Soviet students liked most about their new schools in Canada were the buildings, the relaxed atmosphere, and the flexible curriculum. They were happy not to have to wear uniforms and to discover that the adults in the school were approachable. However, they were upset by what they perceived as excessive permissiveness with respect to clothing, smoking, drinking, and drugs, and disturbed by the lack of manners. They were also critical of the Canadian students' lack of concern for the school premises and for the school "collective". Although they liked their new teachers better as human beings than the ones they had known in the Soviet Union, they preferred the Soviet teachers as pedagogues, respecting them for their commitment to the profession and for the way in which they tried to ensure that every student did as well as possible in his or her schoolwork.

Meanwhile the parents of the Soviet children complained about the lack of regular communication between the school and the family. In the USSR, while they had not been used to having any say in the running of the school or to criticizing the job that the school was doing, they *had* been accustomed to a continual flow of information that kept them up to date on the academic performance of their children and their in-school behaviour. In Canada they often learned too little too late to be effective in helping their children. Informal comments by teachers of the current wave of Soviet immigrant children to Canada suggest that the situation described by Dr. Markus has repeated itself a decade later.

In comparison, I talked to a family of Canadian children who had been to a Soviet school in 1981-82, when their father, a mathematics professor, had been in Moscow on an academic exchange. Three years later, I sat with them in the kitchen of their Montreal home and listened to them talk about their school life in Russia. The oldest girl, Jeanette, who had been thirteen or fourteen at the time, had been placed in one of the senior grades and had kept a daily diary. The others recalled one incident after another as she read from it. I had met these children many times in Moscow, so it was interesting to see them again after they had had time to reflect on their adventures. All of them, except for four-year-old Georges, who had spent a blissful and uncomplicated year in *detsky sad* , had found the first few weeks in the Soviet school difficult and confusing. Although they had studied Russian for a year before going to Moscow, total immersion in the school environment came as a distinct shock. Luckily the school they attended was one of those that specialize in French, so there was at least one class during the day in which they could shine and in which someone could translate when it was really necessary.

Each child had found the school friendly and welcoming, although Josiane, in the first grade, had probably adapted most quickly both to the language and to the class collective. She made many friends and spent most of her time, both in school and out of it, in their company. Jean-Paul was placed in the fifth grade. His eyes lit up with mischief as he remembered his Moscow days. He had a good Soviet friend and they were constantly together. He recalls gambling with imported chewing gum during recess and the distinction of being able to bring it from the Embassy. He was passionately interested in geography and still remembers what an interesting and exciting class that was. Jeanette found her strength in mathematics, where the language is universal. As an adolescent, she found Russian more difficult to speak than her younger siblings, but she was more perceptive about the school atmosphere.

All the children were struck, in retrospect, at least, by the extraordinary bonding that had taken place among the members of their class, even to the point that children would cheat on exams on each other's behalf. Teachers were "out there". In fact, sometimes they were not there at all; they were away sick, and there were no substitutes. The Canadian children thought that their Soviet teachers were good, they were attentive and professional, but they never became "pals" with the children. Jeannette laughed about the school dances because they were so closely chaperoned, and Jean-Paul shook his head when he thought about the food in the cafeteria. While they decided that, on the whole, their experience had been a positive one, they had chafed under the reins of the school administration and the lack of flexibility. When I asked Jean-Paul what he thought was missing from the Soviet school in comparison with a Canadian school, he thought for a long moment and then he said, "Not enough wild time."

None of our own children was school-aged during our posting to Moscow. They were already at university or beginning their careers. However, I know that they would have echoed Jean-Paul's words, especially my son, who had a very "wild time" at the American school in New Delhi when he was eleven years old. I know they would have especially resented the idea of criticizing their schoolmates for moral shortcomings, something neither they nor I was ever encouraged to do. One of my Soviet friends grimaces now when she remembers the judgements she formally imposed on "weaker" children. Children should *never* be authorized to sanction one another's behaviour, as they are in Pioneer councils, particularly at an age when experimentation is as necessary for growth as breathing. There is much to recommend in the structure and content of a typical Soviet school, much that is of real benefit to the social and emotional well-being of the children who attend it. But, in my view, being "exacting towards one another" is never a "socially useful" activity for any developing child and I am encouraged by reports that the children of *glasnost* are no longer being pressured into it.

CHAPTER FIVE

Boys and Girls Together

Moscow in May, emerging from the dark winter, basks in the warm sun. The seams of the city are stitched with pale green, and the parks embroidered in purple and white. The lilacs are in bloom. The Embassy *dvorniks*, two strong young men whose charge it is to keep order in the yard, bring me great armfuls of blossoms cut from the gnarled trees in our small garden. Massed in bowls on polished wood, their fragrance floats through the formal rooms of the Residence. The lilac has a lovely name in Russian—*siren*—and never have I seen it in such beauty and abundance as in and around the city of Moscow. During two or three weeks each year, old women stand on street corners, selling drooping branches out of pails, and the Sunday Metro is full of children perched cautiously on brown leatherette seats, cradling their country bouquets wrapped in *Pravda*.

On a Saturday in late May 1983, I came up out of the Metro into Nogin Square. As I walked through the park to the side entrance of the Polytechnical Museum, I found myself in dappled sunlight, breathing warm lilac and dodging the drunken bees. Appropriately enough, I was on my way to a public lecture about sex education in the schools. Boys and girls in the Soviet Union are growing up more quickly than they used to. Soviet doctors have calculated that the onset of puberty in girls occurs, on average, two years earlier today than it did before the Revolution. Current Soviet data also suggest that adolescents are becoming sexually active at a younger age. Unplanned teenage pregnancies are on the rise, as is the incidence of sexually transmitted diseases, all of which sounds only too familiar to Western ears. But while the elders lament, the professionals look for solutions. A major cause of these problems has been ignorance about sexual matters; so, at the beginning of the 1980s, a decision was finally taken to teach the physiology of sex to the fifteen-year-olds in grade eight and to offer a course called "The Ethics and Psychology of Family Life" to students in their last two years of high school.

People are divided on the issue of sex education in the USSR, just as they are in North America. In Canada and the United States, I have heard sex education called a "communist threat to the sanctity of the family". In the Soviet Union, there are those who rail against the idea of discussing sex in the classroom for fear of encouraging Western "bourgeois licentiousness". Luckily, in the USSR, common sense has prevailed and, somewhat timidly, a unit on the physiology of sex has been incorporated into the biology course called "Man and Human Health", which is taught in grade eight. I had been told that this unit would be the subject of a lecture at the Polytechnical Museum that sunny morning in May and I was eager to hear it.

The massive and ornate Polytechnical Museum was erected in the centre of Moscow in the latter part of the nineteenth century. While the main body of the museum is filled with display cabinets celebrating enlightened scientific and technological progress, the building also contains lecture and concert halls reserved for the All-Union Society of Knowledge (Znanie). Znanie, a manifestation of the Soviet state's belief in the efficacy of public education, has branches all over the USSR. Its purpose is to bring, in the form of lectures, concerts, readings, and discussions, the most "advanced" scientific knowledge, the most sophisticated artistic culture, and the most burning social concerns to the consideration of the masses.

A Soviet woman friend was waiting for me just inside the entrance and we climbed the stairs together to a light, airy

room on the second floor. Before the lecture began, I examined
with interest a booklet I had picked up at the desk downstairs
containing the calendar of the month's events, many of which
were concerned in one way or another with children and families.
The offerings for May included a presentation on the psycho-
social problems of divorce, a panel discussion on law and the
family, a lecture on relations between parents and children,
and a workshop on educating gifted children. Both the State,
which is ultimately responsible for the Society of Knowledge,
and the public, who turn out to these events in droves, were and
are preoccupied with these problems, and even in those pre-
glasnost days the State was willing to approach such issues in a
straightforward, non-ideological manner.

Growing Up Male and Female

Our lecture hall was one of the smaller ones, and it filled up
rapidly. A slim, dark-haired young woman with an intelligent
and expressive face mounted the platform and began to talk.
She spoke rapidly and, my Russian being what it was, I began
wondering if I could possibly be understanding her correctly.
Her topic was not sex education, as I had anticipated, but the
problem of sexual identity in children, more specifically, in young
boys. What I seemed to be hearing her say was that weak or
absent fathers and bossy mothers were creating confused sons,
uncertain of who they were or how they were to behave. "We
should not have ignored the theories of Freud with respect to the
psycho-sexual development of children," she said, adding that
serious social problems have now emerged related to the fact
that boys are growing up with a tenuous male identity. This line
of reasoning brought her to say that women must become more
"feminine". (No, I didn't actually hear her say "submissive".)

After the lecture, there were questions from the floor, handed
up to the front on slips of paper, as is the Soviet custom. The
lecturer unfolded them, smoothing them out on her lectern as
she prepared her reply, which she gave after reading the question
out in a clear voice. The questions ranged from the very personal:
"What should I do about my nine-year-old daughter who spends
all her time on the telephone pursuing the boys in her class?"

(Answer: "Don't interfere. Try to understand what is happening. Perhaps there are not enough men at home?") to the very general: "Is it all the fault of the West?" I applauded her response to that one: "How can it be? We don't really know enough about Western culture to assign blame. No," she went on, "our children's sexual identity problems come from changes in our own families, easier times, and to a certain extent, from the 'masculinization' of women."

When the question period was over, my friend and I went out into the sunshine and sat down on a park bench under a lilac bush to discuss what we had just heard. I had noticed since my arrival in Moscow that many Soviet women reminded me of myself in my younger days, happily "socialized", as the women's movement would have it, to be a mother and a helpmate to my husband, supporting him in his career and pursuing my own work and interests in whatever time was left over. Like many other women in North America, exposed to more than twenty years of consciousness-raising and, in my case with four independent daughters, I can never return comfortably to that state of mind. But I can remember what it was like and I can still recognize, almost with nostalgia, the characteristic contours of that old emotional landscape. Could it be that in this land of revolution, of work for all, of legal and economic equality, Soviet women feel more at ease in that psychic territory now than I do? And was the lecturer actually suggesting that, for the sake of a healthy Soviet male child, that was where they ought to remain?

Of course, I did not pose my question to my friend in exactly those terms. But after confirming that I had understood the lecturer correctly she was genuinely surprised that I would question what I had heard. She said that, of course, Soviet women wanted to be feminine. And having observed them for nearly three years I thought that I could understand why. Older women in the Soviet Union must be weary of their historical burden, weary of doing double duty while their men disappeared into the camps or went off to the wars and got themselves killed. And they must also be fed up with having to do so much physical labour, with driving tractors and running heavy machinery, with cleaning roads in summer and chopping ice off sidewalks in winter, with doing so many tiresome jobs at the lower end of the salary scale that drained their energies and spoiled their looks. As for the younger women surely they were weary of not having enough time for their children, of not having enough time to do both their jobs and the housework, of not having enough time to get their hair done or to stand in line to buy a new pair of shoes from Hungary. I could well imagine that Soviet women might want to be feminine, especially if that meant being courted, even pampered.

My friend nodded, but she hastened to add that wanting to be feminine did not mean that Soviet women were uninterested in furthering their education or achieving professional competence, nor did it mean that they wanted to stay at home to be housewives. But she, herself, was not ambitious for power and, indeed, I never met a Soviet woman prepared to proclaim her interest in pursuing a political career to the highest level.

As I travelled with my husband throughout the USSR, however, I met some of the women to whom I think the lecturer was referring when she spoke of "masculinized" women. Most were of an older generation and would have been indistinguishable from their male counterparts had it not been for their ample bosoms and their bleached, back-combed, bee-hived hair. In positions of managerial responsibility, they came across to me as capable and powerful, but inflexible and doctrinaire. Not all the Soviet women in authority I met were like that, of course, and I have a certain sympathy for those who were, being aware of some of the circumstances that forced them to steel themselves on their way up.

Almost all older Soviet women alive today have been badly scarred by Soviet history. They have undergone personal experiences of extraordinary and often devastating emotional intensity, experiences from which most North American women have been mercifully exempt; children lost, fathers, husbands, lovers, and sons imprisoned or dead. Millions of men suffered too, and millions died, leaving behind widows and orphans as well as vast numbers of women for whom there never were nor ever would be husbands and children. Some of these husbandless women, armed with the skills they had acquired performing superhuman tasks in extraordinary circumstances, eventually made their way up the managerial ladder. If they were "masculinized" it was because, replacing absent men, they found they had to adopt the masculine model of authority to be successful. There are also some younger women who have become "masculinized", although for somewhat different reasons. As a result of a number of social changes, including the fact that they are rarely the unique family bread-winner, many men have retreated from roles they once played in the family, and women have had to take up the slack. Because some women put on the attributes of men as they pick up the roles men abandon (or have been deprived of, depending on the point of view) sons, according to the lecturer I had just heard, were growing up badly confused.

It is impossible to know what proportion of contemporary Soviet women hold traditional female attitudes to power and authority and what proportion have been "masculinized", assuming authority according to a male definition. As I sat talking to my friend, I wondered about the middle ground between these two positions. Were there no Soviet women prepared to assert that a feminine perspective on politics, power, and world affairs was not only valid but necessary in the contemporary world? It is true that Marxism-Leninism provides little basis for the kind of confidence that I now possess with respect to the legitimacy of the feminine point of view, since, theoretically, consciousness is determined by *class* and not by *sex*. Nevertheless, many Soviet professionals, both men and women, have recently been asking the same question. Since Gorbachev's coming to power, the debate about femininity and masculinity has widened and more people are staking out positions on the middle ground. Although there is still tremendous concern about the "feminization" of little boys as a result of the refusal of women (particularly mothers) to fit the stereotype of the nurturing female, I think that the young girls who have grown up in the 1980s will have more real options with respect to defining their femininity than their mothers or their grandmothers had.

As I proffered this last thought to my friend in the gardens outside the Polytechnical Museum, I was conscious of two ghosts stirring beside me on the warm bench. For several generations, Soviet women have had at least two powerful female models who broke all traditional stereotypes, both in their lives and in their art, two of the greatest poets of the twentieth century, Marina Tsvetaeva and Anna Akhmatova.

Early in 1921, Tsvetaeva mounted the worn steps of the Polytechnical Museum to the largest lecture hall and boldly proclaimed that she was "a rebel in head and womb". And, in May 1944, Akhmatova, passing through Moscow on her return to Leningrad after spending the war years in Tashkent, received such a standing ovation in the concert hall for a writer who had not been published for fifteen years that she brought herself to the attention of Stalin, thus setting into motion a campaign that culminated, two years later, in her expulsion from the Union of Soviet Writers and her public denunciation as "half nun, half whore".

Both of these women sing of the world of love and death in poems of great beauty. Both lived lives that hold profound meaning for any Soviet citizen, experiencing agonies during the Revolution, the Stalin years, and the Second World War. Only recently has all of Akhmatova's poetry been published in the Soviet Union, yet it, as well as Tsvetaeva's, has long been known to women growing up there. While Tsvetaeva, dying by her own hand in 1941, is buried in the Volga region, and Akhmatova, heart-stricken in 1966, lies in a grave near Leningrad, their ghosts linger in Moscow.

Women writers have been important to the growth of feminism in the West. However, for cultural and historical reasons the influence of poetry and poets in the Soviet Union is much wider and deeper than it is in North America. For years, adolescent girls have memorized the poems of these two great poets, and their feminine consciousness has been shaped by them. Try as it might, the State could never exorcise their ghosts and now they are more powerful than ever. Tsvetaeva and Akhmatova sing in a different voice from their male counterparts and Soviet women, when they listen, are affirmed.

Sex Roles and Stereotypes

Dr. Igor Kon, an eminent Soviet philosopher, ethnographer, and social psychologist, was the person who was able to explain the Soviet dilemma with respect to sex roles, sex stereotypes, and sexual identity most clearly to me. Contemporary Soviet society, he said during one of several conversations I had with him, is trying to disentangle and come to terms with three distinct but interrelated categories of phenomena. First, there are the psychological distinctions between boys and girls based on biology and affected by their differing rates of physical maturation. Second, there are the roles of the two sexes as they have been historically determined by changing economic and social relations. Third, there are the culturally based but enduring stereotypes of masculinity and femininity. By looking at these three categories, it is easy to see how the Soviet Union differs from the West.

I found Kon's comments most enlightening, and his insights inform much of what follows. My life experience has convinced me that some biologically based psychological distinctions between boys and girls are real and that they are just the same in the Soviet Union as they are in the West. But in Canada and the United States stereotypes of masculine and feminine behaviour are crumbling even though legal and economic equality between the sexes has not yet been secured. In the Soviet Union, that process has been reversed.

The Revolution established a new form of economic relationship between the sexes by bringing women into the work-force. According to Marxist theory, a new, improved social relationship should have followed. What actually happened is not, I think, what was intended. By being more equal, marriages should have become happier *and* more productive, but this was not the case. And what's more, the traditional Russian stereotypes of masculinity and femininity have held surprisingly firm. A study published in Russia in 1850 stated that, because Russian women were characterized by "sensitivity, love, and modesty" while men were known for "honour, energy, and intellect", women were better suited to provide "comfort in times of suffering" than men who were expected instead to be more "active" and to accomplish deeds of valour. Official Soviet documents written more than a hundred and thirty years later echo the same message.

It is hard to know whether these stereotypes could have survived as long as they have, had it not been for the war. Ceremonies held throughout the USSR in 1985, to commemorate the fortieth anniversary of the hard-won Soviet victory over Nazi Germany, underscored the degree to which the "Great Patriotic War" still occupies the hearts and minds of ordinary Soviet citizens. These ceremonies, and the publicity that surrounded them, held up, once again, the model of the male as the authority figure; tough, active, and incredibly brave. Women were shown as equally courageous but modest and self-sacrificing, comforting where possible and, where not, suffering and grieving.

Social reality in the Soviet Union, however, has come unstuck from these stereotypes. Women under thirty (older ones as well) no longer fit the approved model of femininity. This may be because the demographic situation has placed women of marriageable age in a position of choice for the first time in two generations. For every hundred boys born in 1960 only eighty-five girls were born in 1963. Men now have to compete harder for wives. In addition, girls are better educated than boys and the gap is widening. More than 54 per cent of university students are now female. Young men go off for their military service for two years, and young women get ahead of them. Of all those with a professional education in 1985, 59 per cent were women. Nowadays there are more and more women engineers, for example, placed in jobs that may lead to management positions.

Young women also have wider cultural and social interests than their male contemporaries. They go to more theatres, concerts, and museums and take a larger part in various forms of community action than their husbands and boyfriends. Many young wives complain that their husbands are boring. The lecturer at the Polytechnical Museum was probably correct when she said the problems that boys and young men are confronting with respect to their sex roles and their sexual indentity are new ones. It is women who are still having to deal with the old ones. One Soviet expert told me that research must be done on men's adaptation to their new sex roles before it is too late to prepare the young boys who are now growing up. He is forward-looking; not surprisingly, the State is less so. Although it recognizes that problems exist, it is far from ready to discard the old stereotypes.

Above all, the State is concerned to restore stability to the institution of the family and thus protect both production and reproduction. It has been noted that unhappiness at home affects a worker's productivity and that women who are not sure they want to stay married are reluctant to have children. The State is wary of any new definition of what goes on between men and women. It is attempting, instead, to reduce the high incidence of divorce and its unwelcome economic and social consequences, by urging boys and girls to practise the communist "virtues" of hard work, collectivism, and patriotism, and to hang on to the traditional stereotypes of "noble, active" males and "gentle, loving, nurturing" females. These injunctions, with all their contradictions, are incorporated into both the sex-education program and the course in the "Ethics and Psychology of Family Life" to which I will now turn.

Sex Education

Three weeks after the lecture at the Polytechnical Museum, the lilacs had gone and Moscow was into a new season; *pukh topoliny*, Muscovites call it, the time when the poplar trees go to seed. I have never known anything like it. All over the city downy puffs float through the air forming cottony billows that swirl back and forth across the ground. After the devastations of the Second World War, planners, who wanted to beautify the badly damaged cities as rapidly as possible, planted the quick-growing, wide-spreading poplar along the main boulevards and in the parks. No one stopped to consider what would happen during those few weeks in June when the poplar sheds its seeds. The offending trees may one day be replaced with another variety whose seeds will not clog car radiators or drift through open windows to cover the desks of bureaucrats. But until that happens, the clarity of June in Moscow will continue to be obscured.

Authorities are also planning to plant "trees of knowledge" to replace the current obfuscation about sex. But it will also take a long time for that fluff to be cleared off. When I went to the Institute of General and Pedagogical Psychology in central Moscow to follow up on the lecture I had heard, I had to wade ankle-deep through poplar down to reach the main door. And the psychologist who received me in her tiny office, T. I. Yuferova, was still not prepared to talk to me about sex. She wanted instead to tell me about her role in helping to develop the family-life education course that was about to be introduced into Soviet schools. It was a question of priorities. She agreed with me that basic sex information was essential for adolescents but insisted, as did all the other experts with whom I spoke, that ethics and psychology must accompany biology in any presentation of the subject to students. We must, she said, be clear about our approach before we begin to teach the young.

One of Yuferova's assignments in preparing the course in family-life education had been to conduct polls in Moscow schools with respect to children's images of "male" and "female". She described her results with some amusement. The young boys who participated expressed traditional attitudes. Perhaps because they missed their mothers after school, their "ideal" woman worked less and was more often at home. Older boys were looking for "kindness, understanding, and tenderness". Young girls, however, said that they wanted to "do everything and know everything"; from their point of view, the "ideal" boy was one who would help them get what they wanted. Older girls were more romantic and wanted a man to be a "knight" and to protect them.

It was clear, said Yuferova, that young people in the Soviet Union were ripe for a course that would help them clarify their ideas about marriage and family life. The course was set up to combine the very latest medical and scientific data on human sexuality with psychological studies on human development and research into interpersonal communication. Sociological data had been added as well as insights into human behaviour gleaned from the treasury of world literature. The course structure was designed to encourage students to discuss relations between the sexes primarily from a moral and psychological perspective. It was not the place to talk about sex.

So I asked Yuferova about the classes in sex and hygiene that were supposed to precede this course. She didn't know very much about them. In fact, it took me several more months to uncover the curriculum. It was no use asking students. One of them told me her class had missed out on sex because the course had not been introduced when she was in grade eight; another just laughed. Their parents were even more tongue-tied. Since no one has been allowed to talk openly about sex for such a long time in the Soviet Union, most people have grown up unaccustomed to discussing the subject frankly in public. As a result, it is much easier to learn about what people should do than about what they are actually doing. Many parents are acutely uncomfortable with the subject and public images of sexuality are rare. Sexually explicit magazines are forbidden. Even the scantily clad performers in the ever-popular circus, although undeniably sexy, have a curious air of innocence. Not that students are as inexperienced as adults would like to think. On the contrary, a great many of them are sexually active at an early age. The data are irrefutable. But Soviet adolescents have not been very knowledgeable about what they have been doing, and a great deal of unhappiness, to say nothing of unwanted pregnancies and sexually transmitted diseases, has been the result.

The best thing that can be said about sex education in Soviet schools is that it is taught at all. In the United States, up until the recent AIDS epidemic, only a few states had made sex education mandatory, and the situation in Canada had not improved much since my own high-school days more than forty years ago. At that time, the girls in my class were taken to a local movie house, confronted with the disastrous consequence of a tumble in the back seat, and shown, in full technicolour, the awful symptoms of venereal disease, thus assuring our nervous chastity until well beyond our high-school years.

Soviet educators initially took their cue from Anton Makarenko, who had written in the late 1930s: "My experience says that special, deliberate, so-called sex education can only lead to regrettable results", adding, "no talks with children about the 'sex' problem can add anything to the knowledge that will come of itself in good time". Today, they have come to their senses. Drawing on his knowledge as an ethnographer, Dr. Kon comments that, until recent times, the sharing of the "facts of life" with young children was a community affair, either through specific initiation rites or, less formally, through the child's observation of the sexual behaviour of surrounding adults. In the modern era, however, children spend most of their time excluded from adult society although they are closer than they used to be to their own parents. Parents, however, find it extremely difficult to discuss sex with their children because, according to Kon, they have trouble achieving the necessary tone of neutrality to convey information without embarrassment. Therefore, he says, "if one takes a sober view of matters...then one sees that the school...is the only institution where modern and effective sex education can be conducted within the framework of the process of moral education and of preparing youth for family life."

Having decided, at last, to teach sex in the schools, what is the information that Soviet adults feel it necessary and proper to give to young adolescents? I read large extracts from a book by A.G. Khripkova and D.V. Kolesov called *Devochka-Podrostok-Devushka* (*Little Girl–Adolescent–Young Woman*). Along with a companion volume called *Little Boy–Adolescent–Youth* , this book sets the tone for the course. Khripkova, a member of the Academy of Pedagogical Sciences, was given overall responsibility for the entire three-year sex and family-life program. Her guidelines with respect to what to teach about sex are quite sensible. The information, she writes, must be "comprehensible to the students, have a natural science orientation in substance with an emphasis on the moral aspects, be interesting and sufficiently exhaustive so that the pupil is satisfied with the amount of information conveyed and will not seek other sources of information, and it must be correct.... Children are keenly sensitive to lies and halftruths and don't want to be taken for a fool."

I also bought some of the sex manuals for young couples that are now being sold in limited editions in the Soviet Union. Through them I have gained an idea of what is and is not openly discussed. The information they convey is substantially correct, if inadequate. The basic details are there, but, as one of my friends told me scornfully, the "how-to" is pretty primitive.

Parents in the Soviet Union need not worry that sex education is arming their children with a panoply of erotic techniques or in any way encouraging them to experiment early. On the contrary, "teenagers must be taught that an early sex life carries the threat of venereal disease". There is no reference in any of the manuals to homosexuality, and one can be sure that the subject is not raised in the sex-education course. Until very recently, male homosexual behaviour was illegal in the Soviet Union (no legislation ever referred to female homosexuality), and the subject remains touchy. Dr. Kon's textbook for sexologists and other professionals, published in 1988, contains the first non-judgemental description of homosexuality yet to appear in print.

Here is the actual course in sex education as outlined in the new biology curriculum approved in 1986: after a general overview of the human organism and fifty class periods devoted to the other systems of the body, the students finally spend four hours on "Reproduction and Development". In this short time, they are expected to learn all about "the reproductive organ system. Fertilization and intrauterine development. The birth of a child. Infant growth and development. Breastfeeding hygiene. The Soviet government's concern for mother and child. A description of adolescence. Hygiene for young men and women."

Dr. Kon's response to this abbreviated course is a sigh of despair. "Our sexual culture is inadequate," he wrote in 1987, "and this seriously inhibits sex education…. The experience of other countries…shows that a good school system of sex education that introduces students to contraceptive measures reduces the number of teen-age pregnancies and abortions. We are not ready for such a program in this country." He goes on to explain that the majority of parents and teachers would still be against it and furthermore that there are not enough trained professionals to teach it. "What kind of moral education can we talk about if teenagers are not given the truthful information about their own psychosexual development? Our silence on this score," he concludes, "is essentially immoral."

However, I fully expect that the scientific information about sexual development and about reproduction conveyed to young people in biology classes will gradually expand and, as it does, it is to be hoped that the accompanying messages about the "approved" social behaviour of men and women will moderate. Otherwise they are bound to exacerbate marital difficulties later on, no matter how "knowledgeable" the two young partners become. For example, the text addressed to young girls that I read emphasizes *female* responsibility for the outcomes of sexual activity and therefore, by implication, reinforces the old double standard. Of course, a young man is exhorted to be "honourable" and to protect a young woman's virtue, but when he can put the blame on her for being "provocative", it is too easy to rationalize. "Women do not *customarily* begin to court men. This contradicts female *nature,"* say Khripkova and Kolesov (italics mine). "For a male to display his activism, however, a woman must attract his attention and this requires that she demonstrate her characteristically female receptivity in sufficient measure." Furthermore, "Modesty in a woman is attractive but is not acceptable in a man...modesty in a male may be perceived as a sign of sexual weakness." The authors also state that "occasionally even very small girls consider it their duty to lecture, admonish and criticize little boys. Some older girls are also inclined to scold young men. What all this leads to is obvious."

I need not go on. This stereotypical approach is not helpful in the present-day context of Soviet male-female relations. Most of the younger Soviet women I know are contemptuous of such statements. It is interesting to note that in a number of short stories now appearing in popular Soviet magazines, women are frequently portrayed as sexual aggressors. In paragraphs of panting prose, lustful predatory women pounce on hapless men. No longer are they temptresses or seductresses (traditional if immoral female roles) but ravishers, out for their own pleasure. Popular fiction is usually nourished by currents in the social environment. It would appear, then, that it is useless to preach "modesty" and better to reflect upon and to address what is really going on.

The Ethics and Psychology of Family Life

Now that Soviet teenagers are finally learning some of the basics of sex in class, what are they subsequently being taught about the dynamics of family life? The textbook I studied was written before the course became compulsory in 1985 and it reads as if it had been written in June during the period of the *pukh topoliny*. A blanket of muffling rhetoric covers its solid substance. Nevertheless, there is much in it that is interesting and valid, and in the hands of wise and understanding teachers this course could be of real benefit to the uncertain young. Revised textbooks for the course are less tendentious, and I expect that they will continue to improve.

It is worth spending some time looking at this course because it reveals so much about the general climate of relations between men and women in which the Soviet child of 1980s grew up. It is designed to be taught in thirty-four class hours, seventeen in each year. Its general aim is to prepare boys and girls for what Soviet authorities and experts have determined should be the norm for marriage and family life in the Soviet Union. Alternative life-styles are never mentioned.

The course opens with some discussion of the significance of the family in socialist society. Marxist-Leninist rhetoric claims that only a socialist society is capable of promoting the "harmonious development" of every side of the human personality (intellectual, moral, physical, aesthetic, social). In the first classroom hour, students are asked to reflect on their good fortune in being born into such a society and are given to understand that readiness for family life will be one of the most important consequences of their successful education. In order to make this clearer to them, the next three hours of the course focus on the interrelated themes of personality, society, family. This introduces the students, in broad outline, to Soviet psychological theories about personality and human development. In the final hour of this first section of the course, pupils are taught that "the most important task of the contemporary family is the formation of the personality of children", and emphasis is laid on the solidarity of the family collective as as a prerequisite for human development. Young people are reminded of their obligations to other family members, respect for parents and grandparents, and responsibility for younger siblings.

The second section is devoted to interpersonal relationships and feelings, the very stuff of adolescent life. Students are asked to think about the difference between functional and personal relations and then to examine flirtation and infatuation and to distinguish both from true love. They are also expected to talk about friendship and how having real friends is different from just being popular, discussing all these topics as freely as they wish with the teacher acting as a moderator. No marks are given for any part of the course.

A substantial segment of the second section of the course is given over to the theme of communication. The young people are asked to examine what the Soviets describe as the "culture" of communication; the ability to listen and the wish to understand the other person. This involves, they are told, respect for his or her outlook, thoughts, moods, abilities, and aspirations, and a desire to feel *with* him or her. Students are taught that the "culture" of communication also involves developing some skill at conflict resolution.

Boys and girls then discuss the nature of "masculinity" and "femininity". If, as Dr. Kon writes, sexuality is more polarized during adolescence than it is at any other time in our life-cycle, then attitudes that are reinforced at this time have a good chance of becoming set. This is surely what the authors of "The Ethics and Psychology of Family Life" hope will happen. Young people are asked to present their views of the "ideal" man and the "ideal" woman. Boys are told about their duty to preserve the virtue and honour of girls, and boys and girls alike are instructed on the special role of the girl in preserving a healthy climate in the collective. The teacher is required to expose any "incorrect presentation of masculinity" or "false understanding of womanliness".

Finally, the class turns to "Thoughts of Love". They are told, as if they did not already know it, that love is both the highest and the most complex of human feelings. They learn that the ability to love is the expression of the "highest level of development of the personality". They talk about first love and about love as the basis for marriage. They are warned against mocking those who are in love. They are instructed to nurture their feelings and take care of each other and not to ruin their relationships with "looseness".

The remainder of the first year of the course (six hours) and the first ten hours of the second year are occupied by the topic of marriage and married life. Students are introduced to the fundamentals of Soviet family law. Then they are expected to spend a couple of hours struggling with what it means to be psychologically ready for marriage. Following whatever limited success they may have with that task, they will be asked to look at the history of the family in the Soviet Union and at the special virtues of the socialist family as opposed to the "exploitative" nature of the capitalist one. During the last two classes before the end of the school year, the young people are warned of the difficulties that often erupt during the first year of any marriage and then asked to think what kinds of problems are most likely to arise as two personalities adjust to each other and strive to become a couple.

At the beginning of the second year of the course, the young people, who are now seventeen or about to be, and who have had a whole summer to mull over what they have learned, to fall in and out of love a couple of times, and perhaps to engage in a little sex, have to confront the heavy issue of family duties in the Soviet state. Brushing away lingering echoes of the last music tape they listened to or memories of fumbling in the bushes, they are expected to focus instead on the role of the family in combating "bourgeois" ideology and in reinforcing the "moral code of communism" among its members. Before they get too restless, the teacher will move on to a discussion of the psychological climate of the family and thus open up again the topic of interpersonal relations that adolescents everywhere find so endlessly fascinating. Students are encouraged to discuss whether or not the family is a true source of human happiness and why it is so important to have a home atmosphere of "loyalty, trust, compassion, tact and sensitivity". For homework, students are asked to prepare a debate on the theme of happiness using the following quotation from Pushkin: "They say that misfortune is a good school. Perhaps. But happiness is a better university."

Now students are asked to consider practical questions. Soviet families are supposed to be "working collectives" in which every member is expected to show proper respect for domestic labour and to perform his or her share of the household tasks. Students are expected to learn in a couple of sessions how to keep a family budget and how to organize the work that has to be done: shopping, cleaning, cooking, and so on. There is no presumption in the curriculum text that these tasks are sex-related. The Soviet stereotypes of masculinity and femininity refer to personality traits and attitudes rather than to task allotment. The fact that women end up doing so much of the housework is lamented by experts and officials alike, in principle, that is.

Class time is also set aside at this stage for a discussion of leisure time, how to plan for vacations, or to organize family outings, for example. Students are encouraged to think of the families they are going to form as miniature "culture clubs" in which family members will share many kinds of cultural experiences: reading, attending plays and concerts together, going to the movies, watching television, playing games. The messages contained in this section of the course are reminiscent of those that surrounded me and my friends during the 1950s. The notable difference is that it is assumed that both parents will be away during the working day. The experts who put this course together have nevertheless been realistic enough to realize that their message of 1950s "togetherness" has to be complemented by an acknowledgement of possible failure. And so the final hour devoted to the theme of "the Soviet family today" will allow students to focus briefly on marriage breakdown and discuss reasons for divorce.

Seven class hours are left. The last theme is "children". Students are introduced to the basics of child-care and the principles of "upbringing". Certain points are emphasized by the textbook. First, it is hoped that students will learn and understand that a child requires a structured environment for optimal development and needs to know that there are consistent family rules that are to be respected. Second, students are taught that they must never use physical punishment or any other disciplinary measure that might humiliate or devalue a child. Third, they are told that they must understand the different characteristics and typical activities of each stage of the child's life and act appropriately in order to draw the child up to the next stage. Children cannot be left to grow spontaneously or they will not develop "harmoniously".

Students are introduced in this section to the differing roles of mothering and fathering in the child-rearing process. They are asked to think about the special influence that each parent has had on his or her "spiritual" development. (The word "spiritual" does not carry the exclusively religious connotation for the Soviets that it usually does for us. *Dusha*, the Russian word for "soul", is frequently used in ordinary speech to refer to that innermost part of one's being "where the meanings are".)

Mothers are considered more important than fathers with respect to the spiritual things of life. Motherhood is held in high esteem throughout the Soviet Union. This is, of course, partly sentimental and traditional. Yet, the respect for mothers is quite genuine. When people in different parts of the USSR asked if I had any children and I told them about my five, I could see myself rise in their estimation. This respectful attitude to motherhood is so fundamental to Soviet society that I expect it will endure for some time even as relations between men and women change. It is certainly being reinforced in Soviet children. A young person is taught to value his or her mother not only for her "inexhaustible" love and support throughout childhood, but also for her "spiritual friendship".

Fathers, of course, also have their role, and the authors of the family-life course have made an effort to accord it as much value as possible. It is through the father, they say, that the child looks outward to society. This means that his model as a socially responsible citizen has a very strong influence on the shaping of the child's developing attitudes. Father is presented as the "guarantor" of mother's authority and the guardian of the family's honour. Students are taught that the roles of fathers and mothers are distinct. Fathers are not supposed to be motherly, and mothers should not have to play both roles, although this is increasingly the reality in the Soviet Union, as in the West. One of the intentions of the family-life course is to convince young people before they marry and have a family that children should grow up with two parents.

The last theme of the course is the relationship of the family to other institutions participating in the upbringing process. Young people, whom the State hopes will one day be parents, are given the message that the whole of Soviet society will be there to share with them the task of raising their children. Students taking part in this class are about to leave behind them the whole network of children's institutions in which they have spent so much time during their formative years. Now, in the final hour of the course, they are asked to take on, with respect to the next generation, the role that their parents are presumed to have played with respect to theirs. Once they are parents, they, too, must co-operate with the *yasli* and the *detsky sad*, the school and the extracurricular organizations, such as the Pioneers and the sports clubs, in the task of raising socially active, responsible, patriotic citizens, convinced and energetic "builders of communism".

Soviet students are given a great deal of homework in every subject and the family-life course is no exception. Before they discuss the "Culture of the Behaviour of Lovers", for example, they must prepare themes based on maxims given in the textbook. The following are typical:

> "Only lovers have the right to be called human." Alexander Blok

> "Before loving the woman in a girl, one must love the person in her." V. Sukhomlinsky

> "Nature says to the woman, be beautiful if you can, be knowledgeable if you wish, but you must, without fail, be sensible." Pierre de Beaumarchais

> "When a man is disrespectful to a woman it almost always means that she was the first to abandon herself." Denis Diderot

There are many other literary quotations scattered through the textbook, but few by women and none by my haunting ghosts. And yet, who knew better than Anna Akhmatova and Marina Tsvetaeva the raptures and regrets, the tragedies and ironies of love? Who gave better expression to all the aspects of love that women know? After all, the course, "The Ethics and Psychology of Family Life" is not intended for boys alone. And if knowledge is going to help to build better marriages, then young people should learn about love from the female as well as from the male perspective.

Urgench is an arid little town on the plains of Central Asia. In 1983, we spent two nights at the Intourist hotel there while we visited nearby Khiva, a museum-town of Islamic architecture. Our guide, a slender young woman wearing blue jeans and a flight jacket, told us that she had inherited her bright blue eyes from her strong-minded Ukrainian mother. However, she had been born and raised in Urgench, and although she did not care much for Moscow where she had gone for her Intourist training, she was restless in her hometown.

We spent the day with her, visiting Khiva's empty palaces, deserted mosques, and surprisingly full bazaars. Later, we went to the hotel dining-room for dinner. She was already there, seated at a crowded table, celebrating her birthday with her friends and her younger brother. During dinner she came to our table several times, bringing us champagne and pieces of birthday cake. Then she asked my husband to dance. Afterwards, she sat down with me to tell me about her life. That day she had turned thirty, and now no young man in Urgench would want to marry her. She was too old and too well educated. But then she didn't want to marry a man from Urgench anyway. The married men of her age had long since started leaving their wives at home to go out with their friends. She said that a Japanese businessman had been in love with her for nine years and kept coming back to Urgench. What should she do? I was moved by her plight, but what could I usefully say? Brought up in the Soviet Union, she was still convinced that her future depended on a man.

Five years later, in 1988, just before International Women's Day
(March 8), a baby named Masha was born in Moscow. The weekly
newspaper *Moscow News* asked four women to express wishes
for her future. Irina, a researcher, said: "I hope that, whether you
become minister, cosmonaut, lawyer, captain, scientist or builder,
you find your feminine happiness in marriage and maternity,
that you are tender, true, and faithful, understand suffering and
struggle, and that you strive and achieve." Nadezhda, a worker,
wished Masha a large family, adding: "for this it is essential that
she works less and her husband earns more." Yelena, a teacher,
wished her more choice with respect to the subjects she would
like to study. Olga, a physician, did not want Masha to do jobs
men are supposed to do: "If women can do everything," she said,
"it doesn't mean that they must do everything. The main thing for
them is to remain women at all times." Then she added that if a
woman is to bring joy to others, she needs warmth herself, so
"I want Masha to have a wonderful husband who will make her
happy".

When Masha turns thirty, the new century will already be into
its second decade. How different will her situation as a Soviet
woman be from that of our unhappy blue-eyed guide in far-off
Urgench? As children and youths grow up in the Soviet Union
today, they are finding themselves in the middle of social turmoil
as far as sex roles, relations between the sexes, and sexuality
are concerned. Boys and girls at home and in the classroom are
being pulled this way and that by a variety of forces. Some of
these forces are physiological. We have all known them. They
are as old as the human race. Some of the forces are cultural;
of these, some are quite new. Real changes in the behaviour
and attitudes of women after seventy years in the work-force
are contradicting stereotypes of masculinity and femininity that
many men (and women, too) continue to hold. The problem is
that "women want to live in the new way but feel in the old
way", as one Soviet commentator has put it, "and men want to
love not a colleague but a woman". Yet, "in a society of equal
responsibilities a woman doesn't feel like being self-sacrificing,
tractable and gentle." And "having divided their rather tiresome
burden in the work-place with women, men finally received a

real opportunity to take a breather—and they weren't slow in taking advantage of it", which means that many of them have rapidly discarded habits of responsibility for women and children. Some of the other forces that are buffeting Soviet children as they sort out their sexual identities are political and ideological. The political power structure is still predominantly male and is only just beginning to show some signs of acknowledging the existence of women who think in a new way. All these forces are reflected in "The Ethics and Psychology of Family Life". The course contains solid scientific knowledge, profound literary insights, real human compassion and understanding, all of which coexist somewhat uneasily with fixed stereotypes of what it is to be male and female with an ideology that has no room for the idea that the wisdom of women is as valid as, yet different from, the wisdom of men.

Officially sanctioned models of masculinity and femininity in the Soviet Union today will have to become more flexible if they are going to fit Soviet reality and permit girls such as little Masha (and boys, too) to grow up and fulfil themselves as individuals, as partners, and as members of Soviet society. Dr. Kon was asked, "Does the optimal model for the conduct of boys and girls exist?" "Yes," he answered. "It does. But each couple develops it and hence the model is optimal just for this couple." This does not mean that there are no ethical standards by which a couple should abide or that truth about the relations between men and women is always relative. What it means is that young people will continue to need help from their elders and from the collective wisdom of society but that, in the end, it is they who must decide about how to conduct their own relationships. For this decision, education about sexuality is essential. However, if the factual knowledge about being male or female and about sexual reproduction is to be translated into wisdom, it must be accompanied by "trust in oneself, one's feelings, emotions and creative potential". The courses in human reproduction and in the ethics and psychology of family life that are currently being offered in the Soviet school system are only a start.

Dr. Kon likes to quote from the Russian writer Mikhail Prishvin (1873-1954) when he talks about this subject. I will too: "Love is an unknown country to which all of us set sail, everyone as captain and sailing his own sailboat. No one can chart the exact route to this country for another individual but…it would help if everyone knew the fundamentals of navigation."

CHAPTER SIX

Growing Up Human: Soviet Theories of Child Development

Every Tuesday and Thursday morning, from October to June, during the three years I lived in Moscow, I would climb into my blue Zhiguli and drive the short distance from the Embassy to Alexey Tolstoy Street for a forty-five-minute exercise class. In a small gymnasium behind the solid bourgeois mansion that the Ministry of Foreign Affairs now uses for official entertaining, I would join a dozen or so other diplomatic wives in a concerted effort to control the impact on our bodies of our busy social schedules. Too many lunches, dinners, and national-day receptions made some of us look at ourselves uncomfortably in the mirrors that lined one wall of the gym. It was a relief to turn our backs when we could and gaze through the large windows opposite into the playground of the nursery school next door. Our moveable exercise bars stood so close to the windows that I would often come up from a deep knee-bend and find myself nose to nose with a small child in a tasselled wool bonnet, peering in curiously at our motley collection of moving female forms. We would waggle fingers at each other and smile. Another child would come running up to join the first but, inevitably, one of the teacher-upbringers would call to them and they would turn obediently and go back to play in the narrow enclosed yard.

Although our beautifully slender and incredibly agile instructor kept us in almost continual motion, my attention frequently strayed to the playing children. On most days, there were twenty or so two- to three-year-olds on the playground with three or four adults (women, or course). The timing of my exercise class obviously coincided with their fresh-air period because they were outside even on the coldest of winter days, when they were so bundled up that it was hard for them to do anything but stamp and blow. Usually the children were involved in unstructured play. When there was no snow, and even when there was, the little boys pushed trucks and other toy construction equipment along the ground, and the little girls dug in the sand-box with shovels, filling pails and little plastic moulds. The upbringers, or *vospitateli* as child-care workers are known in Soviet pre-school establishments, moved among them quietly or sat together on the edge of the sand-box, chatting and keeping an eye out for improper behaviour. Occasionally, they would stand up and organize the children into exercises with balls and rings or form them into circles for round games.

One morning I watched them play a game that took me back to my own early childhood. Looking at them, it was easy to imagine myself sitting beside them on the grass, hunched over a bit, tense between the shoulder blades, anticipating the poke on the back that would send me flying to my feet to race around the outside of the circle in a desperate attempt to get back to my place before another child could sit down in it. I could feel again the intense satisfaction that flooded through me when I made it, although most of the time it was I who became "it".

Dreaming about the past, I came to with a start when I realized that the object with which the children were poking one another was not just the ordinary twig that I remembered from my childhood. It was a pink plastic gun. I expect the use of a toy gun was quite incidental to the game. It was probably a water-pistol or perhaps an elastic-band shooter, like the one with which my older brother often tormented me. It was a part of this particular game only because it had been the object closest to hand in the treeless yard when the upbringers were rounding up the children.

Still, to see any gun in that peaceful environment brought me up short and made me think.

Suddenly, it became important to me to find out what was going on in the heads and hearts of these and other little children in the Soviet Union as their personalities were developing and their minds were being formed. My momentary identification with their game had reminded me that there are some things, like play, that are a universal part of childhood, yet my surprise and my sense of unease at the sight of the toy gun had forced on me an unwelcome reminder of adult conflict. Before my eyes I could see the children grow up and the gun become real. If the experiences of early childhood are as vital as I believe they are, then what these small children were learning on the playground that morning would stay with them in one form or another for the rest of their lives.

Bringing up my own children I found I needed some understanding of what I was doing, as well as why, in order to avoid making too many mistakes. So when they were grown, I returned to university to take a master's degree in educational psychology to help me consolidate and make sense out of twenty years of hands-on experience. But none of the theories of child development I studied in my courses in the 1970s satisfied me because they did not pay adequate attention to a phenomenon I had seen with my own eyes: children developing as human beings through an unending process of minute exchanges between themselves and their surrounding social world, countless small moments like the one I had just observed. Nor, in my view, did these theories take sufficiently into account the fact that children influence and change those who are caring for them almost as much as we think we are influencing them. Finally, I found them limited in their ability to explain the similarities and differences I had discovered among the children of the several cultures in which I had lived. In India, I eventually turned to the study of Indian religious thought to gain insight into the Indian children with whom I worked. Would a study of Soviet rather than Western theories of child development help me understand what it means to grow up human in a Soviet context? I decided to find out.

The Institute of General and Pedagogical Psychology

The first thing I did was seek an interview with Dr. V.V. Davydov at the Institute of General and Pedagogical Psychology because I was told that was where the most interesting contemporary Soviet research on child development was centred. This institute has a long and distinguished history. It was founded at Moscow University in 1911 as the Institute of Psychology. After the Revolution, a number of gifted young investigators, prepared to be challenged in new directions by the theories of dialectical materialism formulated by Marx and championed by Lenin, came together within its walls. Among these young men were Alexander Luria, Alexey Leontiev, and the brilliant Lev Vygotsky. Under Vygotsky's leadership, these men and their followers developed the ideas and theories that inspired the work that was being done at the institute at the time of my first visit in 1981.

However, Vygotsky's importance to the fields of developmental and educational psychology had not been easily established. Like so many of the bright intellectual starts that sprouted in the young Soviet state, Vygotsky's innovative ideas and those of his companions and followers were driven underground during the Stalinist period. It is a tribute to their vitality that they survived and in the late 1950s returned to flourish in the very place where Vygotsky, Luria, and Leontiev had first developed them. In the meantime, the Institute of Psychology had become attached to the Academy of Pedagogical Sciences (1944), and its name changed to the one by which it is known today.

The first time I visited the institute, I knew nothing of the dramas that had marked its early years. Nor was I aware that a new struggle was underway between Davydov, one of Vygotsky's most distinguished heirs, and certain members of the academic establishment. However, my journal records that he arrived late to our last meeting in a highly emotional state. In my presence, he channelled his rage into angry complaints about "the people" who underrate the ability of young children to deal with abstract thought. Then, we went on to discuss his recent work with primary-school pupils. I was very impressed by the vigour of his mind and the originality of his ideas. A short time later,

Davydov "resigned" as director of the institute—"for reasons of health", I was told—and transferred to the Institute of Pre-school Education. In the meantime, on his recommendation I visited experimental classes in School no. 91, the Moscow school with which he had been associated for more than twenty years. There I watched in awe as ordinary ten-year-olds tackled algebra with gusto, teaching one another concepts that I did not meet until I was in high school.

Several years later, I discovered that rumours I had heard at the time were true and that Dr. Davydov had, in fact, been forced out of the Institute of General and Pedagogical Psychology by his enemies. An article called "Catching Up with Davydov—A Pedagogical Drama of the 1980s" appeared in *Moscow News* in the spring of 1988, deploring the fact that Davydov's work had been blocked by "five or six" persons in positions of academic and administrative authority in the field of psychology who had succeeded in closing down his innovative classes, an act described as a typical example of the "intolerance of talent" that had marked the "stagnation period" of the early 1980s.

Now Davydov is active again. He heads a "laboratory" uniting researchers from several of the institutes of the Academy of Pedagogical Sciences in the task of laying foundations for a new comprehensive program for the primary school. If his proposals, and those of his colleagues, gain acceptance, it will mean that the influence of Vygotsky will spread throughout the whole Soviet educational system and no longer be restricted to pre-school institutions and experimental classes in general schools, as in the past. Judging by the success enjoyed by Davydov's students from School no. 91 at higher levels of education, this will benefit the whole country.

The opposition experienced by Vygotsky and his successors, including Davydov, is typical of the difficulties encountered by so many other scientific innovators throughout Soviet history. Yet the stimulus of Vygotsky's extraordinarily creative mind survived, and scholars and researchers such as Davydov have been inspired by his ideas to devise exciting programs for educating Soviet children that have worked, even if they have not been widely implemented. Davydov's ideas excited me and so I decided that if I was going to understand (from a Soviet point of view) what was happening inside the hearts and minds of the children at play behind the diplomatic gymnasium (and by extension, inside all the children in all the pre-school programs in the USSR), I would have to become better acquainted with the theories of Lev Semyonovich Vygotsky.

Lev Vygotsky and Soviet Psychology

Vygotsky burst onto the Soviet scene at the Second Psychoneurological Congress held in Moscow in 1924. He startled the psychologists present, upsetting some and exciting others, by refusing to accept the view that man's conscious behaviour could be fully explained by making reference to conditioned reflexes as so many at the time were trying to do. The rejection of all that was "bourgeois" by the revolutionaries had meant that explanations for human behaviour containing religious concepts or elements of philosophical idealism had become unacceptable. There could be no forces other than those of the natural, material world operating in human life. The mind-body, spirit-matter split that had characterized the view of human nature favoured by Church and State in nineteenth-century Russia had no place, according to the leaders of the Revolution, in the naturalistic scientific thought favoured by Marx. Although "consciousness" was a term used rhetorically by Lenin and his followers (as in "raising the consciousness of the masses"), as a scientific term it was highly suspect. It was considered a "mentalist" term associated with that mysterious and non-materialistic entity known as the "mind". In post-revolutionary Russia psychologists were supposed to focus on the physical brain and on neurological functioning in order to explain behaviour.

It was about consciousness, however, that Vygotsky chose to speak. Alexander Luria, who was present at that meeting as a very young man (Vygotsky himself was only twenty-seven at the time) described in his memoirs how stimulating it was to listen to him. Speaking without notes, Vygotsky stated that the concept of consciousness had to remain in psychology because it is conscious behaviour that distinguishes human beings from animals. Then he announced his determination to discover why, in the natural world—the only world that science according to Marxism-Leninism could accept—humans are cultured conscious beings, and animals are not.

Like Freud in late-nineteenth-century Vienna, Vygotsky was thoroughly grounded in the social and political climate of his time. Artists and scholars of his generation, the first to be active after the Revolution, had been well trained by the last generation of pre-revolutionary professors. These men, in spite of tsarist control and religious bigotry, had generally been serious researchers seeking the truth about the worlds of nature, art, and human conduct through their chosen disciplines. The universities of Moscow and St. Petersburg were centres of excellence that resembled the other great European universities of the period.

Psychologists educated in Russia before the Revolution came to their profession from two quite different disciplines; philosophy and medicine. However, those who had based their work on philosophic idealism, or were even thought to have done so, were not allowed to do so for very long after 1917. Many soon left the country on their own and, in 1923 and 1924, a large number of psychologists were exiled to the West, along with other Russian intellectuals, for "allegedly sticking to idealism". While Vygotsky came to psychology from philosophy and the humanities, he was not a philosophical idealist. On the contrary, he was one of those who had been energized by the intellectual currents that were brought to the surface by the Revolution. Inspired by Marx and Lenin, freed (or so they thought) from the oppressive hand of the past, excited by new discoveries in science and technology, these scholars and intellectuals were optimistic. Many of them were convinced that not only could they comprehend and transform nature, and especially human nature, within a few years, but that it was their moral duty to do so. "With Vygotsky as our acknowledged leader," wrote Alexander Luria, recounting what happened after Vygotsky was persuaded to join him and Leontiev at the Institute of Psychology, "we undertook a critical review of the history and current status of psychology in Russia and the rest of the world. Our aim, overambitious in the manner characteristic of the times, was to create a new, comprehensive approach to human psychological processes."

Vygotsky brought to that challenging task a wide educational background as well as some practical experience with both normal and handicapped children. He had graduated from Moscow University in 1917, just before the Revolution, where he had studied literary criticism, linguistics, and jurisprudence. From 1917, until he appeared in Moscow in 1924, he taught in the Pedagogical Institute of Gomel, a provincial town in Belorussia. There he worked with children with congenital defects, helping them to advance by building on what intellectual and other strengths they had. In Moscow, in addition to the other two men who had formed with him what Luria called "our Troika", he gathered around him a large group of eager young scientists and scholars to work on his theories about the historical-cultural development of consciousness in children.

To test his theories, Vygotsky and his colleagues conducted large-scale experimental studies, using normal children, mental patients, and the nomadic peoples of Central Asia as subjects. They were encouraged by the results of their research, but in the early 1930s, as the shadow of Stalin descended, most of them moved away from Moscow to Kharkov in the Ukraine so that they could continue to work as freely as possible. Vygotsky commuted back and forth to Moscow, where he was the director of research at the Institute of Defectology (devoted to what we call "exceptional" children) until he died from tuberculosis in 1934, aged thirty-seven.

Even before his death, Vygotsky had been severely criticized by the guardians of communist ideology. In 1936, his work was officially blacklisted in association with a Communist Party decree condemning "pedology" (a term describing the interdisciplinary study of children that had been so productive during the 1920s) as "bourgeois" and overly individualistic. After the end of the Stalinist period, Vygotsky was rehabilitated, and, in 1956, his two former colleagues, Luria and Leontiev, published some of his works in an edition for which they wrote a joint introduction. Since then, the work of Vygotsky and his group has framed the best of Soviet research in both cognitive (learning theory) and developmental psychology, and principles derived from his work have been incorporated into the educational program wherever possible. Unfortunately this has not been easy, particularly in the secondary school where until recently the techniques of social upbringing approved by the Communist Party have taken precedence over methods based on Vygotsky's insights into how children actually learn. As a result, as Dr. Davydov lamented when we spoke in 1982, the school system as a whole was not responding to the normal developmental needs of youngsters, ten to fifteen years of age, for greater freedom and more opportunities to experiment. The consequence, he said despairingly, was "too many heads stuffed with useless knowledge" and not enough creativity, spontaneity or, indeed, compassion.

Growing Up Human

Vygotsky produced many detailed studies of intellectual functioning, but it is his views about the psychological development of children as human beings that most interest people like myself who have a practical involvement with children. How does an apparently helpless newborn infant develop the consciousness that, according to Vygotsky, distinguishes human beings from the rest of the animal world? In formulating his answer to this question, Vygotsky was inspired by Marx who wrote that, unlike the rest of the world of nature, man as a species no longer evolves by natural selection but by the selective use of human culture. And what is human culture? According to Marx, it is the product of the physical and intellectual activity of men and women, their physical and mental "labour", the means by which they grasp and control both the physical and the social environments in which they live and turn them to their own purposes. As human beings change their environments through their creative activities, they, in turn, are changed by them.

The genius of Vygotsky was to use the dialectical method of Marx to understand how what he called the "higher" mental functions (the functions of deliberate memory, selective attention, and decision making, which comprise the concept of consciousness) develop in an individual child. The dialectical method led him to speculate that just as the human race has developed historically through a dynamic process of interaction with the products of its own activity, so the individual child must develop psychologically through his or her own activities in social interaction. The limited reflexes (rooting and sucking) and indeterminate sensitivities with which a baby is born combine with its biological need for nourishment to bring it to its mother's breast (or to a bottle). The mother's first response opens the baby's social life. During infancy, the baby's dependency on and need for human contact will lead it to develop ways of attracting and maintaining closeness and communication and it will use all its mental faculties to do this. From then on, the baby's intellectual as well as emotional development is inextricably tied to communication with other human beings either directly, or through the cultural "tool" of language.

Vygotsky was exceptionally sensitive to "the varied and changing roles of language in the child's mental life". He studied with particular care the manner in which the child makes use of and relies upon "the psychological tool of language in making new skills its own". As a result, Soviet psychologists of Vygotsky's school urge parents to involve themselves closely in their children's language acquisition. I remember being generally advised to talk to my children and to read to them, but that was about all. Soviet parents are given specific recommendations as to how to reinforce the language skills of their children so that they can use them to organize their inner life, their emotions, and their will, as well as their ideas. The richer a child's language, the stronger and more flexible will be the "tool" with which he or she can manipulate and interact with the outside environment.

Language is essential for human communication, and communication and collaboration are considered by Vygotsky and his followers to be essential conditions for the psychological growth of the child. Dr. Davydov writes that the "ideal" result of a child's emotional experience in infancy is that "the need for communication is formed and methods for constructing communication are worked out". One of his colleagues at the Institute of General and Pedagogical Psychology, I. Dubrovina, adds that "the ability to learn can be formed only in the course of communication with teachers, parents, classmates".

A child's collaboration with his or her classmates in purposeful activity is considered to be essential for all aspects of that child's development. The learning that takes place during shared communications within a group and is then internalized by an individual child is the psychological justification for the child collective. The child collective may have ideological significance for the authorities of the State, but, for Soviet psychologists, its role is primarily developmental.

The Vygotskian model of child development is an optimistic one, more optimistic than many religious models that emphasize sin and guilt or psychoanalytic ones that focus on the failure of primary relationships. Generally speaking, we, in the West, are not as confident about the human potential for intellectual development as Soviet theorists are. Yet, Vygotsky's faith in the capacity of children to develop their mental faculties by their own activity—in collaboration with others, of course—has led to some quite remarkable achievements with respect to handicapped children in the Soviet Union. I will describe these in the next chapter.

Vygotsky's hypothesis that the higher mental functions are socially formed using the tools of human culture, if true, puts great responsibility on the shoulders of every adult and older child who interacts with a younger one. According to this theory, if children are to grow up to fulfil all their human capacities, then the persons who surround them must be more than just guardians and loving caretakers. They must also be active planners and educators, careful architects of suitable learning environments. Furthermore, they must monitor their own behaviour in order to be the most humane of models. The challenge for parents, and for educators, is to create situations in which children can be stimulated to progress to the highest level of performance possible for them.

The Ages and Stages of Growing Up Human

When Soviet psychologists look at growing children, what they see does not, on the surface, differ much from what parents anywhere in the world see: stretches of relative stability, cheerfulness, and steady progress alternating with short periods of unusual agitation, tears, and difficult and inexplicable behaviour.

But what causes these shifts in behaviour? It is in addressing this question that Soviet psychologists begin to differ most obviously from their Western counterparts. Vygotsky, inspired by Marx, interpreted these stages, and the crises that mark the transition from one to another, as part of a dialectical process. "Not a single researcher," he wrote more than fifty years ago, "can negate the fact that these distinctive periods exist during childhood.... It is impossible not to note that all children during their critical periods become relative problems in comparison with their own behaviour in their adjacent stable periods." He further notes that external events can exacerbate these crises, something to which I can unhappily attest, since I always seemed to be moving from one country to another when at least one (if not two or three) of my children was going through a crisis. He described the negative elements of these crises in ways that brought them right back to me; how younger children become "stormy and impetuous" and older ones "obstinate, stubborn, capricious and selfish", full of contradiction and inner conflict. The way other people interact with a child during this period can enable the child to resolve that particular crisis and rise to a higher form of stable behaviour. Vygotsky's views about the ages and stages of child development are persuasive and have proved fruitful for his colleagues and followers.

To describe the ages and stages of growing children as the Soviets see them, I have chosen recent books by two Soviet women psychologists. Although both are academics associated with the Institute of General and Pedagogical Psychology, their books are intended for general readers, especially for parents and teachers. Both *Child Development and Education* by Lada Aidarova and *Growing Up Human* by Valeriya Mukhina are available in English, but it is clear that the texts were designed for Soviet, not Western, readers.

Infancy

Soviet psychologists characterize developmental stages by describing the way in which, during that particular period, a child is most receptive to learning. In infancy, it is the emotional contact between the baby and the adults on whom it is totally dependent, especially the mother, that focuses the baby's learning. When adults are loving and playful, when they hold the baby closely and pick it up when it cries, the baby will thrive intellectually as well as emotionally. The responsiveness of parents, and others with whom a baby spends its days, will lay the foundation for the baby's emerging personality because, according to Soviet theory, parental response determines the way the baby perceives itself. When parents show their approval of the baby's efforts to learn, their approval makes the baby giggle with pleasure. This, in turn, calls forth from parents (and others) the kinds of communication that a baby needs to develop in a healthy and normal manner. The baby "itself begins to give birth to its own developmental environment, arousing a specific attitude towards itself among the people around it." If love and approval are not forthcoming, it is easy to see what may follow. Both Mukhina and Aidarova emphasize the child's need to be loved as its first social need and recognition as its second. "Without this, being loved by parents and others, a child will come to mistrust people, which will have a telling impact on how his personality will develop in future."

Mukhina does not believe that maternal love is spontaneous. It comes to different people in different ways. Her references to the journal in which she recorded the progress of her twin boys sent me to my own not so scientific records. After the birth of my first daughter in Paris in 1954, I wrote in a journal: "When I came to after brief anaesthesia there she was, all wrapped up with her eyes wide open and Geoffrey [my husband] looking very pleased. It is a strange feeling when the baby is born and no longer part of one. I didn't feel any particular sense of accomplishment or anything ecstatic.... Mostly I had a sense of *her* complete individuality.... There she was, already a separate individual whom I shall grow to love more and more." Mukhina writes: "My first acquaintance with my sons did not draw any particular enthusiasm out of me. When they were brought home and unwrapped...I can't say that the unceasing movement of four arms and four legs aroused a flood of maternal tenderness." Rather, she discovered that maternal sentiment developed slowly in her—as it did in me—but develop it did, as the rest of her journal clearly shows. Mukhina is honest in her writing. When she makes a mistake, she records it and tries to learn from it. She both observes and tries to assist the growing differences in the personalities of her two sons. She is very careful to point out how unlike they are, and how one response was right for the boisterous and impatient Andryusha but was quite inappropriate, even inhibiting, for the quiet and gentle Kiryusha.

Early Childhood

Now "the child focuses his attention on the surrounding world of things discovering for himself their basic qualities." The emotional quality of the child's social world remains important and so does interaction with those who are close. However, the "direct communication of emotions gives place to exchanges because of objects and toys, the joint activity of the adult and child." The basic accomplishments of this period are the "mastery of upright movement, the development of actions with objects and the mastery of speech". According to Aidarova, "psychologists believe that by two years of age, the child gets almost as much information about the outside world as he is to get during the rest of his life."

As a child's third birthday approaches, the focus of learning shifts back from the world of objects and their properties to the world of human relations. Memory has developed as a result of manipulating objects, and the child has become more and more consciously aware of himself or herself as a continuing *subject* of actions, as an "I". All along the child has been internalizing adult reactions to his or her behaviour and thus forming a sense of identity, which leads the child to want and need to be recognized as a person in a world of people, to be independent. If parents and other adults are not sensitive to this need at the right moment, there will be a crisis marked by unruly behaviour. I have no quarrel with the Soviet interpretation of this crisis point, the "terrible twos" as I remember them.

The Play Age

When the crisis of independence is temporarily resolved, children enter a new stage where the leading activity by which they come to know the surrounding world is play. It is through play that children grow to understand the world of social relations, and further develop the mental functions they will use to control their conscious behaviour. This period normally lasts from the age of three until the age of seven, or whenever the child is genuinely ready for school. The seeds of play activity were already sown in the previous stage. Most of us might think that what the child was doing then was play. However, according to Soviet theory, activities that look like play do not really become play until the child has developed the capacity to use an object as a substitute for something else, particularly for something that has a place in the adult world. The bright object with a long handle that the baby sees, clutches and bangs, listens to, sniffs and tastes, may be the very same one that the toddler, unsteady on his or her feet, pushes along the floor to try out new motor skills. The older child, however, takes hold of this rolling, tinkling object by its protruding stick-handle and rides it around the room like a pony. This signals that important changes are taking place in the child's mental development. "The symbolic function of consciousness begins to evolve. Instead of actions with objects, actions are performed with substitutes", and the child is now ready for the development of the imagination, the stage in which play is the leading activity.

Because the play age marks the birth of the imagination, it has a particular fascination for people who reflect upon or write about what it means to be human. The faculty of imagination lies at the heart of all art, all invention—and all deception. Deceit in animals is mere camouflage, and babies don't lie. But who knows where the young child riding on his stick is off to?

Vygotsky wrote: "Children's play is imagination in action." Maxim Gorky said that play is really "children's path to understanding the world in which they live and which they are called upon to change". Mukhina and Aidarova are more specific. Mukhina emphasizes some of the motivations that engage small children in play: "In play the need for recognition manifests itself on two planes. The child wants both 'to be like everyone' and 'to be better than everyone'. These desires stimulate his development" through play, when both needs can sometimes be satisfied at the same time. Aidarova looks at the consequences of play for the child. She says that the principal significance of play in the child's mental development is that "role-taking in play is the leading activity in the course of which children get a basic idea of human activities in general". On this point, Western and Soviet theorists agree; play is fundamentally important for growing up human in a world of people.

In Soviet theory, play becomes the leading activity in the formation of the child's consciousness when the growing child begins to experience "unrealizable desires". Leaping to see how far one can go before touching the ground is no longer enough. The child now wants to leap up and over the moon. The things that gratify immediately no longer satisfy all of a child's needs. Now children want greater freedom of action. They want to enter the adult world but can't, so they begin to play at it. And as they play, at first on their own or parallel to other children (that is, engaged in the same activity but not interacting) and later with them, they begin to sever the meaning from one object and transfer it to another. The names of the horses they will not be permitted to ride in reality are transferred to a pile of sticks, and away they go, triumphant, in a cloud of dust. Thus the imagination is born. However, the sticks have to be brought back to the stables because games have to have rules copied from real life or they won't be any fun. Vygotsky emphasized the role of pleasure in play and said that children slowly impose more and more complicated rules on their play because that gives them greater pleasure than to play without rules. In role-playing games such as "House" or "Doctor" or what Soviet children call "Cossacks-and-robbers", the structure comes from the social situation that is being copied. However, as children get older, they begin to play increasingly abstract games with formal rules, such as checkers, chess, or *lapta* (a traditional Russian game played with a ball and a bat); it is winning by playing according to the rules that now gives the greatest satisfaction. The pleasure of abiding by formal rules in play is one of the things that carries children into the next stage of development, the school age, when the leading activity will be formal, systematic study.

The Soviet view of play as a leading activity in the development of conscious behaviour made me reflect on my own childhood. My earliest memory has to do with an object, a toothbrush, actually, that had a little doll attached to it. I received it at my second Christmas. Almost all of my other memories up until the time I went to school have to do with play. I remember the baby doll I could feed a bottle of water to and squeeze out over my long-suffering dog. I remember the stuffed animals, the ones I was given and the ones I made myself. But most of all I remember the social games: dressing up in all the tinsel and finery that my mother could find for us and performing our invented plays in front of our ever-patient parents. Then there were the games we played outside all through the long summer evenings, where, although I was younger than my brothers and usually the only girl, I would be accepted as "one of the boys". Sometimes I even beat them. All over the soft grass of the front lawn that became slippery with dew as night came down, we played "Frozen Tag" and "Prisoner's Base" and "Red Light" and "May I?". All kinds of things were going on across the street and around the corner but my home was secure and my world was play. When I ask my old friends about their early childhood they, too, growing up in different parts of Canada before the Second World War, mostly remember play.

For my children, memories of play jostle for place with others (the cobra in the garden, the lizard on the wall) owing to our many moves and the stresses they created. But their childhood was as unusual for their time as mine was normal for mine. I wonder, though, about North American children today. I hope there is enough room in their lives for real play, for, as Tolstoy said in describing the long winter evenings of his childhood, "If you only go by what's real then there won't be any games. And if there are no games, what is left?"

Child psychologists in the Soviet Union insist that the play stage should not be rushed. Children who are pushed too early into the kind of learning that properly belongs to a later stage when the child is in school, may miss out on some other aspect of their development and their personalities will suffer. Mukhina says: "Unlike physical birth which occurs in a specific year, a specific

month, and a specific day and hour, one's personality is born
over a period of many years of life, in one's day-to-day existence,
in ups and downs, in overcomings and indulgences, in joyous
satisfaction with oneself and despair at one's frailties." In the
formative years, social, emotional, and intellectual development
should proceed together or children will be unbalanced and their
personalities unstable. The notion of the all-round harmonious
development of the personality is a prominent one in all Soviet
writing about children. A child should not be hurried out of the
play stage before he or she is ready because not only does play
develop imagination and social understanding in children, but it
also develops moral understanding and behaviour in ways that
are pleasant and non-coercive.

Mukhina quotes Soviet research to demonstrate that, in joint
play, "children learn the language of social intercourse, learn
to coordinate their own activities with another's and learn to
understand and help one another". They also conform to moral
standards and rules far better than they do in everyday life
situations. When children are really interested in a game, and
want to take part in it, they will make mutual concessions because
they know that if they can't agree, the game will collapse. You
can always pick up your marbles and go home but then nobody
will like you and you won't have much fun.

Finally, because children want and need to play, play in-
fluences the development of other voluntary psychological
processes: attention, for example, and memory. The need to be
understood by children of one's own age also stimulates the development of coherent speech. However, Soviet scholars are most
interested in the function of play in enabling the child to know
and understand the meaning of human relations and actions.
Adults are important in play, but only at one remove, as models rather than as actors. They provide the conditions for play
but they should not interfere too much. Later on, though, they
must. As the child moves into the school age, adults are needed
as teachers and trainers. They have the knowledge and the skills
that the child, who is now ready for systematic learning, wants
to acquire.

The School Age

I have devoted considerable space to the concept of play because in the West it is not always accorded the respect it deserves as the most important activity by which pre-school children learn. Vygotsky and his followers believe that what children *want* to do is the activity that will best enable them to learn. And for children between three and seven years of age, it is unquestionably play that engages their emotional energies. But then, from seven to ten years of age, children want more structure and are eager to study symbolic systems and the human culture they represent: reading, writing, arithmetic, other languages, music, and so on. This is when school becomes the best environment for intellectual development.

Young adolescents (eleven- to fifteen-year-olds) are very social. According to Vygotskians, the development of the mental functions that determine conscious behaviour in this age group, such as logical thinking, judgement, imagination, and will, are most strongly influenced by what young people discover about themselves and others through social interaction. Soviet children's organizations, particularly the Pioneers, regard this period as one during which they can exercise maximum influence on the growing child.

Childhood's end is marked in virtually all industrialized societies (including the Soviet Union) by the assumption of political responsibility, the right to vote. For most boys in the Soviet Union, it is also marked by the beginning of military service. The final stage of childhood begins around fifteen and ends at eighteen. During this stage, the focus of young people is assumed to shift from social relations to preparation for the adult world of work, including the acquisition of work-related skills and knowledge. This period of vocational choice is usually marked by a personal identity crisis, the resolution of which points the young person in the general direction of his or her lifelong work activity.

Since several other chapters focus on school-aged children and various aspects of their development, I want to return for a moment to the pre-schoolers and comment on the contribution of their parents. Here is a final quotation from Aidarova. Speaking of parents she says: "The more generous they are, the richer is their child. It is what the parents give that makes the child emotionally rich and moulds an endowed personality.... It is essential for the adult to understand and, if possible, create for each age, those ideas that are to 'feed' the child and to form his new attitude to the world."

In this chapter, I have concentrated only on those of Vygotsky's ideas that have been most fruitful for Soviet research on normal child development and have subsequently found their way into Soviet practice. Most of us pay little attention to the impact of "ideas" on the structure of our day-to-day lives. It is unlikely that contemporary Soviet mothers give much thought to the influence that Vygotsky's ideas have had on shaping the environments in which their children are growing up and being educated. It is just as unlikely that the young mothers I watch from my kitchen window in Ottawa, pushing their baby-strollers along the sidewalk, are paying much attention to the theories about education and psychology that emerge from universities and other centres of research in North America and find their way into the schools. Yet the social and institutional environments in which we live and work are not random creations; they have been constructed over time by the power of human minds. Sometimes, as in the years of intellectual excitement and turmoil that followed the founding of the Soviet state, those minds have been remarkably focused, and geniuses such as Vygotsky have been able to come up with ideas that are innovative and exceptionally productive.

It will be obvious that I have found much that has merit in Vygotsky's ideas about child development and in the ideas of his intellectual descendants at the Institute of General and Pedagogical Psychology. I have learned things from them that have expanded my understanding of how *all* children, not just Soviet ones, grow and develop. I have reservations, but they relate less to Vygotsky's ideas than to the modifications imposed on them by his followers and by the ideological climate of the Soviet Union, which, for such a long time, blocked children's opportunities for social experimentation and for free debate by refusing to recognize the essential role these activities play. Vygotsky appears to have had a mind of exceptional vigour, open and flexible. It is certain that, had he lived and had he been able to conduct unimpeded research—which would have been a double miracle in these terrible years—he would have continued to expand his theories, possibly in unexpected directions.

What about his intellectual descendants today? That many of them are scholars of distinction there can be no question. One is aware, in talking with them, of the presence of great intellectual energy. They have survived difficult periods and now, in the new climate of *glasnost,* they should acquire much greater freedom for their research as well as many more opportunities to test their theories in practice. Davydov's recent appointment (in January 1989) as vice-president of the Academy of Pedagogical Sciences is an encouraging sign.

The opportunity to test their theories in real-life situations is more important, I think, to Soviet researchers in developmental psychology than I have sometimes found it to be among researchers in North America. But of course the unity of practice and theory is one of the central concepts of Marxist thought. It is usually identified by the use of the Greek word *praxis*. According to Marxists, "thought and action are inseparably bonded in the experience of life itself". Theory provides insights that lead to effective action, which in turn keeps the theory alive and dynamic. The problem is to assure that the relationship between theory and practice is so well balanced that neither dominates the other. In the early 1980s, one could detect a certain staleness in much of the psychological literature. With the changing climate there is a freshening wind.

The reader may have found this chapter overly theoretical. Yet theory is important. I could understand what was going on with my own children only when I began to read about child development. And understanding the children of another culture requires even more theoretical knowledge than understanding our own because the culture itself is strange. What I have just described is how, by and large, Soviet psychologists see the formative years of Soviet children. Let's see how it helps to make sense of the scene on the playground with which I started.

With our eyes opened by Vygotsky, what do we see now? Little boys dumping truckloads of pebbles and little girls shaping sand are revealed as learning about human activity in an objective world and as developing mental structures to retain and classify the information they are receiving in play. This is a universal developmental process. The children gently summoned back from their brief encounters with me at the window, however, were learning about relationships with foreigners on the Soviet model current at the time. The pink plastic gun we now see as harmless because it was not used as an instrument of violent aggression in the circle game. As a result, the children would not have thought about it that way. According to Vygotsky, a stick used as a gun would convey more messages to children about man-made violence, would be more "loaded", so to speak, than a gun used as a stick.

What we can also see now is that the adult-child interactions on the playground were not frequent enough, and, when they did happen, they were too interventionist for active learning to take place. The Vygotskian model of child development demands a well-designed environment for children to play in and thoughtful adult collaboration so that children can learn through the activities in which they are engaged. Adults should present children with challenging games, play with them, and then help them internalize their experiences. They should not tell them what they are supposed to learn, but learn with them. A pre-school institution that really operated on the Vygotskian model would be a vital place. Of course, children also have to be allowed to play on their own or freely with other children. They may even have to be encouraged to do nothing but daydream if they don't appear to know how. But a well-planned nursery school would enable all these activities to take place in an appropriate and balanced manner. What I saw from the window of the diplomatic gym was only the shadow of such a school. What I, and many of the people most concerned about children in the Soviet Union would like to see now, is the real thing. Judging by the pre-school institutions that I saw in the early 1980s, the children of *glasnost* had an unexciting start. But, as Soviet society continues to open up, they will now have a chance to examine what they themselves have learned and use their insights to change the culture of the next generation.

The Best Interests of the Child

CHAPTER SEVEN

Special Schools for Special Children

In the month of September the lands of European Russia begin to turn yellow beneath the northern sun. The air is soft, neither hot nor cold. When I lived in Moscow, it was my favourite time of year. The Russians call it *zolotaya osen* (golden autumn). The colour starts in the north and spreads slowly southwards until it reaches the Black Sea coast. The warmth of summer lingers in Black Sea waters long after it has left the Gulf of Finland, yet on either shore September is a lovely month, a time of hope and of new beginnings; little children are off to school.

One fine day in the golden autumn of 1983, I gazed out at the Gulf of Finland from the park of Peter the Great's summer palace near Leningrad. Once known as Peterhof, now called Petrodvorets (Peter's palace), this "Versailles of the North" was constructed at the beginning of the eighteenth century to impress the rest of Europe with the grandeur of the Russian tsar. During the Second World War, when Leningrad was under siege, Petrodvorets was occupied by members of the German general staff. In 1944, when they were forced to retreat, they tried to destroy it and they almost succeeded. But, as soon as the war was over, the Soviet state set about to resurrect the ruined palace and restore it to its former glory. Canals and fountains were cleared of debris, classical statues regilded, and once again the gardens were opened to the people.

The sun was shining on the day I was there and the park was crowded with strollers making the most of the last warm weather. All older children were in school, of course, but there were plenty of overdressed toddlers to chase after the dancing yellow leaves. I bought a *buterbrod* , as the Russians call a sandwich, and a small cup of thick coffee and sat down at a little round table to relax in the sun. I had just spent the morning at a residential school for severely retarded children and I needed to collect my thoughts. The school director had suggested that I eat my lunch in the peace and beauty of Peter's elegant seaside garden. He told me he often took groups of his students there so that they, too, could take pleasure in the dazzling fountains, the golden statues, the wide green spaces, and the broad avenues of trees. As I sipped my coffee I found myself hoping that he also encouraged them to play with Peter's water tricks.

These "tricks" are simple stone structures placed here and there in the lower gardens that conceal mechanisms, designed by Peter to use the many streams of water descending from the ridge above. Peter liked to lure unwary visitors onto the paving stones that activated his mechanisms, and then roar with laughter as they got soaked. I knew these trick fountains still worked because, on an earlier visit to Petrodvorets, I had watched young boys racing back and forth over the stones, dodging the sudden sprays.

I was intrigued by the thought that handicapped children in the 1980s might be able to enjoy a practical joke invented nearly three centuries before by Peter the Great. What would have happened, I then wondered, if Peter had been born in 1972 instead of 1672? Forget for a moment that he was the son of a tsar. From all accounts he was an exceptional child, greatly gifted and full of intellectual curiosity but also violent and subject to uncontrollable rages. A Peter growing up in Leningrad in the 1980s would almost certainly have been sent to a special school. The question is, which one? A foreign-language school to prepare him for the conduct of foreign policy? A maths and physics school to discipline his aptitude for science? A special sports school to train him as an athlete? Or a "forest" school (cum treatment centre) for his emotional problems?

All of these schools exist in the Soviet Union today as part of the State educational system. Everyone knows of the Bolshoi Ballet School, and I have described a school specializing in foreign languages in an earlier chapter, but until I began to look into the situation of the exceptional children at the other end of the spectrum—the physically and mentally handicapped—I had no idea of the variety of educational opportunities available to them. The responsibility that the Soviet state assumes for exceptional children is not just a question of social justice; it also reflects the Marxist-Leninist tenet that human beings are perfectible if the right social conditions can be created. This belief in perfectibility underlies not only the Soviet system of special education but also the child-health system (where it contributes to the focus on prevention and health promotion) and the child-welfare and juvenile-justice systems.

Of course, Peter the Great was privately tutored as a child and never went to school at all. State schools did not even exist in Russia until he himself established them. Now, however, the Soviet state promises appropriate education to each and every child, including those who are exceptional. Soviet educational authorities recognize that children are not all alike. Nevertheless, they believe that every child can be enabled to make a contribution to society. This goal presents a challenge not only with respect to handicapped and disabled children, for whom special educational provisions are clearly necessary, but also with respect to exceptionally gifted children whose unrealized talents would be a double loss, to themselves and to society.

The Soviet Science of Handicap: Defektologiya

Defektologiya is defined as "an integrated scientific discipline that embraces the study and education of all handicapped children and adults.... Children who are classified as handicapped are those with physical or mental defects that hinder their optimal development within the conventional system of education for children: blindness or impaired vision, deafness or impaired hearing, significant speech impediments, locomotor defects, and mental retardation." Also included in the classification are children with multiple defects and the very large number who suffer from a temporary delay in mental development but who are otherwise normal. About 11 per cent of the school population are considered disadvantaged for learning owing to handicaps or developmental delays. But less than 1 per cent are accommodated in special schools. Some are in special classes within ordinary schools and others have to make do in the regular classroom. One day, the State hopes that there will be enough facilities and enough trained specialists so that every child will be properly educated.

Living in Moscow, I was surprised to see so few handicapped children around. True, I occasionally noticed a deaf child signing or a child with Down's syndrome on a family outing, but not once did I see a visibly handicapped child in an ordinary school. "Where are they?" was my first question for Dr. T.A. Vlasova, the director of the Institute of Defectology, when I went to call on her in 1982.

Dr. Vlasova, a woman of warmth and intelligence, clearly committed to the potential of handicapped children, made haste to assure me that they were all studying somewhere, many of them in schools that had been specially designed with their particular handicap in mind. After the Revolution, the few existing charitable institutions for handicapped or disabled children were brought into the State educational system. At first, resources were so limited that only the deaf, the blind, and the mentally retarded could be accommodated. Today, there are ten different types of schools for all categories of disability serving well over 500,000 students. Most of these schools provide students with a complete secondary education, although it may take longer for some to cover the curriculum than for others owing to the time that they have to spend developing abilities to compensate for their defects. The deaf, for example, take an extra two years to cover the entire program because they need more time than children without impaired hearing to acquire the necessary language capacity. Technology can now shorten that time, and hearing aids have made it possible for many hard-of-hearing children to attend ordinary schools. Children with a mild degree of mental retardation attend what are called auxiliary schools where they are given an elementary-level education along with the labour-training that all Soviet children receive. These children take eight years to complete a standard curriculum, which is usually covered in four. Most special schools are boarding schools. Children go home on weekends and during long holidays and parents are encouraged to visit regularly and to serve on school committees.

"But why," I asked Dr. Vlasova after she had described the system of special schools to me, "do you insist on educating these children away from their normal peers? Why not integrate them into ordinary schools as we do more and more often in the West?"

First she gave me practical reasons. By grouping children with similar disabilities into special schools, she explained, a teacher, a qualified defectologist, can work with each individual child. This is not possible in an ordinary classroom unless every teacher has specialized training. What usually happens in such classrooms is that handicapped children are expected to learn in much the same way as all the others. But, because their teacher is unable to teach them properly, they fall behind and begin to misbehave out of frustration. It is much better for them to be with others with similar handicaps so that the successes of their peers will challenge them to try harder, to "emulate" them. Soviet defectologists, Vlasova among them, believe that handicapped children can be stimulated by being given learning tasks that are just a bit too difficult for them to manage *without* the help of others. Because they come to rely upon one another for help, the collective spirit is reinforced.

Another practical advantage to the special school is that it can be equipped with workshops for labour-training that are adapted to specific handicaps. Furthermore, a special school, particularly a boarding one, can be made into a "therapeutic" environment designed to meet the handicapped child's needs rather than those of adults. And, of course, when medication and physiotherapy are prescribed, it is much easier and probably more effective to provide them to children who are living together with others requiring the same treatment.

Other reasons for differentiated education are theoretical, deriving from the work of Lev Vygotsky who, when the Institute of Defectology was founded in 1929, was its first research director.

Studying the development of different catgories of disabled
children, Vygotsky observed that each type of handicap changes
the handicapped child's relationship to his or her social world in
certain specific ways. Since he believed that the higher mental
functions related to consciousness start to develop only through
social interaction, he was sure that distortions of that interaction
would almost inevitably interfere with normal development. The
social interaction that matters to Vygotsky, of course, is not
the amiable but undirected get-togethers that characterize so
much of human "socializing", but the important moments of
shared purpose when children and adults come together in a
teaching-learning situation.

If a child cannot hold a cup, or cannot see it, or cannot hear
his or her mother's voice, then the social interaction by which a
child normally learns the specifically human custom of drinking
out of a cup will change. Mother may get cross and lose patience,
or she may become over-protective and feed the child herself. In
either case, the child will become a passive rather than an active
partner in the process of learning to eat according to the cultural
traditions of the human species. As a result, the child's mental
development, which depends as much on the child's initiative in
learning as on the adult's teaching, will be hampered.

The example of the cup is a simple one; learning to speak and
then to read are processes of much greater complexity in which
social interaction is even more likely to be distorted by a physical
or mental handicap. Unless careful attention is paid to the quality
of the social interaction that adults and older children have with
the developing child, a primary handicap will very often lead
to one or more secondary ones. These will usually manifest
themselves in abnormal, often antisocial, behaviour. Inspired by
the Marxist understanding of the nature of the world, Vygotsky
envisaged the education of a handicapped child as a dialectical
process depending as much on the social learning environment
as on the child's innate abilities or on the curriculum that is used.

The current practice of special education in the Soviet Union
is infused with Vygotsky's ideas. Thus the highly structured
environment of the special school is considered much more
desirable for handicapped children than the North American

practice of "mainstreaming". In North America, we are concerned with a disabled child's perceived need to study with, and be accepted by, his or her normal peers. The Soviets, however, are more concerned with a disabled child's relationship to the teaching adults who are so important for his or her growth and development to fully functioning adulthood. Of course, peers are important and every Soviet cihld is expected to be part of a children's collective. But, a collective of similarly afflicted children is considered by Soviet experts more likely to be supportive and able to give the disabled child a sense of his or her own self-worth than a collective of normal children who might be either too protective or not sufficiently tolerant of the child's special needs.

Special Schools for Children with Physical Handicaps

In May 1986, I spent a morning at Spetsialnaya Shkola no. 17, one of two boarding schools in Moscow for children with motor difficulties. I sat through several classes, admiring the aplomb with which the students were able to work under observation. In one room, a little boy with short misshapen arms performed miracles with paper and scissors while helping his companions. In another, children with shaking hands laboured patiently at the blackboard with chalk and sums.

None of the 350 or so students in School no. 17 (who range from six to seventeen years of age) is able to move normally. They suffer from cerebral palsy, from a variety of birth defects, or from spinal-cord or other injuries that affect bodily movement. However, all of them are ambulant. Children who are paralysed and confined to wheelchairs are either taught at home by a special teacher (if their mothers do not have to work and are thus able to care for them) or live and study in a home for invalid children or in a sanatorium run by the Ministry of Health. School no. 17 has access to such a sanatorium where its pupils can go during school holidays. There are also special kindergartens for disabled toddlers.

The aim of schools for the physically handicapped is not only to take disabled students through the standard Soviet curriculum but also to rehabilitate them so that they will be able to manage adult life with a minimum of artificial aids. Two things struck me in particular as I walked about this school. The first was the normalcy of the atmosphere. All the children at the school had problems. But somehow they did not *seem* different. There were a lot of them about. At break time, when I arrived, most children were in the halls or playing outside in the yard. When we passed a couple on the stairs, they smiled at us and stood respectfully but carefully to the side. The school has several floors and the teacher who was showing me around explained that the children benefited from the additional exercise as they mounted and descended the stairs and also learned how to cope with a physical environment they were bound to encounter outside of school, because few apartment buildings or public places have ramps or other facilities for the physically handicapped.

Everything about the school program, including the extensive physiotherapy incorporated into almost every aspect of the curriculum, is aimed at normalizing the children. They study the same subjects as their age-mates all over the Soviet Union and they take part in many of the same extracurricular activities sponsored by the Pioneer organization. They compete in sports and other events with a neighbouring general school and share social activities with the children there.

The second thing in the school that particularly interested me was the little museum on the third floor. Each generation of students is encouraged to identify a disabled person who has had a successful life and to collect material about him or her to put on display. This activity is intended to help them and their schoolmates to see the possibilities and challenges of living with a handicap. The museum celebrates a blind poet, a paralysed mathematician, a one-armed "hero of socialist labour", and many others. Some of these people visit the school, and a photograph of the event is added to the collection. The most intriguing figure in the museum is Valentin Dikul, a weight-lifter in the circus, and now a member of the Soviet Children's Fund. He was totally paralysed by an accident in his youth and condemned by doctors to a life of immobility. Instead, he developed his own set of exercises, restored himself to activity, and returned to the circus. Now he performs astonishing feats of strength, including lifting cars. Everywhere the circus goes he visits hospitals and schools to encourage disabled children to try harder. Dikul attributes his success not only to his determination but also to his study of physiology. A scientific understanding of how the body works is an essential characteristic of the Soviet approach to physical handicap.

A special school that has had particular success with severely disabled children is the boarding school for the deaf-blind in Zagorsk, a small town some seventy-five kilometres northeast of Moscow, best known in the West as the site of the great Trinity monastery of St. Sergius. (Sergius was a fourteenth-century monk whose miraculous help enabled Prince Dmitry Donskoy to defeat the Tartar hordes at the famous Battle of Kulikovo Field.) This school and its program are fully described in *Awakening to Life*, a book written by a twentieth-century miracle-worker named Alexandr Meshcheryakov, who was the school's inspired director for many years.

The condition of being both deaf and blind, a rare one, is the supreme test of methods and techniques aimed at overcoming the handicap to normal development posed by physical abnormalities. A postscript to Meshcheryakov's book was written by four former students, all of whom graduated from Moscow University's faculty of psychology in the 1970s. These remarkable deaf-blind individuals believe that their productive careers are living proof of the validity of the theories derived from Vygotsky on which Meshcheryakov based his work at the school. "Now I am convinced," writes one of them, Natalya Korneeva, "that the teaching of deaf-blind children is not a miracle but a logical, practical application of scientific knowledge." That being said, one still gets the sense that for Natalya her own rescue by Dr. Meshcheryakov from a life of loneliness and isolation remains a miracle.

Meshcheryakov often used a suggestive simile to convey his belief that human consciousness can only be constructed through interaction with the outside world. "A deaf-blind child," he would say, could "be compared with a safe by those who did not know any better and these same people would maintain that all that needed doing was choosing the right key for the safe so as to open it and glimpse the untold wealth within. Yet we know in advance that the safe is empty. At first a good deal has to be put inside so that there is something worth taking." For a deaf-blind child this involves being exposed as soon as possible to common objects and common routines so that he or she can experience them directly and repetitively and so begin to build a representation of them in his or her head. A teacher will model for the child actions such as using a fork, drinking from a cup, dressing, making a bed, over and over again, until the child is able to do these things on his or her own and thus enter the world of human culture. Eventually the deaf-blind child learns signs for these objects and activities and can begin primitive but purposeful communication with surrounding adults. The adults at the school must be constantly alert for the smallest show of initiative on the part of the child and encourage it because an active two-way teaching-learning process is crucial for the child's further development. Signs give way to words as the child learns to finger-spell. Words are so much more flexible than signs that for a long time Soviet scholars were convinced that only with words could the deaf-blind child enter the true world of human knowledge and culture and grow up as a fully realized human being. Now signing has acquired new respectability as a psychological tool and is being more fully developed.

Soviet defectologists insist that all handicapped children acquire the fullest possible control of their native language. To grow up able to function with a minimum of technical assistance, children have to be energized and motivated to carry out the immense task of building internal compensations for their handicaps. Soviet practice suggests that language is indispensable for this. With help, as at Zagorsk, handicapped children can talk themselves into performing actions that normal children take for granted.

Special Schools for Children with Mental Handicaps

The schools I visited for children with mental handicaps were marked by the same positive outlook and structured learning environment that I had encountered in the schools for the physically handicapped. There are several categories of children who have difficulty learning owing to some degree of mental handicap. In the Soviet Union, these children are grouped on the basis of their prognosis for adult functioning. For the most severely retarded children, known as *oligofreny*, there is little likelihood of a productive adult life outside of an institution. Their mental retardation is caused by a defect in the central nervous system of such a nature as to prevent them from ever learning as other children do. Mildly retarded children, known as *debily*, or those with difficulties in learning associated with an organic disorder such as epilepsy, have a much better prognosis. Children suffering from temporary delays in mental development have an excellent one. There are schools especially designed to provide the most appropriate education for the children who fall into each of these three categories.

The school near Petrodvorets that I had just visited on that sunny September day when I began to speculate about Peter the Great is for children from the Leningrad area who are considered so severely retarded that few, if any, of them will ever be able to live or work outside of a sheltered environment. It is set in open fields not far from the highway that links Petrodvorets to Leningrad. From outside the school looks uncompromisingly functional, even ugly. But inside it is bright and, considering that it was built in 1974, unusually well planned for its special population.

My visit began with the usual discussion in the director's office accompanied by coffee and chocolates to moisten the facts and sweeten the figures. The director was neither a medical doctor nor a psychologist but, he told me, an ordinary school principal doing his duty for the Party. Not that he was complaining. On the contrary, he enjoyed the challenge the Party had set him. His professional staff, most of whom were trained in defectology, were supposed to supply the expertise he lacked. He had 4 doctors, 21 nurses, and 57 teachers as well as 200 others, to look after 420 children between the ages of four and eighteen.

The director professed sympathy for parents who have to accept the fact that they have a child so mentally disabled that he or she may never be able to learn to read or write but he was highly critical of those who abandon their disabled children at birth, as many still do. The school tries to maintain ties between families and their retarded children, encouraging parents to make regular visits to the school and to take their children home from time to time. Unfortunately, he said, after a while, some parents seem not to care.

All children at the school arc given basic education up to the level of their ability. They are organized into groups of fifteen to eighteen. Twenty-one of these groups attend class, and three are unable to. Those who go to class master some words and a few simple intellectual tasks. They look after themselves and their simple belongings and help out in the daily routine of their own small collective. They also learn some productive activity, such as making boxes, sewing bags, or packing and assembling small metal items. The older children are paid for this work and when they leave the school they will continue the same activities in a sheltered workshop while living in an institution. Only a very few are ever able to live on their own. All the costs of this school (and of the other special schools) are borne by the State, in this case, by the Ministry of Health.

When I asked about the children's social life, the director replied that he ran a tight ship, trying to schedule the day to keep the children constantly occupied with pleasant and satisfying activities. Otherwise they were apt to become disruptive and to undo all the efforts that were being made on their behalf. Adolescents, particularly boys, caused the greatest difficulty because some of them had powerful sexual urges and could become violent when aroused. The building is structured (with double stairways, for example) to minimize confrontations between different groups of children mainly by keeping them apart.

We toured the school so that I could meet some of his pupils. First he showed me some tidy dormitories and small cheerful lounges. Then we sat in on a couple of lessons. The classrooms were uncluttered and the teachers and students appeared fully engaged in joint activity. Some of the children had Down's syndrome, and others were physically as well as mentally handicapped, but they all wore bright colours and becoming hairstyles, and had clear eyes and open faces. The teachers were very well dressed. The director tried to convince me that this was not for my benefit but to show respect for the children.

The curriculum is simple. A class of nine- or ten-year-olds was working with coloured wooden shapes. The teacher was both patient and persistent. She encouraged each child to speak, no matter how haltingly, and she acted so positively towards all the children that I felt sure they must be making steady progress. The director shook his head. Children would often advance for a couple of months, he said, then forget everything they had learned, and have to start all over again. However, he praised his teachers and said that they refused to give up. The children looked up at him and smiled.

In a sunny corner of the second storey, the entire floor is a coloured game-board. Small children were jumping about from square to painted square according to directions called out by their *vospitatel* (upbringer): two squares forward, one square back, and so on. Directed physical movement is considered an effective method for improving the higher mental functions of retarded children, so every day is filled with games and physical activity. The school's facilities for this are impressive. In addition to play areas, there is a gymnasium and a swimming pool. I watched little girls in gym shorts, climbing bars and tumbling on brown leather mats. A small hunchbacked girl, her eyes alight with determination, was helped to turn her somersault by a good-looking young gym teacher. In the swimming pool several teenaged boys practised their strokes. In the assembly hall younger boys and girls were learning a folk dance. ("An exercise in order and rhythm," commented the director.) Music is considered to be as beneficial for these children as physical activity, and the school has a music as well as a physical-education specialist.

In the last classroom that I visited I was introduced to some adolescents who were making small grey cardboard boxes of the kind I had often examined critically in Soviet souvenir shops. Watching these boys at work made me think again. They were making boxes on order for a local factory, one of their industrial patrons. The boys were visibly proud of their handiwork. The director told me that these particular students had learned quite a lot over the years from their work experience in the school. It had made them feel useful and had given them a simple trade to offer to society.

I left the school impressed by the resources that the Soviet state appears prepared to expend on these severely handicapped children, yet concerned about their future. The general population is not comfortable with retarded adults. When I asked people I met about them they would respond to my questions in ways that reminded me of attitudes current in Canada a generation or two ago. As a result of the work of voluntary organizations, the International Year of the Handicapped, and a concerted effort at public education, attitudes in Canada have now changed, to everyone's advantage. This kind of consciousness-raising is only now beginning in the Soviet Union. In the meantime, retarded adults are kept out of sight.

In May 1986, I visited an auxiliary school for retarded children, accompanied by Professor Vladimir Lubovsky, a distinguished psychologist and a modest man of considerable personal charm, who speaks excellent English. Shortly afterwards he replaced Dr. Vlasova as director of the Institute of Defectology and, in January 1989, was made a member of the Academy of Pedagogical Sciences.

Special School no. 486 is hidden away on a quiet street lined with untidy trees in one of Moscow's faceless residential areas. Outside it looks like an ordinary general school, the usual two-storey functional block, but inside it is distinguished by the careful display of attractive wooden objects—wall plaques, sculptures, chairs, and tables skilfully ornamented with coloured inlays—all made by students in the school.

The school director was a forceful woman who, talking very quickly, told me in short order that she was responsible for three hundred children in eighteen classes, that her school offered an extended-day program for children in the primary grades, and that the students had three good meals a day. The most severely retarded children study language, simple arithmetic, and technical drawing. The others have a more advanced experimental program designed to bring out their potential to the highest degree possible. All children have labour lessons from the first to the third grade and then start some sort of productive labour in the fourth. By the time the children have been in school for eight years they are spending a month at a time on a worksite.

The director then told me about her forty-two teachers, only eight of whom were male (a situation she regretted). All of her teachers were trained in defectology and earned at least 20 per cent more than ordinary school teachers. They were expected to follow a prescribed curriculum and to use methods developed by the Institute of Defectology but they were also urged to work creatively on their own, developing a separate program for each student. A teacher is responsible for an individual child for several years, a responsibility that includes maintaining contact with the child's parents.

I was interested in parent involvement in the school since I had been told that many parents are reluctant to send their children to special schools. The director confirmed that parents are not obliged to send their child to a special school although they certainly are encouraged to do so if a recommendation for placement has been made by a medical-pedagogical commission. If the parents accept the placement, the school works closely with them to help them deal positively with their mentally handicapped child. School no. 486 is a day-school and the students go home every night. They are also with their parents during holidays although they will probably spend the month of June in a Pioneer day-camp. Most of the children at this school come from nearby and there is an active parents' committee. The majority of parents are co-operative, said the director, once they recognize that the school is acting in their child's best interests. Caring parents are vital co-partners in the successful education of handicapped children, but unfortunately there are some who, for a variety of reasons, refuse to take part.

I enjoyed my tour of the school. In the classrooms the children were cheerfully occupied. I was pleased to note that there were boys among the girls in the sewing room where the students were learning to tailor clothes. Considering their disabilities, and the absence of exciting Soviet models, the clothes on display, which had been designed, cut, and sewn by the students themselves, were remarkably stylish. In another classroom, the director tousled the hair of a slight, wiry young adolescent whom she introduced to me as Alyosha, a boy with a "character disorder". She told me that he was erratic and disruptive in his behaviour and that when he first came to the school he frequently skipped out. However, his condition had now greatly improved and I was struck by his responsiveness and his apparent sociability. He certainly did not look "cowed". In fact, nowhere in the several schools for the handicapped that I visited did I see sullen or withdrawn children.

The students at Special School no. 486 have difficulties with the normal curriculum owing to quite serious mental handicaps and associated behaviour problems. The school program is designed to enable them to graduate with a trade and with sufficient social and emotional skills to live a useful and productive life in society, even though most of them will always be limited to some extent by their disability. However, there is another category of afflicted children who may start out in life with a disability but who should be able, with appropriate education, to catch up to and even surpass their normal peers. These are children who suffer from what the Soviets term "a temporary delay in mental development".

Dr. Lubovsky has conducted research into the problems of these children for many years, and it is from my conversations with him and my study of his writings that I have garnered most of the following information. I myself have long been interested in these children, whom we usually call "learning disabled" in Canada. I have known many and have observed, in some cases, the lamentable consequences of late identification and inappropriate education for these children's social and working lives. The situation in Canada has much improved in recent years, as it has, thanks to Dr. Lubovsky and his colleagues, in the USSR.

Dr. Lubovsky told me that the identifying feature of the child with a temporary delay in mental development is the functional immaturity of his or her central nervous system. This may have been caused by an illness during pregnancy, by a premature birth or a birth trauma, by an illness during infancy, or perhaps by an inherited weakness. These children are not ready to respond to their surrounding environment in developmentally appropriate ways. They have tremendous difficulty in filtering sensory perceptions when they are very young. Thus they are easily overwhelmed by noise and movement and become agitated and anxious at a time when they should be enjoying and learning from their sensory experience. These children also show a characteristic lag in the way they play. They do not role-play like other children of four and five, preferring to play on their own. Thus, when they should be learning to play according to the social rules imposed by games such as playing house they are still at the object-handling stage. This retards their social development.

The Institute of Defectology has been studying children with developmental delays since 1960. At that time, it established a special boarding school and began to experiment with various compensatory methods to enable these children to function normally as quickly as possible. Teachers tried to restore the specific dynamic of a particular stage of development by taking the child through it in a structured way. At the play stage, the period between three and seven years of age when, according to Vygotsky, children learn best by playing, children with a temporary delay in mental development have to be patiently encouraged to move from construction sets to games that engage them with other children and teach them about social interaction. It is also very important to reduce unnecessary stimulation and confusion in the environment until a child's central nervous system is strong enough to cope with it. This is why early identification and placement are considered so essential for children with developmental delays as well as for other handicapped children, any one of whom may develop an additional developmental problem if he or she does not enter an appropriate educational setting.

Correct identification and placement are crucial to the successful education of handicapped children. All Soviet children undergo a series of compulsory examinations at their district polyclinic during infancy and early childhood. Children cannot enter school without a complete polyclinic record. These regular multidisciplinary screenings should ensure the early identification of most handicaps—provided that the required specialists are all available at the polyclinic and that they know what they are doing. Any medical specialist, upon determining the presence of a handicap that is serious enough to interfere with learning in the regular classroom, may refer the child to a local medical-pedagogical commission in order to decide where the child should go to school. This commission is usually made up of a representative from the local education authority (which is responsible to the city or the district soviet), a pediatrician, a psychoneurologist, a speech therapist, a psychologist, a defectology teacher, and the director of a particular school under consideration. The commission will make a recommendation to the child's parents. It would be an unusual parent who would defy such a formidable array of experts in order to keep his or her child in the ordinary school system. Nevertheless, it is painful to be told that your child has a severe learning difficulty, and many parents do, in fact, insist, against all evidence, that their children are normal.

Children handicapped by a temporary delay in mental development can be distinguished from those who are retarded by means of a teaching experiment. Since, according to prevailing Soviet theory, the mental development of children is conditioned more by social interaction than by heredity or by environmental factors, it is more important to discover how well a child can learn *with* adult help than to test the same child's unaided performance.

A teaching experiment involves observing the child in a natural setting (the kindergarten, say) being taught a specific task that is slightly in advance of the child's current performance ability, a task that lies in what Vygotsky called "the zone of next development". On the level of unassisted performance, a retarded child and a child disabled by a temporary delay in mental development might score the same. With assistance, however, the developmentally delayed child consistently out-performs the retarded one. A teaching experiment may also enable examiners to detect the specific nature of a child's learning disability and thus guide them in the preparation of the most appropriate teaching plan. Each child in a special school for delays in mental development is supposed to have an individual program carefully tailored to his or her needs. As in all special schools, the classes are much smaller than they are in ordinary ones.

There are far too few schools in the Soviet Union for children with temporary delays in mental development. There ought to be about two thousand in all, a number equivalent to the auxiliary schools for the mentally retarded that currently exist. When the Ministry of Education accepted the need for such schools in the early 1980s, it was expected that they would expand rapidly even though it costs the State three to five times as much to educate a child in a special school as in an ordinary one. This optimism was based on the good results obtained by experimental schools in Moscow, Gorky, and Kiev. A little over half of the children in these schools take an extra year to complete the primary cycle, but then are able to attend an ordinary school. Although the others require specialized teaching until they graduate, as graduates they have successful records of employment and of socially useful activity, records that are decidedly better than those of their peers with similar problems who were not able to attend special schools or classes, or who had not been identified until they had experienced school failure. By 1989, only 88 special schools for children with temporary delays in mental development had, however, been created. Instead, more and more so-called levelling classes had been established in ordinary schools. This is less costly, of course, but there is a danger, according to the experts, that by being easily accessible they will become "dumping grounds" for difficult children instead of challenging settings for children who are temporarily disabled for learning.

Childhood Autism

Some children in the Soviet Union need special education because they suffer from mental disorders that are characterized by strong emotions and unusual behaviour. In the case of a serious mental illness such as childhood schizophrenia or clinical depression an afflicted child will be treated and educated in a mental-health centre or a sanatorium. The son of one my Soviet friends suffered a nervous breakdown in early adolescence and spent two years in a "forest" school—the Soviets believe strongly in the health-restoring properties of fir trees. He recovered eventually and returned to his former school. His treatment consisted of tranquillity, medication, and some psychotherapy, but there was nothing special in the education program at the sanatorium. The young patients all studied the universal Soviet curriculum, taught to them in the usual way.

There is, however, one mental disorder in childhood that requires special education wherever it occurs—childhood autism. Autistic children are both a puzzle and a challenge to all who come in contact with them. Why do such children shut off normal interaction with the rest of the world? Can anything be done to encourage them to establish healthy social relations with those who love them? The Institute of Defectology has been seeking answers to these questions for some years, and in 1989, I visited the institute's centre for autistic children, located in an unpretentious ground-floor apartment near the Metro station Kirovskaya. The space is very home-like, not like a school at all, which makes it much more welcoming to autistic children who are easily disturbed by strange surroundings.

The centre serves 170 children who come two or three times a week for special sessions. Most of the younger ones stay at home with their mothers who draw a small pension from the State for having an invalid child, but 67 per cent eventually enter either a general or an auxiliary school and a few even continue to post-secondary education. The children and their families maintain contact with the centre at least until the child reaches the age of fifteen because the centre believes that long-term support is essential if an autistic child is to achieve his or her potential.

The children who come to the centre are the most severe cases, many of them subject to aggressive fantasies and hallucinations and manifesting strange ritualistic behaviours. Nevertheless, Soviet researchers have discovered that outcomes can be positive if corrective work is begun early enough. They have also found that the children who have been referred for help from a *yasli* or a district polyclinic have better prospects than those who have been hospitalized before diagnosis, separated from their parents and expected to function in a large dissimilar group.

Soviet experts believe that the condition of childhood autism is a constitutional one and is probably related to any one of more than thirty identifiable anomalies arising in the brain of a baby before birth. The effect of these anomalies on a baby's developing central nervous system is that an autistic child is born with a much lower sensitivity threshold than a normal child. This means that autistic children are very easily frightened and distressed. Even the most commonplace events of infancy and early childhood can be absolutely terrifying to such children. To protect themselves, these children isolate themselves from the outside world and from emotional contact with others. They lose (or never acquire) the ability to distinguish between animate and inanimate objects. They behave among people as if they were alone. Autistic children develop ritualistic behaviours and make rigid demands of the environment to ensure that it never changes. If they speak, their speech is strange. They make varied and contradictory statements and rarely use speech for communication.

How can these children be helped? Obviously early childhood is a crucial period for autistic children and so is the family environment. However, according to Soviet experts, autism is seldom clearly established until two or three years of age. After that, the condition tends to remain stable for another two to three years. The best opportunities for change present themselves between six and ten years of age because a tendency towards compensation seems to emerge at this time. One-quarter to one-third of the cases observed by researchers at the centre became more socially adapted during this period. The best prognosis is related to autistic children with high intellectual potential who are not mute. These children, in fact, are often unusually gifted and can become extremely valuable members of society.

Dr. K.S. Lebedenskaya, the director of the centre, showed me over her somewhat restricted premises where I observed children playing a variety of games, each with his or her own special teacher. She explained that the centre's approach is to lead the child away from his or her fears into pleasant yet purposeful activity undertaken in co-operation with adults. The teacher or parent is instructed to stimulate other parts of the child's brain so that it will be able to compensate for biological inadequacies. Certain games are recommended to raise the child's emotional "tonus" because the child's mental activity can be best promoted if emotional appeal is added to sensory experience. Games that have proven to be successful are those that involve music, light, and water, such as balloon games or blowing soap bubbles or playing with sun "bunnies" (a Russian expression for the dancing light reflected from a hand mirror). These games help to improve the quality of the autistic child's contact with adults by making that contact more enjoyable.

Another primary task is to decrease the continual sensory and emotional distress experienced by autistic children. This is why the atmosphere of the centre is so calm and peaceful. The surrounding environment is arranged to protect the child from such traumas as bright lights, loud sounds, strong smells, or abrupt gestures. Parents are told that it is important to remove any object that might remind the child of an earlier frustration. The adult should try to find out what it is in the child's physical world that frightens him or her. Since such children feel they are surrounded by enemies, even the most innocent-looking toy may be terrifying. So the adult should walk through the child's habitual environment, holding his or her hand, and note the moments of greatest tension. Certain games played in enclosed places may be able to reduce the child's fears and enable him or her to express the content of those fears.

All interaction with autistic children must be carefully structured, Lebedenskaya insisted. The children should become used to quiet rhythms in work and play. A gentle musical accompaniment will minimize over-excited reactions. The autistic child needs ready-made patterns of behaviour that he or she can learn through play. Games should reproduce everyday situations and they should always include adults. If the child can be encouraged to play the role of a classroom helper then he or she can begin to be made aware of the positive dynamics of purposeful joint activity. Gradually, the centre's research has discovered, the child will begin to feel a need for the adult, and his or her state of anxiety will diminish.

The adults (teachers, parents, or psychologists) who work with autistic children at the centre learn to detect the smallest, most primitive movement that such children make towards contact and respond to it with real but gently expressed pleasure.

Once contact is made it is patiently reinforced over and over again. Medication is also used: tranquillizers and neuraleptics to decrease psychomotor excitability and anxiety; other drugs to stimulate mental activity. It is recognized that living with an autistic child is an exhausting experience for parents, so every effort is made to share the therapeutic task. The centre is encouraged by the results of its research with autistic children and their families, which it willingly shares, but support and money are not yet available to open similar centres in other parts of the USSR. It is most unfortunate that the Soviet Union does not yet have the resources to build on its many strengths in the field of special education.

The Gifted Child

Not all exceptional children have difficulties in learning or suffer from physical or mental handicaps. There are also the exceptionally gifted. The Soviet educational system has adapted over the years to provide for them as well. Although younger children are not streamed in school according to tested ability as they often are in the West, there are many opportunities for them to enrich themselves through the extracurricular activities that are offered both inside and outside the school. A "young naturalist" can join one club and study the migration of birds. A "young technician" can join another and learn to make small radios. A child who loves to sing can join a children's chorus at the local Pioneer palace. Children with literary and artistic interests have endless opportunities, from writing poems to play-readings, from painting to photography. Most of these activities take place in *kruzhki* (circles). Children are discouraged from the solitary pursuit of their interests. These *kruzhki* are very widespread and offer a lot of stimulation to a lively and curious young mind. But they are not really what either I or the Soviets would call "educational" provisions for the gifted child.

The *kruzhki* were created by design to respond to differing tastes and abilities so that the school curriculum itself could remain uniform and open to all. In the early days after the Revolution there was a determined effort to abolish élitism. In fact, children from advantaged homes were actively discriminated against and the children of workers and peasants were promoted. This is why there were no in-class opportunities for the intellectually gifted. The situation was different for artistically talented children or those with athletic promise. It was easy to argue that these children should have special educational provisions so that their gifts could be developed for the glory of the State. Besides, such talents could be discovered in children from any sector of the population, so a special school for dancers or painters or athletes would not necessarily favour one social class over another. On the contrary, the world's first socialist state could show that a child from the poorest of families had just as good a chance as any other to become a great violinist or a world-class swimmer.

It was much less acceptable to admit that one child might have greater intelligence than another. That was considered a bourgeois notion. It was not until the 1960s that the debate opened up with respect to the intellectually gifted. Many leading scientists felt that the by then traditional means of fostering talent through extracurricular activities was too low-powered and episodic for the gifted minority. In 1961, some schools began to specialize in foreign languages and others to focus on science and mathematics. While these schools ostensibly serve the catchment areas in which they are located and therefore do not discriminate among children from different social classes, an almost inevitable process has taken place since they were established. In the USSR there are no independent private schools of the kind that flourish in the West. So ambitious parents, perceiving the schools with special programs as superior to the other 90 per cent, strive to get their children admitted.

A university professor described this process to me quite graphically one day after admitting that she, herself, had taken advantage of it. We were in the Cheryomushki (southwest) section of Moscow where many academic institutes are located. When this section of the city was built twenty or so years ago, apartments were apportioned so as to ensure a complete social mix. However, through the swapping and bargaining that goes on all the time with respect to living quarters, more and more intellectuals moved in and blue-collar workers moved out to get closer to their factories or to have more room. As a result, the school population became more "advantaged" and the local school, which has a French program, more highly regarded. Better teachers were attracted and the quality of the school continued to improve, leading to the very élitism that the authorities had hoped to prevent. The parents of these students are able to pay for the extra tutoring that is usually necessary to get their children into the best universities and institutes. One can be sure that these children will do the same thing in turn for their own offspring.

Special schools, including language schools, serve the State well since knowledge of a foreign language, English in particular, is essential for success in world affairs. Nevertheless, in the new spirit of *glasnost*, cries of "élitism" have arisen once more. In 1987, students were detected arriving at school in the chauffeur-driven cars that were then provided to senior government officials, and other parents and journalists cried "foul!" After a lively debate, the future of existing special schools was more or less assured but no new ones will be opened for the time being.

There is no perfect solution to the dilemma of equality versus excellence, which will always arise, in my view, because some parents care more about education than others do and have either the money or the clout to go after it for their own children. The best answer is to raise the quality of all schools by adding extra resources to those that are not good enough. Unfortunately the problem of inequality in education is further complicated in the Soviet Union by a serious rural-urban split that persists in spite of, or perhaps because of, increasing migration to the cities. Few teachers are eager to serve in remote areas if they have to forgo the amenities and opportunities of the city.

It is against this background of "creeping élitism" that the debate about special education for the intellectually gifted in the USSR should be seen. In the early 1960s, a proposal was made to open a special school for physics and mathematics at Akademgorodok, the famous "science city" in Western Siberia. Many people were opposed. Both academics and politicans warned about the undesirable social and educational effects "of segregating a privileged group of *Wunderkinder*". They also argued, being ideologically opposed to the use of IQ tests, that it was very difficult to assess talent. However, in the early 1960s the country had such need of innovative and highly qualified scientists that resistance was overcome and the first physics and maths school was opened in Akademgorodok in 1963, to be followed shortly by the founding of similar schools in Leningrad, Moscow, and Kiev. By 1975, there were nine more.

The school in Akademgorodok is the prototype. It takes students for their last two years of secondary school, five to six hundred of them. Priority is given to children from the more remote areas. They come from a variety of social backgrounds, from twenty-eight to thirty different nationalities, and have differing levels of school performance. The selection criterion is not intellect per se, but originality. Every year, a special science "Olympiad" is held for young Siberians. The first round is conducted by mail. In November, problems set by the Olympiad organizing committee are printed in the newspapers that most young Siberians read. Anyone can compete. The questions are constructed in such a way as to pick out the children who can think unconventionally, clearly, and originally. Tens of thousands of fifteen-year-olds enter the first round. For the second round they have to compete in person by coming to one of the big cities in Siberia. Teachers from the Academy of Sciences in Akademgorodok attend this round so that they can speak to and personally assess the interest of the competitors. Winners of the second round attend a summer camp in Akademgorodok and prepare for the third round. There they can meet distinguished scientists and get a feel for the scientific atmosphere so that they will know what they are getting into if they opt for a life as a scientist. The questions for the third round are extremely complex. Successful candidates then enter two demanding years of study at the physics and maths school. They can choose their own scientific speciality and work one day a week at one of the nineteen scientific institutes in Akademgorodok. The standards of teaching are very high, the school atmosphere is stimulating, and the success rate in terms of students continuing into future scientific work, most satisfactory. As one might expect, there are some social problems in the school. A number of children cannot settle into boarding-school life and competition is often fierce.

Of course, the number of children who attend such schools is minuscule in relation to the total school population. Far more attend schools that have advanced teaching in particular subjects. However, many intellectually gifted Soviet children find no special encouragement at school for their talents. Nor with the increased focus on polytechnical education that characterizes the current school reform, and the continuing debate about élitism, are special curriculum provisions for academically gifted children likely to increase in the near future. The vast majority of these children will continue to receive the same basic schooling as everyone else and will have to depend on extracurricular activities, planned or unplanned, for stimulation and enrichment.

The Bolshoi Ballet School

For the artistically gifted, the situation is better. There are many special schools for them offering training in music, the visual arts, the theatre, even circus arts. Two in particular have never had their existence questioned: the Bolshoi Ballet School in Moscow and the Vaganova Ballet School in Leningrad. The children who attend these schools are very special indeed. I visited the former on a snowy day, in February 1983, and came away enchanted. Of all the performing arts, I most love the dance. My life in Moscow was greatly enriched by evenings at the Bolshoi Theatre. While I missed some of the excitement that is provided by the more imaginative modern dance troupes in the West, I never failed to be awed by the technical brilliance of Soviet dancers or moved by their profound musicality. *Spartacus, Macbeth, Ivan the Terrible,* and *The Golden Age* were among the full-length contemporary ballets that astonished and delighted me. But the most magical performance I ever saw was *Swan Lake* danced by the Kirov Ballet of Leningrad. The artistry of the dancers, both soloists and corps de ballet, was of such perfection on that particular night that the whole audience was transported. I have never seen a classical performance in the West to equal that evening. How do the Soviets do it? My visit to the Bolshoi Ballet School helped me to understand.

Sofya Golovkina, the director of the school at that time, was once one of its students and then she danced for twenty-five years before returning to take over the school, which moved to a new building in 1967. A short woman, blonde and a little stout, she seemed a bit severe at first, but during the course of the morning I saw her transformed by her pride in her students and the satisfaction she gained from working with them. At the time of my visit she was sixty-seven years old, but she revealed so much energy and such interest in every aspect of "her" school that she seemed much younger. She was still there five years later. The parts of the school that I visited were imbued with her personality and her ideals. I saw discipline combined with warmth, high expectations for individual artistic excellence and a sense of community. Everybody appeared to know everyone else. The children in the corridors greeted Mme. Golovkina cheerfully and respectfully, and she always responded in a friendly and direct manner. No doubt there were personal dramas being enacted within the walls of the school that I could not see. In an atmosphere of such intensity, that would be inevitable. However, in her presence they were firmly under control.

The Bolshoi Ballet School was founded in 1773. At that time, "theatre dance" was not a profession for ladies, so at first classes were offered at the Moscow Orphanage. In the nineteenth century, the classes were organized into the Imperial Ballet School. In 1920, after the Revolution, the Commissariat for the Enlightenment (Narkompros), which had responsibility for both education and culture, set out "Rules of the State Ballet School" and admission was opened to all talented children in the USSR, regardless of background.

Today the school has six hundred students, with an equal number of boys and girls. Every year, auditions are announced and two or three thousand youngsters apply from all over the USSR and abroad. The school's examiners look at each applicant carefully so that the interested children will feel that they have been given a fair chance even though it is clear from the outset that some of them will not do. Indeed, most are turned down after the first try-out. The remainder are examined by various specialists, including medical doctors, to see if they have the proper physical endowment. Ninety are then selected. These children enter the school at ten years of age. After eight years of study, sixty-five to seventy members of the entering class will graduate as dancers. Some join the Bolshoi Ballet Company, many go on to dance in other Soviet ballet troupes or return to the countries from which they have come. A few turn to teaching. Three hundred students live in the boarding unit of the school and three hundred somewhere else in Moscow. Tuition is free but a small fee is required for board. Financial assistance is available from the State for the purchase of dance clothes and shoes, particularly if the child's family has limited resources.

The school day begins at eight. During the day, there are six hours of dance class, rehearsal, or practice. In addition, students must complete a secondary-school education with emphasis on relevant subjects such as music, history, dance theory, and French. A child with academic problems will be assisted as much as possible. There are few failures. Children leave the school because of illness or for personal reasons but only rarely, Mme. Golovkina told me, are they expelled for misbehaviour.

After tea and explanations with Mme. Golovkina in her office, I was shown around the school. Although it was a grey wintry day, there was light everywhere. The classrooms and the practice halls open off a corridor carpeted in light blue and walled with glass. I was shown a small gymnasium, a library, and some rooms for crafts (great emphasis is placed on the development of all aspects of the student's "creativity"). The school also has its own theatre for rehearsals and performances with a stage made of pine planks and canted to the exact same degree as that of the Bolshoi Theatre.

There are three hundred staff members. They include medical professionals for the attached polyclinic and dietitians who supervise special diets for the students. The Soviets are scientific about this sort of thing. I remarked on the long necks of the girls and was told that special exercises had been designed to elongate them. Noticing that all the older girls were tall and slender, I asked what happened to those who did not grow. I was told that they were discouraged from continuing because no ballet troupe wants a short dancer unless she is truly exceptional.

The best part of my visit, of course, was seeing the students in class. The quality of the teaching is captured in the school's brochure: "The work of a classical ballet teacher is similar to the jeweller's art. With patience and care, diligence and inspiration, they polish their student's talents day after day."

I watched a small class of twelve-year-old girls. Before the forty-five-minute class began in earnest, one of them came in with a watering can and sprinkled the wooden floor near the bars. As the mother of four girls, I have watched my fair share of dance classes but this one was of an altogether different order. The teacher, in ordinary street clothes, never paused for a moment. She knew the strengths and weaknesses of each girl and somehow managed to work with her individually at the same time as she worked with the whole class. She was almost more interesting to watch than they were. There were twelve of them in pink body suits with their hair neatly rolled up in back. A pixie-faced girl with red hair may have been embarrassed by having her winged ears exposed but she never stopped smiling. The girls all had slender bodies but each one was at a slightly different stage of development. They were totally absorbed by what they were learning. During the thirty minutes that I was there, the teacher kept them at it continuously, but whenever the tension became too great she broke it with a little joke. The class seemed to function as an organic whole. The accompanying pianist was as involved as the teacher and her students and required no spoken instruction as she shifted tempo and mood.

The last class I visited was Mme. Golovkina's own. It was made up of seventeen-year-olds, in their seventh year of study. One more year and they would graduate. Over their blue body suits they wore knitted leg warmers of different colours, and each of the nine faces was distinct and memorable. This class, which lasts for ninety minutes without a break, had already been in session for an hour when I arrived, and two of the girls had had to stop and sit down for a few minutes. Mme. Golovkina scolded them for not eating any breakfast and confessed to me later that eating disorders are a problem for some of the older girls.

Mme. Golovkina had just recovered from the flu. At one moment, she told the girls that just because they had been working with someone else was no reason for lumping around like elephants. To my eye no comparison could have been farther off the mark. Mme. Golovkina is an extraordinary teacher, tremendously vital. At her age she does not leap about, but every move is a speaking illustration of her vision of what her students are capable of. And these students were capable of anything. This was the director's special class and the girls knew it. There was one who had such a sensuous and beautiful face and such grace of movement that I could scarcely keep my eyes off her. Only when she smiled, which was rarely, did I remember that she was still a school girl.

I left the school thoughtfully. There is always a human price to pay for excellence. The Soviets know that as well as we do. They try to minimize the cost somewhat by surrounding the developing dancer or the budding scientist with a normal school program in addition to his or her special curriculum. All the other special schools for the artistically gifted, the music conservatories, the art schools, are run on the same lines. But, in the end, it is almost inevitable that the talent will be nurtured more than the child.

With the Bolshoi Ballet School I come to the end of my tour of special schools for special children in the Soviet Union. Whether or not one agrees with the concept of differentiated education for children with special needs and talents there can be no doubt that the Soviets have developed some effective techniques for teaching exceptional children. I was as favourably impressed by most of the institutional settings for the handicapped that I visited as I was by those for the gifted, yet I know there are many others that I would have found inadequate, poorly staffed, and depressing, particularly those that look after children who have been orphaned, abandoned, abused, or neglected by their parents. Such institutions are likely to be unhappy places in any society. If there is no parental or community involvement and if the supervision by the State is half-hearted, then the risks of misery are increased. While the centre for severely retarded children near Petrodvorets and the school for the deaf-blind in Zagorsk appear to be models of their kind, an auxiliary boarding-school in Moscow has been recently exposed as a place of almost Dickensian conditions, little more than a holding-pen for difficult, unwanted children. In 1988, an investigative reporter published an article in *Sovetskaya Kultura* deploring the prison-like conditions of School no. 98 and the disdainful attitude that the director and some of her staff were displaying towards the child-inmates. This article, supported by the testimony of others, led to significant improvements in the school's conditions. The authorities have undoubtedly responded not only to the public outrage but also to the fact that the school was being managed in a manner contrary to the prevailing philosophy of the State. This philosophy clearly states that handicapped children must be educated so that they will be able to live full lives as adults and contribute to Soviet society. And to do this they must be taught to communicate properly with other people, something that is unlikely to happen if they are badly treated.

The prevailing philosophy in Canada is somewhat different. We, too, stress the need for exceptional children to be able to live independent and personally fulfilling lives but we do not always expect them to make a contribution to society as well. For purposes of a brief comparison I have studied the provisions for exceptional children that are offered by the Ottawa Board of Education. Since the proclamation of Bill 82 in 1983, school boards in the Province of Ontario have been obliged to provide education for *all* exceptional children, as is the case in the Soviet Union. The trend is to mainstream disabled children if possible by placing them in ordinary classes with special assistance or in special classes within ordinary schools with specially qualified teachers. There is, however, one special school in Ottawa for children with physical handicaps and another for the mentally retarded. Vocational schools for slower learners are also available. Separate educational provisions are made for children who either are in hospital with long-term illnesses or suffer from such severe mental or behavioural disorders that they have to be kept apart. If and when these children get better they are reintegrated into the ordinary schools. All the children in the region who have been diagnosed as autistic are taught together in a local school. The intellectually gifted are placed in special classes in a small number of schools or allowed to proceed through the curriculum more rapidly than their age-mates. There are other enrichment possibilities including a special high school for the arts. And, of course, there are independent schools for those who are able and willing to pay.

As far as I know, teaching strategies designed for exceptional children in Canada do not have an overall theoretical or philosophical base aside from a general adherence to Jean Piaget's theories of intellectual development and Erik Erikson's stages of emotional growth. The present system for exceptional children has emerged as a result of the various pressures that characterize democratic pluralism, including strong lobbying by parents. As such, it represents the nature of our society, where both the rights of the individual and tolerance are cultural values. Those who strive for the total integration of handicapped children into the mainstream are convinced that the long-term interests of such children are best served by such a practice. I am sure that normal children in Canadian schools are much more accepting of handicapped children now than was the case when I was growing up, and that the daily life of handicapped children has been enormously facilitated by all the measures that have been put in place in recent years. This is particularly true with respect to people with physical handicaps. The situation of people with mental handicaps or mental illness unfortunately still leaves a great deal to be desired.

In the Soviet Union, attitudes to handicapped people among the population at large are marked by ambivalence. Many people express compassion and active concern, yet more often the reaction is one of embarrassment or a confused sense of guilt. Differentiated education has tended to keep handicapped children out of public view, so public awareness about and acceptance of disabled people is not as high as it should be. The quality of the schools that we visited came to my Soviet translator as a distinct and agreeable surprise. More public education is necessary and the improvement of public facilities for the handicapped is part of that education. However, I do not think that in the Soviet context "mainstreaming" handicapped children is the answer. The Soviets do not have the resources to give all handicapped children special attention in an ordinary school as we try to do. Nor do they believe "mainstreaming" is in the children's best interest. Physical and mental abnormalities are either handicaps or gifts, according to social definition and by comparison with other individuals in a given society. The Soviets have developed a system of special education that reflects some of the best of their cultural values just as ours does some of the best of ours.

After studying the special schools in the Soviet Union, however, I am doubtful that any one of them would have been able to manage the brilliant, volatile child who became Peter the Great. There are obviously some children who are so exceptional that no schooling is totally appropriate. Nevertheless, I like to think of the mentally handicapped children from the school near Petrodvorets being taken regularly to Peter's garden by the sea to play his water tricks. Because when one of them steps on the loose stones that release the streams of water, a special man reaches forward across nearly three hundred years to make a special child laugh.

CHAPTER EIGHT

Child Welfare and Juvenile Justice

In 1959, the General Assembly of the United Nations adopted a Declaration of the Rights of the Child. In so doing, states with radically different political systems agreed to recognize that all children on this earth need protection and nurture and have the right to expect that the countries into which they have been born will do their best to ensure that their basic needs are met. Hundreds of millions of children have been born since the declaration was adopted but, unfortunately, millions have also died because the ideals of the declaration remain as far beyond the reach of most member states today as they were thirty years ago. Yet, these ideals persist. Spurred by the International Year of the Child (1979), the declaration was redrafted as a convention that was adopted by the General Assembly on November 20, 1989. Countries that sign and ratify it will now be bound by international agreement to incorporate its principles into their domestic legislation. On January 26, 1990, a first group of nations signed the document in New York. The Soviet Union was among them.

The rights of the child addressed by the U.N. convention arise from the fact that childhood is a preparation for adulthood and that all children have needs that must be satisfied if they are to grow up as caring and responsible human beings. The economic, social, and cultural rights of children include the right to adequate food and shelter; to medical care; to special services for the handicapped; to education; to participation in cultural activities, play, and recreation; and to protection from exploitation, cruelty, and neglect. The prescription of these rights recognizes the vulnerability of children and the fact that their physical, mental, social, and emotional development is at a formative stage. Civil rights, which are the ones that we in the West tend to think of first when we think of "human rights", are also spelled out in the convention with the intention of promoting the concept of the child as a human person. The civil rights of children include the right to a name and nationality, the right to be consulted in all matters affecting him or her, freedom of conscience, expression, assembly, and the right to privacy. The novelty is that all children are assumed to have these rights because they are born into the human family. Any restrictions placed on their rights in view of their level of maturity or because of conflict with the rights of their parents will have to be justified. As for political rights, however, the convention's definition of childhood precludes them. These are acquired in most societies when children attain the age of majority and are able to vote, that is, when those who are granted these rights are no longer children.

How Soviet legislation responds to the needs of children and guarantees their rights is a fundamental strand of the web of culture that surrounds Soviet children from the day they are born. Laws are part and parcel of any society they regulate, offering a unique perspective on its values. The evolution of a country's laws also reflects the structure of social change. Under Gorbachev the Soviet constitution is being amended to move the Soviet Union away from the rule of the Communist Party towards the rule of law. An independent judiciary and more defence lawyers, if they materialize, will greatly strengthen the protection of individual rights. But children, highly valued by both Soviet society and the Soviet state, have long been better served by the system than adults. At the time of the Revolution the majority of children in what is now the Soviet Union lived in dire circumstances. They were poor, hungry, unhealthy, and unschooled, and were often beaten or exploited. After the Revolution, it was many years before the material conditions of children's lives showed much improvement. During the last thirty years, however, the Soviet Union has moved close to guaranteeing *de jure* and *de facto*, in law and in fact, most of the rights now accorded to children by the U.N. convention. Given the situation of children in most of the rest of the world, particularly in Africa, South America, and Asia, this is a notable achievement.

The Soviet Constitution

On October 7, 1977, the Soviet Union adopted its current constitution. To celebrate this event, and to underscore its importance, October 7 became a national holiday. Each year, as the date approached, Soviet schoolchildren were asked to study their country's constitution and to reflect upon it. Their teachers presented it to them in glowing terms and encouraged them to feel sustained and protected by its provisions. It is a model teaching tool for social studies. Everything is clearly laid out— the political and economic system of the Soviet Union, social and cultural structures, the status of the nationalities, foreign policy and defence—and all in a way that makes it easy to memorize. In addition, throughout the 1980s, a compulsory course in the eighth grade of the Soviet general school called "The Fundamentals of State and Law" took a whole year to make sure that Soviet children knew the constitution inside and out and had some understanding of Soviet law.

In 1989, the Supreme Soviet set up a commission to draft a new constitution for the USSR, a task which will be enormously challenging in view of political change. In the meantime, the 1977 constitution, with some remarkable amendments, continues to be the base on which all Soviet legislation is constructed. Like the society it structures, and, to some extent, still mirrors, this constitution evolved out of the revolutionary ideas that were embodied in the original Soviet constitution of 1918. The "supreme goal of the Soviet state" is still the same: the building of a classless communist society in which the people will be self-governing. The preamble states: "The main aims of the people's socialist state are: to lay the material and technical foundations of communism, to perfect socialist social relations and transform them into communist relations, to mould the citizens of communist society, to raise the people's living and cultural standards, to safeguard the country's security and to further the consolidation of peace and development of international cooperation."

General principles are established in individual branches of Soviet legislation in accordance with the constitution. The "Fundamentals of Legislation for the USSR and the Union Republics on Marriage and the Family" or "on Health" or "on Public Education" are prepared in Moscow and then ratified by the Supreme Soviet of the USSR. Individual republics draw up and adopt their own legal codes and laws, which must conform to these "Fundamentals". A certain amount of leeway is allowed in areas where tradition is strong. There is also flexibility with respect to the use of the local language. However, such practices as dowries or bride-price, which used to be common in Central Asia, do not conform to the socialist principles of marriage as established in the constitution and therefore cannot be permitted by the law of any Union republic. The codes of the Russian Federation (RSFSR) that I quote will illustrate how this relationship between the fundamentals and the codes works in practice.

Children's Rights Under Civil Law

During my second year in Moscow, I spent a morning exploring children's rights in the Soviet Union with two women lawyers, specialists in children's legislation. We met in the offices of the Soviet Women's Committee, near the centre of Moscow. One function of the Soviet Women's Committee is to provide opportunities for voluntary work by women, and many dedicated professionals are attracted to it for this reason. The two women with whom I spoke had freely contributed their time and expertise to a book on Soviet legislation and children's rights published in 1979. A revised version in English was produced by Progress Publishers in Moscow in 1982; it was this book that provided the guidelines for our discussion. In 1988, I met in the same place with another lawyer from the Institute of State and Law in order to update my information. In talking with Z.A. Yakovleva and S.V.

Polenina and later with A. Litvinova, I focused on points of civil law that are likely to have the most impact on individual children.

We began with the most individual right of all, the one addressed by Article 2 of the U.N. Convention on the Rights of the Child, the right from birth to a name and to a nationality (where nationality is understood as citizenship, not as ethnicity). Under Soviet law (Law on Citizenship of USSR, Article 10) citizenship is acquired at birth, which is when the child becomes a legal entity capable of having civil rights. This is known as legal capacity. Legal ability (or competence)—meaning the right to enter into legal contracts—comes with the age of majority, which is eighteen in the Soviet Union.

The right to a name brought up the question of Russian names, which, as anyone who has ever read a Russian novel knows, are complicated. Non-Russian Soviet citizens have had to adopt Russian practice in order to fulfil the requirements of civil registration forms (birth, marriage and divorce, death). When the birth of a baby is registered, his or her first name is normally followed by some version of the father's name (*Petrovich*, son of Peter, or *Petrovna*, daughter of Peter) and then by the family name. Most people are known in everyday life by name and patronymic (except to their intimates, who may call them by any one of the innumerable diminutives of common first names). The family name is reserved for formal use when it, too, has a masculine and feminine variant, as in *Karenin* and *Karenina*.

But what happens, I wanted to know, when a baby is born out of wedlock? Is he or she considered illegitimate? No, was the answer. If the father admits paternity, then his name will be entered in the official register of births, the baby's patronymic will be based on his first name, and he will be liable for maintenance (Fundamentals of Legislation of USSR and Union Republics on Marriage and the Family, Articles 17 and 18.) Alternatively, the mother can, with proof of paternity, secure a court order to register the father's name. Paternity can be established using a blood test (negative evidence), letters, or some evidence of having shared a common household. Since the State becomes responsible for the father's share of maintenance if the paternity cannot be known or proved, legislation was prepared in 1988 to admit new forms of evidence for paternity. If the father is unknown, the mother can supply whatever patronymic she chooses and register the baby in her own family name. The baby of a married couple can also carry the family name of the mother in the Russian Federation as long as both parents consent (RSFSR Family Code, Article 51). As a result, my informants concluded, triumphant, "The way in which births are registered has done away with the concept of illegitimacy!" I said that this looked to me like a sleight of hand and they had to admit that unmarried mothers still encounter social disapproval, but their children less so.

Custody and maintenance orders issued at the time of divorce affect children profoundly. Although marriage in the USSR is supposed to be based on "a voluntary...union of man and woman and on mutual love, free from materialistic considerations and on friendship and respect for all family members" (Fundamentals, Marriage and the Family, Article 1), divorce has been common since the time of the Revolution, except during the most oppressive years of Stalin's regime. Many divorces take place between young childless couples and these are simply and cheaply accomplished at the State Office for the Registration of Acts of Civil Status, commonly referred to as ZAGS. Whenever there are children, however, a court decision is mandatory. A husband cannot even apply for divorce without his wife's permission while she is pregnant or until one year after childbirth (Fundamentals, Marriage and the Family, Article 14). The custody of the child (or children) is supposed to be decided in the child's best interests. In general, and not only in divorce proceedings, "Parents rights may not be implemented against the children's interests" (Fundamentals, Marriage and the Family, Article 18). Children must be consulted when custody is being awarded (RSFSR Family Code, Article 55), but they are not always considered able to determine their own "best interest". While there is no presumption in Soviet law that either the father or the mother has a preferential right to the child, custody is, in fact, almost always awarded to the mother. I was told that this is true in at least 90 per cent of the cases, particularly when children are small. The older the child the better the father's chances. One of my friends admitted that she would never have divorced her husband if she had not known for sure that she would be granted custody of their daughter.

No matter who is granted custody, the other parent is guaranteed access and so, technically, are grandparents (RSFSR Family Code, Article 57). Unfortunately, mechanisms for controlling access are poor, and so the law, as in so many other cases, is better than the practice. Even if it does not always succeed, my informants suggested, Soviet law strives in principle to protect the natural bonds between parents and children and to preserve connections between the child and all other close family members. Close family members are responsible in law for looking after one another when necessary (RSFSR Family Code, Articles 82, 83; Constitution, Article 66). Relatives are always the first to be called upon to take care of adoptable children; brothers and sisters must maintain underage siblings; children are responsible, if it becomes necessary, for supporting parents and even grandparents; and so on. Also, siblings must not be separated in custody decisions, when put up for adoption, or when being placed in a children's home (Model Statute on a Children's Home, USSR decree October 12, 1978, Articles 2.3 and 2.4).

I was curious to know whether non-custodial parents ever "kidnap" their children in the Soviet Union. Yakovleva and Polenina were uncertain about this, although I have since learned that it is not an uncommon occurrence. Legislation has existed since 1960 (RSFSR Criminal Code, Article 125) that addresses the abduction of children, and the two very different levels of punishment called for (one when there are "vile" motives and the other when there are not) suggest that one form of the crime is considered to be much more serious than the other. Nevertheless, kidnapping, no matter what the motive, is a gross violation of a child's civil rights and is bound to be traumatic. The first case of "classic" kidnapping (for ransom) was recorded in the USSR in 1978. Since then, the number of such kidnappings involving children has begun to rise, particularly in the Caucasus and in Central Asia where children possess a traditional value for the family. Tragically, the statistics show that a third of such victims die.

After the divorce there is, of course, the question of child support. According to the Fundamentals of Legislation on Marriage and the Family, Article 18, both parents share the responsibility for maintaining and bringing up their children, whether they are living together or apart. Maintenance orders are very strict. They are based on a percentage of family income. Since both parents normally work, their total income is taken into consideration. Of that, one-quarter is designated for one child, one-third if there are two, and one-half if there are three or more (Fundamentals, Marriage and the Family, Article 22). Even in a well-patrolled state like the USSR, fathers try to avoid paying. They do not declare their whole income, or they run away from their responsibilities. I was told by Litvinova, the lawyer with whom I spoke in 1988, that on the initiative of the Soviet Women's Committee and the State Committee on the Conditions of Labour, an all-Union alimony fund was set up in 1984 to ensure that regular child-support payments are made. The State pays the custodial parent (usually the mother), and the other parent (usually the father) repays the State, with interest.

With respect to adoption, my two lawyers confirmed what I had already been told by others, that in the USSR, just as in Canada, there are far more childless couples wanting to adopt children than there are children to be adopted. In fact it is probably even more difficult in the USSR for a non-related family to obtain a child. If there are no relatives, and if the parents are dead or have formally relinquished the child, then he or she (or they) may be adopted by a couple who are deemed, on a variety of criteria, to be potentially model parents. Only recently have single women been considered suitable to adopt children. An older child who is adopted will, of course, be aware of his or her status and over the age of ten must give consent (RSFSR Family Code, Article 103). But in the case of adopted babies, both social and legal opinion lend support to the idea that it is best to keep the adoption secret from the child. In fact "persons revealing the secret of adoption without the consent of the adopter may be made answerable in a court of law" (RSFSR Family Code, Article 110; RSFSR Criminal Code, Article 124.1). There are now many who question this practice, and the legislation may change.

Litvinova told me that all legislation with respect to adoption was being re-examined in order to pay attention to the developmental needs of very young children.

The last thing we talked about that morning was a subject of particular interest to me in view of the alarming incidence of child abuse in Canada: the protection of children at risk. In a society such as the USSR that has such a protective attitude towards children, and where privacy is at a premium, it seemed to me unlikely that gross physical abuse could continue for long unchecked but I was sure that it existed in some form. I told the lawyers that legislation in Canada now obligates people to report any reasonable suspicion of child abuse to child-welfare authorities. I asked them if there was need for a similar law in the USSR. They looked at me wryly and commented that in the Soviet Union the problem was to *discourage* people from making unfounded reports. However, abuse certainly exists and has to be dealt with.

Child welfare is the responsibility of the executive committee of a district or city soviet (council) and is delegated to a commission for the affairs of minors, which appears to combine the roles of our child-welfare agencies with those of probation officers and others concerned with crime prevention and with children in trouble with the law. A suspected case of abuse or neglect will be reported to an inspector for the affairs of minors associated with the commission. The inspector must, in urgent cases, remove the child or children from the home to a reception centre within eight hours of being informed of the situation (Duties of Inspectors for the Affairs of Minors, USSR decree, February 15, 1977). On investigating the circumstances, the inspector may have a court order issued (Fundamentals of Legislation on Marriage and the Family, Article 64) to take the child into care, if he deems it necessary for the child's well-being, and to find alternate living arrangements. The law requires efforts to be made to maintain contact between the parents and the child. If it can be established that either or both parents "have neglected their duties in bringing up the children or abused their parental rights, maltreated the children, exerted a harmful influence on them by their immoral antisocial behaviour and also where the parents are chronic alcoholics or drug addicts", then they will be deprived of their parental rights by court order and the child or children will be placed in the custody of the child-welfare agencies (Fundamentals of Legislation on Marriage and the Family, Article 59).

Under Soviet law, parental duties and rights are viewed as symbiotic in nature. A Soviet child is not only a member of a particular family but also a citizen of the USSR. Parents must bring their children up with this in mind. If they don't, then the State will intervene. If parents are not looking after their children as they should or not giving them the proper education, they can be officially reprimanded by a comrades' court (a tribunal set up in the work-place) or censured by the commission for the affairs of minors in whose jurisdiction they live. It is only when the failure to perform their duties is extreme that parents are deprived of their rights. The restoration of parental rights will be ordered by the court when it is deemed to be in a child's best interest. Court orders with respect to both the deprivation and the restoration of parental rights must be carried out with the participation of the child-welfare agencies (Fundamentals of Legislation on Marriage and the Family, Article 66).

The admission that some Soviet children are physically abused is a recent phenomenon in the USSR, and I have not yet seen any public discussion of sexual abuse. However, in a proposed reform to the criminal code, the violent sexual abuse of a child, defined as the rape of a minor, is one of the six remaining criminal offences that will still warrant capital punishment. Four of the remaining five are crimes against the State: high treason, espionage, sabotage, and terrorism. (The death penalty is also being retained for certain premeditated murders.) Since the seriousness of the crime is so clearly understood, it is to be hoped that other sections of the reformed criminal code will address the physical and sexual abuse of children with the careful attention that such a complex and painful issue demands.

Children in Care: The Children's Home

Most children who are taken under the care of the child-welfare agencies are assigned by court order to guardians or trustees (usually other family members). A small but gradually increasing number are placed in foster care. The rest are sent to children's institutions; infants' homes, children's homes, or boarding-schools. In 1987, of approximately one million children in care in the USSR, 300,000 were in institutions. Infants' homes accept babies from birth to three years of age. A child who has not been returned to his or her parents, placed with a relative, or adopted, then "graduates" to a children's home.

There have been children's homes in the Soviet Union ever since the Revolution. Their continued existence has reflected ("like a mirror" according to Albert Likhanov, the founder and chairman of the Soviet Children's Fund) the tragic history of the country—the misfortunes and deprivations of the Civil War, collectivization, the purges, the Second World War, and the difficult post-war years. Now, when the "scientific-technological revolution" has at last brought some prosperity to children, it has been accompanied by social trends that deprive many of them of adult care. In Soviet children's homes today, the children being cared for are rarely orphans, as they once were. They usually have living parents who are unable to cope. There are even, apparently, a growing number of foundlings left behind at maternity clinics. This latter fact is sad evidence that the support systems that would enable a reluctant mother to become attached to her baby do not exist and that the laws governing adoption are unhelpful. This is why, Litvinova told me, the laws will have to be changed so that such babies can be placed in adopting families more rapidly after birth.

Even before *glasnost*, I was aware that many people were seriously concerned about the condition of the children's homes. In the mid-1980s two excellent movies, *The Mistress of the Orphanage* and *Games for Adolescents*, both of which vividly depicted how children and teenagers live in such places, brought the issue into the open. There was a flurry of articles in the press. Albert Likhanov was then the editor of *Smena* magazine, a monthly journal for young people, and he published a number of critical accounts.

Likhanov and others described Soviet children's homes as intolerable, claiming they were badly built and improperly staffed, that

the child inmates were often emotionally neglected and sometimes even physically mistreated. A noted educator from Georgia,
S. Amonashvili (now a member of the Children's Fund) commented that the prevailing mood in the children's homes was
one of "adult imperialism". "*Zapugat, potom vospitat* (intimidate,
then educate) was the motto of such homes," he said, adding
that "these accounts sometimes made me think of Dickens' *Oliver
Twist* ." According to these commentators, it is hardly surprising
that in recent years a large number of children from children's
homes have "graduated" into penal institutions.

However, many children's home directors are prepared to do
everything in their power to make the children under their care
as happy as possible, although the task is a formidable one.
One woman became personally involved in a children's home in
Leningrad in the early 1980s. Her cousin, a friend of mine, sent
me a newspaper clipping that described the experience.

> Children's Home No. 53 is located on a quiet street in
> a building erected at the beginning of the twentieth
> century. The director...who considers the children her
> family and often stays to pass the night told us "Our
> children's home is not the best but neither is it the
> worst."... Nine of the 220 children are orphans but the
> majority has mother, father or even both deprived of
> parental rights....
>
> Teachers who worked at children's homes during the
> post-war period and are not yet retired confess that it
> was much easier to work then. Whatever hard lives the
> children of those years had, it was the war from which
> all suffered that made them orphans. But how can one
> explain to children today the terrible reason for their
> orphanhood with their parents being alive?...
>
> Olga V. came to the children's home four years ago.
> As it sometimes happens with people she suddenly
> paid attention to the neighbourhood house marked
> with a sign that should have been rooted out from our
> life.... If they had been hungry or poorly dressed she
> would have easily known how to help them, but what

they did was to quarrel over the right to take her hand
during outings....

Olga V., a doctor of biological sciences, often told
her colleagues at the laboratory about her "own"
children's home but her talks were not popular. The
good intentions of her colleagues were limited to the
books and toys they bought for the children. Some
people expressed the opinion that her Sunday visits
could not solve the problem on the whole, that the
structure of the children's homes and public attitudes
toward such parents should be radically changed. But
for such people, children's home remained merely an
abstract notion and for her this home was associated
with real boys and girls.

Considerable progress has been made since this article appeared in 1984. People and organizations have responded
generously with both time and money. With the creation of the
Soviet Children's Fund greater resources are available and the
material conditions in children's homes have improved. When I
visited a children's home on the outskirts of Moscow in 1989, a
minivan with the logo of the Children's Fund stood outside. Inside the sleeping rooms and common rooms had been freshly
painted and imaginatively decorated. The children looked healthy
and were very friendly. The director introduced me to one particularly lively little boy whom she told me later was about to be
adopted. But what about the others? Was there anyone to care
just for them?

The Soviet Children's Fund is changing the system of children's
homes so that a child's right to love and affection can be better
protected. It has lobbied for the creation of a number of children's
villages to replace some, at least, of the large institutions in
which so many small wards of the State are obliged to live.
These village communities comprise ten or more semi-detached
houses in which couples live with their own and several foster
children. There are garden plots, playgrounds, and a community
centre, and the village is close to a regional school that the
children attend. Such a village has the status of a children's

institution. Housemothers are paid a child-care worker's salary with allowances and pension. Housefathers may work in the factories or farms that are the patrons of the children's village. In the Soviet context, this sounds like an excellent solution to the problem of children in care.

"Protection and Encouragement of Motherhood"

Among the Bolsheviks who accompanied Lenin into power, my favourite is Alexandra Kollontai. An early feminist who cared about children and a beautiful woman with a history of passionate love affairs, she ran afoul of sexual puritanism within the Party and was sent abroad by Stalin in 1922 to spend most of the rest of her life as a diplomat. In 1916, she published a book called *Society and Motherhood* in which she spelled out a system of institutional support for the protection of working mothers and their children. Her ideal was that

> every working woman [be] guaranteed the possibility of giving birth to her child in healthy conditions with the appropriate care for herself and the child, the possibility of looking after the child during the first weeks of its life, the possibility of feeding him herself without the risk of loss of pay...that state and community...provide medical consultations for mother and child...and a broad network of creches, nursery schools and children's centres where the working mother could leave her child with a quiet mind...that Soviet legislation attach due importance to the protection of female labour...a short working day, break periods for nursing mothers...and, finally, that the community would guaranteee to mothers during pregnancy, birth and the nursing period material assistance sufficient to meet the needs of both her and the child.

Seventy years later, Kollontai's dream has been embodied in the Fundamentals of Legislation of the USSR on Marriage and the Family, Article 5, and protected by the codes of the Union republics. The law intends that no woman in the Soviet Union should be discouraged from becoming a mother by material difficulties. In practice, the financial support provided under the law is far from adequate, but the leave provisions are welcome. The significant improvement in the complete family-benefits package that has taken place in the 1980s has been partly spurred, of course, by demographic concerns. There are simply not enough babies being born, particularly in the European part of the Soviet Union. Up until 1983, the birth rate had been declining steadily. Then there was an up-turn, but the increased number of births turned out to be an echo of the Soviet baby boom of the early 1960s rather than proof that women were actually having larger families. According to Soviet experts, even more measures to encourage child-bearing and to support young families will have to be implemented in the near future.

In addition to generous maternity-leave provisions (starting in 1990, partially paid maternity-leave was extended to eighteen months, with another eighteen months of unpaid leave available to mothers who want it), family allowances are being augmented, as are support payments to single mothers. While the sums involved are not great, they certainly help, as do the privileges accorded to young families such as a priority placement on waiting lists for new housing. In 1987, two new laws were enacted, partly as a result of pressure from the Soviet Women's Committee. One requires the work-place to establish flexible schedules for working mothers. The other permits a parent to take fourteen days of fully paid leave to care for a sick child. What is notable about this second piece of legislation is that, for the first time in Soviet law, fathers are accorded the same status as mothers and either may apply for the leave.

The process of implementing these new laws will be closely monitored by 230,000 Zhenskye Sovety (women's councils) that have recently (1987) been established in industrial enterprises and residential areas. During most of the Soviet period, the cause of the worker has taken precedence over separate work-place concerns of men, women, and children. The women's department of the CPSU, led by Kollontai, was abolished soon after the Revolution on the grounds that it was no longer needed. With the re-emergence of women's councils as a force to be reckoned with, women once again have a distinct and much-needed institutional voice to address their special needs in the work-place as well as in the building-complexes in which they live. These are not women's advocacy groups in the sense that we have them in North America, but they can play a significant if narrowly defined role in improving the lot of women and children.

Children in Trouble with the Law

In every *militsia* (police) station in the Soviet Union there is a room set aside for minors, known as the "Children's Room". Children who are caught violating the law are brought there so that a decision can be taken as to how they should be made aware of the seriousness of their transgression. Soviet law enshrines the innocence of the very young. The age of ciminal responsibility is fourteen for the most serious crimes (RSFSR Crimincal Code, Article 10); otherwise it is sixteen. When children are small, others must be held responsible for their misdemeanours. "Responsibility for the harm inflicted by a minor under the age of 15 years shall rest on his parents or guardians unless they can prove that the harm was incurred through no fault of their own" (RSFSR Civil Code, Article 405). Parents will be penalized for their children's misbehaviour in a number of ways, including public reprimands, and the obligation to pay fines or compensation.

Statistics that have been collected in the Soviet Union in recent years with respect to young offenders appear to justify this legal presumption of parental responsibility. They show a powerful correlation between juvenile delinquency and broken homes, low parental authority, poor supervision, and parental drunkenness. According to one authority with the Institute of Crime Prevention in Moscow, 90 per cent of all juveniles who commit violent crimes come from troubled families where violence is the norm. This situation has led to an elaborate system of prevention involving not only the parents (one highly successful experiment organized by the procurator's office has been directed specifically at educating or re-educating fathers) but the community at large.

The commission for the affairs of minors includes among its statutory responsibilities the organization of "work to prevent neglect of and infringement of the law by minors". But if this fails with respect to a specific youngster, then there is recourse in the "institution of public tutors", established by statute in the RSFSR on December 13, 1967, in order to increase the part played by the public in educating minors who have committed offences. Any persons with enough "experience of life or of work with children" may qualify for the position. The main task of a public tutor "is to give assistance to parents or persons acting *in loco parentis* , to re-educate offenders who are under age in the spirit of respect for and observance of the law and the rules of socialist society".

I was unable to visit a *militsia* station to inspect a "Children's Room" during the time I lived in Moscow because people were still defensive about the existence of juvenile crime. However, during a visit to the USSR in 1984, I attended a session in juvenile court. I am not a lawyer and my experience of the law is limited. The only courts I have been to in Canada are family courts, not criminal ones. On each occasion, however, I was genuinely impressed by the due process of law. The cases were difficult ones—custody and wardship—but the judges were thoughtful and patient, the claims and counter-claims clearly presented, the evidence was there to be weighed, and the judgments were wise and compassionate. A similar atmosphere permeated the court session I attended in the Soviet Union.

The court building was older and shabbier than the one I had been in at home and, situated next to Moscow's City Zoo, it was certainly smellier. The courtroom, however, had style. Daylight flooded through tall windows, and the court furniture was impressive, particularly three high-backed chairs lined up on a red-carpeted platform for the judges to sit on. I sat facing the platform in one of fifty or so public seats. The courtroom was the judicial chamber of the Moscow Oblast (District) Court that considers appeals in cases involving juveniles. The one we were about to hear was nothing out of the ordinary, of vital interest only to the boy and his closest friends and family. Several people entered and sat down at two opposing tables in front of the high-backed chairs. Then the judges filed in. The senior one, an older man with a pronounced limp, had to be assisted on to the platform. He sat down between two women colleagues and signalled for the session to begin. The procurator, a slim young woman in a smart black suit, rose and stated the facts in a clear voice, reading from her hand-written notes. Oleg lived in a small town north of Moscow. He was fifteen years old. In April, he got drunk and threw stones at a girls' hostel, breaking a few windows and generally creating a disturbance. He was picked up, charged, and released into the custody of his parents until the time of his trial. As the date approached, he lost his nerve, got drunk again, and boarded a train for the Ukraine. When he reappeared and came before the court in September for his postponed trial, he was sentenced to two and a half years' deprivation of liberty. His lawyer and his parents thought that the sentence was too severe and so did the State procurator in his home town. An appeal was made (within seven days, as required by Soviet law) and two weeks later we were present as it was being heard.

The boy's lawyer spoke next. He said that the lower court had not taken into account the fact that it was Oleg's first transgression, that he had confessed immediately and had repaired the damage himself. He said that his failure to appear at the date set for this first trial could be understood and that his development as a socially responsible person would not be assisted by sending him to an educational-labour colony, where he would have to remain until the age of eighteen. He explained that the boy's parents had not come to the appeal because it was rather far from their hometown, but he gestured to the man who was sitting beside him in a rumpled suit and a frog-green shirt, and introduced him as "the people's defender". "The people's defender" is a representative of the community in which a juvenile lives who is prepared to speak on his or her behalf. Oleg's defender stood up and stated that Oleg was a regular student at the *tekhnikum* (vocational school) where he was a teacher, that the boy was constant in his attendance at Pioneer meetings and generally of good character. He added that the school was willing to be responsible for him if his sentence was suspended. The proceedings lasted about half an hour.

I heard this case in the company of the president of the court, A.S. Markova, and afterward we climbed the worn steps to her top-floor chambers. We sat down at a heavy, polished oak table to discuss the case we had just observed and to await the judges' ruling. Markova told me that Judge Orlov, the senior judge, was a war veteran, a former pilot, and that he walked awkwardly because he had artificial legs. He was a wise man, she said, who had teaching as well as legal experience. In fact, she went on, all judges in juvenile court are expected to be teachers or psychologists, or to have had other professional experience with children, in addition to legal training. Judges are elected for a period of five years, at the same time as other municipal district officers, and Judge Orlov had already been re-elected several times. When he arrived to join us twenty minutes later, it was apparent that he really liked young people and had a good deal of sympathy for them. He had a twinkle in his remarkable blue eyes, which I had not been able to see when he was sitting in judgement.

He told us that he had suspended sentence on Oleg, that a telegram had been sent to the reception where he was being held, and that he should already be in the process of being released. He had read documents concerning the case before the hearing, and the presentation of the appeal had persuaded him that Oleg's best interests would be served by placing him under the supervision of the school. The judgment was in accord with Article 39 (1) of the RSFSR Criminal Code as amended in 1977. This amendment, laying out conditions for suspending sentence on minors, had been welcomed by people involved in the juvenile-justice system. Now minors charged with less serious crimes can be kept in the community and re-educated rather than sent to a labour colony where they might come under the influence of experienced young criminals. The weight of the law with respect to juveniles has shifted to diverting the young offender away from criminal activity and reforming him (or less frequently, her) rather than condemnation and incarceration.

Have these measures and the other efforts at prevention I discussed earlier had any noticeable effect on the rate and the character of juvenile crime in the Soviet Union? The evidence suggests not. Now that the Moscow police are briefing the press weekly on crimes in the city, it is possible to have a better idea of the extent of the problem. While the actual number of murders, rapes, burglaries, or automobile thefts in any one week constitute only a fraction of what happens in New York, a city of comparable size, an increasing percentage of crimes are being committed by teenagers. There is also evidence that the nature of the crimes committed by the young has changed over the years. At Oleg's trial, Markova told me that the majority of criminal charges laid against contemporary juveniles have to do in some way with the automobile: theft, joy-riding, or accidents with injury. Then there are thefts of electronic equipment: television sets, radios, and so on. Another category of serious crimes includes rape. Alcohol is a factor in most juvenile crimes and 54 to 56 per cent of them are committed by groups. The use of illegal drugs is rising, with all that that implies. With the advent of *glasnost* and with more information available about drugs, people who are concerned with young drug-users are better prepared to deal with them, but the problem continues to grow.

Oleg's crime fell into the category of non-malicious hooliganism, which is not considered to constitute a "great social danger", and therefore can bring a suspended sentence and/or "compulsory educational measures" rather than criminal punishment (RSFSR Criminal Code, Article 10). These "measures" may include the obligation to apologize to his victim publicly; a severe reprimand or warning; some reparation for damage by the young person in money or work; strict supervision; or placement in a special education or treatment institution (RSFSR Criminal Code, Article 63). When the crime is more serious, young boys or girls may be sent to an educational labour colony with an "ordinary" regime. For grave crimes that have incurred a sentence of more than three years, boys (only) will be sent to colonies with a reinforced regime (RSFSR Criminal Code, Article 23).

These labour colonies have a very mixed reputation. In *Ogonyok*, the flagship journal of the *glasnost* press, a long article in January 1988, entitled "Barbed-Wire Sky", exposed the worst type of labour colony. Over the years this colony had been characterized by harsh rules and brutal treatment, a regime totally inappropriate for essentially deprived youngsters of fourteen to eighteen years of age and one that was almost guaranteed to produce hardened criminals rather than reformed delinquents. All labour colonies have three components: a custodial regime, productive labour, and political upbringing work. In many colonies, the custodial regime is rigid and inflexible, the labour almost always boring assembly-line production, and the upbringing peformed by untrained and unmotivated *vospitateli* (counsellors).

There are, however, others that correspond more closely to the intention of the law to rehabilitate difficult youngsters. The youth newspaper *Komsomolskaya Pravda* described one of these as "a brick headquarters building, a fence, watchtowers" containing young boys convicted of "robbery, rape, malicious hooliganism...the absolute majority raised by a mother alone or by a mother and stepfather; many parents were drinkers and changed jobs often." A bleak picture, perhaps, and at one stage of the colony's history it looked hopeless. "No measures had been able to establish order here: on the surface regulations were observed but deep down the ineradicable yeast of another life known only to the teenagers themselves fermented." But an imaginative director, calling on the experience with delinquent boys of the famous educator Anton Makarenko, changed the situation. He identified the ringleaders and made a tremendous effort to understand them: "The entire teaching staff focused its efforts on these informal leaders and found 'keys' to the majority." With great patience the boys were involved in creating a colony collective with detachments and divisions competing for the creation of better conditions for everyday life. "Now the inmates have a splendidly designed assembly hall and hockey arena and they created all this themselves without any help from professional builders or designers."

In a widely shown documentary made in Latvia in 1986, called *It Is Not Easy to Be Young*, there is a moving scene in which seven young people convicted of hooliganism and the destruction of state property after a rock concert, hear themselves being sentenced to varying periods of deprivation of liberty. For them and their families the experience is devastating. They are anything but hardened criminals, and as I watched the film I found myself hoping desperately that they would not end up in a labour colony like the one described in "Barbed-Wire Sky". If they did, then what had begun as a prank might easily end up as a sentence to a life of crime. The law does make provision for the "conditional release or the substitution of a lighter punishment with respect to persons who have committed a crime when under the age of eighteen years" (Fundamentals of Criminal Legislation, Article 45). But it is unlikely that the labour colony will be abandoned in favour of other forms of correction for young male offenders who have committed serious crimes. Only if enough public attention can be drawn to the situation by such organizations as the Soviet Children's Fund will it be possible to press for the improved conditions that might bring the practice of the juvenile-justice system closer to the principles of prevention, diversion, and rehabilitation that inform Soviet law with respect to young offenders.

The Three "P's"

When children's rights are grouped under the traditional headings associated with human rights, it will be seen that the Soviet Union has made remarkable progress in enshrining them since the time of the Revolution. Leaving aside political rights, many civil as well as most economic, social, and cultural rights of children appear to be safeguarded by Soviet legislation.

There is, however, another way of grouping children's rights that casts a different light on the subject—namely, to categorize them in terms of the three "p's": provision, protection, and participation. While Soviet children are reasonably well provided for under Soviet legislation and protected by law from acts and practices that would harm them, their rights of participation are limited.

Participatory rights include the right to have an effective voice in matters affecting one's life and the right to express oneself. Soviet legislation continually refers to "the best interests of the child" and in some cases guarantees that a child may express his or her own desire in custody or adoption cases. However, I have been unable to discover full guarantees in Soviet legislation for the rights addressed by Article 12 of the U.N. Convention on the Rights of the Child. This article states: "States parties [to the present convention] shall assure to the child who is capable of forming his or her own views the right to express his opinion freely in all matters affecting the child, the views of the child being given due weight in accordance with the age and maturity of the child." This right is spelled out further in Articles 13, 14, and 15.

Article 13 states that "this right shall include freedom to seek, receive and impart information and ideas of all kinds, regardless of frontiers..."; Article 14 addresses the right of the child to freedom of thought, conscience, and religion; Article 15 addresses the rights of the child to freedom of association and to freedom of peaceful assembly.

One of the basic principles of the U.N. convention is that children's rights, like all human rights, should be understood as reflecting "the interrelation of individuals in society, all of whom have the same right". This suggests that every right carries with it a responsibility to see that other people's rights are also respected. One of the greatest challenges confronting parents and society at large is to encourage children to assume the responsibility for their own lives in ways that will make them responsible, productive citizens in an adult world. A basic theme of this book is that Soviet society has not yet found out how to resolve this important problem.

During one of my visits to Moscow, a distinguished woman scholar asked me if I thought that Canadian children were more independent than Soviet children. When I replied that I did, her reaction surprised me. "How," she asked wistfully, "do you do it?" I thought about all the protections guaranteed to children under Soviet law and then about the highly protective nature of Soviet society that these laws reflect. It's not that I would like to see the protections and provisions diminished, but I do think that rights to participation should be increased. The most positive, competent, and outgoing young people I know have told me that as they were growing up they were always consulted when family decisions were being taken that would seriously affect their lives and that they were encouraged to take charge of minor ones from an early age. So I replied, "Children need to be protected but they also need to participate and experiment. This is the only way they can learn how their rights fit in with those of other people.

In Canada, we sometimes take risks with our children. We allow them to speak out, we give advice but then we expect them to find their own way home."

CHAPTER NINE

In Sickness and in Health

In the grey mists of early November we travelled westward to Minsk. It was the beginning of our second year in the Soviet Union and we were making an official visit to Belorussia. Riding the Moscow train into the city in the early morning hours was like slicing into forty years of Soviet history, back to the worst days of the Second World War. As we neared the outskirts, we passed through a landscape dominated by giant cranes lifting up the skeletons of new highrises. Then we were in the suburbs where tall apartment blocks, set out at angles to one another, stood guard over the low buildings that everywhere in post-war Russia house kindergartens, polyclinics, and food stores. From the train window, these apartment buildings were striking, each façade broken by an oblong of deeply coloured tile, navy blue or burgundy. As we approached the station, the multiple-dwelling units became plainer and shabbier, functional blocks thrown up quickly for a homeless population after the end of the war. In the very centre of the town, we found a few scattered pre-war buildings. Minsk was more than 90 per cent destroyed during the Second World War, paying, like the rest of Belorussia, a heavy price for blocking the way to Moscow. Scores of towns and villages were totally destroyed, and two and a half-million people (one-quarter of the population) were killed.

The peaceful, rolling countryside around Minsk is dotted with poignant memorials to the tragedy of war. On the second day of our stay, we were driven to the place where once a little village named Khatyn had been home to a score of peasant families. Of each cottage, only the hearth now remains, marked by a slender chimney surmounted by a bell, which, every thirty seconds, clangs out dolefully into the vacant air. Each dwelling site also carries a plaque with the names and ages of all the family members who were living there on the cold morning in March 1943 when they were hauled out and herded into a barn by soldiers of the German army. The door was bolted and the building set on fire. Inside there were 149 villagers, including 75 children. One man, Iosif Kaminsky, was away at the time. When he returned, he found his dying son among the ashes. On our arrival at the memorial the first thing we saw was a sculpture of Kaminsky, which depicts him staggering forth from the village, holding in front of him the limp body of his dead child. Unlike some of the other monuments we were shown as we travelled about the USSR, Khatyn is not an oversized tribute to the Soviet Army. Rather, like Piskaryovskoe, the mass cemetery that holds the remains of 600,000 victims of the siege of Leningrad, or like the green memorial park in Kiev that covers the bones of Babi Yar, it is a haunted place to remember a suffering population and the little children lost.

I was deeply moved by my visit to Khatyn, reminded of the vulnerability of civilian populations and of the fragile lives of children in times of war and of other disasters. Since the turn of the century, the people who live in what is now the Soviet Union have had more than their share of these events. There have been two world wars, a civil war, a man-made famine, two major nuclear catastrophes (Belorussia was downwind from Chernobyl and many of its children are still affected), and several natural disasters, the most recent being the devastating earthquake in Armenia in December 1988. Who knows how many millions of children have been killed or maimed by these events? In North America it is hard to imagine how people must feel who have experienced so many human shocks. No wonder they care so much about the health of their children.

When we returned to the city of Minsk from our trip to Khatyn, I asked to visit a children's health centre, and the hospital I was taken to, with its attached polyclinic, was so typical of how the child health system is structured in the USSR that I will use my tour of it to introduce the two main thrusts of health care for children in the USSR: prevention where possible, and if that fails, a systematic program to rebuild the weakened organism so that it will resist further illness.

Following the Revolution, the major health problems that faced the new Soviet government were typhus, cholera, and smallpox, problems that could be attacked best by soap, clean water, and vaccines. With one-quarter of the existing doctors lost to emigration and with medical schools in disorder, the implementation of preventive measures was the only way in which the emerging state-controlled health service could have any impact. Since "a harmonious personality in a healthy body" was a stated aim of the Soviet upbringing process from the beginning, prevention also had to be a key component of the child health system as it evolved from the difficulties of those early years. It has remained a byword of the system ever since.

The Soviet Union has never had the resources to focus, as North America has, on the technological cure of disease. This is one of the reasons that it has chosen to emphasize prevention and the use of natural elements in treatment—fresh air, water, good food, and sunshine—"the best proletarian doctors," as the old Bolsheviks used to say. The experience of the Second World War reinforced Soviet interest in rehabilitation and dramatically increased Soviet knowledge about how to repair and strengthen injured bodies. Soldiers had to be sent back to the front as soon as possible. Since the end of the war, other problems such as primitive medical facilities, severe shortages, and inadequately trained doctors—all problems the current Minister of Health, Dr. Yevgeny Chazov, is only too aware of—have kept the focus of the child health system on prevention and promotion rather than on treatment. This has led to the creation of a network of polyclinics and of convalescent and rehabilitation facilities for children unlike anything we have ever known in Canada; "forest" hospitals, seaside sanatoria, mountain rest homes, and children's health camps. Under the circumstances, this approach has probably benefited more Soviet children than would have been possible any other way.

Children's Health Centres: The Hospital and Polyclinic

There are thousands of children's health centres in the Soviet Union but they vary greatly in quality, if not design. In rural areas, particularly in Central Asia, facilities are often primitive. Some even lack running water and proper sewage systems. New guidelines drawn up in 1987 by the Ministry of Health promise that a concerted effort will be made until the year 2000 to upgrade them all. While this is being done, Children's Hospital no. 4 in Minsk can serve as a model. The hospital is located in a section of the city where there are a great number of factories and many young workers live there with their families. The November day on which I made my tour was so raw and blustery that the painted swings and battered slides on the grounds of the hospital stood empty. However, the deputy director, Ekaterina Dimitrieva, who met me at the front steps, quickly bundled me into her warm office and helped me off with my coat. Then she started, as Soviet managers always do, to load me with statistics. "Today," she began, "all 360 beds in the hospital are occupied and there is a full complement of babies in acute care." But when she told me that her oldest patients were fifteen years of age, I stopped listening, struck by how often fifteen marks the end of childhood in the Soviet Union. It is then that children begin to compete with adults for everything including health care. Their period of grace is over.

Dimitrieva took me to see the babies in the intensive-care ward: inert bundles in steel cots watched over by a nurse at a glass-enclosed station. Anxious mothers were sitting next door, wearing slippers and smocks, talking a little and watching television. If they wished, they could stay overnight and we were shown the little dining-room in which they would have their supper.

Each children's hospital in a region concentrates on certain specific illnesses and medical problems so that the specialists can be brought together in one place rather than spread throughout the system. The ward I saw was for babies with acute gastro-enteritis. Another specialization of this particular hospital was opthalmology, including corrective eye surgery. Since I had had a child of my own whose wandering eye was first spotted in France, misdiagnosed in Canada, and in the end successfully corrected by an operation in Mexico, this section of the hospital was of particular interest to me. Most of the young patients were up and about, talking to their mothers or playing with other children in a bright playroom full of toys. Almost all of them had one eye covered by an Elastoplast eye patch. How familiar they looked! The children came from all over Belorussia and the hospital was organized to keep them as long as necessary.

By our standards, people are often kept in hospital for an excessively long time in the USSR. Hospital costs are much lower than they are in North America, as are salaries, and there is not so much expensive equipment. Costs are borne by the State, not the individual, so there is no economic compulsion for a patient to leave. As both parents are usually working, there is no one at home to look after a convalescing child. Besides, medicines are more reliably available in a hospital setting. All this encourages long stays.

The atmosphere of this hospital resembled that of almost every institutional setting for children that I visited in the Soviet Union. The difference betweeen staying on in a hospital, where parents may visit frequently and school work and other interests can be pursued, and recuperating at home is not as great as it would be in North America. The young children I saw in Minsk were shy of me as a foreigner. Otherwise they appeared to feel at home, relatively content in the hospital environment. I talked at some length to the young eye surgeon. He was knowledgeable and enthusiastic and very proud of his equipment, some of which was Swedish. His section of the hospital, which included examining rooms and a little operating theatre, was spotless.

Children's Hospital no. 4 specializes in general surgery and traumatology as well as opthalmology and gastro-enterology. But if a child has a kidney disease, he or she will be sent to another children's hospital where the appropriate specialists can be found. Many of the children's hospitals in the Soviet Union are quite new. During 1979, the Year of the Child, the proceeds from the annual *Subbotnik* (the Saturday—usually the one in April nearest to Lenin's birthday—on which people throughout the country either work on community projects or donate their day's wages to a worthy cause) were directed to the needs of children. Children's health centres, libraries, sports complexes, and so forth were constructed with the money. In 1981, the earnings from the *Subbotnik* (116,900,000 roubles in all, more than $200 million) were directed to maternity homes, women's consultation clinics, and children's polyclinics. In the twelfth five-year plan (1986-91) 30 to 35 per cent of the budget of the USSR Ministry of Public Health will be channelled in this direction, more in Uzbekistan and other parts of Central Asia where the need is greatest.

I left the hospital and crossed the courtyard to the polyclinic. The polyclinic is an Eastern European solution to health care, functioning best where all medical personnel are on the State payroll and few doctors have their own surgeries. A children's polyclinic combines diagnosis and treatment with prevention and health promotion. There are examining rooms, laboratories, and lecture halls as well as gymnasiums and swimming pools.

Opening the door, I entered a lobby slightly steamy from the damp overcoats and muddy boots of the many children gathered there. The polyclinic receives five hundred little patients a day, along with their mothers and assorted relatives. Children who are not yet in kindergarten come for obligatory check-ups and immunization shots. If a mother does not bring her baby or toddler when she is supposed to, she will be telephoned or visited at home. Older children also come for regular check-ups or are sent to the polyclinic by a school pediatrician for a more detailed examination than can be performed in the school setting. Other children come for physiotherapy or for corrective gymnastics in the little gym. A physiotherapist and a speech therapist will be among the paramedical staff of any polyclinic, along with nurses and technicians. In rural areas there will also be *feldshers*, paraprofessionals with two and a half years of post-secondary specialized training.

One of the polyclinic doctors, a motherly woman in a white cotton coverall who was wearing the characteristic Soviet medical cap—a stiff hair-covering affair that more closely resembles a chef's hat than anything we normally associate with health professionals—took me to every corner of the polyclinic. I saw little children in various states of dress and undress, although, except when swimming, the girls never abandoned their stiff white nylon hair bows. Some of the children were bouncy, some sulky, some visibly apprehensive, like children everywhere. Water therapy is popular in the Soviet Union, and communal steam baths traditional, so I was not surprised to see children exercising in the special swimming pool or, visible through a glass window, taking a hot bath in a room full of vapour. But when the doctor opened the last door, I was presented with a sight as unexpected as it was delightful. A square tub edged with tiles and full of warm water rose up from the marble floor. Four young women in flowered smocks knelt beside it, their hair tied back, their sleeves rolled up, their arms plunged in the water, their hands joined. And there, safe above the woven net of their mothers' arms, their heads supported by coronas of brightly coloured styrofoam cut into little squares, was a floating bouquet of beaming babies, splashing and kicking, naked and fat. What an antidote to Khatyn!

Best Babies Possible?

Children's hospitals and polyclinics are only one part of the unified child health system in the USSR. They are complemented by many other components. It is hard to say where it all begins. With the child's arrival in the world? With pregnancy? With the little girls who will one day be mothers? With the little boys who will one day be fathers? The birth of a child seems the most logical starting-place. During the years I was living in Moscow, I used to walk up from the Embassy two or three times a week to Prospekt Kalinina, the broad avenue lined with shops that was cut through the Arbat district in the 1960s, before the Society to Preserve Old Moscow could get itself organized. Early on, I discovered that one of the old buildings that had not been torn down to make way for the new department stores was a maternity hospital. This became clear one day, when, having noticed that there were always two or three young men rocking back and forth on the curb, I followed their eyes upwards and saw young women in dressing-gowns holding well-wrapped infants up to the window.

I had heard that birthing procedures in the Soviet Union were antiquated. This frequent sight of excluded fathers did nothing to dispel that rumour. Nor did my conversations with women who had had babies in Soviet hospitals. A Spartan experience, they told me, no anaesthetic, no comforts, and inadequate after-care. Most were not too keen to repeat it. Recent reports are only slightly less critical. In 1987, Dr. Chazov complained that out of the thirty-three maternity hospitals in Moscow only twelve met contemporary standards and norms. And this in spite of the fact that high standards are established by the All-Union Institute of Mother and Child.

I interviewed the institute's then director, Dr. Eltsov-Strelkov, on a rainy spring morning in 1983. He was an affable man who, although he came out from behind his desk to join the rest of us around a table, reminded me rather too much of other male European obstetricians I have known, charming but unwilling to share power, least of all with a mother. Nor was he willing to contemplate the presence of fathers at the actual moment of childbirth, although he said that new courses now being taught to expectant parents try to involve fathers more with the mother's pregnancy and with the newborn baby. Some maternity hospitals have even begun to experiment with allowing fathers into the hospital although not yet into the delivery room. Hospital practice is slow to change, particularly in the Soviet Union, so I expect that wistful fathers will continue to balance on the curb of Prospekt Kalinina for some time to come.

Dr. Eltsov-Strelkov emphasized that the purpose of his institute, which includes a hospital for women with reproductive problems, is "best babies possible". To encourage the development of healthy foetuses, mothers at risk are sought out no matter where they live and put into contact with the clinics that are associated with branches of the institute throughout the USSR. Their progress is followed closely and everything is done to try to keep the babies *in utero* as long as possible. Successes and failures are carefully documented and researched.

Dr. Eltsov-Strelkov regretted that the remarkable perinatal units he had visited in North America were beyond the financial means of the Soviet Union. Without such support it was vital to do everything possible to prevent premature births. A public-information campaign had been established by the institute to persuade women to declare pregnancy as soon as possible so that they could be monitored. District centres for consultation on marriage and the family had been created to instruct young couples about the sexual side of marriage and to offer genetic counselling. The doctor hoped that, with the help of this kind of education, it would be possible to lower rates of infant mortality and illness in early childhood. Besides, he added, if the satisfactions of marriage are increased, the population may go up!

Concern for the illness and death of little children is very real in the USSR. The infant mortality rate for 1989 was 25 deaths for 1,000 live births. While that shows improvement from the rate of 38 deaths for 1,000 live births in 1960, it still places the USSR fortieth among the nations of the world and compares badly with the rates of 10 deaths per 1,000 in the United States, 9 in Great Britain, and 8 in Canada. Nor has the rate in the USSR shown a steady decline. On the contrary, in the early 1970s, the rate began to rise again. This increase was detected by American demographers who used their own methods to analyse available data because the Soviet Union ceased the publication of all-Union infant-mortality statistics for a decade. Soviet demographers admitted the increase, but attempted to explain it away as the result of improved methods for garnering statistics from rural areas. In fact, causes must have been multiple. The mothers of the 1960s and 1970s were born during and after the war, and the acute deprivations they suffered in infancy, as well as the malnutrition of their own mothers, may have had some effect on their ability to carry babies to term. There is also a suggestion that influenza epidemics in the early 1970s contributed to the rise. Furthermore, there are special risks to women of child-bearing age when they are doing heavy or dangerous physical work or being exposed to toxic environments. A far larger proportion of Soviet women has been involved in the labour force over the last seventy years than has been the case in most other industrialized nations, and it is only recently that any of us have become aware of the foetal damage and genetic mutations that are brought about by industrial pollutants. Soviet trade unions and the Soviet Women's Committee, working with the standing commissions of the Supreme Soviet, have established a list of more than four hundred jobs from which women ought to be excluded in order to protect them as mothers. Labour legislation has also been enacted (1987) to lower production norms for pregnant women and to allow them to switch to less strenuous jobs. The problem is that the mechanisms do not exist to ensure that the regulations are enforced.

Smoking and alcohol are also implicated in the birth of underweight, premature, or unhealthy babies. Young people are now being warned of the consequences of their "harmful habits". The number of women who smoke rose enormously during the 1970s from one in ten in 1969 to four in ten in 1977. "Scientists recently studied 16,000 newborns and found that the mortality rate of infants born of smoking mothers was considerably higher.... Don't believe your mother or father if they try to convince you that they smoked like chimneys and produced a child that was healthy in every respect," the author of one article about smoking warned his young readers, who must have bridled at his tone, especially when he added, "children of smoking parents are twice as likely as those of non-smokers to show marked deterioriation in their psychological development."

Alcohol is considered even more dangerous. In fact, "alcohol is considered the most toxic of all known poisons where the human embryo is concerned.... Breast-feeding also has dire consequences for the child where the mother is intoxicated. The term 'breast alcoholism' has actually come into usage." The stringent campaign against alcohol launched by Gorbachev very soon after his accession to power in 1985 was enthusiastically welcomed by all those who care about children, even though it has not proved as successful as they would have wished. Still, in 1987, *Izvestia* was able to report that the number of unhealthy newborns had declined by 8 per cent. Nevertheless, the number of low-birth-weight babies born to mothers with such life-style problems as alcoholism, smoking, poor nutrition, and, less frequently, drug addiction remains far too high.

The high abortion rate in the Soviet Union is another factor in reproductive problems. It is not uncommon for a woman in her early thirties to have had up to five abortions. Repeated abortions, complicated by post-abortion infection (the use of antibiotics with this procedure is minimal), can damage the uterus or lead to an "incompetent" cervix, infertility, or premature births. Dr. Eltsov-Stelkov said that he wished that the rate of abortion would decline, and other doctors with whom I spoke at the clinical Institute for Adolescent Gynaecology said that they would prefer all first pregnancies to go to term, even in very young girls, to prevent the damage that might be caused by an abortion. But in 1988, approximately 80 per cent of all first pregnancies were still ending in abortion.

Abortion is a difficult issue for the Soviet authorities. It was legalized after the Revolution as a means of liberating women from the domination of the patriarchal "bourgeois" male. It was outlawed again during the Stalin period, from 1936 to 1955, except for medical conditions. It was reintroduced after Stalin's death, partly as a matter of principle and partly as a result of the infertility and health problems created by the large number of illegal abortions. The State is committed to allowing women to continue to choose whether or not to carry a pregnancy to term. According to one doctor, "We regard any form of coercion— whether a woman is made to get rid of her future child or is forbidden to do so—as immoral and inhumane. In our country the right to make either decision is left to the family. The physician can only voice his misgivings and give his advice."

Soviet doctors are concerned about the long-term physical effects of abortion on women's reproductive systems. The Soviet state is concerned about the birth rate. But to have any effect, these concerns must translate into greater financial resources for the manufacture and distribution of contraceptive devices. This is happening very slowly indeed. Only in 1989 did "Family and Health" clinics begin to open under the aegis of the Children's Fund to encourage and assist responsible family planning. The

birth-control pill continues to be underused by women partly
because they are nervous of its effects and partly because they
are afraid that if they start to use it, supplies may run out. As
for condoms, I was informed that they are either too thick or
full of holes. Besides, they, too, are often hard to come by.
One Soviet professional told me that men no longer feel the
responsibility for contraception that they did in his post-war
generation, an attitude that is not confined to the Soviet Union.
There are no vasectomies, he told me; tubal ligations, while they
are occasionally performed, are not common. Furthermore, it is
quite clear that medical concern about women's reproductive
systems has not yet penetrated the economic-planning apparatus
of the State. Not only are contraceptive devices in very short
supply but there are almost no decent sanitary supplies for
women available in the market-place.

The First Three Years

On our daily walks through the streets and lanes around the
Embassy, we would often meet pleased parents out with their
new babies. They might be on their way into a neighbouring
apartment house to visit the set of grandparents with whom they
were not currently living, carrying their baby bundle enveloped
in white cotton and lace and tied up with pink or blue ribbons.
Or perhaps they were just giving the baby some fresh air in
his or her new carriage, coloured if a Soviet one, or black,
slightly more elegant, and twice the cost, if East German. In
spite of parental pride, these babies were almost invisible under
blankets and covers, their little faces enclosed by woolly bonnets
and punctuated by pacifiers. The overall impression was one of
protective adult concern.

This protective attitude is official as well as personal. Once a
healthy baby returns home from the hospital, neither the family
nor the State will take any chances. As soon as the baby is
installed, a public-health nurse comes to visit the apartment. In
fact she will have already been there, if she is doing her job
properly, to see whether or not the parents have prepared a place
for the baby and have the appropriate clothes and furniture ready.
Within twenty-four hours, the baby will also be visited by the

pediatrician to whom he or she has been assigned at the local polyclinic. Pediatricians usually spend three hours a day at the polyclinic and the rest of their working day making home visits. When I was visiting Moscow in the spring of 1989, I went with a close friend and her fifteen-month-old son to her local polyclinic. Although the building was shabby, the interior was clean and the atmosphere, warm and welcoming. Her son had been regularly and carefully checked and twice, when he had a fever, the doctor had come to her apartment. Andrey has already had most of his immunizations against tetanus, diphtheria, whooping cough, measles, and polio. Babies are also routinely given the BCG, the anti-tuberculin vaccine. My friend showed me a stack of information sheets she had received from the polyclinic and had read attentively. She told me that her own mother was not so sure about all the advice she was getting with respect to child-rearing. As an attentive grandmother, she was occasionally resentful when her advice was ignored in favour of the more "scientific" dicta of the doctors. But my friend is persistent, determined that there will be no mistakes.

Scientific advice on child development is widely available to parents who care as much as my friend does. As I could see for myself, her polyclinic's walls were plastered with charts illustrating good nutrition, baby exercises, appropriate clothing, and daily schedules for every age level. And I used to watch, as she does, some of the TV programs that are shown regularly about all aspects of children's health geared to the changing seasons. In winter, parents are taught how to prevent colds amid images of children throwing snowballs. In summer, they can learn what to watch out for on a Sunday outing in the country.

There are also some brightly illustrated manuals on child care available, although they tend to sell out very quickly. Dr. M. Studenikin, the director of the Institute of Pediatrics in Moscow, is responsible for *A Book About the Health of Children*, which has come out in several editions. It has been a long time since I relied on the comfort of Dr. Spock but the tone of Dr. Studenikin's book aims to be equally reassuring. Everything is carefully laid out; in fact, the child's first year is scheduled almost to the minute. Soviet experts believe strongly in the importance of structure in a child's life and the need to acquire good health habits. They also believe that parents are of prime importance. I particularly like the section in Dr. Studenikin's book about exercises for little babies. Even Dr. Spock did not give me that kind of advice, and my babies would have profited from it. The Soviets have done an enormous amount of research on the physical development of the human body, and the practical implications of what they have discovered are widely disseminated to parents and teachers.

If new parents cannot obtain one of the child-care manuals or are too busy to watch the television, they can easily subscribe to the monthly magazine *Zdorovie* (Health) and find numerous articles related to children. Medical problems fascinate people all over the world so it is not surprising that this popular journal has a circulation of more than sixteen million (and rising). Unlike our health columns, which usually find their way onto the women's pages, *Zdorovie* is aimed at the whole family and has just as many articles for men as for women. When the subject is children, an effort is made to address both parents. The contents of the magazine are presented to a general readership in an interesting and informative manner, with lively, entertaining, and remarkably non-sexist illustrations. Consistent with the nature of the health system in general, the emphasis is on prevention and the responsibility of the individual for his or her own health. Articles on physiology and common diseases alternate with personal stories and practical advice given by a wide variety of doctors. Since the advent of *glasnost*, the contents have become franker and the tone less moralistic. During 1988, for example, the issue of contraception was fully explored and various methods described. AIDS was also graphically presented as a serious health problem. However, the focus on children is as strong as it was in the early 1980s when I first began to read the magazine. Each issue contains a tear-out sheet on child care. When the year's sheets are assembled, parents will have a reliable booklet to keep on their bookshelf. The magazine also addresses children directly, which was not the case earlier. Stories appear every month about *Stobed* ("A hundred disasters"), a naughty wooden doll whose escapades always end up by teaching him a health lesson. "How

Stobed decided to kill germs but fell ill himself" is the title of one characteristic tale.

Zdorovie is not the only journalistic source of advice for parents. All of the most widely read periodicals contain columns about child-related issues. The Soviet Children's Fund now puts out a newspaper called *Semya* (Family) that is unusually informative; in the spring of 1989, for example, it published a Russian translation of an excellent French manual for pre-adolescents on how babies are conceived, develop, and are born. However, it is one thing for parents to know about children's health in general and quite another for them to obtain information from the medical profession about an *individual* medical condition, their own or their child's. Soviet doctors still appear reluctant to release an explicit diagnosis to their patients, particularly if the prognosis is poor.

The Health of the School-Aged Child

The pediatric team at the neighbourhood polyclinic will monitor a child's health until he or she enters an institutional setting. Then the centre of preventive health care shifts to the *yasli* (day-care/nursery school), *detsky sad* (kindergarten), or *kombinat,* where the *yasli* and *detsky sad* exist together. Every one I visited was scrupulously clean, and in every building there was a cheerful doctor with a brightly lit office. Outside her door, there was always a bulletin board for parents covered with useful and up-to-date information on various aspects of child health, including information on how to keep the whole family healthy. Nevertheless, many parents are so concerned about the health problems that crop up among children in day-care that they keep them at home as long as possible, relying for child-care on a grandmother or a woman pensioner living in the neighbourhood. Almost every young working mother with whom I came into contact complained of the colds and sniffles and other illnesses to which their children succumbed when they left home. These are justifiable complaints. According to Soviet pediatricians, respiratory diseases are the most important public-health hazard for children when they first enter the pre-school system. There is also a high incidence of gastro-intestinal disorders. In North America, we do not have a massive state-supported day-care system, and our young children's cases of coughs, wheezes, and diarrhoea are not so well documented. However, research is now beginning to show that, in many large day-care centres, there are similarly high infection rates.

The climate of the USSR is harsh for the very young. Throughout most of the country, winters are long and dark. And for the large number of children who live above the sixtieth parallel, in such towns as Murmansk and Norilsk, there are particular hazards. Northern children take regular sunlamp treatments, standing at attention in their underpants, their eyes protected by dark glasses. However, there are too few citrus fruits in shops during the winter months and no chewable multivitamins. I read about the incidence of rickets, and a Canadian physical-education specialist, who was visiting kindergartens and watching the children change into their gym clothes, noted the slight bruising that is characteristic of vitamin C deficiency. I have no doubt that both the knowledge and the goodwill are there to improve the health status of young children once they enter school. What is missing is the proper management of available resources. The poor distribution of fruits and vegetables in the winter, for example, is a major impediment to good nutrition. The difficulty parents have in arranging to stay home with a sick child and isolate him or her from other children is another problem.

Medical staff at pre-school institutions and in schools do what they can to keep children healthy. They also continue the regular physical examinations that children have been getting since birth. Since children's check-ups are recorded at the polyclinic or at school throughout their school days, the statistics accumulate. I went to the Institute of Child and Adolescent Health to find out what they had to say. This institute was set up by the USSR Ministry of Health in 1959 to study the influence on children and adolescents of their surrounding environments: physical, occupational, and social. To gather information for this book I visited many research institutes because they seem to play a more important part in the evolution of State policy in the USSR than they do in North America. They make recommendations based on their research to the ministries that fund them, and establish standards that are often, although not always, accepted. They do not engage in public controversy, as many institutes in North America do, yet they operate as important channels for critical thinking.

The Institute of Child and Adolescent Health occupies one arm of a crumbling U-shaped building, very typical of nineteenth-century Moscow. Its long, low, dusky yellow façade is ornamented with stained white pilasters and surmounted by a classical pediment. I met with Dr. Grombakh, the institute's deputy-director, in a pleasant ground-floor office shaded by trees that have been growing in the central courtyard for nearly two hundred years. He was very forthcoming. First of all he explained the institute's mandate. One part, he said, is to set health standards for buildings that are specifically constructed for children, such as schools, kindergartens, children's homes, and sanatoria. Another is to undertake research to determine the toxicity of various materials, particularly man-made ones, and to issue regulations for children's toys, clothes, and other articles with which children have frequent contact.

The institute also studies school-related stress in children. In 1982, I heard Dr. Grombakh say that in spite of opposition from teachers and school directors the institute was strongly recommending that the stress-creating study-load be decreased. After the implementation of the school reform in 1984, institute researchers began to see even more evidence of stress. Pressures on young children had increased rather than decreased. During their obligatory medical examinations, 50 per cent of first-graders complained of fatigue and many were showing signs of cardiovascular distress. As a result, in 1987, the institute announced that its standards with respect to children's health should have the force of law. What clout it can wield on this issue remains to be seen.

Dr. Grombakh then went on to tell me about the institute's large-scale population studies, which he hoped would enable researchers to define more efficient ways of safeguarding the health of the young. A classification system had been devised based on four principles for evaluating child health: first, the presence or absence of chronic disease; second, the level of

normal value of vital functions; third, the level of resistance of
the organism (how often the child is sick); and fourth, the level
of physical, psychological, and mental development. Using data
generated by the compulsory, regular medical examinations and
on the basis of this classification system, the institute and its
affiliates throughout the USSR have been able to determine that
20 per cent of Soviet children are well, that approximately 30
to 35 per cent have some functional deviation (wear glasses, for
example), that another 30 to 35 per cent have chronic diseases but
are able to function, and that a small percentage (2 to 4 per cent)
are so severely disabled that they require special schools or long-
term hospitalization. According to doctors I have spoken with in
Canada, nation-wide statistics that would enable us to compare
the situation of our children with those in the Soviet Union are
not readily available. What we do know, however, is what we
spend on hospital care for children. A much larger percentage
of our health budget is allocated to the most expensive kind of
hospital care than is the case in the Soviet Union; only 3.5 per
cent is invested in prevention.

On the basis of its population studies, the Institute of Child and
Adolescent Health has determined that the most efficient steps
to improve the health of the "rising generation" include implementing preventive measures among healthy children, improving
the system for early identification, reducing acute respiratory ail-
ments in pre-school institutions, and developing further measures
to stimulate the participation of children and youth in physical
activity. These steps have now been earmarked as a priority concern for the Soviet state and will undoubtedly take precedence
over the development of high-tech medicine in the years to come.

Health Education

Education is among the most effective of preventive measures,
and the health-education curriculum for Soviet schools is evolving
rapidly. At the beginning of 1980s, Doctors A.G. Khripkova and
D.V. Kolesov were lamenting "today's children, adolescents and
youth know a great deal about the world around them—conquest
of space, atomic energy, laser beams and many other things.
Often, however, they do not know how to avoid various diseases,

how to take care of themselves when they are ill, how to organize their daily routine sensibly or how to keep themselves fit for a high level of work output. They lack a knowledge of how their bodies function, of the physiological and psychological differences between the male and female sexes and so forth."

These concerned doctors then recommended a concerted educational campaign to develop good health habits and to eliminate bad ones. Good health habits include proper work and study routines, regular sleep, daytime schedules that start with early-morning exercises, and well-balanced meals. Bad habits include smoking and drinking, procrastination, and (heaven forbid) laziness. From the Soviet point of view, a habit is acquired when an action has been repeated with sufficient regularity for it to become a real need. Good habits are considered to be liberating because they enable a person to do what he or she is supposed to do without expending too much energy. The Soviet emphasis on habit-formation is partly a result of Soviet psychological theories and partly a consequence of Lenin's ideas about the need to internalize the rules of Soviet society. And it also finds an echo in the heart of every worried parent who has ever said, "Stop smoking!", "Don't drink!", or "You'll ruin your health if you continue to stay out so late!"

Anti-smoking education is quite recent. The Soviet staff at the Embassy were not warned against smoking for health reasons when they were young so there were few among the thirty or so employed there during our time who did not smoke. Out of respect, however, they would hastily stub out their cigarettes whenever I came on the scene. When I returned to the Embassy in 1988, Nikolay, the Residence steward, told me proudly that he had given up smoking. Several others complained that their children were now nagging them to stop. The climate for smoking is changing even though 40 per cent of minors aged fifteen and sixteen take it up each year. Alcohol is considered to be a much more serious problem. Large numbers of children and young people have experimented with alcohol, and many of them have gone on to become heavy consumers. Gorbachev's anti-alcohol campaign has had limited success in controlling consumption but it is essential to deter the young from acquiring the habit of drinking.

The new grade-eight biology program, entitled "Man and Human Health", has been drawn up with this in mind. For one school year (two classes a week), boys and girls study the human organism and the major health issues related to it. Studying the skeleton and the muscles, they learn about the importance of physical exercise and also how to apply first aid. With respect to the circulatory system they learn how innoculations create antibodies. They also learn how important it is to donate blood (which can be done through the Soviet Red Cross/Red Crescent Society after the age of eighteen). Particularly emphasized is the "deleterious effect" of smoking and alcohol upon the cardiovascular system.

A study of the respiratory system carries the same message, of course, as well as warnings about the dangers of air pollution. Students are taught artificial respiration. Looking at the liver in the study of the digestive system brings another warning about alcohol. This section also encourages a discussion of the prevention of dental disorder. And so it goes for the rest of the body's systems, including reproduction.

Drug abuse and AIDS are new subjects for education. The use of illegal drugs among the young has grown in the Soviet Union during the 1980s, partly as a result of the intervention in Afghanistan (where 50 per cent of Soviet soldiers allegedly used them). The number of young registered addicts is still small but growing. AIDS is potentially another extremely serious problem. So far, according to health authorities, the incidence is low. Yet, tragic events such as the careless handling of syringes in a children's hospital in southern Russia that resulted in 26 babies becoming HIV positive in 1988 show how vulnerable the Soviet health system is. So, once again, prevention is crucial. One of my friends sent me a pamphlet that she had been given in a Moscow street in 1987 called *What One Needs to Know about AIDS*. This small folder contains essential information presented with simplicity and clarity. The first printing was of five million copies and it was distributed everywhere, including in schools. I was impressed, given some of the hysteria about children with

AIDS in North America, that the folder makes it very clear that AIDS cannot be contracted at school by normal contact with an afflicted child.

Nutrition

Children and adolescents in North America are putting on weight. Since 1960, the incidence of obesity among six- to eleven-year-olds had increased by over 50 per cent. Nearly a third of white males in this age group are overweight. Malnutrition is a problem in Canada and the United States, not because children do not have enough to eat, but because many of them eat too much of the wrong things. To learn about the Soviet situation, I met with a small group of nutritionists and doctors, all women, at Moscow's Institute of Nutrition. Over tea and rich chocolate éclairs, we spent a couple of hours discussing what children and expectant mothers ought to eat. At the time of our meeting, the institute had just established new standards for nutrition during pregnancy and lactation, calling for more protein than is present in the average Soviet diet and additional vitamins. Mothers-to-be are urged to absorb these naturally, rather than through supplements, which are hard to obtain.

Breast-feeding is customary in the Soviet Union, where it has always been encouraged. Factories and other enterprises are required by law to provide space for babies to be nursed, and to allow mothers time off to feed them if they decide to return to work while they are still lactating. It is estimated that about 20 per cent of mothers are unable to breast-feed for some reason, but fresh bottled breast milk is supposed to be available for sale at a reasonable price in special diet kitchens. Unfortunately the supply is not reliable. Supplies of infant formula to supplement or replace breast milk are more reliable, although the formulas are not always appropriate. The institute considers six months the optimal duration for breast-feeding but under the circumstances, most women are wise to continue, if they can.

Vegetable purées are introduced at four and a half months, and meat at seven. Babies are weaned to canned milk if fresh milk is not available, although in Moscow, at least, there are special supply depots for children under two where the quality of dairy products is remarkably high. Prepared baby foods can be purchased, but are in short supply, so mothers are encouraged to prepare food themselves, especially in the winter when fresh fruits and vegetables are hard to find. Mothers get endless advice about what to feed their children, in the hope that a plethora of propaganda will turn them into good cooks and that they will have the time, energy, and funds to make the necessary purchases for recommended meals and be able to find the ingredients in the first place.

Children are provided with breakfast and lunch in nursery schools and kindergartens at a minimal cost to their parents. At school, there is a hot snack for those who do not stay on and lunch for those who do, again at a minimal cost. Guidelines are set out by the Ministry of Health, based on standards established by the Institute of Nutrition. However, the actual menu in each child centre or school is made by the "diet sister", in consultation with the cooking staff and the school doctor. The diet sister has trained as a dietitian with a specialization in children's nutrition. Nevertheless, as we all know, no amount of book knowledge will guarantee a tasty meal, and school meals are a subject of constant complaint.

One of the women at our meeting, Dr. Baryshneva, was a specialist in childhood diseases related to nutrition. The diseases she now sees most frequently are food allergies and obesity. Children in the Soviet Union are also putting on too much weight. Diseases of undernutrition, once so common, have been replaced by difficulties associated with overeating. Nevertheless, my hosts were very interested by what I had to say about *anorexia nervosa*. A few cases had begun to crop up in urban centres, more than a few, I learned later from a Soviet psychiatrist. I suppose it is not surprising that at an age when the young person is unusually self-conscious, emotional disturbances follow international social trends. The new Soviet girl wants to be thin.

Food habits during adolescence are a problem anywhere. Junk food may not be as readily available in the Soviet Union as it is in the West, but even the most casual observer will notice the quantities of bread, ice cream, soft drinks, and sweets that are bought and consumed by the whole population. Nutritional education directed at schoolchildren is not what it might be. Nor is the example of the adult population one to be emulated. Still, the quality of the food is now much better than it was in earlier generations. As a result children and young people in the USSR today are taller, better proportioned, and slimmer than their parents. Many of the girls have wonderful skin. It is mostly among boys that one sees acne and pimples.

Teeth, however, are not in good shape. It is ironic that one of *our* most successful preventive programs, the control of dental caries in children by the addition of fluoride to water, has not been widely implemented in the USSR. A Canadian dentist visiting the Embassy had a good look at some dental facilities and said that, although the dentists were quite knowledgeable, their equipment was outdated. Certainly the adults I met were *very* unhappy about going to the dentist, and the frequent flashing of gold and steel teeth is a testimony to major problems.

An angry article in *Izvestia* in 1985 laid responsibility for the inadequacies of Soviet dentistry squarely on the shoulders of the director of the Central Dentistry Research Institute. He was accused of blocking progress for twenty years. Instead of focusing on the recommendations of the World Health Organization concerning the prevention of periodontal disease and caries, he directed research into the study of general changes in the vascular system, and other issues of only tangential importance to the practical problems of dentistry. Researchers who objected were forced to leave. The director also abolished the use of amalgam for filling teeth and replaced it with "flimsy plastic which is destroyed in six months to a year", leading to a need for frequent replacements and overworked, discouraged dentists. The institute was shaken up, the director forced to resign, and the Minister of Public Health issued an order outlining a whole series of practical measures, including the mandatory use of local anaesthesia during painful dental procedures. In view of what I said earlier about the role of institutes in the USSR, it is fascinating to learn that one man held that much power over a whole profession for so long. Of course, the article undoubtedly overstated the case and, as a result, as a Soviet doctor told me later, a flood of threatening letters arrived in the editorial room of *Izvestia* from people who were eager to do in the unfortunate man. Years of aching jaws were seeking revenge! Still, dental care is now improving, and the new generation may be able to wear more gold on their fingers than in their teeth.

Folk Remedies

No discussion of the Soviet child-health system would be complete without some allusion to folk medicine. Over the centuries, a country such as Russia, where most inhabitants live close to the land, inevitably creates a healing tradition based on medicinal herbs and other "natural methods". Given the disappointments of the public-health system the persistent use of folk remedies is hardly surprising. Many people I knew remained faithful to the memory of the herbal brews their grandmothers had prepared for them when they were little. *Zdorovie* has a regular illustrated feature on the identification and use of medicinal plants, and if you don't collect your own, all kinds of natural powders, leaves, barks, and roots can be found in the farmers' markets, to be used (usually in the form of infusions) to keep your family healthy all winter. My cook used to arrive at work with a cut clove of garlic strapped to her wrist when she had a toothache. If I was sick, the whole staff would produce remedies for me. *Balzam*, a strong, unpleasant (to my taste) liqueur from Latvia, would be poured into my tea or mustard plasters provided for my chest and back.

Homeopathic medicine is officially recognized as part of the Soviet health system, but in addition there are spiritual healers and other unorthodox practitioners who carry on ancient traditions. Sometimes they are prosecuted, and sometimes they are protected by the powerful. I met Dzhuna Davitashvili, a slender young Georgian, at a diplomatic gathering and was struck by her exotic appearance. She was alleged to be applying her "healthy touch" to Brezhnev at the time. Now she has a State business licence to "teach" healing and is a member of the Soviet Peace Committee.

Folk remedies are usually employed for common childhood complaints: chills and sniffles, toothache, cuts and bruises. In addition to the infusions and the mustard plasters, many families resort to *banki* (cupping), which is supposed to increase the circulation. If a child is very ill and does not respond to normal medical treatment, then a healer may be sought out. When, for whatever reasons, the scientific approach of the State fails, people in the Soviet Union are likely to fall back on the wisdom, or the superstitions, of their ancestors.

Mental Health

Bringing up a large family in the foreign service has made me more than normally conscious of the vulnerability of all children to emotional stress and strain. It has also convinced me that some children are constitutionally more at risk than others. As a result I have been involved for more than a decade in the development and implementation of a preventive mental-health program based in the elementary school. This personal experience has taught me a great deal about the field of mental health and about the positive management of social and emotional disorders in young people.

However, when I asked people I met in Moscow about children's mental health, the response was usually the type of anecdote about a niece or the son of a friend, told to me in hushed but dramatic whispers, that I remember from my childhood. The Soviet public is as uneasy about people (including children) who are mentally ill as they are about the mentally disabled. An exception is Dr. Marat Vartanyan, the director of research for the All-Union Institute of Psychiatry. At a reception for visiting Canadian doctors, he talked to me enthusiastically about the institute's new children's mental-health centre and offered to show it to me.

We drove there on a pleasant August day in 1983. On the way, Dr. Vartanyan told me that Soviet doctors are optimistic about mental illness in children, believing that with proper diagnosis and appropriate treatment outcomes will be positive. The purpose of the fifty-bed children's mental-health centre we were on our way to visit, he said, was to observe and diagnose child patients correctly, draw up treatment plans for them, and recommend appropriate educational placement; it was not a long-term treatment centre. Children rarely stay for longer than three months. Then they are either sent home with a treatment plan or on to a sanatorium. In the Soviet Union, efforts are made to treat children on an out-patient basis if possible. In fact, Dr. Vartanyan wanted me to know, the USSR pioneered community mental-health centres for day patients more than sixty years ago. Children in hospital are expected to go home for weekends and during the holidays.

Children usually come to the centre on referral from a poly-clinic. Once there they will be examined by a multidisciplinary team of specialists who will classify them (according to their symptoms) as oligophrenic (mentally retarded), autistic, epileptic, schizophrenic, or suffering from a variety of emotional or behavioural disorders. If these disorders are neither organic nor constitutional in origin, but caused by problems in the social environment, then a ready response to appropriate therapy is expected. Children with such disorders are usually recommended for out-patient care and sent home at once, as long as adjustments can be made to the classroom or to the family environment to change the adult behaviour that gave rise to the problem in the first place. If the disorder is a long-standing one, therapy will be initiated in the hospital setting, and the child will not return home until he or she is stronger. The regime of the hospital and its physical environment are designed to create a state of tranquillity in the child. Behaviour is modified by the use of what Soviets call "therapeutic pedagogy". Each child is placed in a class of ten to twelve children, and every effort is made by the teacher to create a strong children's collective so that the disturbed children will be able to provide emotional support for one another. The regular school routine is used to create an atmosphere of normalcy.

We pulled to a stop in front of a low modern building with many large windows. After meeting with the medical director, we walked along a wide pale green corridor, pausing to admire the airy semi-private rooms for adults, until we reached the children's wing. The children were in class, so we inspected their living quarters first: tidy dormitories, dining-rooms where little tables were already set for lunch, and pleasant playrooms with stacks of neatly arranged toys and healthy green plants. All was clean, ordered, and yes, peaceful! Then we entered a couple of classrooms. One class contained children of various ages with Down's syndrome. A teacher moved quietly among the desks, talking briefly to one child and then to another. Apparently she was trying to ascertain the level of teachability for each one in order to recommend the most appropriate long-term educational placement. In the other classrooms, the children were less obviously afflicted and appeared to be working diligently at a variety of paper-and-pencil tasks. I was told that their seemingly normal classroom behaviour was the result of the therapeutic use of the children's collective led by the specialized teacher-diagnostician. Their specific disorders would be treated separately in sessions with psychiatrists or other specialists.

Western observers are struck by the Soviet emphasis on the role of constitutional, hereditary, and social as opposed to emotional factors in the evolution of psychiatric problems in children. Childhood schizophrenia, for example, is viewed primarily as an organic disorder, "a disruption of the co-ordination of activities between the hemispheres" of the brain resulting in a drastic reduction of the energy potential of the central nervous system. This leads, in turn, to a profound disturbance in the functional systems "responsible for speech, perception, thinking, acting, as well as other finely organized behaviours". Bizarre behaviour, which is antisocial in nature, can lead quite quickly to a diagnosis of schizophrenia. But what constitutes bizarre behaviour? Socially deviant behaviour in adolescents, commonplace in North America, is very seriously viewed in the Soviet Union, where, of course, it is culturally, indeed ideologically, defined. Under Gorbachev, the growing tolerance for unorganized behaviour, particularly in young people, will modify at least some diagnoses.

As for treatment, Soviet psychiatric practice relies heavily on medication. Many other physiologically oriented therapies are also recommended for both children and adults. Hydrotherapy, vitamin dosage, and galvanotherapy are all popular. Hypnotherapy, autosuggestion (bio-feedback), and elaxation techniques are more widely used in the USSR than they are in North America. Play therapy with younger children has become routine in recent years. I asked about family therapy, and Dr. Vartanyan assured me that it, too, was coming into common usage. What kind?

I wondered. He wasn't sure, although he told me that child psychiatrists are aware of most Western therapeutic techniques, in theory, at least, if not in practice.

Although Dr. Vartanyan assured me that the principles of prevention and rehabilitation underlie the Soviet approach to children's mental health, just as they do the Soviet approach to children's physical health, problems persist. In fact, there is evidence that mental-health problems are becoming increasingly serious in the USSR. There is a growing incidence of self-destructive behaviour: drug and alcohol abuse, so-called wild games such as "Pass-out" and "Gasoline Hood", juvenile prostitution, and attempted suicides. These problems, judging by Western experience, are related as much, if not more, to abuse, neglect, and sheer unhappiness in childhood as they are to physiological or constitutional factors. The Soviet Children's Fund is beginning to focus on these problems, but as yet, and as far as I know there is no "institute" for the prevention of child abuse in Moscow. As for sexual abuse, public awareness is just beginning. Only when the violence that is done to young children by adults and older children, who are sometimes unaware of the enormity of their acts, is fully exposed to public view can the Soviet Union, or any other country, begin to heal the psychic wounds we inflict on our own young.

The health system is the first State institution with which the Soviet child comes into contact. Since the coming of Soviet power the State has managed through its preventive health measures to ensure that fewer and fewer children have to undergo the trauma of serious illness. Soviet children are taught that the health system is the instrument of a State that is protective and caring, and the fact that health care is free is supposed to reinforce this message. As they grow up, children become accustomed to frequent medical examinations at the polyclinic or at school and to a flow of fundamentally sensible advice. The system has enormous shortcomings but it also has much to recommend it.

I admire the emphasis on prevention and on rehabilitation, even when the latter takes place in an institutional setting. From our perspective, lengthy stays in convalescent homes are undesirable, however much they may "strengthen" the organism, for we are conscious of the effects that prolonged separations from their parents may have on children. In the USSR, however, children leave home on a daily basis at a very early age and soon learn to draw emotional support from the children's collective. This may well mitigate the effects of being away from the family. Besides, there is now a trend towards encouraging mothers to stay in hospital with children when they are undergoing active treatment. The Ministry of Health has directed hospitals to "enlist the help of mothers more widely in the care of sick children" and to make it possible for them to remain there at night. Of course this may be partly to relieve the shortage of qualified nurses but it usually works to the benefit of the child.

Dr. Chazov was appointed Minister of Health by Gorbachev in February 1987. Previously, he had been the heart specialist of the Kremlin hospital and co-chairman of International Physicians for the Prevention of Nuclear War. He has travelled widely in the West and is well acquainted with the best of what is available for health care in other countries. Once in office he took a good, hard look at the Soviet health system and then told the Soviet people what most of them already knew. He listed the major problems: shoddy facilities that often do not meet sanitary norms; a severe shortage of medicines and modern equipment; unreliable medical education; inefficient, inappropriate, and inflexible management procedures; and a low level of medical science, except in a few notable research institutes.

After six months, the new minister published his ideas for reforming the system: improved medical education; higher salaries for doctors and nurses; more autonomy for regional health authorities; more money to buy equipment abroad while building up the Soviet Union's domestic production; "mighty" centres of research. These and many other proposals initiated a nation-wide debate on the public-health system that involved more than a hundred million people. Maternal and child health emerged as a concern of the highest priority. There was little criticism of the main thrusts of the child-health system: prevention and rehabilitation. The major complaints were about the quality of service.

The Armenian earthquake has reinforced everything Dr. Chazov has had to say. The Soviet helath system was clearly incapable of responding to such a major disaster without outside help. This help has been enormously appreciated. The suffering of the Armenian children who were hurt or who lost their families is almost unbearable to contemplate. Yet, the outpouring of sympathy from people all over the USSR is a reminder of how much children are valued in that country. And, on a positive note, the influx of sophisticated equipment and medical knowledge will spur on Dr. Chazov's reforms. If his proposals are implemented, if more money is invested in health care (up from 4 per cent of the national income in 1987, to 6 per cent by the year 2000), then by the end of the century the maternal- and child-health system as I have described it should be considerably strengthened. This will be of considerable importance to the children of *glasnost,* especially the girls, who will no longer be discouraged (for health reasons, at least) from having children when their time comes.

During a visit to Moscow in 1984, I spent a morning at a children's polyclinic in one of the new residential suburbs. It was a sunny day but chilly, and the children who flooded in and out of the three-storey building, accompanied by parents or relatives, were warmly bundled in brightly coloured coats, caps, scarves, and mittens. The doctor-in-chief was young and brisk, a well-trained woman who bombarded me with information until I stopped her flow of statistics and convinced her that what I really wanted to do was *see* the children, not *hear* about them. She took me first to the education clinic. There, amid the informative posters, a toddler was playing with blocks while her mother was being gently instructed as to which toys were most appropriate for her daughter's age. Then we visited a session of corrective gymnastics where we watched a dozen prostrate youngsters stretch their legs shakily upwards off the mat. Finally, we found ourselves in the pool room where ten or twelve mothers and a grandmother or two stood waist-deep in the water, teaching their babies to swim. A large cheerful blonde in a flowered two-piece bathing suit made sure that I was watching and then plunged her beaming son head-first down to the bottom of the pool and up again, spluttering and squealing with delight. The air was full of sunlight and laughter and an almost palpable sense of emotional connection and physical well-being.

I closed the door of the pool room behind me with regret and, leaving the polyclinic, I went out thoughtfully among the high-rise apartments. The Soviet children's health system is far from perfect, as even its propagandists will now admit. The high-tech equipment is missing, children are still dying. But millions of children are getting a better start than would have been possible in the past and, if they can learn to take care of their own health and surmount the many emotional problems that beset them, then, chances are, they will thrive.

Body and Soul

CHAPTER TEN

Games Children Play: Physical Culture, Sports, and Recreation

We never meant to go to Bratsk. But, as we were approaching Irkutsk on a July evening in 1983, our plane suddenly banked and veered to the north. Descending slowly over dense Siberian taiga, we eventually landed, without explanation, at the wilderness city of Bratsk. Only then were we told that there was fog in Irkutsk and it was soon clear that ours was not the only flight that had been diverted; the terminal building was overflowing with stranded travellers. No one was expecting us, so it looked for a while as if we might have to spend the night on the floor. Fortunately a local Party official had been on our plane, and he made a quick phone call. Before long, a minibus arrived and we were transported some distance away to a pleasant guest house with clean, comfortable beds.

Next morning, we awoke in sunshine to discover that we were on the shores of a large lake. As we were eating breakfast, a good-looking man of about fifty, very trim and fit, appeared at the door with a bouquet of late-blooming lilacs. He introduced himself as Anatoly Zakopyrin, the chief executive officer of Bratskgesstroy, the large engineering enterprise that had been responsible for the construction of Bratsk's huge hydroelectric power station. He had come to show us his town.

Before the dam was built in the 1950s, a small village existed on the site of what is now the city of Bratsk. Thirty years later, this village had grown into a booming town of more than 250,000 inhabitants. To Zakopyrin, it had become home. He was not a native Siberian, he told us, but after living in Bratsk for twenty-five years he had no desire to live anywhere else. He pointed at the beautiful lake "his" dam had created. Sailboats skimmed across its surface, and we could see beaches along the shore. Man and nature had combined to provide recreation, and the people of Bratsk were able to enjoy their short summers. But what about the winter? "How do you and your family endure the long, cold months?" I asked Zakopyrin. "We ski," he replied. I assumed he meant cross-country skiing, but he corrected me. All of his family were avid downhill skiers and spent as much time as they could on nearby slopes. Bratsk has some excellent ski runs, he told us, and more facilities are being built all the time for every kind of winter sport. "I am going to retire here," he announced, "and make sure before I die that the Winter Olympics come to Bratsk." Sensing his energy and determination, I looked at the forested hills around me and thought, "Why not?"

When the XVth Olympic Games were held in Helsinki in 1952, it was the first time Soviet athletes had participated. Since then, the Soviet Union has won more medals than any other country. If this phenomenon was only the result of the highly specialized training of a few promising youngsters at the expense of all the other children in the USSR, then it would scarcely be relevant to this book. But it is not. The desire to excel in international competition is only one of the reasons why Bratsk is developing Olympic-class sports facilities. Zakopyrin has attended Olympic games more than once and he spoke with pride about Soviet athletes but he emphasized that his interest was in health and fitness as well as in sport and that he was particularly interested in children.

Today, it is taken for granted that Soviet athletes want to show off on the world stage. But this has not always been the case. Indeed, for some time after the Revolution, leaders of the new Soviet state viewed international competition with "bourgeois" athletes with disdain. What mattered to them was the degree to which sport could promote the health, physical fitness, and all-round harmonious development of the new Soviet citizen. The Soviet state's original commitment was to physical culture for all rather than to success for a few and this commitment helped the Soviet Union to become a strong and versatile sporting nation. The State is still committed to health and fitness for all, but now, like so many other countries, it has been caught by the lure of Olympic gold. In recent years, these two quite different goals have competed with each other to shape a system of physical culture in which every Soviet child who has grown up in the 1980s has participated.

Physical Culture

Physical culture is a wide-ranging concept, comprising physical and health education as well as sports and organized recreation. It even includes civil defence. Soviet experts have long accorded it almost as much importance for good child development as they have the culture of the mind, basing their support on one of the tenets of Marxist-Leninist thought: that physical and mental states are interdependent. This means that not only is physical culture expected to stimulate mental activity but it is also supposed to play a positive role in the "moulding of morally sound and socially active people". The importance of physical culture for Soviet ideology is what underpins the Soviet Union's unified system of physical education, sport, and "organized rest". In the West we observe the results of this system in the stellar performances of Soviet athletes. However, the outstanding successes of the "Masters of Sport of International Class" are only the tip of the iceberg. Below them lies a nation-wide system that touches the life of every Soviet child.

Before the Revolution, only 45,000 Russians belonged to sports organizations. Seventy years later, more than 70 million people participate in the "physical culture movement". What this last number reflects, of course, is primarily the fact that a system now exists that enables people engaged in some form of sport or planned recreational activity to be counted. It says nothing about the quality of their participation. None the less, almost any child who has the talent and the will can now pursue an internationally recognized organized sport. Before the Revolution, this would have been possible only for a child of the leisured class. Not that pre-revolutionary peasants and workers were physically inactive or unable to enjoy games. The long history of national folk sports such as wrestling (Central Asia), horse racing (the Caucasus), and the Russian games *gorodki* (a game like skittles), and *lapta* (a ball-and-bat game) testify to that. But ordinary folk—the vast majority of the population—were excluded from the sports clubs that organized the sports that were included in the Olympic games when they were revived in 1892.

After the Revolution, the new Soviet government decided that everyone should be included in the physical-culture movement, especially the young. With this in mind, in 1925 the Party issued a document that defined the principles from which all subsequent physical-culture policies have derived. These are: first, the promotion of health and physical fitness; second, character-training for the builders of communism; third, military training; and, fourth, group identification for social and political activity.

The principle of using international sports competitions to demonstrate the superiority of the socialist system had no place in this initial document. On the contrary, the Party favoured mass demonstrations of physical activity that combined propaganda with exercise. Competition was included only to attract more people. Today, the situation is reversed. Mass displays are still featured at sports festivals throughout the Soviet Union but only as an adjunct to the competitions. During the 1930s, sports competitions were restricted to the Soviet Union or to meets with "communist" athletes from other countries. Party approval for international competition with "bourgeois" athletes came only after the Second World War, when it was decided that the success of Soviet athletes could help demonstrate the superiority of socialism over capitalism and thus influence the choice of developing nations. The Soviet Olympic Committee was formed in 1951. The rest is history.

Soviet successes at the Olympics, and at other international competitions, have created a quandary for those in the Soviet Union whose commitment to the concept of physical culture for all is based on their concern for the healthy development of children. Can the Soviet Union maintain its competitive edge internationally without diverting resources away from the physical-culture movement in general? Or will the children of Central Asia, say, have to go without school gymnasiums so that a few children have the facilities to become world-class athletes? Or is it possible to provide both? Yury Vlasov, an Olympic weightlifting champion of the 1960s and now a people's deputy, suggested just before the 1988 summer Olympics that the Soviet Sports Committee (the organization that controls all sports in the Soviet Union) should be divided in two; one organization to deal with "big-time" competition and the other with popular sport.

But even if that happened, a second quandary would exist. Many people in the Soviet Union are just as concerned about the dishonest use of performance-enhancing drugs among Soviet athletes as we have become in Canada since the disgrace of the Canadian sprinter, Ben Johnson, at the Seoul Olympics. For some years, Soviet efforts to control the situation have had limited success because neither the resources nor the will have existed, first to screen out, and then to punish athletes who test positive. This is now changing, especially in track and field. But pressures to excel are still excessive, and many children are pushed too far too fast by coaches and others who want them to win, no matter the cost to their physical and psychological development. The broken neck that paralysed the young gymnast Yelena Mukhina just before the Moscow Olympics is a tragic reminder of the price talented youngsters anywhere often end up paying for the ambitions of others.

A third quandary also exists for people who care about children in the Soviet Union. Partly as a result of changes to the concept of physical culture brought about by political pressure to prove the value of the Soviet system at international competitions, it has become less clear where the line should be drawn between organized and unorganized sport and recreation. The Russian word for recreation is either *otdykh* (rest, relaxation) or *razvlechenie* (amusement, entertainment). Both are obviously necessary for good physical and mental health. However, organized sport (which produces world champions) and organized

recreational activities (which promote the goal of group identification) often interfere with the informal games and creative
play that Soviet psychologists recognize as vital to the healthy
development of children.

While adults in the USSR wrestle with these three quandaries,
children arrive at their own solutions. Most of this chapter is
about physical culture in its organized form but it is clear that the
children of the 1980s have made their own choices about what
to do with their leisure time. In the next decade, young Soviet
athletes may no longer win all the competitions, but perhaps all
Soviet children will have more fun.

Physical Education and the GTO Complex

The component of the physical-culture system that affects the
greatest number of Soviet children is physical education; no child
is exempt. Even those who are disabled or have medical problems
are expected to participate twice a week in a modified PE class.
The first goal of physical education, of course, is health and fitness
for all. A second goal (nearly as important in the eyes of the
State as the first one) is the physical preparation of young Soviets
for labour and defence. It is this second goal that has given the
GTO complex—"GTO", for *Gotov k Trudu i Oborone* (Ready for
Labour and Defence) and "complex", the set of physical skills a
boy or girl should develop in order to be ready both for the world
of work and for national defence—the importance it has in the
PE curriculum. And it is the GTO complex that gives the average
PE class the special twist that makes it characteristically Soviet.
When I was at school, I learned to toss a ball so that I could play
baseball, not in order to be able to toss hay or, though Canada
was at war at the time, to toss a grenade.

In the Soviet Union only pre-school children are not expected
to think about labour and defence since the GTO standards are
not in force before grade one. However, parents are urged to
accustom their infants to regular exercise and when they enter
the *yasli* , even very small children take part in organized physical
education. Toddlers are taught to march, run, and jump, and
they are sent out of doors in very cold weather to increase
their resistance to disease. They also play active group games

although they will not have the necessary concentration and co-ordination for playing competitive games until they are older. Prime objectives for physical education in the *yasli*, in addition to health and fitness, are good posture (with special attention being paid to the arches of the foot and to the development of respiratory muscles by proper breathing exercises) and the enduring association of physical movement with pleasure.

In the *detsky sad,* children are introduced to the twice-weekly PE classes that will be a part of their school life until they graduate from high school. They stretch their arms and touch their toes as do children anywhere, but, as a special feature, they are taught to use their collective wits to solve physical problems such as how to get the whole class across a ditch without a bridge or how to stand several children upright on a tippy bench. And they have to memorize the basic rules of physical hygiene. In Moscow and other northern cities, older kindergarten children are taught cross-country skiing; during the winter I would often meet lines of bundled-up four- and five-year-olds learning to slide their skis forward on the snow-covered pathways of the Garden Boulevards.

Skating is also popular in the northern part of the Soviet Union. There are small skating rinks in most residential areas, and in the major parks warm changing houses and large, well-maintained skating surfaces encourage families to come out. I was particularly impressed by the low parallel bars set up each December in the corner of one of Gorky Park's larger rinks. Using them for support, little children were able to venture onto the ice with real confidence.

Once children enter the general school, physical education becomes formalized. A typical class starts with a five-minute warm-up period during which the teacher prepares the students physically and psychologically for what is to come. The teacher introduces the children to the principal objectives of the lesson, which usually include developing a specific motor skill, preparing for one aspect or another of the GTO complex, and training a moral quality such as self-discipline. Then thirty to thirty-five minutes are devoted to the main activity of the lesson, which could be gymnastics, a mobile game involving running and jumping, a sport such as volleyball, or an outdoor excursion on skis. Finally, a short period of three to five minutes allows for cooling down and for the children and the teacher to assess the results of the class together. I don't recall ever being asked to *think* about what I was doing during my PE classes and I certainly did not have written homework. In the Soviet Union, however, a good PE instructor will expect his or her students to work on the theory as well as the practice of physical culture.

In the mid-1980s, a ten-minute period of physical exercise became compulsory before the start of classes, an acknowledgement that children rarely do morning exercises on their own. Between classes there is often a *fizkultminutka* (physical-culture minute). A slightly longer *fizkultpauza* (physical-culture pause) may take place during the long break in the middle of the morning. One day, I walked in on a class of eight-year-olds who were performing languid arm movements to a scratchy recording of *Swan Lake*. I was told that they were unwinding after a taxing mathematics class.

Connecting physical education and daily exercise to labour and defence is the task of the GTO complex, which was first introduced during the 1930s. A "defender of the Motherland" needs speed, strength, stamina, and flexibility; the PE curriculum focuses on games and exercises specifically designed to develop these qualities. Soviet children are taught to jump, climb rope, throw balls, swim if possible, cycle, run or ski cross-country, and they are expected to reach the level of proficiency established for their age-group by the norms of the GTO complex. These norms are set every ten years or so, the last time being in 1985. When students are ready to be tested, they engage in competition outside of school hours. If successful, they earn a GTO badge. If very successful, it will be a gold one.

Universal compulsory physical education as it exists today was also designed to create a broad base of physical competence and fitness on which the pyramid of Soviet sports achievement at the international level could be built. It is true that international champions have emerged from every corner of the USSR, but it is not at all clear how much credit for this can be given to the PE program. In fact, it now appears that the program (with its

GTO component) has fallen far short of the primary goal of health and fitness for all. According to recent data, Soviet children are by no means as healthy as they should be. The poor physical condition of eighteen-year-olds entering military service is a cause for particular alarm.

The truth is that there have long been serious shortcomings in Soviet schools with respect to both PE teachers and PE facilities. Most of my friends reported that they found their PE classes boring and their teachers uninspired. But, because they had grown up in cities, at least they had a gym to do their knee-bends in. Many rural schools have no facilities at all. The State now promises that every school in the country will have a sports hall, or, at least, an outdoor court for games by the end of the century.

As for the quality of teaching, at the beginning of the 1980s physical-education specialists confessed that "physical culture lessons are still relatively ineffective because they are poorly organized and the wrong methods are used". By 1984, however, or so I was told during a visit to the Sports Institute in Moscow, 80 per cent of existing PE teachers had been qualified, and new ones were being trained all the time. As a result, every school in the country should soon have at least one properly trained PE teacher on staff. Sports have a good deal of prestige with the general population so competent young people, many of whom are active in one sport or another, are attracted to teaching physical education, often bringing their special enthusiasm to the schools to which they have been assigned. Although the time allotted to PE in the curriculum was slightly shortened by the 1984 education reform, the syllabus has become more varied. In addition to activities associated with the GTO complex, students are being taught recreational sports so that they can better enjoy their leisure time.

The Making of a Champion

In spite of all its shortcomings, the PE program does help to identify potential athletes. However, it is the second component of the physical-culture system, organized sport, that is really geared to the making of champions. The story of the great hockey goalie, Vladislav Tretyak, is an example of how this happens.

My husband's appointment as Canadian Ambassador to the Soviet Union coincided with Canada's decision to join the other Western nations who were boycotting the 1980 Moscow Olympics in protest against the Soviet intervention in Afghanistan. We did not arrive in Moscow until the games were over, but when we did we discovered that the city had been left with impressive new Olympic-class sporting facilities. The choice of Moscow as a site for the Olympics had given an enormous boost to the physical-culture movement in the USSR, and particularly to Soviet sport.

Once we settled into the Embassy, we soon discovered that, despite government boycotts, the world of international sport has a dynamic all of its own. Canadian athletes, along with their coaches, managers, and chaperones, were among the most frequent (and often the most welcome) visitors to the Embassy during our stay there. We would host a reception for them in the Residence and then cheer them on as they competed at international meets that took place at the various Olympic sites in the city. There were gymnasts, synchronized swimmers, figure-skaters, boxers, and wrestlers. And then there were the hockey players.

Everyone knows that ice hockey is Canada's game. Certainly the Soviets thought so when they started to play what they called "Canadian" hockey in 1946. Up to then, most Russians played (and many still do) bandy hockey, a skating game that uses a ball rather than a puck. The first time Soviet players confronted native Canadians was in Stockholm in 1954. Our team was made up of amateurs, eager but underqualified, and the Soviets defeated them. It was not until September 1972 that the Soviet national team finally met the professionals of the NHL (National Hockey League). There was a series of eight games, four in Canada and four in the Soviet Union, and the populations of both countries were glued to their television sets for every game. With only thirty-six seconds to play in the very last game, Paul Henderson shot and scored and won the series for Canada. The Soviet goalie who was able to hold off the Canadians until that last dramatic moment was a remarkable young man, a twenty-year-old named Vladislav Tretyak.

Since that time the Soviets have played Canadian professionals in an international series that takes place every three or four years called the Canada Cup. In September 1981, the Soviets won. In November, my husband was called upon to present the winners with a replica of the Cup during a brief ceremony that took place before one of the regular Soviet major-league hockey games in Moscow. The game was between the Central Army team and *Dinamo*, the team associated with the Ministry of the Interior. As my husband stepped cautiously onto the ice to hand the heavy trophy to Vladislav Tretyak, he was watched by Leonid Brezhnev (who often came to Army games) and by 150 million television viewers. "Canadian" hockey is a big sport in the USSR, and Tretyak, like the Canadian forward Wayne Gretzky, is a superhero.

Tretyak and Gretzky are friends. We met them together at the rink of the the Central Army Sports Club in June 1982, and two days later, on the first of July, they came together to our national day reception. The Canadian and Soviet members of the Embassy staff were equally delighted to have them there and lined up indiscriminately for their autographs. In 1987 Gretzky wrote an introduction to the English edition of Tretyak's autobiography, and in 1988 Tretyak came to Edmonton for Gretzky's wedding. In October 1989, Tretyak became the first athlete from outside of North America to be inducted into Toronto's Hockey Hall of Fame.

The development of Tretyak into a superb goalie is an excellent example of how the Soviet system of physical culture and sport identifies and promotes outstanding athletes, whenever and wherever they appear. Born in 1952, Vladislav Tretyak grew up in a small town near Moscow. One of the first things he emphasizes in his autobiography is that his parents were not overly protective, as so many Soviet parents are, and that he and his brother were encouraged to be adventurous in their play when they were still very young. He was also helped by the fact that his mother was a physical-education teacher who had once played field hockey. As soon as he was old enough, he went to a summer Pioneer camp, where he spent at least half of his time engaged in sports. At school, he participated in a great variety of sporting events; he admits that he wanted to win them all. At the age of ten, he heard that there were some openings for young hockey players in the children's section of the Central Army Sports Club and he went to try out. His hockey career thus began on the same ice where we met him with Wayne Gretzky twenty years later.

For the first few years, Tretyak trained at the Army Sports Club three times a week after school for an hour and a half. He also played regularly on a skating rink near his home. He recalls those years as happy ones during which he was fully occupied by his school work and by his passion for hockey.

Research in the West has shown that the lives of children who grow up to be outstanding performers in either the arts or sports are characterized by certain essential factors: aptitude, personal ambition, supportive parents—and a mentor. By the time he was fifteen, Tretyak had attracted the attention of the head coach of the Central Army team, Anatoly Tarasov. In Tarasov, Tretyak had found his mentor. Tarasov convinced the young Tretyak that he believed in him, and Tretyak responded to his encouragement. Tarasov was going to make him the best goalkeeper. "The best in the country?" Tretyak recalls asking. "In the whole world," Tarasov answered, and then told Tretyak, "Remember this once and for all: in the world!"

Tarasov was a hard taskmaster but an intelligent one. He made Tretyak train incessantly. He was thoroughly scientific in his approach. He studied the techniques of successful goalkeepers from other countries and adapted them to the abilities and the personality of the boy he was training. Over and over again he challenged him to use his head, to *think* about the game of hockey. "Always learn—every hour, every minute," he exhorted the young Tretyak. "Be hard on yourself, don't deceive yourself with your success, find the roots of your failures. March forward step by step."

Tarasov was not the only one who supported Tretyak. He was surrounded by encouragement from the time he entered the Central Army Sports Club. Later on, as a member of the national junior team, he had easy access to advisers and models. In his book, he remarks on the determination, strength, and courage that these people demonstrated both on and off the ice and tells how he came to link these qualities with "patriotism, loyalty to traditions, honour of the flag, selflessness and respect for the rival". Retired from active competition since 1985, Tretyak is now taking his turn to encourage the hockey players of the future.

Tretyak's youthful experiences in hockey illustrate how sports are organized in the USSR for children and young people. The system as it exists today was shaped in the 1960s. Experts in the field could see that the path to the Olympic gold lay through mass training and through competitions that would enable the best to arrive at the top. Under the tutelage of the Communist Youth movement—the Pioneers and the Komsomol—nation-wide competitions were organized involving more and more youngsters every year. Some of these are sponsored by the media to give them maximum exposure. The newspaper *Pionerskaya Pravda* sponsors an all-Union ski competition, and the radio program "Pionerskaya Zorka" ("Pioneer Dawn") sponsors a skating contest. These competitions all have names and children are urged to form or join clubs with the same name so that they can participate. Some examples are the Leather Ball (soccer), the Golden Puck (hockey), the Neptune (swimming), the Silver Skates (skating), and the White Rook (chess—which is classified as a sport in the USSR). The first level of a Golden Puck competition, say, will be held at school, at a Pioneer palace, in a residential area, or at the facilities of a local sports complex. At this level millions of youngsters may be involved. The winners move on to city and district competitions and then to regional and Republic ones. At the all-Union finals, the successful team will be presented with a golden puck.

In addition to single sport competitions, there are others involving several events, such as the Hopeful Starts competition, which was organized for the first time two years before the 1980 Moscow Olympics. This competition requires children to enter a minimum of seven events. It has become associated with the all-Union Schools Spartakiad, which now takes place every year.

All of these sporting events taken together involve more than seventeen million children every year. One can only guess at how many other people, professionals and volunteers, help to organize them. I was told that many of these people are ranked athletes or Masters of Sport able to scout for special talent in their own sports disciplines. Tretyak does not say in his book whether he, himself, ever took part in a Golden Puck competition. The first one was held in 1965 and by that time he was already training at the Central Army Sports Club. Tretyak's years at the sports club were crucial to his development as the "Greatest Goalkeeper in the World". Given its resources, the Central Army Sports Club is one of the best, if not the very best in the country, but throughout the USSR there are thousands of other sports clubs for children who want to take part in a sport.

There are also several types of sports schools. The most exclusive are the boarding-schools for training exceptionally talented young athletes, schools that function like the other special schools for gifted children I have described. In 1984, there were forty of these. Students follow the standard Soviet curriculum and undergo intense training in their specialty, under close medical supervision. These schools concentrate on Olympic sports (plus chess) on the assumption that world champions should be nurtured in controlled circumstances, an assumption particularly relevant to those sports in which international records are being set by younger and younger competitors, such as gymnastics and swimming. General schools that promote sports in the same way as those that specialize in foreign languages are more numerous. These schools are attended by a normal cross-section of children, but they focus on physical culture and sport by providing extra classes, better-trained teachers, more in-school organizers, and so on. There are about four hundred of these. Finally, there are around eight thousand after-school sports schools.

In September 1984, I visited a school of this latter type located in south Moscow. The building was new but, like many structures in the Soviet Union, shoddily constructed. The lobby, offices, and changing rooms were unimpressive, the cafeteria and dormitories for visiting teams decidedly spartan. But the quality of the two gymnasiums was first class. The flooring was excellent, as was the equipment, and there was plenty of natural light. This "school" specializes in basketball. In one gymnasium, some young boys were warming up with preparatory exercises. In the other, girls were dribbling balls.

The director of the school, a Master of Sport of the USSR, was open and direct. He explained how the school functioned. Students come after their regular school day to train for an hour and a half, two or three times a week. Those who are talented, and interested in playing the game competitively, will come more often, particularly during periods of active competition. This school, like all other such sports schools, has a distinct sports curriculum that must be followed by the children who attend it. This is what distinguishes a sports school from a sports club or "circle". Students do not have to have unusual ability to be accepted at the school, but those without any at all drop out after a year or two.

The director called to some girls who were passing the ball to tell me why they were there. One said she had been recommended by her school, another had come because her sister had, a third had come on her own because she loved playing basketball. The school can accommodate at least three sessions a day, so two or three hundred children are enrolled at any one time. The best and keenest also go to at least one session of a summer training camp that the school maintains in the country.

Attendance at sports schools, and use of equipment, is free. Costs to an individual child for engaging in any sport, including an expensive one such as downhill skiing, are kept to a minimum so that no one need be excluded on that ground alone. Actual costs are assumed by the State or by a trade union. Trade unions have a tradition of supporting physical-culture centres for children, obtaining funds for this from the dues of their members.

The staff of all types of sports schools include trained professionals and ranked athletes. This combination of personal experience with professional knowledge may be one of the reasons why so many of these schools are successful. The thoroughly scientific manner in which training schedules are developed for every sport would be quite useless if the trainers were unable to communicate the reality of competition to children. During their active careers, athletes in the Soviet Union are pressured to pursue post-secondary education at pedagogical colleges and sports institutes. Many of them thus emerge from their years of competition as qualified teachers, ready to train a new generation of champions. Those who have not kept up with their education during their competitive years, for one reason or another, may have serious emotional and job-related difficulties later on, a problem the Soviet Union shares with many other sporting nations.

There are two other aspects of Vladislav Tretyak's youth in sports worth mentioning. One is his military connection. Tretyak is an army officer, and the army has supported him materially ever since he began to play competitive hockey. Tretyak is also a Soviet patriot. From the point of view of the children and youth for whom he is a hero, his association with the army serves to cast a glow over the military and thus to reinforce the association of physical culture with defence. Because he has none of the belligerent qualities of the stereotypical warrior, his impact on girls is probably as strong as his impact on boys. He appears to be honourable, brave, and caring, and is an effective model of Soviet virtues because he is also credible. His modesty and the frankness with which he admits to fear and weakness combine with his undeniable athletic achievement to make him very persuasive. He is now a member of the Board of the Soviet Children's Fund and an indefatigable "ambassador" of Soviet sport to the outside world.

Organized Recreation: Pioneer Palace and Pioneer Camp

The third component of the physical-culture system in the Soviet Union is organized recreation. The physical-education program is aimed primarily at health and fitness (or, in association with the GTO, at preparation for labour and defence). Organized sport is designed for character-building and for the making of champions. Organized recreation for children has as its goal the reinforcement of group identification through pleasurable activity. Almost every Soviet child spends part of his or her childhood at one or the other of those two quintessentially Soviet institutions, the Pioneer palace and the Pioneer camp. The Pioneer palace enables children to engage in a wide variety of extracurricular activities during the school year, ensuring that they take place in a group setting. The task of the Pioneer camp is to keep groups of children physically active, productively occupied, and collectively entertained during the school holidays.

The term "palace" is a surprising one for a children's institution but it was chosen quite deliberately because it has connotations of "specialness" and it conjures up images of pleasure and privilege. After the Revolution, the new Soviet government decided that it would be a splendid symbolic gesture to transform some of the palaces that had belonged to the aristocracy into playgrounds for the children of workers and peasants. In Leningrad, Pioneers still make use of the magnificent Anichkov palace that once belonged to the family of the tsar, and in Irkutsk, I saw sturdy Siberian youngsters stamping their heels on the resilient ballroom floor of a nineteenth-century merchant's mansion. In recent years, however, new "palaces" like the one in Moscow have been designed and constructed with the specific needs and interests of modern young Pioneers in mind. These buildings are usually more satisfactory for their purposes than the converted mansions, and, if they are still called "palaces", it is because the term continues to affirm the fact that children are a privileged class.

The first Pioneer palace that I visited was in the city of Kiev during an official visit we made there in April 1981. Leaving behind a Moscow trapped in the grimy last stages of winter, we entered a city enveloped in pale green gauze. The chestnut trees and the lilacs, the pride of Kiev, were already in bud. Unlike Minsk, many of Kiev's fine old buildings survived the German occupation, but the city owes most of its beauty to its natural setting, a setting that has been enhanced by an extensive system of public parks on the heights rising above the Dnieper River. The Pioneer palace has a choice location in one of these parks.

As I drove up, clutching my handful of maple-leaf pins, I saw a large, new building that looked like a ship. "It was designed that way," explained the director as she greeted me on the steps, "so that children will think of boats and learn to enjoy the water." There are pools on the palace grounds, and the Dnieper is good for sailing.

The director turned and I followed her across the lobby to the room of "international friendship" where a group of well-brushed ten-year-olds stood waiting for me. One of them nervously made a speech of welcome, and then we all sat down at a round table while the director talked. She spoke about the Pioneer movement and the admirable job it was doing providing recreational opportunities for all the children in the USSR. She recited the enormous range of activities sponsored by the organization, including sports clubs, festivals, and competitions held all over the Soviet Union, and thousands of summer camps. Then she described her own palace, impressing me with the fact that the city of Kiev was prepared to spend more than a million roubles a year to support its work. The palace has more than ten thousand registered members and, although each sector of the city has its own Pioneer house, the palace is their flagship. There is a paid staff, most of whom are young Komsomol members. They have excellent rapport with the children, she claimed, because they are so close to them in age. In addition, people of many different trades and professions (carpenters, dressmakers, ballet dancers) volunteer time two or three times a week to share their knowledge with young Pioneers.

The children relaxed while the director was speaking, and when she had finished they were prepared to tell me what they knew about Canada. They mentioned hockey, Prime Minister Trudeau, the Rocky Mountains, and 1867, the date of Confederation. I felt like a quiz-master as I rewarded them for their responses with my maple-leaf pins (Soviet children love to collect and trade pins). Then I gave them some books of Canadian children's fiction to help them learn more about their Canadian contemporaries.

Clubs or "circles" of international friendship are a characteristic feature of every Pioneer palace. However, a Pioneer palace the size of Kiev's has more than 150 other interest groups. I was shown where children met to cook and sew, to paint and sculpt, to make model airplanes, develop photographs, dance. My visit was in the morning when most children are at school, but in the rehearsal hall I found an intent group of six-year-old girls pointing their toes under the direction of a young dancer from the Kiev opera. They had come from a nearby *detsky sad* . Later in the afternoon, older children would get their chance.

Children come to circles at a Pioneer palace twice a week. New programs are organized on a regular basis and advertised in all the local schools. Any child is welcome. Parents, however, are not. This is not a rejection of parents (who often take part on committees or work as volunteers) but an affirmation, so I was told, of the right of children to have some degree of control over the roles that adults can play in their special environment. Each Pioneer palace has a children's advisory group, and children are given responsibility for organizing circles. Since so many of the staff members of Pioneer palaces are themselves young, the responsibility given to children, if limited, is quite genuine. However, when I asked whether or not Pioneer palaces sponsor debating clubs like the ones my argumentative children used to take part in, honing their verbal skills by defending positions with which they disagreed, I was told that children should be encouraged to discuss rather than to debate.

I left the palace in Kiev full of admiration for the facilities and for the dedication of staff and volunteers. The atmosphere of this and every other Pioneer palace I visited in the USSR struck me as particularly suited to the natural gregariousness of pre-adolescents and to their need for friendly direction. However, there comes a time when youngsters have to seize hold of their own lives if they are going to mature as autonomous adults and the formalized structure of the Pioneer palace does not seem to allow for this. Most of the children I saw enjoying themselves in Pioneer palaces were between the ages of eight and thirteen. Older teenagers were usually present only in an organizational capacity and, while there were not many adults, those that were there were clearly in charge. A palace is a special place, but privilege has its price; someone is always watching.

While most children attend a Pioneer palace only a couple of times a week, for an hour or two at a time, a Pioneer camp is a complete live-in experience. This is what I learned when I spent a day at "Zorka" ("Dawn"), a pioneer camp about thirty-five kilometres south of Moscow, off the main road to Kiev. The camp director met us at the turn-off from the highway and guided us along a gravel road into the deep woods. With my Canadian camping experience in mind, I was disconcerted to arrive at a locked gate and discover that the entire campsite was enclosed by a wall. Given the overprotective attitude of both parents and authorities, and with a large number of children to keep from straying, I should not have been surprised. The two Soviets who had accompanied me on this visit, one of whom had a fourteen-year-old son and the other an eight-year-old daughter, were horrified when I described my son's white-water canoeing adventures and my daughter's challenging tests of personal survival at an "Outward Bound" camp. While Soviet children are often exhorted to be brave and courageous, they are rarely exposed to the dangerous physical situations that would actually test these qualities. No one is willing to be responsible for allowing them to take such a risk.

At the time of my visit, Zorka was in the charge of a good-natured ex-naval captain who had been camp director for eleven years. He told us that he had washed up on this particular shore by happy accident and that he had indulged his nostalgia for the sea by building a stationary ship in the middle of the camp's shallow pond. Children could play in it for hours, but no one was worried because it would never sink.

Zorka is associated with the oil industry, and the majority of campers, who range in age from seven to fifteen, come from Moscow where their parents work in the oil ministry. Others come from oil-production sites, such as Tyumen in the Urals. The cost per child per shift (as a session is called) is about two hundred roubles. Half the children pay nothing at all while the other half pay ten roubles each, the oil industry's trade union paying the rest.

The camp is active all year around. In the summer there are three shifts of twenty-six days each, interspersed with three- to four-day breaks. Each shift can accommodate 550 children, and some attend two or even three shifts in a row, returning summer after summer. During the New Year holiday, there is another shorter shift during which children concentrate on skating, ice hockey, and skiing. At other times, the camp is used as a rest house for workers and for short family holidays.

The captain had a staff of 150, including service and main-tenance personnel. There were counsellors, instructors, three doctors (pediatrician, surgeon, dentist), and six nurses. He was particularly proud of his highly qualified physical-culture instruc-tors. The expressed aim of the camping experience is to give children a good time in a collective setting, build up their health, and help them to develop hobbies and acquire leisure-time "skills".

The captain took us for a tour. We first admired his "boat" and the fairy-tale log cabin on the pond's shore where a few children were practising folk-dances. Then we walked to a little hut surrounded by bushes where a "circle of young naturalists" was learning to look after animals. The children rushed to greet me, and each one proffered his or her charge (rabbit, guinea-pig, mouse, hamster, chick, turtle) for me to pet. Next, we went to a glass house where the camp soviet (council) meets twice a week to discuss discipline problems and to make plans. At the beginning of each shift, campers form collectives in their dormitories and elect representatives to the camp soviet. These delegates take their responsibilities very seriously, wearing their Pioneer uniforms when they meet. They draw up duty rosters, and ensure that the Party and the camp patrons are not forgotten while the children enjoy themselves. A pair of them guided us solemnly through the camp museum, where we examined the obligatory Lenin corner, some war relics, and a display about the oil industry. An alley of Pioneer heroes (all of whom had died in the last war) took us from the council house to the playing-fields.

All Pioneer camps have sports programs but few have such extensive facilities as Zorka. In addition to a swimming pool, there is a soccer field, two tennis courts, a basketball court, separate areas for volleyball and badminton, a lower field that becomes a skating rink in winter, and a covered facility for rainy days that is used for gymnastics and ping-pong in the summer and tennis in the winter. Children swarmed everywhere. On the lower field, those who were not involved in one or another specific sport, were playing relay games—"cheerful games," they are called. It was a fine day, and everyone, including the young instructors, appeared to be having a good time.

We had lunch with the campers. It was substantial and tasty: fresh vegetable soup with sour cream, meatballs and rice, tomatoes and cucumbers, a fruit compote (*kissel*), which could be drunk, and stacks of dark bread. We were served by the duty Pioneers. There were no other adults to be seen.

As we walked back to the director's office after lunch, loud-speakers blared selections from Tchaikovsky's *Sleeping Beauty*. The captain wanted me to write in his guest-book, so I sat down and wrote, quite truthfully, that I had enjoyed meeting so many busy, cheerful children, and I commended him on his well-organized territory. My other impressions I kept to myself. How could I tell him that I was dismayed by the absence of adventure, when he had been trying to reassure me all along about safety? Or that I was saddened by the functional look of the buildings, when he was so proud of his facilities? Or that I was disappointed that the green spaces looked unkempt rather than rustic, when he was telling me that one of the camp's aims was to encourage the children's love of nature? It was not a question of resources, but of style. I thought of wilderness camps I had known in Canada, even poorly funded ones, where buildings and environment are harmoniously blended, and I sighed.

Zorka, and more than seventy thousand other Pioneer camps in the Soviet Union, provide opportunities for sport and recreation and health promotion to a substantial number of children, without asking whether or not their parents can afford to pay. During the summer of 1986, for example, approximately twenty-nine million children under the age of fifteen went to a Pioneer or a school camp, spent time at a hiking or touring base, or were taken on a trip to the countryside organized by one of the children's institutions. Such high-profile Pioneer camps as Artek on the Black Sea coast and Orlyonok in the Krasnodar area, where only the most meritorious of Pioneers selected by their peers are supposed to go, probably receive more funding than the rest, but facilities overall are improving all the time. Like the Pioneer palace, the Pioneer camp is here to stay.

After I had been to Zorka, I often asked Soviet friends and acquaintances to tell me what they remembered from their camping experiences. Without exception, the women told me that they had suffered from acute homesickness during their first "shifts" but had often enjoyed later sessions. The men, generally speaking, spoke with pleasure about the sport activities. Some people complained of being bored much of the time, although one or two recalled (with a smile) their furtive sexual gropings (the camps are coeducational). On the whole, however, it is clear that Soviet society has created in the Pioneer camp yet another environment where Soviet children can develop individual and group skills but will have as little chance as possible to "eat of the tree of knowledge".

Unorganized Games and Recreation

Now we come to the point where Soviet children's games and pastimes finally escape from the physical-culture system and become a matter of a child's own initiative. Soviet physical-culture specialists still consider unorganized recreation part of their domain but they find it difficult to control informal games and almost impossible to ensure that everything Soviet children do in their spare time contributes to their physical culture. The State can regulate the design of toys and determine what cannot be shown on television. But no authority can fully control how a child plays with a toy or mandate which TV program a child actually watches. At best, the State can try to reach children's recreation through their parents. I used to watch a popular TV program, for example, called "Mommy, Daddy, I", which showed families competing against one another, playing games and running races. It was very amusing and may well stimulate parents to be more active with their children. But many of those who would watch such a program are probably already busy taking their children skiing, skating, or sledding in the winter, hiking in the spring, swimming in the summer, or mushroom-hunting expeditions in the fall.

Parents are also becoming involved with the sports clubs that have appeared in many residential areas since 1975 to give some structure to children's recreation. How many of these clubs are parent-initiated, and how many are State-initiated, is hard to say, but it is striking how often the State had stepped in to co-opt children's activities. Nevertheless, these clubs are welcome in a society in which both parents work. They sponsor a whole range of activities from ping-pong to figure-skating, usually for a small fee.

But when they are not being organized by someone else, Soviet children end up playing the same informal games that I have seen children play in every part of the world in which I have lived: hopscotch, hide-and-seek, ball games, skipping rope, swinging, tree houses, and so on. Most Soviet apartment blocks are designed with large interior courtyards where younger children of various ages can play together in relative safety after school, on weekends, or during the holidays. In this case, there will usually be a *babushka* or some other older person keeping an eye on what is going on. There is, however, one corner that exists (and long may it) completely beyond adult control. This world shared by children everywhere but never with people in authority is the world of children's lore.

Soviet Children's Lore

Almost every week during my years in Moscow, I sat down at a desk in the Residence to write home to my children. The window in front of me faced onto the street, and every so often, as I paused to collect my thoughts, I would stop and stare at School no. 59 across the way. Over time, I observed endless episodes of child's play involving scores of youngsters of different ages who were either gathered on the pavement outside the school or playing in the schoolyard. Watching three little girls whispering together or a quartet of boys hunched over some invisible object on the packed-earth playground, I would wonder what they were up to.

One morning, before school started, my attention was caught by two small boys standing near the curb, looking mischievous. As soon as a girl appeared, one of the boys swung around abruptly and thrust a jointed wooden snake into her face. She jumped back in alarm and then ran giggling into the school while the boys waited for another victim. Small boys teasing small girls. What a classic theme! I thought of all the variations that I had witnessed in France, India, Mexico, the Canada of my youth, and that of my children's childhood, and drew comfort from the universality of children's lore.

Such lore consists of riddles and rhymes, jokes and teases, charms and magic games, all the verbal and physical devices that children have created and passed along for centuries in order to come to terms with the social world around them. As soon as children start school, they discover that life among their peers is different from family life and that their status among other children will be determined by their actions and their personalities rather than by their position in the family. It is the lore that each generation of children passes on to the next, without the intermediary of adults, that best enables them to gain some control over their social situation.

Children invent nicknames to slot other children into categories they can deal with, they play word games to show off, they parody adult behaviour to bring grown-ups down to size. They recite charms to ensure fine weather for a picnic, they share the secret words that distinguish insiders from outsiders, they engage in games that they think no other gang knows how to play. As adults, most of us accept that children's games and pastimes are important, but how quickly we forget what they meant to us! When we were children, we had no idea why we took such delight in all those spontaneous games other children taught us. And when they had fulfilled their function in our lives, we lost interest and they vanished from our consciousness like dreams, although not before we had passed them on to another generation of children.

Children's lore is abundant in the Soviet Union. As I travelled about the country, I glimpsed familiar scenes, but as a foreigner— an adult—I could not be absolutely certain what the children were up to. Luckily, there are Soviet scholars who have long been interested in the topic of children's lore, and I met one of them, a young woman named Mariya Osorina, during a visit to Leningrad in 1984. She told me that, because her mother was a folklorist, she became conscious of the existence of what she calls the "children's tradition" while she was still young enough to be part of it herself. The children's tradition is most active from the time children enter school at the age of six until they are thirteen or fourteen. Pre-school children receive their culture primarily from adults. After puberty, the new concerns that adolescents have lead them to dismiss children's lore as childish. Unless they start collecting it, as Osorina did.

Here are two samples of contemporary Soviet children's lore from her collection. Children frequently recount horror stories at Pioneer camps or in other residential environments, such as sanatoria or boarding-schools. A well-told horror story is able to produce a delicious (and ultimately consoling) shudder in a group of young children adjusting to a communal setting away from home. The children draw emotional support from one another as they huddle around the story-teller (who is close to their own age) and collectively overcome the fears that the story symbolizes. And where had the story-teller learned the story? Probably from an older child at camp the previous year.

Osorina has published a number of the stories she has gathered from children around Leningrad and in the Volga region. One of them, told by ten-year-old Tanya, struck a bell. Reading it, I suddenly remembered my ten-year-old self, miserable at summer camp, whispering in a dark cabin. Then I heard the voice of my cabin-mate chanting: "I am walking around a black, black city. I am walking along a black, black street. I am seeing a black, black house..." Then, "A black, black skeleton lies in the black, black coffin and the skeleton is shouting [here the story-teller grabbed me], 'Give me back my heart.'" How on earth, I wondered, did a little Soviet girl come to know this self-same story and recite it to Osorina forty years later, ten thousand kilometres away, and in Russian?

Secrecy is an essential feature of children's lore. Osorina writes that Russian children (and I have had this confirmed for me by one who is now grown up) love to make what they call "secrets". These are small holes in the ground in which various "precious" objects such as stones or coloured foil candy wrappers are placed under a sheet of glass that is then camouflaged by earth. A child will make a number of these "secrets" in locations that only he or she knows and then visit them from time to time alone, or occasionally with a special friend. Osorina speculates that this may be one way in which children emotionally master the physical territory of their everyday lives. By the same token, she suggests, much of children's verbal lore may exist to define (and carve out a place in) the social territory they share with their peers and with adults.

There are two other common expressions of children's lore in the Soviet Union that I have come to know about, both of which have to do, as Osorina writes, with "demonstrating opposition to the 'proper' and frequently over-powering adult world". The first is the popularity of that widespread topsy-turvy day known in the West as April Fool's Day, and in the Soviet Union as the "Don't Believe Anything Day". On the first of April, Soviet children are allowed to play pranks on adults that would be unthinkable at any other time—and they do. The other form is the joke told at the expense of the heroic adult to bring him or her down to size. Somewhat to my surprise, I learned of the existence of a whole body of scatological jokes about Pushkin common among ten-year-olds. Of course he is known to have been a man of considerable sexual prowess, but who tells that to ten-year-olds? That there are jokes about generals in the Civil War (particularly Chapaev) is more to be expected. If Soviet children have their noses rubbed in the heavyweights of literary and military tradition too often then they are bound to take revenge. Jokes about authority are not, of course, restricted to childhood in the Soviet Union. When we were living there, a new one about Brezhnev, or even about Lenin, would run through Moscow like lightning. Now Gorbachev is coming in for his share.

Children's Pastimes

Living for years in cultures as rich and ancient as those of Mexico and India, I have developed a passion for archeology. What interest me most, however, are not the trappings of vanished kings, but the artefacts of childhood. The dolls, the little wheeled carts, the broken games labelled "children's toys" in museum windows, never cease to fascinate me. I like to envisage Mayan children in what is now Yucatan or little Harrapans near the Indian ocean playing with them in the heat and the dust. This sometimes makes me wonder how the objects of our children's lives will strike future archaeologists. What, for example, will they be able to learn from them about Soviet, as opposed to North American, childhoods in the 1980s?

In the ruins of Detroit, scholars would certainly find far more toys than they would in what was once Sverdlovsk, an industrial town in the Urals. Soviet children have toy boxes that are neither as full nor as varied as those of their North American contemporaries. And, on average, their toys are not as well-made. For that reason, and because they are of simpler manufacture and more natural materials, they will probably not endure as long. Sexy Barbie will still be there with her arms raised, long after the brightly coloured *Matrioshka* nesting dolls have faded and fallen apart.

Nor would the Soviet hearth yield as many dog-tags for, although Soviet children really love animals, it is hard to keep a pet in a small apartment, nine storeys up. Archaeologists would find large numbers of electronic remnants on both sites, though, for television and radio are just as much a feature of a Soviet child's life today as they are in America. But, if my scholar of the future wants to understand what influence the electronic media had on the children of the two cultures in the 1980s, then he or she would have to do more than count shards. For Soviet children do not pass as much time watching television as American children do, and when they do, the concerns of conscientious parents in Sverdlovsk are different from those that preoccupy their Detroit counterparts. Soviet parents worry much more about the time that their children spend watching television (and therefore not engaging in other activities) than about the actual content, most of which is quite safe for family viewing. There is almost no overt sex and very little gratuitous violence at any time of day, nor is there much commercial advertising, and none of it directed towards children. As for the videos that are now beginning to circulate among better-off city dwellers, most of them are equally "safe" because they have been made in the USSR. So far, Soviet school children do not have access to the kinds of violent videos that some thirteen-year-olds are known to be watching in the United States.

Both radio and television are under State control in the Soviet Union. The fare they provide ranges from light variety and sports to educational programs and public affairs. Except in Estonia, where signals from Finland can be captured, it has been almost impossible up to now for Soviet viewers to receive programs beamed in from outside. Radio is different. Millions of ordinary Soviets have short-wave receivers. Older children listen to Western music, and they may also listen to foreign-language broadcasts in order to improve their ear. To get the news, however, young children are more likely to listen to their own program called "Pioneer Dawn", which is broadcast across the country at 7:30 every morning.

Soviet radio has three national networks, and at least one station in each area broadcasts in the local language. Each of these networks is required to provide a certain amount of programming for children and young people. On the second network, for example, there are three hours every afternoon (between 3:00 and 6:00 p.m.) when the target audience is under seventeen. There is news every half-hour, children's music, and talk shows that feature children and invite contributions from listeners. The major cultural channel is the third network, which offers evening programs for young people twice a week, broadcasting either classical music with explanations, or plays, poems, and works of fiction that are on the school curriculum. There are also sports programs for children (a friend recalls how eagerly she used to listen to the play-by-play description of an important chess match). Radio stations receive a great deal of correspondence, particularly from children living in small communities for whom radio is an important source of information and entertainment.

Soviet television provides less program time for young children than does Soviet radio. I was told, when I visited the children's section of Gosteleradio (State television and radio), that medical experts have pronounced thirty minutes the maximum amount of time a small child should be allowed to watch television every day. For more than thirty years, half of that time allotment has been taken up by the nightly show "Spokoynoy Nochi, Malyshi" ("Good Night, Little Ones"), which is usually shown around eight in the evening as a spur to bedtime. Most other children's programs are on in the late afternoon or in various daytime slots on the weekend. Soviet television also has three main channels, two national ones and a regional one whose language varies with its location, as well as a daytime channel for school broadcasts. Some programs appear weekly, some twice a month, some monthly.

I often watched television because it was an activity I could share with millions of Soviet citizens without any barrier, except language. I was especially interested in the children's programs, many of which were excellent. For children between eight and twelve years of age there are a number of magazine-type programs, the longest-running being "Budilnik" ("Alarm Clock"), which has been shown on Sunday mornings at 9:30 for more than twenty years. There is a twice-monthly program called "Eralash" ("Hodgepodge"), which specializes in humour and satire, much of it produced by children themselves. "Avtograf" ("Autograph") is a regular literary quiz for young readers, which is supposed to stimulate child viewers to read more. Then there are the programs that showcase talented children from various republics. In a cavernous studio in the children's section of Gosteleradio, I watched young singers from Latvia rehearsing for a program featuring children's choirs from different parts of the country. I was impressed with the ease with which the producer was able to work with the very young. She told me that it came from years of experience in a well-financed sector that produces nothing but programs for children.

The participation of young people is even more striking in programs for teenagers. I will mention only a few. On a program called "Vesyolye Rebyata" ("Cheerful Kids"), highly talented students deliver clever parodies of standard television and radio programs. This program has a wide audience and not just of young people. "Chto? Gde? Kogda?" ("What? Where? When?") is a long-lasting science quiz show involving young competitors and guest scientists. "Do 16 i Starshe" ("Sixteen and Older") is a provocative discussion program based on challenging real-life situations. A recent episode focused on a boy and girl who were involved in an automobile accident. The girl was injured and hospitalized. The boy felt guilty, yet did not go to visit her. He was interviewed, and so were the girl and her mother. The interviews were then juxtaposed and compared to another case with a different outcome. The studio audience was encouraged to debate the issues raised.

During the 1980s, two new television programs for young people appeared and aroused great interest among young and old alike. "Mir i Molodyozh" ("The World and Youth") was first shown in December 1983. This program is filmed live. The production crew goes out in a van to places where young people congregate: schools, sports arenas, clubs, Pushkin Square near the centre of Moscow. Arriving unexpectedly, members of the crew challenge any teenagers they find to a frank discussion of issues that concern them. The teenagers respond willingly. Love and sex, the chance to earn money part time, heavy-metal music, what to do with their spare time when they don't want to do what everyone else is doing, all of these have been topics of recent shows.

However, it is "Dvenadtsaty Etazh" ("The Twelfth Floor") that created the greatest excitement. The program took its name from the twelfth-floor studio at Ostankino, where it was produced once a month. The idea was to find a group of young people from Moscow, link them by satellite (if necessary) to another group somewhere else in the USSR, and then allow both groups to confront bureaucrats and other people in authority who had been brought to the studio.

"The Twelfth Floor" got off to a shaky start. At the beginning people at Gosteleradio were uncertain how far they should go in allowing authority to be questioned. Friends of mine who watched the first programs with unconcealed delight told me that they often thought that each one would be the last. There was a lot of criticism. A program that challenged the school system, for example, as only young people can, drew outraged letters from "highly respected people" who claimed that "television has a damaging effect on the upbringing of our young people and undermines the hitherto unchallenged authority of the school, the teacher and the textbook."

By 1990 "The Twelfth Floor" had made its mark and its innovative director had moved into adult programming. Forty years of commitment to quality programming for young people is now paying off for the adult population as well.

"Where did you go?" "Out."
"What did you do?" "Nothing."

When a child answers "nothing" to an inquisitive parent, what he or she is really saying is, "You couldn't possibly be interested in all the things I have been doing outside in the yard and I couldn't possibly tell you, so it is much easier for me to say 'nothing'." What the child's "nothing" stands for, then, is the vital personal freedom of child's play, the very quality that makes play such an important part of growing up.

In a perceptive essay on the importance of play for children, the distinguished American expert on child development, Bruno Bettelheim, writes that "developing an inner life including fantasies and daydreams is one of the most constructive things a growing child can do". For this to happen, children must have plenty of time for unorganized play. They should not, Bettelheim goes on, be "continually distracted from the task of self-discovery, forced to develop their talents and personalities as those who are in charge of various activities think best".

The provision of healthy and appropriate recreational opportunities for the whole population is one of the goals of the Soviet physical-culture movement. All such opportunities are intended to reinforce the identification of individuals with collectives or groups. Soviet experts in child development have long recognized that children must play games "just for fun", or take up hobbies out of personal interest, if they are going to grow up to use their leisure time constructively as adults. Soviet political authorities, however, are rarely psychologists and their primary interest is to ensure that children's pastimes are safe, educational, and remain within proper limits. Individual talent may be nourished, but not individualism per se.

This is why it matters whether or not Soviet children have enough time to do "nothing". On the surface, it might appear that they don't because so much of their play, and so many of their games and sporting activities, appear to be under the control and direction of adults. Nevertheless, there are good conditions in Soviet cities, as well as in the countryside, for child-directed activities to flourish. As I observed every time I walked through my front door, there are endless cluttered, partly-enclosed city spaces in Moscow and elsewhere whose very untidiness makes them ideal areas for informal group play. There are also abandoned buildings, collapsing stacks of lumber, old untrimmed trees, all of which promise the secret places young children yearn for.

But can these conditions compensate for the long hours that young schoolchildren in the Soviet Union spend in supervised institutional settings, such as the extended-day programs? I do not know. What I do know is that the creation of conditions for the most constructive kind of child's play is a challenge for all cultures.

I have often returned in my thoughts to our unexpected visit to Bratsk and to our enthusiastic sports-minded host. As we careered around the sprawling townsite, he pointed out the parks and playgrounds with the same pride as he showed off his turbines and generators. I have since learned that Bratsk has a sports school for downhill skiers, as well as one for bobsledders, and an international luge course. I am sure that there are many sports clubs in the area, a local Golden Puck club, for example, for children who want to compete in hockey. With its new "lake" and its old forest, there are plenty of opportunities for both organized and unorganized recreation. I expect that younger children are rarely bored in Bratsk. But for a teenager, "nothing" takes on quite a different meaning. The developmental requirements of adolescents with respect to play and recreation are different from those of children. Adolescents need more scope for risk and experimentation, and more chances to come together informally and spontaneously on territory that they feel belongs to them. This does not mean that physical culture, Soviet-style, with its sports and recreation programs, is to be despised. It is a question of balance. In the Soviet Union, the balance tips towards too much structure. In North America, there is often too little. Adults have to let go as children turn into adolescents. But they also have to be around to ensure that youngsters who run into difficulties have the support they need in order to learn from their mistakes.

For adolescents, the most satisfying and growth-promoting play will involve an element of recklessness. Adults should be prepared to recognize this and approve, which they sometimes do, even in the Soviet Union. I once watched a group of teenaged boys climb up some scaffolding around the bell tower of the Savvino-Storozhevsk monastery in Zvenigorod, not far from Moscow. They made it to a high open platform where a great bronze bell stood on brick and rubble. They rested. Then one of them leaned over, picked up a metal bar and, turning around abruptly, swung it at the bell. The ensuing clang could be heard clear across the valley. We all stood stock-still. The boys peered down at us and smiled at their nervous girlfriends. Then, one after another, they swung the bar at the bell. When they finished, and the almost forgotten sound had died away, there was a long pause and then a ragged round of applause arose from the visitors dotted around the territory of the monastery, all of whom, except for ourselves, were Soviets. The boys descended carefully to the base of the tower, collected their girls, and strolled out of the monastery gates, their heads held high.

CHAPTER ELEVEN

The World of Art

Every day, just before noon, a small crowd gathers outside a grey rectangular building on a segment of Moscow's Ring Road known as Sadovaya-Samotyochnaya. Heavy traffic swishes by in both directions but no one pays the slightest attention. All eyes are fixed on a large abstract metal sculpture over the main entrance. On the first stroke of twelve, it comes to life. A golden rooster crows. Twelve geometric forms centred on a sunburst fly open and fairy-tale characters come out to nod and twist and play on musical instruments as the cock continues to crow the hour. The children and adults on the sidewalk below gaze up with delight until the cock falls silent and the mechanical figures retreat behind their doors. The brief show is over.

This unusual animated clock is the trademark of Moscow's Central Puppet Theatre, built in 1970 for Sergey Obraztsov, the Soviet Union's best-known puppet master. It was the first Moscow theatre we went to after our arrival at the Canadian Embassy in 1980, on the assumption that, because our Russian was limited, it would be easier for us to understand a clever puppet show than a stage play. We thoroughly enjoyed our first performance, a parody of the Soviet television shows we had just begun to watch. So we went back, and when our children came to stay, we went back again.

Puppets appeal to everyone. With a few deft movements, a gifted puppeteer can endow a puppet creation with a recognizable personality and give it such vitality that it will draw even the most resistant spectator into its make-believe world. In Obraztsov's theatre, the puppets are shown on a stage that is just above eye level and are worked from below by sticks. The illusion created is so powerful that when the puppeteers come up the side ramps at the end of a performance, carrying their now-lifeless bundles of papier-mâché, cloth, and wood, they look like giants. Then the illusion fades and they return to normal size. The impact of the puppets' magic, however, lingers on.

Obraztsov's theatre has other marvels. The inner lobby is forested with palm trees; exotic plants hang suspended over pools of golden fish. Between the inner and outer lobbies, a maze of glass cases houses the fascinating collection of puppets Obraztsov has brought together from around the world. Wandering in this small museum, I would be reminded of puppet shows I had seen at other times, in other places. One case would evoke the hot day in Mexico when I watched wooden marionettes re-enact the Mexican Revolution before a handful of barefoot urchins. Another would bring to mind the old story-teller I saw in India manipulating shadow puppets behind a sheet to dramatize an episode from the *Ramayana,* that ancient religious epic that still models the behaviour of contemporary Hindu men and women. Still another would take me back to the performance of "Punch and Judy" I attended one day on London's Hampstead Heath and I could hear again the gleeful sound of children's laughter.

In traditional societies, puppetry communicates established values through familiar tales. In revolutionary ones, it is used to inculcate the new social vision in the young. In either case, puppets are supposed to entertain. After the Bolsheviks took power in Russia, puppet shows became the most popular form of entertainment for children, and Sergey Obraztsov emerged as the most original of the new puppet-masters. He survived the Stalinist period by focusing on his craft and taking a profound interest in the role that art can play in the upbringing of young children.

I went with one of my daughters to call on Obraztsov at his theatre on a snowy December afternoon in 1982. At eighty-one years of age, he was an engaging gnome of a man with an open, mobile face. His office was large and bright and full of greenery. He introduced us to his two canaries. One was lively but the other crouched on the floor of its cage, shabby and disconsolate. Obraztsov gazed at it fondly and told us that, although this bird was blind and could no longer fly, it had been his friend for fifteen years and he wasn't going to abandon it now. Indeed, in his view, one of the primary concerns for children's artists should be to teach children to be kind to all living creatures. He is convinced that there is an indissoluble link between art and morality, and this conviction determines the direction of his work, particularly for children.

Obraztsov is happy about the vitality of puppetry in the Soviet Union. At the time that we spoke, there were more than 130 well-established professional puppet theatres in the country as well as hundreds of amateur groups. They continue to thrive and to develop original and distinctive styles. Obraztsov's own style was influenced by his training as an actor and his life in the theatre. His productions on the puppet stage are brilliant and racy. I have never seen anything like them.

Obraztsov had a message for us, and not much time to give it, so he dropped the subject of puppetry and proceeded to discuss the ways in which theatre and cinema influence the aesthetic and moral development of children. He cautioned us about the emotional power of drama telling us that it must be "administered" to children with care. All of us should pay attention to the absorptive capacity of children, he said, for, like medicine, a dose that will cure an adult may make a child sick. Children should not be overloaded with images nor exposed to material for which they are not ready. Nor should they encounter gratuitous scenes of cruelty. He, too, had seen a "Punch and Judy" show in England but he deplored the scene in which the little pink pig is pushed through a machine to come out the other end as a sausage. He was distressed that the watching children laughed because, in his view, hurting a living thing (even in a puppet show) should never be seen as humorous.

Obraztsov looked at his watch and told us apologetically that
we would have to go because he had to rest up for his great-
grandchild's second birthday party that evening. But he walked
with us down the corridor to the elevator and along the way
we were allowed tantalizing glimpses of theatrical magic through
half-opened doors: puppets under construction, costumes being
sewn, small rehearsals. Then he left us with a friendly handshake.

As the elevator descended, my seventeen-year-old daughter
sighed. "What a pity," she said, "that old people spend so much
of their energy on the recitation of old 'truths'." But I told her
that this was precisely why I had found our visit to Obraztsov so
useful. He had spoken as a true representative of the traditional
Soviet approach to art for children, and his career as a puppet-
master, which spans almost the whole of the Soviet period, is
an excellent demonstration of the value that has been placed on
the arts for children since the time of the Revolution. Although
many of his current productions are designed for adults, it was
Obraztsov's work for children that initially brought him the
support of the State, and without that, he would never have been
able to establish and maintain his theatre. He repays his debt
by remaining faithful to the idea of the moral responsibility of
artists and of the art they create. This moralistic approach to art,
so characteristic of the Soviet Union, is not just a product of the
Revolution. It has long been part of the Russian tradition and is
admirably captured by Leo Tolstoy's essay "What Is Art?" I can
think of no better way to preface my description of the various
art forms that make up the Soviet child's world of art today—
theatre, musical theatre, music, the visual arts, cinema—than by
looking at Tolstoy's essay.

What Is Art?

Three peasant lads posed this question for Tolstoy on a moonless
winter night in the middle of the last century. He had been
teaching them all day in his school at Yasnaya Polyana, and now
he was walking them home along the snowy pathway. Under
the dark trees, the boys drew near and he began to tell them
stories about wolves and Caucasian robbers and how the brave
man sang before he died. "Lev Nikolaevich," said ten-year-old

Fedka, "why does one learn singing? I often think, why, really, does one?" "And what is drawing for? And why write well?" asked Tolstoy, not knowing at all (he admits) how to explain to the boys what art is for. But they talked about "usefulness" and "goodness" and "beauty", and when they parted to go their separate ways, they felt closer to one another than they had ever felt before.

In 1898, thirty-seven years after this incident, Tolstoy published "What Is Art?", a long essay in which he was finally able to lay out to his own satisfaction his answer to the problem that the boys had set him that evening. By this time he had come to the conclusion that the true purpose of human life was to come together with others in brotherly union, and that the true role of art was to transmit such "universal feelings as can unite all men". His experience with the boys had shown that by telling stories he could do just that. Tolstoy is often quoted by contemporary Soviet theorists on art who agree with his definition of art as "a means of human communication bringing people together through shared emotions". They are also attracted by his insistence that the mark of true art is "infectiousness". If a work of art is unable to "infect" its audience with its human values, then it is false art. By such a definition, many of the Socialist Realist paintings produced during the Soviet period claim to be "true" art, truer than most of the abstract or non-objective paintings produced in the West, which make little sense to the average person.

Tolstoy dreamed about a future in which ordinary men, women, and children would be able to enjoy great art and in which the standard for assessing the value of a work of art would be whether or not it was able to satisfy "all those great masses of people who undergo the natural conditions of the laborious life". Like many great artists, he was attuned to the vital currents of his time, and some of the things he predicted about the future of art in Russia, particularly with respect to children, have come true. The strength of the artistic institutions for children in the USSR today is certainly connected to the aesthetic aims of the revolutionaries who, like Anatoly Lunacharsky and his colleagues at Narkompros (the Ministry of the Enlightenment) picked up and used Tolstoy's ideas is to shape the sensibilities of Soviet children, to deepen their awareness of human values, and to incline them towards virtue (Soviet-style). Luckily for Soviet children, and for those of us who accompany them into their world of art, this task is often executed with deftness and humour.

Theatre for Children

The Bolshoi Theatre stands in the centre of Moscow, not far from Red Square. It is a neo-classical building of great beauty, and above the grand pillars that dominate its façade, four splendid rearing horses draw the chariot of Apollo. When this group was sculpted in 1825, the Russian theatre-going public was made up of merchants and aristocrats. Now the god of music and poetry looks out at a massive bust of Karl Marx on the other side of Sverdlov Square and down on the people with no influence who wait patiently before every performance hoping that someone will arrive with a spare ticket. To the left of the Bolshoi, facing onto the square, is the long building of the Maly Theatre. Actors have performed there since 1824. To the right, in a place of equal honour, is the Central Children's Theatre.

It is not by accident that there is a separate children's theatre so close to the Bolshoi. Members of the new revolutionary government, especially Lunacharsky, fully understood the power of theatre to harness emotions and shape attitudes. So, professional theatres for children were created throughout the country during the early years of the Soviet state. Moscow's Children's Theatre was founded in 1921. In 1936, renamed the Central Children's Theatre, it moved to its present site. Despite differences in style and repertoire, it and every other children's theatre in the Soviet Union continue to be committed to their original task of "cultivating moral values and high ideals" in children and youth.

Theatre for young people in the Soviet Union today is professional theatre with actors who have been specifically trained to reach their designated audience. Children are rarely employed (although they frequently appear in children's movies). Instead, the roles of children are played by "travesty" actors and actresses who often become quite famous for their ability to act and look like children. Real children, it is assumed, will find plenty of outlets for their dreams of acting in the after-school drama groups that abound.

All theatres in the USSR, including opera and ballet, are obliged by decree to mount regular productions for children. Most Soviet children are thus assured of at least minimal exposure to these art forms as they grow up. In their own playhouses, about a quarter of the repertoire is occupied by works by foreign authors, both classic and modern. Of the rest, many will be works that are being studied in school, a dramatization of a poem by Pushkin, for example, or of a story by a popular Soviet writer for children such as Arkady Gaidar. In the Union republics there are also "national" theatres for children. In Yerevan, for example, there is a children's theatre that only produces works in the Armenian language. In other cities, such as Riga, the capital of Latvia, the same children's theatre will mount productions in both Latvian and Russian. Plays and musical works drawn from the many national cultures of the USSR enter the repertoires of children's theatres elsewhere in the Union.

Children under five are not permitted to attend professional children's theatres. They are not considered sufficiently mature (or sufficiently well-behaved) to benefit from the experience of theatre-going. Instead, puppet shows and plays are brought to their kindergartens or can be seen in parks. After they enter school, however, Soviet children are encouraged to become regular theatre-goers. The Theatre for Young Spectators in Leningrad, which was established at the same time as Moscow's Children's Theatre, holds a festival to celebrate coming to the theatre for the first time. Most performances for children under ten are held on weekend mornings so that parents and children can come together. The director of the Leningrad theatre at the time that I visited it, Z. Korogodsky, reminded me, as Obraztsov had, that theatre is an art that attacks all the senses and that younger children should have a loving adult beside them to mediate the experience. Theatre tickets for all age groups are very cheap, and more than thirty million children and teenagers attend performances every year. Millions more take part in amateur performances.

In the autumn of 1984, I invited an engaging nine-year-old Soviet girl and her mother to accompany me to a play at Moscow's Central Children's Theatre so that I could see what a professional stage production for children was actually like. We chose a double-bill featuring two of Pushkin's famous *skazki* , the light-hearted verse-dramas he created out of traditional fairy-tales. Western parents know these stories as "The Fisherman and the Golden Fish" and "Snow White and the Seven Dwarfs".

It was just before curtain time when we arrived, and every seat was occupied. Taffeta bows bobbed as little girls settled down. Boys were neat in jackets and ties. It was a chilly September afternoon, and the six-year-old boy who sat between me and his very large, very blonde mama wore white tights under his grey shorts. He did not appear to mind, and he seemed to enjoy the show. So did we—with reservations. When this production had first been mounted in 1966 (most children's productions remain in repertory for a long time), it must have been delightful. By the time we saw it, however, it had been played too many times; the costumes and sets were wearing out and some of the actors had gone stale.

The first tale was best. The poor fisherman (very well acted) caught a life-size golden fish who rewarded him with three wishes for letting it go. His vain wife used up the wishes on outlandish clothes and ostentatious dwellings. She over-reached herself, of course, and was reduced in the twinkling of an eye (and a clever set change) to her former state. The children watched this cheerful but uncompromising moral tale with fascination and applauded spontaneously when it was over. The second play broke the spell. The actors seemed bored, the children grew restless, and the final applause was thin.

During the intermission, we explored the theatre. The upstairs lobby contained photographs of past productions, cases of costumes, displays of children's drawings, all of which were interesting enough to hold the attention of two adults and one child while everyone else waited in line to buy something to eat. And then had to swallow fast, because food and drink are definitely *not* allowed in the auditorium. The Central Children's Theatre will not put up with "uncultured" behaviour. In fact, it has published a pamphlet listing the rules of theatrical etiquette, which it circulates to schools and makes available to young play-goers when they arrive. Children are advised to arrive twenty-five minutes before the curtain rises so that they will have enough time to check their coats and find their seats. They are warned to put their coat-check tokens in their pockets. "Don't play with it for you are sure to drop it in the end and…it will make a disturbing noise and may roll away." Exactly.

After several other carefully explained "don'ts", the young theatre-goer is finally given permission to do something: "If there is something you don't understand in the play, ask the theatre teacher on duty for an explanation." Every theatre has a pedagogical section that works directly with schools to prepare classes for visits. Some theatres also invite parents and teachers to see a new play before it is performed, so that they can help the children appreciate it. And a teacher attends each performance in order to explain the play to any child who cares to ask. If the close association between aesthetics and ethics, that the Soviets are so keen on, is to be maintained, then no educational opportunity must be missed.

The existence of so many theatres for children has engendered a large cultural community devoted to the creation and production of works for the young. Even during the most difficult years of Stalinist oppression some experimentation was permissible in works of art for children. So, artists, to whom other outlets were closed, channelled their creative talents in this direction. Some of these works served as vehicles to carry messages to the population at large. An example is a musical based on *Alice in Wonderland*, with lyrics by the enormously popular balladeer, Vladimir Vysotsky. The translation is very clever. The word-play that has delighted generations of English children adapts quite easily into Russian, a language equally rich and flexible. So does the topsy-turvy logic. When the Mouse dries up Alice's Pool of Tears with a boring lecture, he chooses a history lesson about Peter the Great. But why, sings the Mouse, did Peter open only a "window on the West" and not a door through which it would have been so much easier to pass? The Russian version emphasizes Alice's struggle to hold on to her identity through her unexpected changes in size and shape, and Vysotsky added a sly lyric about time (remember the Mad Hatter's tea party?) that any

Soviet of an older generation will recognize as a comment on the misuses of time in Stalin's days.

Another example is a play that is often produced by Obraztsov at his puppet theatre. Written by Yevgeny Shvarts, a well-known writer of children's stories, *The Dragon* conveys as moral a message as Tolstoy could have wished for, in a light-hearted and unsentimental manner. Only the most unimaginative person, young or old, could fail to be amused by it. And very few could miss its lesson about the corrupting power of tyranny on tyrant and tyrannized alike. The play was written in 1943 but it was performed only once (in Leningrad) before the death of Stalin and not many times afterwards, until Obraztsov chose it for his theatre. It was not written for the puppet stage, of course, but it lends itself well to Obraztsov's imaginative direction. Here is a brief synopsis.

A dragon has terrorized a small town for more than four hundred years until the people have become so used to it that they ritually sacrifice a maiden to it every year, with scarcely a second thought. Enter Lancelot and a talking cat. No one really wants him to destroy the dragon because, as one of the characters says, "The only way to be free of dragons is to have one of your own." Nevertheless, Lancelot (having fallen in love with that year's promised maiden) slays the dragon in a fierce battle. He is badly wounded in the fight and retreats to the Black Mountains to spend a year in the Cave of Records, where all the crimes and miseries of the world are recorded every day. In his absence, the Mayor claims to have been the real dragon-slayer, and the still-subdued population allows him to take over the dragon's place. He imprisons all the creative people and prepares to marry Lancelot's girl to his son.

In the last act, which takes place a year later, Lancelot returns to complete what he started when he killed the dragon. He soon recognizes that his job has just begun. He says to the Weavers, whom he releases from prison, "We have some very tricky and boring work to do, even worse than embroidery. The dragon has to be killed in each and every one." In almost the last speech of the play, the Gardener pleads, "Be patient with us, Sir Lancelot, I do beg you to be patient. Tend us gently. The fires you light will help us to grow. But take out the weeds carefully or you might damage the new roots."

To his credit, Obraztsov staged *The Dragon* before Gorbachev came to power. That he was able to do so is, I think, an indication of the indulgence that Soviet authorities have accorded to art for children for many years. While *The Dragon* was clearly written as an anti-Stalinist statement, its theme is a universal one and its admonitions are as timely now as they were then. I would like to think that its production in the early 1980s in a theatre for children was a harbinger of the current climate of *glasnost*, and of a more critical attitude to authority.

It should be noted, however, that the adolescent population in the Soviet Union is not reached as successfully by theatre as young children are. One reason is that there are not enough plays in the "Theatres for Young Spectators" that deal with the bursting sexuality of teenagers. "To talk about love in all its complexity on the stage of the youth theatre is still considered indecent and anti-pedagogical," laments one theatre director. And another commentator complains that "children's theatres do not trust teenagers". A countervailing force to adolescent disenchantment may be found in some of the theatrical circles that are associated with Pioneer palaces, and particularly with houses of culture. There young people are no longer spectators but active participants, and some imaginative leaders encourage them to invent and improvise and to use theatrical means for the expression of their own values and emotions. These are the groups to watch for the future of Soviet theatre.

Musical Theatre and Opera

Children have helped Natalya Sats to survive. She was only fifteen at the time of the Revolution but, grown-up beyond her years, she quickly found work in the new state, promoting the arts for children. Before very long, she became the director of Moscow's Children's Theatre. In 1936, she achieved a coup by persuading Sergey Prokofiev to compose *Peter and the Wolf* as a way of introducing children to the instruments of the orchestra. She narrated its first performance. In August 1937, during the Stalinist purges, she was sent to prison. Even there, she managed to mount theatricals. After her release, she lived in exile, first in Sverdlovsk and then in Alma-Ata, founding children's theatres in both places.

After the death of Stalin, Natalya Sats was allowed to return to Moscow, but she was not invited back to the Central Children's Theatre. So, with her usual determination, she set out to organize another theatre for children, this time a musical one. As the daughter of the composer, Ilya Sats, she had always loved music. In the early 1930s, she had produced operas in Germany and Argentina. In 1962, she convinced the respected composer Dmitry Kabalevsky to join her in calling for a children's musical theatre. This is how she explained the importance of her plan to the Union of Composers: "With its lively action, imagery and bright colours, theatre will help to attract children to music that sounds on the stage and the orchestra pit, while music will add even more profundity to the ideas expounded in the play." Dmitry Shostakovich also supported the idea and sent, through her, the following message to young people: "Love and study the great art of music. It will open up for you a whole world of lofty feelings and ideas, it will enrich your spirit and make you better." On November 21, 1965, her children's musical theatre opened its doors.

Since then Natalya Sats has gone from strength to strength. In 1979, in celebration of the International Year of the Child, a new building was constructed for her Children's Musical Theatre on Vernadsky Prospekt in the Lenin Hills. This is one of the most interesting pieces of modern architecture in Moscow. Carefully designed with young children in mind, it is set in a wide park, dotted with fountains and story-book figures cast in bronze. At its highest point, the building is surmounted by a stylized bluebird whose upswept wings encircle a harp. *The Bluebird* , one of the most popular opera-ballets her theatre produces, has music written by her father and new libretto by her daughter. I thoroughly enjoyed it. It contains all the elements that Natalya Sats thinks important for introducing children to musical theatre: fantasy, humour, dance, a good story, and a moral.

I met with Natalya Sats in March 1983. At that time she was nearing eighty and, although she had recently been ill, I found her full of vigour, openly defying her age. She was sitting at a desk in a large room on the second floor of her theatre, surrounded by souvenirs of her trips around the world. She turned to greet me with a theatrical gesture, waving a handful of letters. Every day, she announced, a stack of letters arrive for her from children all over the USSR. She tries, she said, to read each one herself so that she can keep in touch with what children are thinking about music.

Mme. Sats described her theatre. If children are going to love the theatre, she said, they have to be caught up in its magic. So she has devised tricks to ensnare them from the moment they enter her doors. Catwalks span the entrance hall, from which costumed actors call down greetings to the arriving children. At one end of the lobby, birds sing out to them from an elegant white aviary. In the cafeteria, gaily painted tables and chairs, just their size, wait for them. In another room, brilliant laquered panels, on which the former icon masters of Palekh have painted fairy stories, hang from ceiling to floor. What child could resist!

The main theatre holds 1,200 child spectators, a smaller one, 400. Performances are almost always sold out. During one week in June 1983, a child could have seen *The Bluebird*, or attended a performance of Puccini's *Madame Butterfly* or a musical comedy based on "Snow White", or a play with music written by the same author as *The Dragon* featuring a wolf who is lonely and frightened, and no longer wants to be the villain of human fantasies. The small hall was offering a one-act opera by Mozart and musical based on "The Swineherd" by Hans Christian Andersen. There are 450 performances a year on two stages watched by more than half a million spectators. These performances are highly professional, the actors young and enthusiastic, the musicians talented. The young audience sits in rapt attention. Raisa Gorbachev took the wives of foreign ambassadors to a performance there on International Children's Day, June 1, 1989. Natalya Sats is still going strong.

Until recently Mme. Sats's children's musical theatre was the only one of its kind (in the world, she claimed). Now there is one in Kiev and another to be opened in Leningrad. Since it was established, her theatre has provided an opportunity and a livelihood for many a musician and composer interested in creating music for children. However, Natalya Sats does not have a monopoly on children's musical theatre. All over the country serious composers, who disagree with what they see as Sats's slightly patronizing attitude to children, have their works regularly performed. One of these is Sergey Banevich, a young Leningrad composer. He has written that the "notion that children are unable to understand 'adult' feelings and they they should be entertained strikes me as completely wrong". But he agrees with Sats that aesthetic education is also ethical education and that "the feelings of joy, pain and compassion evoked by art cannot but leave their imprint in the young soul", even if it takes a long time for a child to understand what it is that he or she has felt.

At the Kirov Theatre in Leningrad, I went to a performance of an opera Banevich wrote for children, *The Story of Gerda and Kai*, based on "The Snow Queen" by Hans Christian Andersen. I read this story many times in my childhood, and it still haunts my imagination. It was my introduction to the gratuitous nature of evil. I have never been able to forget the wicked troll who flew above the earth with a mirror that distorted even the most innocent of human gestures. Nor how the mirror was dropped and shattered and how a glass splinter entered a little boy's eye to blind him to normal human affections. I was curious to see how this disturbing tale could be turned into an opera. Banevich told me later on that he, too, had been troubled by "The Snow Queen" as a child. Stories like these lie dormant in a child's heart until the adult world confirms them. However, since we know that Gerda's love and persistence enable her, after many adventures, to rescue Kai from the Snow Queen, the story's message is not hopeless.

The Kirov produced *The Story of Gerda and Kai* sumptuously. The sets and costumes were lavish, the singing was excellent, and the acting good. The music was melodic and woven seamlessly with the story. If the tenor singing Kai was too plump and "mature" to be credible, the soprano in the role of Gerda was perfect. The little girl sitting next to me (not quite five, admitted her mother) was restless, but the rest of the young audience was extraordinarily attentive to what was happening on the stage. This surprised me because what I saw and heard was an opera produced with all of opera's traditional conventions.

No concessions were made to the age of the audience, no explanations came from the stage. When I met the composer and the conductor afterwards, they insisted that children should be introduced to opera as a serious art form with no apologies. With a sigh, they agreed with me about the tenor (I caught a whiff of backstage politics), but otherwise they were proud of their production. It had been presented that day for the forty-ninth time since 1980, not a bad record for a children's opera in one of the world's great opera houses.

Music

Of all the arts, music is probably the one that is most highly valued in the Soviet Union. Children are taught to appreciate it from a very early age. In kindergarten they sing; at school there is a complete music curriculum. There are school concerts and children's festivals where they can perform and thousands of amateur groups (circles) where they can learn to dance or to play a musical instrument, including traditional folk ones. There are also, at last count, 8,388 children's music schools with a seven-year program serving approximately 1,400,000 children and adolescents. Children go to these schools after their normal school day for as long as seven years, three sessions a week, three hours at a time. They study music theory, music history, and ensemble playing. Every graduate can read music fluently, and play at least one instrument. This type of school, for which there is a nominal fee, replaces the individual or small group lessons that I used to purchase for my own children. Children who attend them often develop a collective of shared interest that becomes more important to them than their regular school collective. After graduating, some students go on to advanced training. An exceptionally gifted child will be encouraged to enter a music conservatory (combining academics and music) as soon as his or her talents are recognized. Most students at these after-school music schools, however, carry what they have learned there into their adult lives primarily as personal enrichment. This kind of music school teaches classical music. The amateur jazz and rock groups that play at parties are more likely to come together at an ordinary school or in a house of culture where drums and guitars are sometimes available for after-school use and where a group of friends can often find a room to jam in.

Classical and authentic folk music and, these days, even jazz, have a much higher approval rating from the guardians of Soviet culture than what we call "popular" music. According to Soviet theorists, it is music of the first category that renders the individual more responsive, more compassionate and high-minded. In recent years, Soviet authorities have been trying to create a strong bias in the general population towards classical music by means of a music curriculum developed for the general school by the late Dmitry Kabalevsky.

Kabalevsky was born in St. Petersburg in 1904. A multi-talented child, he painted and wrote poetry at the same time as he learned to play the piano. He began to compose music in the mid-1920s and then to teach at the Moscow Conservatory of Music. He became a full professor in 1939, and remained on the faculty for the next thirty-five years. He had a successful, if unspectacular, career as a composer. One of my daughters used to practise some of the short piano pieces he composed for children during the years she studied piano, and I became very well acquainted with them. Luckily, as her captive audience of one, I found them delightful to listen to.

Kabalevsky had a lifelong interest in music for children, and towards the end of it, he turned all his energies to mass education. When I interviewed him in 1984 at the Union of Composers in Moscow, he told me that early in the 1970s he lost interest in developing professional artists at the Conservatory and left to devote himself to the musical education of ordinary children. He had often written about music and had spoken at schools, at children's camps, and on radio and television, but now he felt it was time to develop a universal school program for all children. So he went into schools to talk to children and seek their help to crystallize his ideas. Convinced that *every* child is capable of appreciating music and learning the fundamentals of musical culture, Kabalevsky introduced his experimental curriculum slowly, testing it with children every step of the way. By the time I met him, his curriculum (in spite of considerable resistance from the Academy of Pedagogical

Sciences) had become a compulsory part of the school program of the Russian Federation and was being followed by eight million children. He cherished the hope that it would soon spread throughout the whole of the USSR, although he anticipated delays in certain Union republics until its adaptation to the musical traditions of the Soviet Union's many different nationalities was complete.

I asked Kabalevsky what distinguished his approach from the music lessons that earlier generations of Soviet children had known. "The goal of lessons in all the versions of the old curriculum was to develop in youngsters the skills of choral singing," he said, but, while choral singing is "a splendid art and a splendid way of nurturing a sense of collectivism and responsibility", singing alone could not provide Soviet children with a significant musical culture.

Kabalevsky then told me that he had designed his curriculum so that it would start from the life experience of first-grade pupils. "The song, the dance, and the march are the most widespread, most popular and most democratic forms of music," he said, referring to these three musical forms as "the three whales" on which musical culture rests, an image taken from a Russian folk myth that envisages the whole earth supported by three whales. "It is the song, the dance, and the march," he explained, "that connect the entire rich edifice of classical music back to the people and to the soil." From song children can move to opera, from dance to ballet, from marches to symphonic music. In this way they begin to build their musical knowledge.

The music Kabalevsky recommends for use in his first-grade musical curriculum reflects each of these three "whales". The theme of the first quarter is the emotional quality of music and the nature of musical genres. Children are asked: what feelings does music convey? In the Soviet Union, it is assumed that six-year-olds will possess a rich enough vocabulary to answer this question with some subtlety. They should be able, for example, to talk about music being "festive" or "solemn" as well as "sad" or "happy". The question for the second quarter is: *what* does music tell us? Classes during this period are intended to help children understand that music has content that cannot be translated directly into words. The question for the third quarter is: *how* does music tell us things? Children are then introduced to musical discourse and to the means of musical expression: harmony, intonation, rhythm, and so on. The last quarter summarizes what the children have learned. In addition to acquiring listening-to-music skills, they should have come to understand that music always expresses human feelings, but that, because it has its own language, it can only tell us something important if we learn that language.

I was struck by the force of Kabalevsky's conviction that music can change people, ennoble them, and educate their hearts. His own heart was unquestionably "educated". He was the most impressive and perhaps the wisest of the cultural elders whom I consulted about the world of art for Soviet children. When he died in February 1987, I felt a real sense of loss.

Visual Arts

Thanks to Kabalevsky's inspiration, determination, and reputation, the music curriculum he developed is off to a good start. This is not the case with the visual arts. Although an innovative program, similar in spirit to Kabalevsky's music curriculum, has been under preparation for some years, it has encountered considerable resistance. I first learned about this program when I read an article on aesthetic education, published in 1979, praising a program designed by the painter Boris Nemensky. Yet seven years later, in 1986, Nemensky was complaining in *Literaturnaya Gazeta* that he had still not received official approval. In 1987, however, the Academy of Pedagogical Sciences assured me in writing that the program had begun to be implemented and was, in fact, being offered in every school district in the RFSFR, if not in every school. The degree of resistance to Nemensky's curriculum, so much greater than that encountered by Kabalevsky, reflects, I think, the difference between Soviet attitudes to music and Soviet attitudes to the visual arts. Unless it is imitating the song of a bird or the sound of falling water, music is a non-representational art form and no one expects it to be otherwise. But this is not the case for drawing, painting, and sculpture.

In the Western world, art as representation has long since lost whatever privileged status it had, and the free expression of the individual artist is cherished no matter how he or she may choose to exercise it. There was a period around the time of the Revolution when Russian painters, sculptors, and architects were among the most dynamic and creative in the world, constantly expressing new visual ideas. However, the ideology that would make Socialist Realism the only acceptable artistic style for so many years soon began to suffocate them. Many of the best artists who had stayed on after the Revolution, or who had returned to the new Soviet state from abroad, left the country in the mid-1920s to escape its constrictions. Others ceased producing works of any great originality. The Paris-Moscow exhibition held at the Pushkin Museum in Moscow in 1981 was probably the first opportunity for large numbers of Soviet citizens born after 1917 to see the work of these artists.

During the years I lived in Moscow, I saw a number of official and non-official art shows that included many contemporary paintings that were of considerable interest. But only once or twice did I encounter a work that made me look at the world in a new way. I know there is no lack of talent; it can occasionally be glimpsed in the open-air markets recently established in Izmailovo Park and elsewhere. However, opportunities to display and sell are not particularly helpful if there are no standards. Painting and sculpture will only flourish in a rich and varied visual-arts climate that includes critics and collectors with discrimination. The cross-fertilization that took place between Paris and Moscow in the first three decades of the century, with such exciting results, ceased nearly sixty years ago, and there has been nothing to replace it. Our ways of seeing are more influenced by the art that surrounds us than most of us realize. This is one thing I have learned from living for years in cultures as different from one another as those of France, Mexico, India, and the Soviet Union. I suspect that the Soviet officials who are charged with making bureaucratic decisions about the visual-arts curriculum in the schools have had so little exposure to anything other than representational art that they find it almost impossible to grasp that expression must precede form in the formation of a child's artistic sensibility.

I can imagine what their art classes were like when they were children because, when I looked into the visual-arts curriculum for nursery, kindergarten, and primary-school children in the early 1980s, this is what I found: teachers dependent on a manual prepared for them by the Institute of Pre-school Education in 1979 that instructed them to teach art scientifically, using methods that were systematic and sequential. So, three-year-olds, who are nothing if not spontaneous, were sat down at little tables, told to sit up straight, and shown how to hold a crayon properly. Access to the paint-pot was put off until they had learned to dip their brushes in the right way and shake off the excess.

The visual-arts curriculum described by this manual is geared to the development of skills necessary for reproducing the external appearance of an object: its form, size, and structure. Once they have learned to hold their pencils or crayons, a teacher is supposed to lead her little pupils towards representation by means of a particular task. Children may draw strings, for example, for the coloured circles the teacher has painted and thus learn to "represent" balloons. By the end of the year, the children are expected to draw circles themselves. Those who are still having difficulty with this task can be helped by the technique of passive movement, which involves the teacher guiding the child's hand in a circular motion. Teachers are also supposed to encourage their little artists to evaluate one another's work, to point out which drawing looks most like the pretty flower in the vase, and so forth.

Children taught according to this manual are clearly being instructed in techniques of purely representational art. There is scarcely a mention of art as expression. After I had read the manual, I understood why the art work I saw in kindergartens and schools was so conventional. I am told that this "scientific" approach to the teaching of art is what still prevails in the kindergartens and general schools that have not yet been selected to try out Nemensky's method. A Canadian painter I know was so unnerved by the row of paintings of building-cranes he saw on the wall of a classroom in Uzbekistan that he congratulated the child who had had the originality (and the courage) to paint her crane facing in the opposite direction.

Fortunately, the classroom is not the only place where children can learn about the visual arts in the Soviet Union. The delightful paintings, drawings, and models I came across in Pioneer palaces and in theatres, libraries, and exhibition halls often stood out in striking contrast to the art displayed in schools. These works appear to have been chosen for their expressiveness rather than for their technique. Interested children have access to a great variety of out-of-school art activities. Pioneer palaces and houses of culture often have excellent facilities for arts and crafts, and many artists volunteer to teach art to young children. Great museums like the Hermitage have special clubs and there is a monthly magazine called *The Young Artist* with informative articles and fine colour reproductions. There are also a number of four-year after-school art schools for keen students, run on the same principles as the music schools I have already described. And, of course, there are a few highly specialized art schools for the truly gifted.

A practising artist usually understands, from his or her own experience, how to teach art to young children better than an ordinary classroom teacher, who feels safer with a set curriculum. So, a certain amount of tension exists between them, an example of which turned up in *Izvestia* in April 1986. Some Moscow artists had received a letter from a school director seeking their help to decorate the hall of her new school. When the artists arrived to paint a mural for the children, the director was absent. They set to work, and all day long they created marvels while the children crowded around to give advice. When "the vivid fairy-tale drawing which illuminated the hall like a sun" was finished, the assistant director, who had been left in charge of the school, was very upset. She thanked the artists politely but, as soon as they had gone, she called up two other teachers and the three of them took green paint and rollers from the basement and covered up the offending work.

When the children returned to school on Monday morning they were astonished to find a blank green wall. "Where's the yellow horse? Where's the cheerful bird? Where's the fairy-tale?"

they asked. Where indeed? No one knew how to answer them or to explain "why...a person holding some post thinks he has the right to forbid, to destroy or to bar something whose true value he does not know and does not attempt to find out". This cautionary tale indicates the kinds of problems that are bound to crop up as the new visual-arts curriculum is introduced.

The best climate for children's art exists in the non-Russian parts of the Soviet Union, where art as expression has long been valued. Latvians, Lithuanians, and Estonians are well known for their artistic creativity and their sense of design. When I saw an exceptional exhibition of lyrical graphics on the theme of "night" in the lobby of Leningrad's symphony hall one evening, I was not surprised to discover that they were the work of students at the boarding-school for the arts in Vilnius (the capital of Lithuania). This school is named for a revered Lithuanian composer and painter, M.K. Ciurlionis, whose mystical works are as popular now as they were when they were created at the turn of the century. In honour of its multi-talented namesake, this school teaches music and dance in addition to the visual arts and expects it graduates to have a profound knowledge of all three art forms, although they may only practise one.

Georgia and Armenia are also strong in the visual arts, and both republics have children's art galleries that treat child artists with the respect that is normally reserved for adults. Tbilisi, the capital of Georgia, is an ancient city that has been conquered and partially destroyed over and over again. Now money is being spent on recapturing the flavour of the city's oldest quarters. One of the handsome restored buildings on the main thoroughfare has been turned into a children's art gallery. On the day I visited it, the ground-floor rooms were full of lively works from all over the Soviet Union. There was also a small travelling exhibition from the United States. It struck me, as it has in all the countries I have lived in, that children's paintings vary more with a child's age than with his or her nationality. The theme of one room of paintings was sports. I appreciated a Soviet ten-year-old's vision of a hockey game. The only thing that marked it as Soviet rather than Canadian was the fact that the player lying on the ice had

"NHL" on his sweater whereas the group of skaters whose arms were raised in victory had "CCCP".

On the upper floor of the gallery, we found an unusual exhibition, a retrospective show of works by a seventeen-year-old boy who had just died of leukemia. We were led past the paintings and drawings by his black-garbed aunt who spoke of him in funereal tones as "The Boy" and referred reverentially to his deep philosophical insights. He had been exceptionally talented. His works were haunting, extraordinarily intricate, strange visions of another reality. There is a special sense of loss when the life of a gifted young person is extinguished, but it is a fine thing to have a gallery prepared to hang a one-boy show.

At the children's gallery in Yerevan, we saw a group show. This was not a collective show, as are most exhibitions of children's art, but one that included several works by each of seven or eight child artists, hung so that they could be appreciated on their own or in comparison with the others. The paintings were notable for bright colour and large, open compositions, quite the opposite of the work I had seen in kindergartens and schools. The gallery's founder and director, Genrikh Igityan, is a firm believer in art as expression and in the possibility that a child may be just as true an artist at the age of ten as at the age of thirty. He has been publicly agitating for a museum of contemporary art in Moscow for some time, and now that he has been elected to the Congress of People's Deputies, he may have more influence.

When I visited Igityan's children's gallery in 1982, it was preparing to become a full artistic centre. Now the building houses a children's orchestra, a theatre for plays written and produced by children, a film studio for aspiring film-makers, and a museum, as well as a gallery. The staff spoke of their director with admiration, and shared Igityan's conviction that, if children are not given the opportunity to express their creativity and cultivate their talents before the onset of adolescence, their passion for art will be stifled, and everyone will lose.

The children of Armenia are fortunate to have such a centre, but those who are able to take advantage of it are very few compared to the total number of children in the USSR. In fact, according to Boris Nemensky, in the end, and in spite of all the programs I have described, only 3 per cent of Soviet children get involved in serious out-of-school art activities. If more children are to learn to express themselves artistically, and to appreciate great art, then it must be done through the school system.

Those who are pushing for a curriculum in aesthetic education that will "ensure a high level and universality of aesthetic development in school pupils" rephrase Tolstoy's question "What is art?" in their own way. What is the distinction, they ask, between an artistic and a non-artistic depiction of life, between a painting, say, and a documentary photograph taken by an automatic camera? Their answer is that the work of art embodies the thoughts and feelings of the artist in such a way that his or her ideas and emotions can be grasped by others through the material form (pigments, musical notes, dance movements) in which they have been expressed. A documentary can be only a partial record of a real event, whereas a work of art can capture its essence. If children are only taught to copy, or to look at paintings for the "story" they tell, how can they learn to appreciate the *real* relationship between form and content in art? They will remain quite insensitive to the inner meaning of a work of art.

Children should be encouraged to explore any available medium, such as crayons, paint, or clay, to its very limits, and in their own way. They have to experiment. If they feel that blue expresses their attitude to an apple, then they must be allowed to see what a blue apple looks like, and not be criticized for failing to paint it red. They must test how shapes relate to one another, play with colours, turn things upside down. As children grow older, and their ideas develop, then they will feel the need for greater technical mastery in order to express them. They will also begin to pass beyond the ostensible subject matter of a great painting to relate to the feelings and ideas that the artist has expressed through it.

Although these ideas about art education parallel my own, I am paraphrasing them from Soviet sources. I read Boris Nemensky's lament in *Literaturnaya Gazeta* with great sympathy. It is clear that the program that he and his colleagues devised ran into strong resistance because it challenged the whole concept of art as representation, which so many people in the Soviet Union have been brought up to accept. In the new climate of *glasnost,* the program has finally been approved. If it gains the same acceptance as Kabalevsky's music curriculum, then the Soviet Union will have an arts curriculum for school children that few other state educational systems can match. The creative council associated with the Soviet Children's Fund (of which Nemensky is a member) intends to speed the process.

"The Ecology of the Human Soul"

When the young Sergey Obraztsov first began to amuse his friends by putting a doll's head on his fist and cradling it like a baby, Soviet cinema was in its infancy. Now it is a strong presence in the world of art for Soviet children with the potential for touching more of them than any other art form, except literature. Film projectors are available in villages where professional plays and concerts are rarely performed and, with satellite transmission, films that are shown on television can reach children anywhere in the Soviet Union. Soviet children's films vary in quality, and they are so well-regulated that, while there are often romantic episodes between boys and girls, there is almost no sex and very little violence. At worst, these films are harmless bores. At best, they are lively, humorous, and unsentimental. As I watched children's films on television, I noted with interest that the adults in them invariably had secondary roles and that the children were the real heroes and heroines of their own stories.

Whatever their quality, the impact of most Soviet children's films is limited to their primary audience of children. In the mid-1980s, however, several fine films for and about children appeared on the country's screens and became the focus of passionate public debate. These films dealt honestly and sensitively with the problems of contemporary Soviet youngsters, and they shocked the public conscience. The most notable of these films, *Chuchelo* (*The Scarecrow*), is the work of the film-maker Rolan Bykov.

I opened this chapter with Sergey Obraztsov's puppet theatre because to me it represents the best of art for Soviet children that can be classified as entertainment and edification. *Chuchelo*, and the issues it raises, represents an entirely different category of art for children—art as entertainment and revelation. The former category of art has dominated Soviet life since the Revolution; the latter reflects the fact that "art for all" has not managed to humanize the world of adults or, indeed, of children, as Tolstoy dreamed it would.

Eighty years after his death, Tolstoy's utopian vision of a world united in brotherhood seems farther away than ever. The truth is, it is not enough to design music and art curricula for the school system or to provide theatres and cinemas and studios all over the country. Unless the lessons of art in school and out of it connect with children's real-life experiences, they will remain unabsorbed.

Rolan Bykov is a fine actor and a gifted film director who has long been known for his unusual ability to extract natural performances from young children. A generation younger than Obraztsov, he is a man of intense moral passion, although he is not a preacher and does not create his art in order to "improve" his audiences. Instead, his intention is to shake them out of their moral torpor by showing them the consequences of their own actions. He succeeds. I saw his film *Chuchelo* in September 1984 with a couple of Soviet friends. It had just come out and was playing all over the USSR to houses packed with young and old alike. We were lucky to get seats.

The action of this film takes place in an old town on the Volga River during the school break that coincides with the days that celebrate the Revolution (November 7 and 8). In the opening sequence we see a frail young girl, eyes wide with apprehension, descending steps in a riverside park. Behind her, hounding her, is a pack of her schoolmates. She begins to run and they to chase. What is going on here? Lena is a new girl in town who has come to live with her grandfather in an old wooden cottage. During her difficult first days in class, only one person befriends her, the boy Dima. Just before the November break, when their young teacher is away for a day, the whole class, left unattended, goes to the movies. Dima tells on them when the teacher comes back and Lena overhears him. The children are punished by not being allowed to go to Moscow with the rest of the school and they are furious. The unofficial class leaders put extraordinary psychological pressure on their classmates to find out who squealed. In order to protect Dima, whom she cares for, and whose desire to curry favour she understands only too well (she has laughed with the class at her own beloved but eccentric grandfather), Lena takes the guilt on herself.

And so her hounding begins. With the rest of the school away in Moscow, the gang has the park to itself. They bring Lena, blindfolded, to an abandoned chapel. When they uncover her eyes, she sees in front of her a scarecrow on a stick, wearing a dress the children have stolen from her clothes-line. One child pours gasoline on it, and Dima lights the match. While Lena watches the flames in silent agony, the children dance around. It is a very disturbing scene.

The director has already given us glimpses of the unhappy home lives of Lena's tormentors. We realize that their malice is rooted in their own distress. They discover the truth in the end, but by then it is too late. Lena has reluctantly told the whole story to her grandfather, and he has decided that they will have to go away. On the day that school resumes, we see him slowly boarding up the cottage he has lived in for so long. Lena enters the classroom, carrying her suitcase, her head covered. Before the silent children she unwinds her scarf to reveal her shaved scalp. Without her long blonde hair she is, indeed, a scarecrow. The last frames of the film show Lena sitting hunched but clear-eyed beside her grandfather on the riverboat that is carrying them away forever. In the classroom, a child scrawls on the blackboard "Forgive us, *Chuchelo*."

My friends and I were shaken by this film. In fact, the whole audience sat as if stunned for a good moment after the lights came up. Children, twelve-year-olds, with their red Pioneer scarves and their fresh faces, are not supposed to behave like this. And yet I am sure that not a single person in the hall doubted the authenticity of the film. This is where we have come to, it says, with our neglect of the deeper human values, our preoccupation with our own lives and our indifference to the young. *Chuchelo* aroused discussion across the length and breadth of the USSR. Some people resisted the truth that it conveys, but many didn't. Older people found themselves remembering what they had managed to forget, or had idealized. Younger people recognized what they knew. In this film, Bykov has achieved what Tolstoy set as a standard for true art. He communicates his own emotions and attitudes so skilfully through his art that his audiences share them and are deeply stirred. In 1986, *Chuchelo* received a State prize for cinema.

Bykov published an article in *Yunost* magazine about the emotions his film raised. In it, he reflects on the difficulty he had finding a young girl to take the part of Lena. At first, he recounts, he was looking for a girl with naivety and innocence in her eyes. After auditioning hundreds of them, he had to conclude that normal young girls are no longer naïve and he was forced to change his mind about the nature of purity. "The character of Lena Bessoltseva," he writes, "reflects the spiritual sources of a true hero of our time." In today's society a pure person cannot be an innocent but has to be able to combine goodness with strength and character. The actress he finally chose to play Lena, Kristina Orbakaite, portrays this combination with unusual power.

This film marks a shift in Soviet attitudes with respect to art for and about children, and it reflects how both art and children have changed in the seventy years since the Revolution. Bykov speaks for a number of artists and intellectuals who are concerned about the growing materialism and self-seeking of their compatriots; a concern that has little to do with ideology, and a great deal to do with the human values espoused by their nineteenth-century predecessors. Bykov warns, as Tolstoy did, "Now we have art without art and culture without culture, we have morality without any morality and frantic activity without any activity. This is precisely what we call 'mass culture' which replaces true values with their external attributes." The popularity of *Chuchelo* shows, I think, the degree to which many in the Soviet Union share Bykov's concerns. In 1986, the Union of Film Artists elected Bykov chief of its children's section and in 1989 he was one of the five deputies chosen by the Children's Fund to sit in the Congress.

When I met this remarkable artist in September 1987, he eloquently reaffirmed his concern about the moral situation of children in our world-wide era of changing values. There are three overwhelming threats to the future of mankind, he told me: nuclear war, the degradation of the physical environment, and the erosion of childhood. He is writing a book called *The Phenomenon of Childhood,* which will present the insights he has acquired in fifty years of artistic experience (he started acting when he was nine) with respect to "the ecology of the human soul". He uses this term to describe the spiritual environment in which the children of today are growing up. He finds it lacking in nutrients. The behaviour of Lena's classmates would be incomprehensible if Bykov had not shown us the emotional impoverishment of their parents and teachers. In a gesture heavy with meaning, Lena's grandfather, a wise and gentle man who conserves old paintings, donates his collection to the town before he and Lena leave. Obviously the townfolk have more need of the spiritual nourishment of art than they do.

In thinking about the Soviet child and the world of art, I find myself returning again to Tolstoy, and to the predictions he made about the future of art if only every child had access to it both inside and outside of school. This is now the case in the USSR, but in the end, what a difference has it made, all of this enormous investment since the Revolution that the State and so many creative individuals have made in art for children? After all, why should children learn to sing, Lev Nikolaevich, and what is drawing for? And why, we can now add, go to the theatre or see a movie, if not just for entertainment?

Some of the predictions that Tolstoy made about art in his essay have come true. In the vast land in which he lived out his life, "children's art—jests, proverbs, riddles, songs, dances, children's games and mimicry" have become "a domain worthy of art". And all children have some form of aesthetic education and study "music and graphic art" along with letters in the elementary school, just as he had hoped they would. Artists do come from every level of Soviet society, and artistic activity is more or less accessible to all. Tolstoy's descendants value the "infectiousness" of good art, as much as Tolstoy did. But has this raised the "overall level of taste and lowered the demand for superficial and sensational art"? Not according to Rolan Bykov, and to others like him.

Tolstoy had an admirable formula for universal art: "clarity, simplicity, brevity". But what he left out of this formula were the very qualities he himself possessed in such abundance: creativity and originality. Until recently, these qualities were frowned upon by Soviet authorities, and it took an unusual parent, teacher, or mentor to cultivate them in a young child. As a result, generations of children have grown up in the Soviet Union far more knowledgeable about art than their ancestors but not necessarily more discriminating, and certainly not more creative. This is now changing as Soviet cultural life opens up.

However, there is a risk for children in the current cultural climate that, so far, very few people have paid attention to. Up to now, their world of art has attracted a heavy investment of resources and talent, partly as a matter of State policy, partly because people in the Soviet Union really care about children, and partly because many good Soviet artists, unable to work freely for adults, have created fine works for children instead. Now there is the likelihood that some of the "cultural workers", who once devoted their talents to children, will offer them to the adult world instead. I trust that the Soviet love of, and commitment to, children will be strong enough to prevent this from happening at their expense. Like the Gardener in Yevgeny Shvarts's play *The Dragon*, I find myself pleading for patience as the climate changes so that tender new roots will not be damaged. And I also find myself hoping that Soviet children will continue to create their own culture as they always have, in spite of overly zealous parents and teachers, and that they will continue to enjoy it in an unselfconscious manner. Like Bykov and others, I am concerned that Soviet children may be tempted by the "adult" experiences they see in an increasingly open art world to grow up too quickly. Children need to wander freely in the timeless world that art can create especially for them. If they don't, their imaginations may be stunted and their personal creativity destroyed. Whenever I went to Obraztsov's puppet theatre it was not the magical figures dancing on their sticks that enchanted me the most; it was the look on the faces of the children around me, and their delighted, spontaneous laughter.

CHAPTER TWELVE

Books and Young Readers

To the west of Moscow, the countryside is rolling and pleasant. There are woods and meadows, rivers and streams. Before the Revolution it was dotted with country estates and peasant villages. Now there are Pioneer camps, rest homes, convalescent hospitals, and country retreats for the intelligentsia. The Academy of Sciences, the Ministry of Foreign Affairs, the CPSU, all have resorts in the region amid stands of birch and fragrant pine. So does the Union of Soviet Writers.

The Union has created a writer's colony at Peredelkino with wooden *dachas* that are so warm and comfortable some members choose to live there all year round. Boris Pasternak did, as did Korney Chukovsky, the father of Soviet children's literature. The area around Peredelkino was open to foreigners in the early 1980s, and I often drove myself there to walk in summer or ski in winter. Every time I did, I visited Pasternak's grave.

People spend a lot of time in cemeteries in Russia, honouring their dead in the places where they are buried. Most graves are tended by friends and family members, but those of revered writers and artists draw the attention of the whole population. Chekhov's grave in Moscow, Tolstoy's at Yasnaya Polyana, and Pushkin's in a small country churchyard near the northern city of

Pskov, each one is covered daily with a blanket of fresh flowers. Pasternak's grave at Peredelkino is on the crest of a hill under three pine trees. During the years that he was writing *Doctor Zhivago,* Pasternak would often lift his head from his desk on the second floor of his *dacha* and stare across the sloping field at these same three trees silhouetted against the sky. He asked to be buried under them. His gravestone is sculpted with his unmistakable profile, and from a low bench facing it you can sit and contemplate it. Whenever I visited the cemetery, there was usually someone sitting on the bench and I would have to wait my turn. When I made my last trip there, just before leaving the Embassy in 1983, the entire grave-site was occupied. A sombre grey-haired man sat on the bench and passionately declaimed, one after the other, the poems in *Doctor Zhivago.* Seven or eight people stood over him, listening intently.

I stood a short distance away, profoundly moved. Nothing could have demonstrated more forcibly the strength of the Russian literary tradition, or of the special role that poets and novelists play in it, than this scene at Pasternak's grave. From Pushkin onwards, the most gifted Russian writers have shared a belief in the power of words to stir the individual imagination. They have also been convinced that this power, emanating as it does from the writer's own creativity, cannot be controlled from the outside. Both tsars and commissars have tried. Censorship has been the bane of both Russian and Soviet writers and some great works have only reached their public by being published outside of the country. Yet, even in the worst of times, a remarkable amount of fine literature has slipped through the encircling net of State control to reach the growing imaginations of Soviet children.

Among the books read by children in the Soviet Union are some by Soviet authors that rank with the best children's literature in the world. Children also read classics from the Russian tradition and many excellent works translated from the world's treasure-house of books for young readers. "The republic of childhood" is an expression often used to describe the world of the imagination that is created through children's literature, a world unbounded by language or political barriers. Soviet children have access to this domain through the rich bounty of books available to them.

But whether or not children take advantage of this opportunity to transcend the borders of the worlds that confine them depends on the extent to which they have been enabled to become "talented" and discerning readers.

In one of her poems, Anna Akhmatova compares the "mystery" of the individual reader to "treasure buried in the sand". Every year millions of children in the Soviet Union learn to read for the first time, and each one brings his or her unique experience of life and language to the task. What books can they read? Which are the most popular? Do they love them? The answers to these questions can open up the mystery for us. Maxim Gorky, one of the most powerful supporters of children's literature in the early years of the Soviet state, wrote that books "sang their songs" to him like "birds out of fairy-tales", implying that the liberating power of books lies in their appeal to the imagination. But a child's imagination has to be "captured" first before it can be set free. This is a task for the authenticity of an artist rather than for the veracity of a journalist or a writer of popular science. This is why the books I am going to describe are primarily works of fiction. A small child's soul (and character) is not shaped by the scientific fact that the earth is round but by wonder and delight at its infinite and varied possibilities.

Soviet Children's Books

What do Soviet children read? Let's look at the children's bookcase in a typical Moscow apartment. There are two children in this family, a teenager and a child who is just beginning to read. The bookcase is bulging; a quarter of the books published each year in the Soviet Union are for children and they are sold out almost as soon as they arrive in the bookstores. All the books are in Russian but almost half have been translated from another language, from one of the European languages or from one of the other languages spoken in the USSR, possibly even from Arabic or Chinese. Children from most of the other Soviet nationalities will have similar books on their shelves, translated into their own native language. They will also have books from their own cultural tradition, especially folk-tales and contemporary children's stories plus some children's works approved for publication by the editorial boards of native-language publishing houses. These latter books are often translated into Russian for Russian-speaking children. Policies for publishing and distributing children's books in the Soviet Union are supposed to guarantee that all Soviet children share the same corpus of children's literature, with some local variations, and to a certain extent they do.

The bookcase is a bit of a jumble, like all children's bookcases. Some books have been inherited, some received as gifts, and some the children have purchased themselves. But I will try to put them in some order, starting with folk-tales and fairy stories and with works written for children by classical Russian authors. Then come the books for younger children that form the core of *Soviet* children's literature, inspired in the post-revolutionary period by Korney Chukovsky. The next section belongs to the older child in the family and contains adventure stories, science fiction, and romance as well as a certain amount of non-fiction, history, biography, popular science, and so on. Almost a whole shelf is needed for books by foreign authors and books from the other republics of the USSR. On the bottom shelf are the stories that resonate with the emotions associated with certain periods of Soviet history. Finally, there are the inevitable books about Lenin.

Folk-tales and Fairy Stories

V nekotorom tsarstve, v nekotorom gosudarstve ("In a certain kingdom, in a certain land") starts off the tale of Marya Morevna, the warrior queen, and her Prince Ivan and how they combined to outwit Koshchey the Deathless, a story that is a great favourite with my own "feminist" granddaughter in Canada. *Zhili-byli* ("Once upon a time") there was an old woman whose son was a fool...begins another story, a sly tale about greed with a clever horse, a magic tablecloth, and an enchanted horn. These two ritualistic phrases introduce a whole host of fairy-tales that are familiar to almost every child in the Soviet Union. They have existed for hundreds of years, having been passed on from generation to generation by word of mouth until they were finally collected and transcribed in the middle of the last century by Alexandr Afanasyev. Since then, the stories have been told and retold, published singly or severally, in hundreds of different editions and in many languages, including, of course, English. Long before I dreamed I would one day go to Russia, I read to my children the story of the Firebird's burning feather; the tales of Vasilisa, wise and beautiful, and Prince Ivan, handsome and bold. We were fascinated by Baba-Yaga, the witch who flies about in a mortar and pestle and lives in a hut that stands on a chicken's legs. We rejoiced with the triumph of the disregarded younger son, delighted in the tricking of the lascivious old man, the cheating of the cheater. And, like Soviet children today, we laughed delightedly at the stories of the kindly bears, the sly foxes, and the silly sheep.

The oral tradition, from which these stories come, was strong in old Russia. Books were the preserve of the Orthodox Church and they were written in Church Slavonic, a formal language removed from ordinary speech. Before the time of Peter the Great, there were few in Russia who were able to read, so people of every class depended on story-tellers for their experience of literature. Folk-tales and fairy stories were always popular, as were heroic tales in verse called *byliny*. Under the influence of the changes brought about by Peter, the gentry became better educated and their literary tastes more "refined". Folk-tales and fairy stories were gradually relegated to peasants and children. Pushkin heard them, night after night, from his beloved nurse Arina Rodionovna, and Tolstoy's grandfather acquired a blind old serf to tell tales to the little boy until he fell asleep. These greatest of Russian authors were strongly influenced by the stories they listened to as children. In them, they heard the authentic rhythms of Russian speech rather than the artificial cadences of the literary forms that had been imported from Western Europe. Russian children, as well as their elders, have benefited ever since.

Stories that survive in the oral tradition do so because they respond to keenly felt, enduring human needs. Even after they were written down, the tales collected by Afanasyev retained their appeal. No one in the Soviet Union seriously questions the place of fairy-tales in a child's bookcase today, but during Stalin's dictatorship, the world of enchantment came periodically under attack. In his book, *From Two to Five*, Korney Chukovsky recounts the three stages of the "Battle of the Fairytale". In

1929, during the Soviet "cultural revolution", there were many powerful people, including (I am sorry to say) Krupskaya, who sharply criticized the playful, imaginative tales that children love so much as quite inappropriate for children of the proletariat who were supposed to grow up to build communism in a thoroughly scientific manner. Soviet children should not be exposed to fantasies or fairy-tales, they said, but only to stories that contain the "most authentic and realistic facts". This first wave of attack subsided under the influence of Maxim Gorky, and such sensible people as Chukovsky himself, but a new wave arose in the mid-1930s, launched by thick-headed party officials and narrow-minded school directors who considered the "myth or the fairy-tale a threat to Leninism". Finally, in the mid-1950s, even the committee on children's literature in the Union of Writers descended so far (according to Chukovsky, whose own work they were attacking) as to write: "regrettably some of our writers who work in the field of fairytales for pre-school children, actually, for the sake of charming them, make mistakes, assigning to harmful animals, birds and insects qualities of real heroes".

Luckily, common sense and a truer understanding of children's developmental needs won the battle for the fairy-tale, and a contemporary Soviet child now has a vast selection to choose from. Afanasyev's collection remains very popular. And so are European collections, such as those of Charles Perrault ("Cinderella") and the Brothers Grimm. Hans Christian Andersen's stories are especially well known. "The Snow Queen" is required reading in one of the early grades. In addition, folklore from each of the many nationalities that make up the USSR is constantly being translated from one language into another. During the last decade, this sharing of tales within the Soviet Union has quickened because the authorities who give approval for publishing are intent on increasing the Soviet child's sense of belonging to a "family" of nations. In my own collection of children's books purchased in the Soviet Union, I have numerous folk-tales from Moldavia, the Caucasus, the Ukraine, the Baltic republics, Central Asia, and the peoples of the Soviet North. These last-named are full of tales about beginnings as are our Inuit and Indian legends; how Man was made, how the rabbit got its fur, and where the whales came from.

Why are fairy stories so popular and why is it so important that Soviet children hear and read them? One of the best known of Afanasyev's tales is called "The Turnip". The version that most Soviet children know was reworked in a lively manner by Alexey Tolstoy (1882-1945). Grandfather plants a turnip but, when it is grown it is too big for him to pull out himself so he calls first to Grandmother for help, and then to Granddaughter, and then Dog, and then Cat. Finally Mouse arrives and adds his puny force, and the turnip comes out of the ground. Soviet authorities may like this story because they think it shows the collective in action. Children will probably like it because it makes them feel powerful, able to make a difference in the world. It is a mistake to think that folk-tales or fairy stories can be used to teach any specific lesson. They are charged with too many possible meanings. That is what makes them so satisfying. They do not operate at a rational level or at a moral one, but at a deeper psychological one. The story of the turnip, for example, can be read as a dream about the conquest of nature, and the many stories about Ivan the Fool and his magical rings, spoons, scissors, and caps, as a fantasy about how to survive in a hostile world. Other fairy-tales speak to and help resolve the churning emotions that all children have. The stories that feature Baba-Yaga and Koshchey the Deathless enable children to work through feelings of envy, anger, and fear in the company of the threatened Tsarevna and the foolish younger son who eventually wins her hand.

Chukovsky observed that most healthy children are no longer charmed by fairy-tales after a certain age. They enter a stage in which they love to "expose" the irrationalities in such stories. According to him, "the fairytale has now accomplished its task. It has helped the child orient himself to the surrounding world, has enriched his spiritual life, has made him regard himself as a fearless participant in imaginary struggles for justice, goodness and freedom."

Children's Books by Classical Russian Authors

Next to the folk-tales and the fairy stories on the bookshelf is the section reserved for books by classical Russian authors. These are not abridgements or adaptations of adult works but works that were either written specifically for children or have been adopted by children as part of the "republic of childhood". Pushkin, for example, did not actually write his delightful *skazki*, the lilting verse tales that were inspired by his nurse's voice, for children; but children have always loved them. So, as adult readers became more "sophisticated" and these tales lost their status as works for adults, children took them over. The same thing happened to an extraordinarily popular tale known as "The Little Humpbacked Horse", written in the middle of the last century by Pyotr Yershov. The author thought he was writing for adults and, indeed, his work was taken seriously by them, so seriously that it was banned by the authorities for thirty years because its simplicity made them suspect subversion. Once the ban was lifted, it entered the stream of children's culture where it has remained until today. Yershov, who was only nineteen when he wrote his verse tale, never again wrote anything so good, abandoning his natural affinity for folk rhythms in favour of a more "literary" style, which doused his imagination. Ivan Krylov is another nineteenth-century writer who has ended up on the bookshelves of children. He wrote hundreds of fables derived from Aesop and La Fontaine as well as from Russian folklore. They are racy and amusing, and many of his maxims have become common proverbs.

One of his brief fables (it is in the grade-one reader) tells how a swan, a pike, and a lobster came together to move a loaded cart. But the swan flew up, the pike swam down, and the lobster crawled backwards, so in spite of their efforts, "the cart is still stuck there." (*Da tolko voz i nyne tam* is a line that no contemporary Russian will fail to recognize.) Tolstoy's tales are also popular with children. Some are based on Russian folklore and were written for the primers he devised to teach peasant boys to read at his school at Yasnaya Polyana. Others are adaptations of folk-tales from other traditions such as "Goldilocks and the Three Bears". Still others are entirely his own invention. These last tend to be psychologically richer with more fully realized characters than his adaptations. The nineteenth-century educator Konstantin Ushinsky also wrote reading primers for which he sketched charming vignettes from the world of nature. Today, Tolstoy's tales and those of Ushinsky are published and republished in print runs of a million or two at a time.

Many other pre-revolutionary authors can be found in the bookstores, although not in such quantity. Mikhail Lermontov, Anton Chekhov, Sergey Aksakov (whose "Little Scarlet Flower" is a Russian adaptation of "Beauty and the Beast"), and Alexandr Kuprin, all wrote stories for children. Maxim Gorky, known as a Soviet writer, did most of his best writing before the Revolution, did not write the tale called "The Burning Coal" for children but its message makes it required reading for senior pupils and it has been frequently adapted for younger ones. This is the story of a brave warrior whose love for his "tribe" is so great that he pulls his heart out of his chest and holds it aloft where it shines like a burning coal and lights his people out of the dark forest in which they have become entangled. Once they have emerged into the sunshine, the young man dies, exhausted and forgotten. Although not a children's writer, Gorky was an important figure in Soviet children's literature. His childhood experience led him to believe passionately in the power of books. He was a friend of Lenin's, and later had some influence with Stalin, so he was an invaluable ally to those who, after the Revolution, were struggling to establish the highest possible standards for children's literature.

And what of the classical authors of the other national traditions in the Soviet Union? I visited a couple of book fairs in Moscow where a very large display section was given over to children's books in languages other than Russian. My attention was drawn to many books considered classics in the literary traditions of the other Soviet nationalities. Nevertheless, I suspect that Soviet children's literature is dominated by authors who wrote originally in Russian, whether before or after the Revolution.

*From Two to Five: Korney Chukovsky and Books for Very
Young Children*

The undisputed founder of Soviet children's literature is Korney
Chukovsky (1882-1969). At an important moment in Soviet history, he was able to combine his writer's talent with his love for
children and his understanding of how they grow, to set the direction that Soviet children's authors have more or less followed ever
since. Chukovsky began his career as a journalist. In the winter of
the 1903-04, he went on assignment to London, where he discovered all the riches of English children's literature, especially the
nursery rhymes we all know so well. From then until the end of
his long life, he made sure that the best of this literature was translated into Russian and made available to Soviet children. When
I visited his *dacha* at Peredelkino, part of which has now been
turned into a museum, I found many English children's classics
on his shelves: *Alice in Wonderland* , of course, and Edward Lear
and the so familiar slim volumes of A.A. Milne, *When We Were
Very Young* and *Now We Are Six* . Chukovsky's own works were
on display in a small room on the ground floor, in Russian and
in English translations. As I was leaving, his granddaughter gave
me an envelope with a stamp commemorating the hundredth anniversary of his birth, which had just been celebrated. Chukovsky
is now a respected Soviet institution.

But this was not always the case. Chukovsky returned from
his year in England to write critical articles about the deplorable
poetry that was being written at that time for children in Russia.
He found it preachy and tedious. The language that children
themselves use, however, he found fresh and creative, so he
began to study it, writing down the utterances of his own four
children and those of any others he met. Since he was apparently
always able to talk to children on their own terms, he soon
amassed a wonderful collection from which he often quotes in
From Two to Five. He wrote his first *skazka,* "Krokodil" ("The
Crocodile"), in 1916, after being challenged by Maxim Gorky to
do something more for children than write critical articles. He
was not, however, a prolific writer, and composed nothing more
until 1921 when on two succeeding days he produced two more
verse tales, "Tarakanishche" ("The Cockroach") and "Moydodyr"

("Wash 'em Clean"). Altogether, he wrote only thirteen such tales plus a handful of stories in prose.

After the Revolution, Chukovsky fought continually to "establish the legitimacy of children's literature as an art form in the Soviet Union". His major problem at this time was that literature for children was considered too important to be left in the hands of creative artists like himself and his colleagues. The battle for the fairy-tale exemplifies this very well. And the struggle was a draining one. By 1934 Chukovsky had exhausted his creative impulse and was never again to produce such a delightful tale as "Aibolit" ("Ouch-it-hurts") where a character, inspired by Hugh Lofting's "Dr. Dolittle", rushes off to Africa to cure the monkeys and the baby hippos. During the war, Chukovsky fell into official disfavour, which lasted until after the death of Stalin. When he re-emerged, it was as a promoter of children's literature to children themselves. He travelled around the country to read his *skazki* in schools and libraries and received children continually at his home in Peredelkino. His ongoing contact with children kept him young in spirit.

Chukovsky was never didactic. Even his tale "Wash 'em Clean" is much more about the joys of running and jumping and splashing in water than it is about the virtue of cleanliness. He loved small children and, what is more important for his poetry, he *listened* to them with great attention. What he heard was the natural way in which children develop linguistic skills and use them to make sense of the world around them. He did not claim to be a scientist but he was a very careful observer. One of his observations was that "the young child acquires his linguistic and thinking habits only through communication with other human beings". Another was that a child is most "gifted" for language learning between the ages of two and five. It is then that poetry is as natural to children as breathing because rhymes and rhythms are the way in which sounds and syntax are tested for sense and meaning.

In Chukovsky's *From Two to Five*, there is a chapter about what he calls "topsy-turvies". He had noticed that small children from all cultures have a passion for nonsense verse. One has only to think of the Mother Goose rhymes that English-speaking parents still (I trust) read to their children. Some of these rhymes have survived for hundreds of years. Chukovsky asked himself why and then concluded, observing his own little daughter, that small children just beginning to get a handle on the world around them need to strengthen their understanding of what is normal by turning things upside down. The image of "three children sliding on the ice / all of a summer's day" makes them laugh because *they* know better. When children grow older, and their sense of what is real in the world stabilizes, they no longer have the same urge to test it.

One of the most attractive qualities of topsy-turvies is their humour. Chukovsky believed that it is very important to develop a sense of humour in children, "a precious quality which will increase the child's sense of perspective and his tolerance, as he grows up, of unpleasant situations". An example of this is a poem he wrote called "The Muddle" in which the desire of kittens to bark like dogs turns the whole natural world upside down: "Fish are strolling on the ground / Toads are flying round and round."

Chukovsky's poetry was written for very young children and is full of topsy-turvies and word-play. Because so much of it is dependent on the sounds of the Russian language, it cannot be fully appreciated in an English translation. One of my Soviet friends surrendered her much cherished copy of *Mukha-Tsokotukha* (*The Chatterbox Fly*) to me so that I could enjoy it in the original (and I did). Most of Chukovsky's tales involve animals in inverted positions. "The Cockroach", for example, has that insect terrorizing the whole animal kingdom until a gay and carefree little sparrow comes along and swallows him. "It served the nasty giant right / No trace of his moustache in sight."

Chukovsky wrote a number of influential "commandments" for children's poets which he derived from his study of child development and which he followed in his own verse. He instructed aspiring writers to "think in pictures". "Show me!" cries the child who is being read to. The imagery of the poem must be easily translatable into a visual picture. And the poem must contain many such "pictures" because children delight in rapidly changing images. "This verbal painting must also be lyrical," Chukovsky continued, because children love to sing and dance.

He reminded writers to avoid adjectives because small children rarely use them. Most children are far more interested in action than in description. This is not the case, of course, for older children, for whom adjectives serve to enlarge their perception of things. Chukovsky believed that verse for children should be suitable for play and games, and he always insisted that poetry for children be of the highest possible standard in terms of technique. "A bad poem could never be good enough for children," he said. It is by the poetry that is written for them that children can be brought to appreciate the qualities of great poetry in any language.

Poetry and Children's Poets

It is thanks in part to the influence of Chukovsky's "commandments" on the style of other children's writers that Soviet children's poetry is so popular. In a country with such a strong oral tradition and so many great poets, poetry has always been highly respected. This feeling of respect is transmitted to children from the moment their parents begin to read to them, and it pervades their early school experience. Young children are expected to learn poems by heart as soon as they enter school and to recite them eloquently and with feeling in front of the whole class.

Learning a poem "by heart" means that the child will absorb the cadences of his or her native language through the pulses as well as the ear. And what delightful Russian poems there are to listen to and learn! In addition to the verse tales of Chukovsky, almost every Russian child—and probably most children of the other Soviet nationalities—will own a book of poems by Samuil Marshak (1887-1964), the most gifted of Chukovsky's friends and contemporaries. He, too, spent time in England before the First World War and became acquainted with English nursery rhymes. He translated them with brilliance, and it is his versions that are most familiar to generations of Soviet children. In the mid-1920s, Marshak began to write poetry for children himself and to promote children's literature at the Leningrad State publishing house. Like Chukovsky, he ran into trouble with the prosaically minded proletarians but he was defended by Maxim Gorky and, in 1934, allowed to make an important address on children's literature to the first meeting of the newly formed Union of Soviet Writers. Echoing Chukovsky, he proclaimed, "Children's literature must be art. Many of us still do not understand that simple truth." His best poems had been written by then but during the rest of his life he never ceased to encourage young writers of children's literature and to give them technical assistance.

Marshak's poems are remarkably fresh and undated. His poetry abides by all of Chukovsky's guidelines but it is quite different from his friend's in both tone and substance. Chukovsky's verse tales put me in mind of Edward Lear ("The Owl and the Pussycat"), while Marshak's make me think of Robert Louis Stevenson (*A Child's Garden of Verses*). This is particularly true of a collection of poems called *The Rainbow Book*, which is full of gentle humour.

On the whole Marshak's poems are less fanciful than those of Chukovsky. A few are ideological, such as "Mr. Twister" (1933), an amusing poem that describes an archetypal capitalist from Chicago who thinks that he can buy Leningrad. However, his enduring popularity rests on short poems that encapsulate a child's eye view of family, school, and play. They are universal in theme and would appeal to the imagination of any European or North American child.

There are two other children's poets from the earlier period who continue to be popular but who are not, in my opinion, of the same artistic rank as Chukovsky and Marshak. These are Sergey Mikhalkov (b. 1913) and Agnia Barto (1906-1982). Mikhalkov wrote the text for the Soviet National Anthem, and his poetry tends to be didactic as well as patriotic. Verses from his poems are sprinkled throughout the Russian reading primers (as are those of Marshak, Chukovsky, and Barto), and he wrote two particular poems that are bound to be in any Soviet child's library. One recounts the adventures of a brave and kindly giant called "Uncle Steeple". The other, "In the Lenin Museum", describes a little boy's feelings about seeing the precious objects in the Lenin Museum in Moscow and is required reading at school. As far as I know, Mikhalkov no longer writes poetry but he remains a key figure in Soviet children's literature. He works actively to promote it through the Writers' Union and I have often seen his name associated with various committees, including the Soviet Children's Fund, of which he is now a member.

I prefer the work of Agnia Barto. Her sensibility is keener. Her poems relate, with gentle humour, to real-life situations any Soviet child could identify with: a little girl loses her coat-check in the theatre; a dog is left behind at the Pioneer camp; a boy has difficulty getting his homework done; another little boy wonders on the first day of school, as his mother fusses with his school-bag and the flowers he should carry, who it is that is actually going to school, him or her.

A new generation of children's poets emerged during the cultural "thaw" that followed Stalin's death. Among the most popular is Irina Tokmakova (b. 1929). I had thick black coffee and a very sweet pastry with her in the basement cafeteria of the Writer's Union on a warm day in the spring of 1986. I found her to be a woman of an agreeable serenity, confident without pretention. In excellent English, she told me that she had been brought up to be bilingual in Russian and Armenian. As a child before the war, she studied German and at university, English and Swedish. Working as a student guide one summer she met an elderly Swedish professor who had just brought out a collection of Swedish nursery rhymes. He urged her to translate them. She did, and when she took them to a publishing house, they were accepted. Then she translated some Scottish children's folklore. After that, she decided to compose her own poems for children. She married (her husband, Lev Tokmakov, is a children's book illustrator), had a son to inspire her, and continued to write for small children. Her poems are engaging and tender. I particularly like those that express a child's view of the natural world. They are apparently very popular with the age group for whom they are written. Nowadays, she writes mostly short stories and fantasy fiction, always for young children.

Tokmakova admits to being a member of the second wave of Soviet children's writers. I asked her who, if anyone, constituted the third wave. She sounded a little discouraged. She named Leningrad poet Sergey Makhotin, and, for prose, her son Vasily, a forester who writes about nature, but said that few other names sprang to her mind. I asked her how young writers get their start.

She told me that they usually bring manuscripts to one or another of the children's publishing houses, where they are examined by one of the editorial collectives. If a manuscript is accepted, then its author will be encouraged to continue. Of course, she said, there are many writers of little talent who manage to get published only because they are pushy and manipulative. Unfortunately, it is very difficult to become a member of the Writer's Union, a status that virtually guarantees publication. At that moment, she confessed, there were almost as many members of the Union over sixty-five as there were younger ones. Since an application for membership will not be processed unless the writer has submitted a published work and been accepted for consideration by two-thirds of the current members, young writers have traditionally had a hard time. However, she assured me that a concerted effort was about to be launched to bring in younger authors. It is hoped that some of them, at least, will want to write for children.

Fiction

Soviet children are very fond of animal stories, and there are hundreds of titles available. The best are by authors whose personal attitude to the natural world is marked by passion and concern, but who retain the clear eye of a scientific observer. Such writers as Mikhail Prishvin (1873-1954) and Konstantin Paustovsky (1892-1968) fall into this category, and their stories are much loved, even though they are by no means primarily children's authors. Vitaly Bianki (1894-1959) was an author who translated nature lore into brief, lively stories that easily capture the attention of little children who are so naturally protective of birds and small forest animals. The official Soviet stance is that children should be encouraged by art and literature to love animals and to feel compassionate towards creatures weaker than themselves but such an attitude is perfectly natural to the authors I have just mentioned. The love of nature is a powerful force in the Russian literary tradition and good Russian writers need no reminders. After the Revolution, and particularly during the first five-year plans when the drive for industrialization wrought havoc on the environment, economic planners were guided by Marxist-Leninist assumptions about man as the master of the natural world. Nevertheless, sensitive writers, respectful of the delicate balance in the world of nature, continued to write stories for children and to be published. Today, it is a writer from Siberia, Valentin Rasputin, who often leads the charge against environmental degradation. If generations of Soviet children had not been nourished by his fellow authors, many now dead, I do not think he would have been able to arouse the political response from his readership that is helping to make his environmental crusade so effective.

Young children in the Soviet Union also like humorous tales about unlikely characters. *Dunno and His Friends* by Nikolay Nosov (1908-1976) falls into this category. Dunno (*Neznaika*) is a *very* little boy who lives with his friends in Flowertown, under the daisies. This book, which is about the children's collective, presents a social utopia in which there are no parents, no other adults in the village, and no government. All of Dunno's friends have trades or professions. He is the only one who cannot do anything. He gets into mischief because he does not know any better, and he is corrected by the other children in an amusing and light-hearted manner. The message to children is "your friends will help you to learn what you need to know". The same message about friends is central to the stories of Eduard Uspensky (b. 1939) about Gena the Crocodile. Gena, whose daytime job is to be the crocodile in the local zoo, is lonely when he returns home at night, so he hangs out a sign looking for friends. A funny-looking small furry animal with big ears and goggling eyes appears. He does not know who he is until his friends give him an identity and name him Cheburashka. Gena and Cheburashka appear in movies and on television as well as in books and are enormously popular.

A book for slightly older children that fits this category is *The Adventures of Captain Wrungel* by Andrey Nekrasov. Conceived in 1934, this book had a chequered career. It first appeared as a serial in the children's magazine *Pioner*, and it was enthusiastically received by the magazine's young readers. However, it was criticized by adults for being outrageous, full of misinformation and bad examples. The Captain smokes a pipe; the first mate, Lom, likes to drink; and the other crew member,

Fooks, is a card-sharp. It is a marvellous book, a preposterous story, an extended tall tale in the vein of *Baron Munchausen*. For twenty years it was out of print, but since a second edition appeared in 1958 it has sailed, as the author says, "on a fair wind". Captain Wrungel's message to children, if he has one, is that the best way to confront adversity is with good humour, ingenuity, and by calling upon your childhood.

In recent years, Uspensky and Irina Tokmakova have turned to fantasy with a serious message, a message that addresses the social changes that are creating so much stress for young children. Uspensky's *Uncle Theodore* is a funny book about a serious six-year-old boy who leaves home to live on his own with a cat because his parents are too occupied with their own interests to allow him an animal. Tokmakova's book *And There Will Be a Happy Morning* is poetic rather than humorous. Her main character is a little girl who returns to her grandmother's past to bring back a bunch of roses that will stop her parents from bickering.

If younger children respond more to fantasy, older children like science fiction. It is very popular in the Soviet Union with both teenagers and adults, and such authors as Arthur C. Clarke and Ray Bradbury are widely read. There are also excellent home-grown writers such as the Strugatsky brothers, Arkady and Boris, who have written a number of wise and witty stories for adolescents about the delusions of science and of scientists. *Monday Begins on Saturday*, for example, is a fantasy about a group of scholars working at NIICHAVO, The Scientific Research Institute of Wizardry and Magic. "NIICHAVO" plays on the word *nichego* (pronounced "nichevo"), which means "nothing" or "never mind". Two other popular writers are Sergey Snegor who wrote a trilogy called *People Like Gods,* and Vir Bulychev who wrote a series about a doctor on the space fleet *Pavlysh*.

Soviet authors also provide young teenagers with a number of well-written stories focusing on the dilemmas of conscience that are so characteristic of this age group. A story by Lev Kassil called "My Brother, the Hero" is typical of these. A boy in a children's home in a provincial town pretends that a famous aviator of the same family name is his brother until the latter arrives in town one day and the boy is found out. One of the most widely read authors of books of this type for adolescents is a talented writer in the tradition of Tolstoy, Anatoly Aleksin, whom I met at the end of my second year in Moscow. He told me that he tries to help young people between fourteen and seventeen resolve their moral problems by writing long short stories for them that describe real-life events and contain characters with whom they can identify. His stories are about death and divorce and other family crises as well as about situations of moral tension at home and at school. He admitted that the long short story is a challenging literary form that works only if the characterization is good. Aleksin is a talented writer and his works are credible, yet I suspect his range is too narrow to accommodate some of the more difficult problems of today's adolescents in the Soviet Union. Like all the other Soviet authors I have read who are trying to appeal to teenagers, he is entirely too circumspect with respect to sex, to say nothing of drugs and alcohol. He told me proudly that Soviet young people's literature contains no pornography or violence, but I think it could be a good deal bolder than it is without becoming sensationalist.

The World Treasury of Children's Literature

A number of foreign books are shelved with Russian and Soviet ones in any Soviet child's bookcase. Readers in the Soviet Union often acquire books by subscribing to a whole series, and there is a very popular one called *The World Treasury of Children's Literature*. Eventually it will comprise five hundred titles. The books in this series are classics that have been translated from the languages in which they were originally written. Among the best-loved are the English classics I have already mentioned as well as books by Charles Dickens and Rudyard Kipling (*The Jungle Book* and *Just-So Stories*). *Peter Pan* has many fans in the Soviet Union as does *Mary Poppins*. From France come the novels of Alexandre Dumas (*The Three Musketeers* is an all-time favourite) and Antoine de Saint-Exupéry's enchanting *The Little Prince*. From the United States comes Mark Twain's *Tom Sawyer, Huckleberry Finn,* and *The Prince and the Pauper*. There is also a Russian version of *The Wizard of Oz* by Alexandr Volkov, who has included it in a sought-after series of fantasy tales. Cooper's *The Last of the Mohicans* is often read, as is Salinger's *The Catcher in the Rye*. In one children's library that I visited, Hemingway's *The Old Man and the Sea* had been borrowed so many times that it was falling apart.

From Canada the most popular books are those that have to do with nature, the true-to-life animal stories of Ernest Thompson Seton ("Waab, The Grizzly") and the entertaining tales of Farley Mowat (*The Dog Who Wouldn't Be*). From Sweden come *Pippi Longstocking* and *The Tot and Karlsson Who Lives on the Roof* by Astrid Lindgren and *The Wonderful Adventure of Nils* by Selma Lagerlof. "Buratino", the story that Alexey Tolstoy based on his memories of reading Carlo Collodi's *The Adventure of Pinocchio* as a young boy, is loved by every Soviet child. The list goes on and on. Almost all the classic children's books my husband and I have acquired over the years for our five children are available to Soviet children in libraries, if not in bookstores.

Non-Russian Soviet Authors

Foreign books, of course, are not the only books in translation to find a place in a Soviet child's bookcase. A well-known author from Moldavia, Spiridon Vangeli, writes primarily for younger children. His little hero, Gugutse, is a mischievous small boy whose charm lies in his naturalness. He does the things that all little children dream of doing and then he returns safe and sound to everyday life. An Estonian writer, Vladislav Korzhets, writes about Merike, a stubborn and curious five-year-old who is trying to figure out what the adults around her are up to. She is a real child in a real world. I remember myself.

Chik and His Friends by Fazil Iskander, an irrepressible writer from the Abkhazian region of Georgia, is about a young boy who has a number of typical childhood adventures as he and his gang (which includes a crippled lad and a couple of girls) wander freely through his village and the rocky countryside surrounding it. Iskander peoples his books with odd and engaging but quite believable characters, few of whom are the "positive" heroes Socialist Realism requires. He is a gifted and very funny writer whose sardonic portrayal of the interaction of Soviet authority and Abkhazian culture is hardly flattering to the former. As a result, he long had trouble getting the full text of his adult books (irreverent stories about Sandro of Chegem) published. However, his books for young people, which have some of the flavour of Mark Twain, are read throughout the USSR.

Chinghiz Aitmatov, the Kirghiz writer, is not known as a children's writer but his writing for and about children is unusually sensitive and moving. *The White Steamer*, for example, is the tragic story of a young boy abandoned by both of his parents into the care of a loving but ineffectual grandfather who lives in a village in the mountains of Kirghizia. The boy is sustained by the vision of the horned deer sacred to his people (whom his grandfather persuades him will protect him), and by the regular sight of a white steamer crossing the lake below, carrying, or so he believes, his absent father. When his grandfather betrays the sacred deer to some bullying hunters from town during a fit of drinking, the fragile world of meaning the boy has created for himself collapses. Ill and distraught, he plunges into the mountain stream to swim to his father—and drowns. All of Aitmatov's fiction has a powerful undertow of mystic, almost pantheistic meaning and *The White Steamer* is a classic that should be read by any child who is a serious reader.

Books for the Young Patriot

The bookcase is getting crowded, but now there is a gap. There are no religious books. Soviet children are acquainted with some of the legends of Western civilization. The myths of ancient Greece, for example, can be found in school libraries. Teachers believe that ancient mythology "stimulates the imagination, stretches the mind and encourages interest in the ancient past". But until recently children in the USSR cannot buy, or borrow from a library, a book of stories from the Old or New Testament written in faith, or any similar book from the world's other great living religions.

However, all Soviet children are encouraged to read two kinds of books that have "mythic" dimensions and that intentionally cultivate patriotism and identification with the motherland. These are books about major events in Soviet history, and books about

Lenin. Predominant among the first are stories either about the period of War, Revolution, and Civil War (from 1914 to the early 1920s), or about the Great Patriotic War (1941-1945), both of which were times of high emotional intensity and drama that contributed substantially to the forging of the Soviet national identity. The first period was so important in the life of Arkady Gaidar (1904-1941) that it dominates practically every story he wrote. Gaidar's work has always been popular. It adheres to the canons of Socialist Realism (a positive hero overcoming odds to further the cause of "the people") but that alone would hardly keep his books alive in the hearts of children. His secret, and the secret of most other successful works in this genre, is that not only has he created child characters who can practically walk off the page but he has endowed them with the power to do important things. Adults pale by comparison. No child can resist such a vision!

The best known of all of Gaidar's books is *Timur and His Team*. Timur is a young boy who collects his friends into a secret club to do chores and clandestine favours for people whose men (sons, husbands, sweethearts, fathers) are away serving in the Red Army. It sounds sentimental but it isn't. The plot is full of action, the writing taut, and the characterization excellent. The influence of this book was strong during the war, when children, too young to fight, were anxious to be part of the action. They would call themselves Timurites, after their hero, and form similar groups. They still do. This attractive and believable presentation of a working children's collective is one of the reasons that *Timur and His Team* never goes out of print.

The Great Patriotic War gave rise to a host of stories and novels for children and teenagers. One of these, *Search Behind the Lines* by Yevgeny Ryss, was originally published in 1946. Kolya lives with his schoolteacher grandfather in a small town in Belorussia. They take in, as boarders, a soldier's wife and her small daughter, Lena. When the Germans invade, Lena's mother is killed in a bombardment, but Lena and the other two manage to escape and find a safe refuge for two years in an isolated forest hut, living off the land and studying under Grandfather's tutelage. Meanwhile, Lena's father becomes an important general in the Soviet Army.

One day a sinister stranger appears near the hut. The children flee and have many dangerous adventures, which convey the terror of living under the German occupation, without actually overwhelming the child reader. Once again children are the main characters, and many of the adults, except for the grandfather, come across as unreliable and even treacherous. The story ends with the emotional reunion of father and daughter and the rout of the Nazis by Soviet troops. Child readers are bound to be gripped by the heroism of the two children and convinced of the need to defend the native land. As for teenagers, they can read absorbing stories about the war by Konstantin Simonov, Vasil Bykov, Yury Bondarev, and Boris Vasiliev, among others. These are recommended reading in the senior grades.

Books about Lenin are of a different order. They are widely available and read by every Soviet child at school, if not at home. Similar books about Stalin have vanished as if they never existed. Lenin's wife, Krupskaya, wrote a children's version of the life of her husband in her rather leaden prose. *Lenin's Life* by Mariya Prilezhaeva is in the school program. Zoya Voskresenskaya (b. 1907), has devoted her whole career to writing stories about Lenin and his family. These stories have a ritualistic flavour that reminds me of those about the child Jesus that I used to hear in Sunday school—the hero is imbued with just enough naughtiness to demonstrate his humanity but, otherwise, he is wise beyond his years. I am told that Soviet children respond to these stories with some emotion, which is not surprising considering how central the name of Lenin is to their daily life from the time that they enter the educational system.

Voskresenskaya has written several full-length books about Lenin. I read one called *Mother*, which tells the story of the Ulyanov family from the point of view of Mariya Alexandrovna, the mother of them all. Lenin's family was large and close. He had two brothers and three sisters. His father, a progressive provincial school administrator of some social status, died before his children became revolutionaries, leaving his wife to deal with the execution of their eldest son, Alexandr, and all the consequences that flowed from that event. Her children were constantly being imprisoned or exiled, so she obviously had a hard and difficult life, but she survived to the age of eighty-one, much loved, according to Voskresenskaya, by her surviving children. Writing a book from her perspective is an effective way to capture a child's attention. I must say it captured mine as well as I raced along from incident to incident, from Lenin as a five-year-old to Lenin the great revolutionary. The author has done a great deal of research and there is a naturalness to the scenes she describes that would be very appealing to children who have no other basis from which to judge the historical record. These books about Lenin are bound to enhance the emotional aura that surrounds his name even though the child who reads them may eventually grow up to reject his ideology.

Book Illustrations

For very young children (and even for older ones) the impact of a book on his or her imagination will be greatly enhanced by the way in which it is illustrated. In this respect, Soviet children are privileged because the quality of the illustrations in their books has been remarkably high throughout most of the Soviet period. Immediately after the Revolution, when raising the first generation of Soviet children became a focus for serious commitment, gifted graphic artists joined with creative writers such as Chukovsky and Marshak to produce first-class books for children. Later on, illustrating children's books became one of the few areas where artists could indulge in fantasy and experimentation. Besides, owing to the number of new titles produced each year, and the large print runs, a good book illustrator could and still can ensure himself or herself a comfortable living.

There are five artists who, to my mind, best exemplify the qualities of imagination, playfulness, colour sensitivity, and skill that are, alas, missing from so much of the art produced for the adult world in the Soviet Union. Pride of place goes historically to V.V. Lebedev (1891-1967) and V.M. Konashevich (1888-1963), both of whom illustrated many of Marshak's poems. Lebedev lived and worked in Leningrad. Influenced, no doubt, by the exciting avant-garde painters with whom he associated, his illustrations have a stylishness and élan that make them fitting companions to Marshak's humorous and light-hearted poems. Konashevich created subtle and amusing two-colour lithographs that brilliantly capture the flavour of Marshak's translations of Mother Goose rhymes, which were published in a collection entitled *The House That Jack Built.* His fine, nervous line drawings for Chukovsky's works are as well known to older people in the Soviet Union as E.H. Shepherd's drawings of Christopher Robin and Winnie the Pooh are to my generation in the English-speaking world.

My own special favourite among the illustrators is Tatyana Mavrina, who was born in 1902. In one of her most recent books, published in 1983, a set of luminous gouaches accompanies some poems by Alexander Blok. Mavrina is a colourist. I feel that she must have spent hours in the Pushkin Museum staring at the great Matisse paintings that hang there. That Matisse's Mediterranean blue should translate so well to the Russian landscape is astonishing, but it works, perhaps because Mavrina is colouring the sunny landscape of childhood. In 1976 she received the Hans Christian Andersen medal for the illustration of children's books.

Mai Miterich (b. 1925) is also a colourist and an international prize-winner. His illustrations are characterized by splashes of bright primary colours and continual movement. Lev Tokmakov (b. 1928) is more controlled, and the pleasure of his illustrations lies in the unusual harmony of his shapes.

Each of these five illustrators (and there are many more) has understood very well that small children respond spontaneously and happily to pure colour, simple form, and uncluttered line, and that their appreciation of any story being read to them is enhanced by the accompanying visual experience. The wonder to me is not that these illustrators are so popular but that they, and so many other fine ones, have been given such a loose rein. Any Soviet child who has spent time with the books that these artists have illustrated will not be completely at sea in the world of modern art.

The Culture of Reading

Not every Soviet family has such a complete children's library, of course. However, nearly 90 per cent of them claim to have a home library, and if there are young children in the family, it is bound to contain at least some of the books I have discussed. Since I am convinced that one of the distinctive features of growing up in the Soviet Union is the influence of books and literature on the imagination, a few words are needed about how books and children are brought together.

The Soviet Union suffers from a mass phenomenon known as *knizhny golod* or "book hunger". This hunger is only partly a result of an unsatisfied desire for forbidden foreign books. That pales to insignificance beside the hunger for more of their own, for the Russian classics and "the latest 'hot' item in Soviet fiction". The problem lies in the gross inefficiency of the publishing business. First of all, the industry prints unreadable ideological works, and then allows chronic paper shortages to limit the availability of desirable works. Soviet visitors to Canada are shocked by the amount of paper we waste in advertising, but their wastage starts back in their mismanaged forest industry even before the wood becomes paper or newsprint.

The demand for books in the Soviet Union is vast. There were well over ten million subscribers in 1985 for a three-volume edition of Pushkin. During the same year publishers were only able to meet 30 per cent of the demand for children's literature, and this is in spite of the fact that every year Detskaya Literatura, which is the biggest but by no means the only publisher of children's books, publishes five to six hundred new titles, about two hundred million copies all told. Eduard Uspensky, the creator of "Gena the Crocodile", has been told by the libraries that he is the most widely read children's writer in the USSR, but he has trouble believing it because he knows his books cannot be found in the shops. The authorities claim that they are trying to respond to book hunger by increasing the size of print runs as well as by changing the balance in the categories of published books. In 1984, children's books and literature in general, including contemporary fiction, made up 51 per cent of book production, up from 35 per cent in 1975.

This "book hunger" is partly the result of rising levels of education in the Soviet population as a whole and, even more, of the deliberate efforts that have been made for many years to create what enthusiastic librarians call a "culture of reading", an effort in which everyone in the book world has been taking part. Detskaya Literatura, for example, runs a Children's Book House in Moscow that is entirely devoted to familiarizing children with books. It sponsors regular conferences where children tell authors what kinds of new books they would like to read. Detskaya Literatura also encourages children to respond to its books in writing. There is a brief message on the last page of every Soviet book for children that urges the reader to write the publisher. Over 35,000 letters from children are received each year which are carefully answered by staff members at the Children's Book House. I was told that, because children tend to think that if something is in print it must be all right, they are not highly critical of the content of books. However, they complain when they consider the characters unrealistic or when they dislike the language in which a book is written. More girls write than boys, usually about something they have found touching or that they have learned from one of the book's main characters. Many authors answer children's letters themselves, or take part in young readers' circles, so that they can respond directly to children's questions.

People from the House of Books often take books into the classroom for discussion. They conduct polls in libraries and schools throughout the country. They also sponsor competitions. In 1982, for example, all the children's libraries of the Moscow region conducted one on the theme of a "Flight to a planet with life on it". Teams of young readers sought information from the books in the library and then collectively "created" planets. The team that had the most imaginative planet was invited to the House of Children's Books to meet with science-fiction writers who promised to use their "new" planet in a book.

The constant interaction between creative writers and their small readers is an attractive aspect of Soviet children's book culture. Both Tokmakova and Aleksin spoke to me about their regular visits to schools, and other places where children are, and how much they enjoyed them in spite of the time such visits took away from their writing. Children's book publishers in the Soviet Union have always played an important role in the encouragement of new writers and of quality literature for children. This was true after the Revolution under the guidance of Chukovsky and Marshak and later of Maxim Gorky. It was also true during the cultural "thaw" that followed the death of Stalin. The new challenge of the 1980s is to maintain the culture of children's reading, that has been so carefully nurtured for so long, in the face of competing attractions for young people's attention, such as popular music, television, and videos.

I used to see children reading all over Moscow: in the Metro, on park benches, on the riverbank, but most of all in the many children's libraries scattered around the city. Although there are rarely enough children's books in the bookstores to satisfy the eager demand, there are plenty in libraries for children to borrow. Every school has its own library for the use of its students that is supposed to contain copies of all the books on the recommended-reading lists as well as reference works and books about Pioneer and Komsomol activities. The school library also subscribes to the major national and regional children's magazines and periodicals. The fact that a book is from a school library confers a stamp of authority on its perusal. Thousands of other children's libraries serve essentially the same population as the school library but they are geared more to the needs and interests of an individual child. These libraries vary enormously in size and quality. The ones I have seen are friendly places staffed by people who seem to care equally about books and about children (which was not my experience in bookstores).

Looking over the shoulders of children browsing in libraries, and scanning the shelves, I began to get an idea of their tastes. A twelve-year-old girl showed me a book about ballerinas that had caught her fancy. Two ten-year-olds were laughing together over a book of jokes. In one reading-room in Moscow, young adolescents were absorbed by science fiction. In the circular fairy-tale room in the children's library in Kiev six- and seven-year-olds lay on the carpeted floor and listened dreamily to a story-teller. According to the research that has been conducted by the Central Children's Library in Moscow, preferences have changed over the years. Fewer books by classical authors are being borrowed while non-fiction is growing in popularity. There is a new and growing interest among girls in knitting, sewing, and embroidery, and they want "how-to" books to guide them. Boys want mechanical books as well as sports manuals. History, biography, and popular science interest both sexes.

Certain Soviet authors, however, never lose their popularity. Arkady Gaidar continues to head the list for young school-aged children, while Vladimir Krapivin, a romantic author, is the favourite of the twelve- to fourteen-year-olds. My Soviet friends often told me how much they had depended on library books as they were growing up. And their children seem to read as much as they did. The average Soviet child is still growing up in a culture of books.

And it is not only book publishers and libraries that try to nurture the culture of reading. The electronic media are also brought into the picture. There are a number of literary programs on both radio and television aimed at encouraging children to read and to appreciate good literature, although television, improving under *glasnost,* will increasingly compete for children's total attention. Newspapers and magazines, however, have a vested interest in creating young readers and young writers as well. *Vesyolye Kartinki* (Merry Pictures), a magazine for very young children, is full of stories, riddles and rhymes, and the simple pencil games that children find amusing: join the dots, follow the maze, finish the drawing, and so on. *Murzilka* is a magazine for slightly older children (young Octobrists) and *Kostyor* (Campfire) and *Pioner* are magazines for the Pioneer age-group. There is also a newspaper for Pioneers called *Pionerskaya Pravda*, which is published twice a week in Russian and, with a circulation of more than nine million, has a huge readership. The Union republics also produce children's newspapers in their own languages. All of these periodicals print stories and poems by new writers as well as by established ones, and they provide a unique opportunity for children to see their own work in print

(Aleksin, Mikhalkov, and Gaidar all published juvenile works in *Pionerskaya Pravda*). There are child correspondents all over the country and the newspaper makes frequent use of their contributions.

In the last analysis, however, it is young readers themselves who will determine, consciously or unconsciously, the degree to which their behaviour will be influenced by what they read. If they are poor or uninterested readers, it will hardly matter what reading fare is placed before their eyes. However, if readers are "talented"—a concept put forward by Samuil Marshak when he said that "literature needs talented readers for its talented authors"—then there is no end to the possibilities that the books that Soviet children read may open up for them.

Learning to Read

Soviet experts emphasize that the mastery of language is crucial to human development. In order to become fully conscious human beings, children have to master words and their relationship to objective and subjective reality. According to Lada Aidarova, the developmental psychologist whom I quoted in Chapter 6, consciousness is not just knowledge, but knowledge enveloped by the attitude and emotions of the knower. It follows, therefore, that a reader who *loves* to read will be a more conscious and sophisticated reader at every level. As Chukovsky said, children from two to five years of age have a very creative attitude to language. It is during this period that they build up their attitudes to words and to the realities that words represent. This is why children like to play with words so much at this age. Words free children from the environment in which they live and enable them to single themselves out as separate persons, to become subjects of activity rather than objects of it.

Aidarova says that if children are going to love reading then they must enjoy the *process* of learning to read and take an active and creative part in it. Judging by my conversations with primary-school teachers and my examination of the reading primers, it is likely that most Soviet children do enjoy learning to read. A Russian-speaking child encounters his or her first reader at six years of age. Called an *Azbuka* or "ABC", it opens with images based on familiar fairy-tales or on scenes from ordinary life. The teacher says one or two words related to the image and the child is expected to "see" the sound and the pattern of inflection by looking at his or her book, where they are represented by brackets and stress marks. There is considerable classroom discussion about the pictures and the words the pictures suggest. The letters of the Cyrillic alphabet (which most children learn in kindergarten) only appear later in the book where they are grouped according to affinities to sound.

Such methods for teaching children to read appear to be successful. Illiteracy is not an issue I ever heard discussed when I lived in Moscow, nor has it emerged as one during the current airing of social and educational problems. Although schools have been scored for many other shortcomings the fact is that Soviet children *do* learn to read and, more importantly, they do so in a literary context.

The overt political content of the *Azbuka* is minimal. There is a portrait of Lenin, of course, and a number of pictures of mothers and fathers at work on construction sites or in the fields. There is a poem about "my" brother, the border-guard, and his dog, protecting "our" sea, "our" land, and "our" air. There are also a few phrases about "my" grandfather, the war hero. Otherwise the tone is playful or mildly edifying rather in the manner of the primer from which I learned to read in the 1930s. Soviet children are encouraged to say the polite words *Dobry Den*, *Zdravstvuyte*, *Spasibo*, *Pozhaluysta* (Good Day, Hello, Thank You, Please) in imitation of their favourite TV character, Stepashka, the little hare who appears on the nightly program "Spokoynoy Nochi, Malyshy" ("Good Night, Little Ones").

The last section of the *Azbuka* is made up of a series of short readings from most of the authors I have already mentioned. First, there is a poem about the great pleasures that the children will now be able to enjoy because they can read. Then, there is a piece by Krupskaya about how much Lenin loved to read, and how his favourite writer was Alexander Pushkin. This is followed by brief extracts from Pushkin, Tolstoy, Ushinsky, Chukovsky, Bianki, Marshak, Prishvin, Mikhalkov, Barto, Nosov, and a few

others. From the questions that follow each selection it is clear
that the *Azbuka*'s authors assume that the children are already
acquainted with the larger works from which these passages are
taken.

The next reader is considerably more didactic than the
Azbuka. Now that the children have been enticed into reading, there is less room for playfulness, and the serious business
of learning to be a Soviet citizen begins. This text opens with
Mikhalkov's words to the Soviet National Anthem and continues
with a section on the motherland. Where does the motherland
begin? the children are asked. And a poem answers: with the pictures in your ABC, with the neighbours in your courtyard, with
the songs your mother sings to you—and with the image of Lenin.

The rest of the reader is divided into sections marked off by
the various festivals of the Soviet year containing passages that
celebrate the seasons of the year, "our friends" the animals, and
the joy of work. Scattered throughout are prescriptions for how
little Octobrists ought to live. A large number of these texts come
from the same familiar authors. Many of the poems and little
stories are light-hearted and humorous. In themselves they are
hardly moralistic, but morals are carefully drawn by the questions
that are placed at the bottom of the text. Now that they are seven,
it is time that Soviet children learn that literature is more than
entertainment.

In the last section of the book there is a generous selection
of readings intended to introduce children to the great Russian
writers and to literary forms. There are twenty-five pages of
folklore—songs, proverbs, rhymes, riddles, and tales—and then
twenty-five pages of works by Pushkin, the fablist Krylov, and Leo
Tolstoy. The questions on these pages appear to have two aims:
one is to ensure that children actually understand the text; the
other, to encourage oral experience by using the text for role-play
and recitation.

I cannot remember how I learned to read. I know I was reading
by the age of five, but I don't know how it happened. Recently,
however, I came across a primer that was used in the province
of Ontario at the time that I was growing up. I recognized it
instantly, and was able to recapture some of the emotions that

it had evoked in me at the time. I recall the anxiety of reading aloud in class, the curiosity about the next story in the text, and the impatience that progress was so slow. Most of all, I remember the excitement of being able to make sense at last out of those squiggles on the page, and of finding out that they composed words with which I was already familiar, referring to things I knew something about. It was the discovery of meaning in the written text that sped me along until I mastered the necessary skills and was able to read every book I could lay my hands on.

Like my first reader, Soviet reading textbooks assert the primacy of the word. In contemporary Canadian readers, the image tends to dominate. Given the overwhelming influence of television in our culture, this is only to be expected. Nor do I have anything against illustrations, particularly for young children. However, words and images are not exactly interchangeable and I am concerned when pictures overwhelm the text in a book intended to teach children to read. An attractive image may actually discourage a child from putting forth the effort needed to learn a word because initially it appears less meaningful than the picture.

The Literature Lesson

For most of the Soviet period, a price has been attached to school-taught literacy in the Soviet Union: an accompanying dose of ideology. Children are encouraged to read a good deal, it is true, but they are also told what to think about what they are reading. Up until the end of the primary grades, literature is included in the teaching of the native language, but from grade four (when the children are ten years old) it is taught as a separate subject by a teacher who is a literature specialist and who has had ideological training. Whether or not a child will be permanently conditioned by what a teacher says depends a good deal, I think, on whether he or she has become one of Marshak's "talented" readers, knowing how to read for personal meaning. How a Soviet child develops this ability is something of a mystery. It will depend partly on the child's family experiences, partly on temperament, and partly on whether he or she has had the luck to draw a teacher who cares passionately about literature—and there are many. The syllabus is restricted, but it is also rich. If the teacher follows the manual (which many, but not all, Soviet teachers do), the literature included in the syllabus will be taught according to its perceived social value. However, the love of literature is deeply imbedded in the Russian soul and literature teachers are usually well educated. Most Soviets I know can recall at least one inspired teacher from their school days.

For students whose native language is Russian, the grade-four program comprises seventy class hours. The first nine or ten are devoted to folk-tales, riddles, and proverbs. The remainder of the year is divided almost equally between pre-revolutionary and Soviet literature, including four classes on Hans Christian Andersen ("The Snow Queen"). There is also a list of books for independent reading and a list of poems (or prose passages) to be memorized. Eight hours are to be spent on speech development (this means reciting poetry as well as public speaking) and eight hours on the discussion of home reading. Over the summer a grade-four student is expected to read as many as twenty-five books and report on them in the fall. I have the syllabuses of 1970-1971 and for 1987-1988, and there are not many changes.

Nor have there been very many at the grade-eight level. The students are now fifteen years old, and the program is a systematic course in Russian literature from the *Lay of Prince Igor* to Gogol (mid-nineteenth century). Six class hours are devoted to foreign literature; Molière (*Le Bourgeois Gentilhomme*) and Lord Byron (*Childe Harold's Pilgrimage*) and the development of the notion of romanticism in literature. It is the independent-reading list that has expanded to include younger authors and some who were previously omitted. How quickly rehabilitated authors such as Pasternak appear on the school curriculum will be interesting to observe. The latest textbooks being written are expected to include a new section on Soviet literature from the 1950s to the 1980s.

In the senior grades, Soviet students are expected to write a number of themes for their literary classes as well as to take exams and participate in class discussions. Each student has a textbook that contains biographies of the authors on the syllabus as well as the correct ideological interpretation of each work. In writing their themes students are expected to abide by this analysis. The teacher assigns two marks to each item, one for spelling and grammar (most teachers will be very strict) and one for content. In presenting his or her theme the student must first make an outline and then compose five or six pages of text. A young woman I know, who was at school in the 1970s, showed me some of her corrected themes. In grade nine she was asked to write a theme on "a moonlight night in Otradnoe", the passage in *War and Peace* in which Tolstoy describes the romantic longings of the youthful Natasha. "I love Natasha," my friend had written, "for her kind attitude to other people, her noble feelings, her purity, her poetic, spontaneous, sincere, honest, trusting and patriotic nature. None of her actions were motivated by greed or personal advantage. Lying and hypocrisy were incompatible with her nature."

In her graduating year she was assigned the theme "the condemnation of the vices of capitalism in Gorky's early works". Here is her outline: "The power of money that corrupts the soul / Slave labour which makes people cruel / Poverty of the spirit / Soulless attitude to human beings / Indestructible hope for a new human life."

Today, the teaching of literature from a narrow social-utilitarian and Marxist-Leninist point of view has been successfully challenged by respected teachers and specialists in literature. Students are now being openly encouraged to do what so many of them have done privately for years—turn to literature for personal enrichment and private solace. This changing approach was spearheaded by an innovative teacher named Yevgeny Ilyin who has been shown on television and featured in the press, both signs that he has some official support. In an article in *Komsomolskaya Pravda*, in August 1986, he had this to say about the use of themes in the literature class: "We should proceed not from 'The Image of the Oak in the novel *War and Peace*', but from the spiritual needs of the real, perceivable student—from his pain and his inner drama (of which he may not even be fully aware), from the demands of present-day reality mirrored in his pain and from our own passionate response to this pain and this need. As for Tolstoy—he will help us. He will help! And so will Pushkin, and Turgenev, and Fadeev."

Seventy years after the Revolution, the Soviet Union has become a "nation of readers". Given the conditions of pre-revolutionary Russia, where the overwhelming mass of the population was illiterate, this is a very substantial accomplishment. But how do books affect children growing up in the Soviet Union today? In my view, it is an illusion to believe that the contents of a book can influence child behaviour directly. The edifying (or corrupting) potential of literature is vastly overrated by the keepers of children's morals. It is from people, not from books, that children learn to be good or bad. If a boy is brought up in a family where his father and mother respect one another and where both respect him, then a pornographic book is unlikely to corrupt him into acting out his fantasies on a female victim. By the same token, a young girl who has been either overindulged or neglected by uncaring or unthinking parents is hardly likely to be turned into a hard-working collectivist just because she has read a couple of stories (although this may happen if those stories are true literature and are read and then explained to her by an adult, a teacher, perhaps, who cares for her). Nevertheless, literature can and does influence children's behaviour in an indirect way. The route is through the child's imagination. By touching the imagination of a child, a good book can penetrate and light up the soul so that there is a difference, as Emily Dickinson once wrote, "where the meanings are"; or, to use Gorky's metaphor, "the wings of words attached to the spines of good books will fly with a child's soul so far into the realm of the imagination that the child will never be earthbound again."

In the Soviet Union today, there is still a certain distance between a child's public or institutional experience of literature and his or her private, personal experience. Because the private experience is the one that is nourished within the child's family when the child is very young I am certain that it is the one that will dominate later on *if* that experience has been a rich one. Families rarely teach mathematics or physics at home, but they can and do "teach" literature. As long as they care enough themselves, they can find in the Soviet Union of today as rich as treasure-house of books as any child might need.

In May 1987, there was another gathering at Pasternak's grave in Peredelkino, this time to celebrate the poet's restoration to the Writers' Union from which he had been ignobly ejected in 1958, two years before his death. During his darkest years Pasternak, like so many of his predecessors and contemporaries, had been sustained by his belief in the prophetic role of literature and by an equally strong belief in his own vocation. I was told that at one point in this long overdue ceremony someone recited "The Nobel Prize", the last poem Pasternak is believed to have written. Most of this poem reflects the author's anguish when not only State authorities but some of his fellow writers attacked him for winning the Nobel Prize for Literature. Under virulent pressure he was forced to refuse it, yet in this same poem, the great poet found the strength to write:

> Even so, one step from my grave
> I believe that cruelty, spite
> The powers of darkness will in time
> Be crushed by the spirit of light.

The Young Citizen

CHAPTER THIRTEEN

The Young Worker: Labour Education and
Perestroika in the Schools

The most famous schoolhouse in all of Russia is the Smolny Institute in Leningrad. Every Soviet schoolchild knows its name. Before the Revolution, it was a highly respected school for the daughters of St. Petersburg's noble families. But none of them put the name of Smolny into the history textbooks; a man did, a certain man who sat at a desk in an upstairs room on a certain day in October 1917 and launched a revolution.

It was Lenin, of course, who brought fame to Smolny. The school was closed in February, 1917 and in early August the building was occupied by the Bolsheviks, who turned it into the headquarters for the Revolution. On October 24, Lenin left his hiding place north of the city and came to Smolny to change the course of history. The next day, cruiser *Aurora* fired its historic shot, the Winter Palace was stormed, and the provisional government collapsed. Later that night, Lenin stood up in the gold and white assembly hall and announced to the world, "The workers' and peasants' revolution, the need of which the Bolsheviks have stressed time and again, has been accomplished."

Students never came back to Smolny. After the Revolution, the building was dedicated to the service of the new state. From

November 1917 to March 1918, it was the seat of the Bolshevik government. Then Lenin and his commissars moved to the Kremlin in Moscow. Local Bolsheviks stayed on in the building to govern the region and now Smolny houses the Communist Party Committees of Leningrad and the surrounding region, which maintain it, in part, as a shrine to the revolutionary events that took place there.

The building is a handsome one. Its long yellow façade is broken by a double row of white pillars crowned by a classical pediment. The approach to Smolny is along a wide treed avenue and on a cold day in January 1983, we drove up to its front steps under an arch of bare branches, black against an opalescent sky. We were met by a small delegation—my husband was making an official call—and taken directly upstairs to see the rooms that had been sanctified by the October Revolution.

First, we were shown the set of rooms that had served as Lenin's command post. A small plaque on the door still reads *Klassnaya Dama*—a teacher had lived there when the girls were at school—but the furniture is spare: plain wooden desks, straight chairs, an old-fashioned typewriter, a metal telephone. The atmosphere was hushed, but I had no trouble imagining the noise and clatter of that fateful day: messengers rushing in with reports, tense discussions, rapid decisions, orders going out. In the assembly hall, which we visited next, I did not even have to imagine the presence of Lenin because a huge portrait of him hung on the far wall obliterating any hint of the young girls who used to dance beneath the crystal chandeliers.

From the assembly hall we walked down a very long corridor, past offices that had once been classrooms, to a small apartment at the back of the building where Lenin had lived with his wife, Krupskaya, during the early months of Soviet power. The stuffed chairs on which Lenin and his colleagues sat to discuss the institutions of the new state are still draped with the white muslin sheets that covered them then. The couple's iron bedsteads have not been moved. Lenin and Krupskaya must have taken their personal possessions with them when they left for Moscow, but a few objects remain. Among them is a small fan propped open on a side table set against the wall. It is painted with a view of Niagara

Falls. A young soldier, so we were told, found the fan behind a bed in a student dormitory and brought it to Krupskaya as a gift. One of our hosts picked it up and turned it over. "Look," he said with a smile, pointing at the small, neat lettering, "a souvenir of Canada".

I doubt that the people who now work in Smolny's former classrooms are even interested in the fact that their office building was once a schoolhouse. At most they may occasionally ponder the events that took place there during and after the Revolution. But visiting this building, with its combination of traditional elegance and revolutionary history, made such a strong impression on me that I have thought of it ever since as a symbol for the way in which the Russian past became fused to the Soviet present in the crucible of the Revolution. This was certainly true in the field of education, for the Soviet school system as its exists today was not made up out of whole cloth in 1917; it was patched together out of many ideas and practices current at the time and then sewn up with Marxist-Leninist ideology. The strongest thread used for this task by the early Bolsheviks was the concept of labour-oriented polytechnical education.

The idea of training young workers for the benefit of the State was hardly new in 1917. But the Bolsheviks gave it a special twist. As followers of Marx, they accorded "love of work" the status of an ultimate human value. Labour education, therefore, had to be an end in itself, not just a means to something else. According to Lenin and his colleagues, the personal worth of citizens in the new Soviet state would be determined by their participation in "social production" and by the contribution their labour made to the well-being of Soviet society. If work was to be considered the central activity of human life, then it would also have to become the central focus of education.

The challenge for Krupskaya and her colleagues, who began to plan the new "socialist" schools that were to replace the old "bourgeois" ones while she was still living in Smolny, was to design a school environment capable of transforming a young child into a qualified worker who would understand the fundamental meaning of "labour" (in the Marxist sense) and become a highly motivated builder of communism. The ideal society the Bolsheviks envisioned would never be able to come into existence without the help of a strong economy that could produce enough goods and services to go around. Finding the right mix of work-oriented experience, academic training, and social upbringing was impossible for those early educational planners, though, because material conditions in the young state were too hard. And finding the right mix has defeated authorities ever since, in spite of numerous minor reforms and a few major ones. At the moment the State is trying again.

All states, of course, hope that their public-education systems will deliver the increasingly skilled workers the modern world requires. However, when a school system is unable to respond to the human needs of its pupils at the same time as it trains them, then this hope is bound to be disappointed. In the Soviet Union, the needs of a command economy administered from Moscow have long made short shrift of the needs of individual children in all parts of the Soviet Union for a flexible, nourishing environment in which to develop. This was also true of public education in Russia before the Revolution owing to the tsarist regime's long tradition of educating skilled workers and socially useful citizens, ideologically convinced of the primacy of the State. During the Revolution, this social-utilitarian and ideological tradition became fused with the Marxist-Leninist vision of the ideal state. Most of the school reforms of the Soviet period have been introduced to ensure that schools have the structure and the curricula to graduate workers who can respond to the needs of a planned socialist economy. In this social-utilitarian ideological tradition, any conflicts that arise between the needs of the State and the needs of the child are generally resolved in favour of the State.

Fortunately, another Russian educational tradition was taken up at the time of the Revolution by Krupskaya and her colleagues as they designed the new socialist schools. I call this second tradition "pedagogical humanism" because it has generally been represented by people who have taught and cared for children. From the nineteenth century until the present day, this tradition has been upheld by an unbroken stream of remarkable teachers and writers who have appreciated the special conditions that children require for growth and development. In the event of conflict between the needs of the State and the needs of the child, these people have tried to resolve the situation in favour of the child.

Naturally, there is continual tension between these two traditions fuelled by the "objective" (to use a Marxist term) necessity of responding to one set of needs without totally denying the other. Occasionally, the tension is resolved. Two of the greatest teachers of the Soviet period, Anton Makarenko and Vasily Sukhomlinsky, were able to develop educational methods to satisfy individual needs in their students while at the same time helping them to become the productive and committed workers required by the State. And I visited several classrooms during my years in the Soviet Union where the State's needs for scientists and linguists clearly coincided with the students' needs for mastery, for verbal self-expression, and for social interaction.

With respect to labour education, educational planners of an ideological bent tend to look at the needs of the State and recommend ties between the school and the work-place from that perspective. The pedagogical humanists, while not denying the usefulness of school-work-place ties, look at them from the perspective of the child. They observe what happens when children become involved with productive labour and reflect on its educational implications for each individual child. Both of these perspectives exist within the Soviet educational system today, interacting and pushing for change as they have since the time of the Revolution. In the past, the voices of the pedagogues have often been muted, even though they have always been there, somewhere, protecting the "child" in the "pupil" being taught by the State. Today, in the new climate created by Gorbachev, they are being heard again.

The Russian Roots of Soviet Education

Peter the Great founded state education in Russia. Determined to westernize his backward country and to expand the Russian empire, he drew up a formal program for educating the young of all classes so that they would develop the requisite skills and acquire the up-to-date scientific knowledge that would enable Russia to compete with the rest of Europe. Education became obligatory for advancement in State service and, as a result, the upper classes were forced to educate their sons, if not their daughters. When the Church opposed his educational goals, Peter responded by forcing the clergy who taught in church schools to become salaried employees of the State. By this means, without actually suppressing the teaching of religion, he introduced the secular note that is characteristic of the Soviet educational system today.

Catherine the Great was more interested in educational theory than Peter had been. She read many of the liberal tracts on pedagogy that were written in Germany and France during the second half of the eighteenth century and discussed them with her European correspondents, including Diderot and Voltaire. In 1764, she founded the Imperial Society for the Education of Noble Girls, better known as Smolny. Then, in 1786, "Statutes for Public Schools in the Russian Empire" announced the creation of a public elementary-school system that was modern (by the standards of the time), utilitarian, secular, and open to all sections of the population, including girls.

A guide prepared for the teachers who were to be employed in the new system clearly reflected Catherine's attitude to moral training. "The rank of teachers," it said, "obliges them to try and make from their students useful members of society and to do what is necessary to frequently encourage youth toward the observation of their societal duties, to enlighten their minds, and to teach them to think and to act wisely, honourably and decently." Throughout Catherine's statutes relating to public schools, there is the same insistence on patriotism and loyalty to the State that I have found in every Soviet government document on public education I have ever read.

The pedagogical humanist tradition arose later than the social utilitarian one and is represented in the nineteenth century, notably by Konstantin Ushinsky and Leo Tolstoy. Konstantin Ushinsky (1824-1870), who has been described as the "father of Soviet pedagogics" and "the founder of scientific educational theory", was a Ukrainian who came to Moscow to study at the university. A fine-looking, sensitive man with an attractive personality, he was widely read and full of progressive ideas. In

1859, he became the inspector (the academic director) at Smolny, and set about to modernize the school's curriculum. For a brief period, his apartment in Smolny became a meeting place for students, teachers, and writers, everyone in St. Petersburg who was interested in new pedagogical ideas. But Ushinsky was too radical for the authorities, and after three years he was sent away from Smolny (on full salary, it must be said) to study the education of girls abroad. A victim of tuberculosis, he returned to Russia in 1867 and devoted the three remaining years of his life to the St. Petersburg pedagogical society.

Ushinsky was a strong advocate for scientific humanism at a time when the authorities clearly were not. He respected the needs and rights of children at a time when "pedagogues (and others) have...forgotten that a child is not only being prepared to live but is *already* living". In his major work, *Man as the Object of Education*, he deplored the teaching methods current at the time as quite inappropriate to the ages and stages of growing children. He wrote that teaching methods should correspond to the natural development of children as it is revealed by psychological studies rather than to a preconceived image of adulthood. This developmental approach to teaching is upheld by the teacher-innovators who are such an important feature of the current educational scene.

According to Ushinsky, education should devote itself primarily to the formation of character. His articles, handbooks for teachers, and texts for children are full of suggestions to this end. Underlining the importance of the teacher's personal influence, he wrote "The teacher must feel he is a living link between the past and the future and understand that...kingdoms rest upon his work and that whole generations live by it."

Ushinsky also believed that work should be an essential component of education. If children are to grasp the psychological significance of work and appreciate the meaning it will give to their subsequent lives, then they ought to have some direct experience of labour at school. He insisted, however, that children be free to choose their own vocations, thus focusing squarely on the child's needs rather than those of the State.

The ideas of Leo Tolstoy (1828-1910) on the subject of education and labour were particularly influential at the time of the Revolution. Tolstoy had a great respect for manual labour, which he had acquired, he used to claim, by walking behind a plough at Yasnaya Polyana, his country estate. He believed that children should be taught to appreciate labour and the people who perform it. "I think that the first condition of a good education is that a child should know that all he uses does not fall from heaven ready-made but is produced by other people's labour."

Tolstoy was an extraordinary teacher. He set up a school on his estate for peasant children and then set about to entice them into learning. "Children should be taught as little as possible," he would say. "A child...can learn when he has an appetite for what he studies." And then he would whet that appetite by sheer force of personality. Witnesses have described the extraordinary energy that he and the children generated between them. He taught regularly at Yasnaya Polyana from 1859 and 1862 and then from 1870 to 1876. In between he wrote *War and Peace*.

Tolstoy loved teaching children and wrote marvellous little stories to introduce them to the joys of reading. It is through these stories, as much as by anything else, that his genius reaches down to small children today. By the end of his life, nearly one million copies of his readers had been sold, and today, every Soviet child, no matter his or her nationality, learns to read with the assistance of one or two of Tolstoy's brief but clever stories, full of folk wisdom and humour.

Tolstoy spoke up for the peasants (which is one of the reasons Lenin admired him) and he valued work, but he knew children well and his defence of their personal rights remains fresh because it stems from his recognition of certain developmental needs that are common to all children at all times and in all places, not just to peasant children in nineteenth-century Russia under the Tsar.

Four Architects of the Soviet School System: Shatsky, Blonsky, Lunacharsky, and Krupskaya

During the five months that Lenin and his fellow Bolsheviks were based at Smolny, their main task was the consolidation of Soviet power, but at the same time they were engaged in laying the foundations for the major institutions of the new state. Education was accorded a high priority, and Lenin's comrade, Anatoly Lunacharsky, was appointed to the government almost immediately as People's Commissar for Enlightenment. His commissariat, commonly known as Narkompros, was given responsibility for the arts and for education, both of which were important means of enlightening the masses with respect to their new historic role. Lenin's wife, Krupskaya, was very busy during this period, formulating objectives for the new, labour-oriented Soviet school.

When Lenin and Krupskaya and the new Soviet government moved to Moscow, the work of Narkompros was enriched by two educators, both of whom had been influenced by Tolstoy: Stanislav Shatsky (1878-1934) and Pavel Blonsky (1884-1941). Shatsky, a man of many talents, was an unusually innovative teacher. The child of an impoverished minor official, he had studied in a classical gymnasium. He was later to write that his passion for educational reform came partly from his "keenly felt personal experience from school which gave him the clear right to judge how children should *not* be taught."

Before the Revolution, Shatsky worked with children from workers' families in clubs, settlements, and summer camps and began to develop the ideas about work-centred schools that he later built into the plans for the new Soviet school system. He and some colleagues slowly came to associate themselves with the Revolutionaries because they decided that only under revolutionary conditions could they really help the poor children with whom they spent so much time. His wide intellectual background (he had been able to travel in Western Europe before the First World War and to study educational systems there), his practical experience with children, and his commitment to labour-oriented education made him invaluable to Narkompros as it struggled to construct the new school system. He worked closely with Krupskaya whom he admired.

Shatsky was a pedagogical humanist and his fortuitous presence at the birth of Soviet education promoted the continuation of that trend in the educational system. For him, as for Ushinsky, the concept of labour education involved the development of the human personality. In an article he wrote in 1918 entitled "First Steps to Education Through Work", he stated that "school is a place where the findings of our own personal experience are to be processed, systematized and compared with the findings drawn from the experience of others.... Schooling through work is constantly extending the range of children's first-hand experience." The work he envisaged for young students included practical tasks appropriate to the child's age and state of development, meaningful to both the child and to society, and, to the degree possible, organized by the children themselves.

Blonsky was the theorist of the new system. A psychologist with, by all accounts, the temperament of a philosopher and the convictions of a reformer, he was determined to create a radically new type of school for the children of the Revolution, one that would incorporate the Marxist vision of the true value of labour along with some of the pragmatic ideas of John Dewey (by whom he was greatly impressed). *The Labour School*, which was published in 1919, established the model for the polytechnical labour school that the first educational decrees of Lenin's government had called for. In it Blonsky wrote, "The goal of education is to introduce the child to contemporary industrial culture," and the method is to work from the practical to the theoretical. A period in a factory will introduce a youngster to tools. This should enable him or her to understand the working principles of tools and then lead on to physics. Bringing in the harvest should raise questions that will introduce the student to the principles of agriculture. Through polytechnical education, Blonsky asserted, students will learn first hand about the social relations that characterize the world of work and thus come to understand, from their own experience, the advantages of socialism over capitalism.

Anatoly Lunacharsky (1875-1933) was the first Commissar of Enlightenment and, as such, had a special role to play with respect to the foundation of the Soviet school system. A long-time colleague of Lenin, he was an immensely civilized man who read voraciously and spoke eleven languages. Under the influence of Marx, Lunacharsky embraced the idea of labour-oriented polytechnical education as fundamental to the new school system for which he was responsible. In a speech to the First All-Russia Congress on Education in 1918, which adopted the principles of the Unified Labour School, he said, "A man lives not in order to labour but he labours in order to live like a human being. In this…lies his touch of the divine, his dignity, that which distinguishes him from the animals." He then went on to talk about labour both as a school subject and as an educational method. He said that labour should be kept of such a nature in the school that "it can, with gentle care, make out of a little person, a full grown worker in a socialist society".

Of all the founders of the Soviet school system, Nadezhda Krupskaya (1869-1939) was the one who remained most faithful to the educational ideas of the Revolution. Not surprisingly, she saw herself as the translator of Lenin's ideas on education into action. Lenin, the son of an educator, firmly believed that universal schooling was essential to the creation of a classless society, so when he assumed power, he gave priority to the education of young children. His early edicts made it possible for Krupskaya, Shatsky, Blonsky, and others to implement their programs rapidly where conditions permitted. As they formulated their projects, educators like Krupskaya were quite open to ideas from the rest of the world. They studied the works of Maria Montessori and Friedrich Froebel to learn about the techniques these famous teachers had developed to sensitize children to the material world around them. American educators, notably John Dewey, were even more popular for their hands-on approach. Krupskaya was impressed by the way in which she understood that the productive labour of children was organized in the United States. She read about American children gardening in teams, sorting and distributing letters, cleaning streets, preparing food, and so on. She wanted similar activities to be part of the new Soviet school system with the proviso that children engaged in them also learned how what they were doing fitted into the overall pattern of social production.

My girls still giggle when they remember how they learned to sew buttonholes in grade seven, a skill which, as far as I know, they have not used since. Here is Krupskaya on the teaching of sewing: "Hours can be spent teaching pupils how to make even stitches or buttonholes. This is teaching a craft. But sewing can also be taught in an altogether different way by linking it to the study of materials and tools so that the child could clearly see that different materials require different tools." And with respect to machine sewing: "Pupils can just be shown how to turn the wheel, insert the shuttle...or the teaching of machine sewing can be linked with the study of the machine itself and of similar machines. Thus sewing can be taught either as a craft or it can be linked to an analysis of materials, tools, motors...which is the polytechnical approach to education."

Anton Makarenko—"The Work Collective"

Although the plans for the new Soviet school system were full of progressive ideas they had to adjust to a terrible reality, a reality of homeless, miserable children in a country torn by civil war, famine, and disease, with a largely illiterate population and a haemorrhage of intellectuals to the West. In 1922, Blonsky wrote: "Children have classes in half-ruined buildings, wet and cold...teachers starve...there are no textbooks.... Who teaches? Young, scarcely educated women without experience." How could new ideas be properly implemented in such conditions? By the end of 1923, there were fewer than four million pupils in primary schools, down from nearly seven million in 1921. The rest were wandering the cities and the countryside. They were called the *besprizornye*, the "wild ones".

Anton Semyonovich Makarenko (1888-1939) was among a few unusually talented teachers who rose to the challenge of these circumstances. But the students he was responsible for were, in some ways the *least* capable. In 1920, having first taught for many years and then studied educational theory, Makarenko was asked to take charge of a labour colony for juvenile delinquents in the Ukraine. He recognized that the life-style of these young people was a product of the disorders of the times and he set about to change it. Inspired by the ideology of the new State, he developed a way of educating adolescents through the self-imposed discipline of a labour collective that had remarkable results.

Makarenko was an extraordinary figure, tough and demanding. But he was fond of his wild charges and he believed in their capacity to reform themselves. In the beginning he had few material resources, yet his colony was expected to become self-sufficient through its own efforts. This led to a tense situation, which he tried to resolve through various experiments. What worked in the end was dividing the young people into groups and giving them collective responsibility for certain tasks. They had to organize and execute their own work plans with minimal guidance.

Because Makarenko gave so much responsibility to his young-sters, he ran into trouble with the authorities, who preferred to see discipline imposed from above. But Makarenko said "Discipline based on...dogma and command inevitably tends to turn into blind obedience and mechanical subordination to one adminis-trative person." He had no intention of taming his wild children by breaking their wills. Instead, he helped them to harness their explosive energy by encouraging them to direct it into the col-lective and share it with others of their own age in a constructive work activity. His first labour colony was an agricultural one, but the second was involved in light industry. Nowadays, educa-tional reformers recall with undisguised envy that "fourteen- and fifteen-year-olds at Makarenko's factories manufactured cameras meeting world standards."

Makarenko's charges would arrive at his colonies in a dishev-elled condition with little more than the clothes on their backs. To restore a sense of personal pride, he encouraged his student collectives to set themselves military standards of order and neat-ness. It was this aspect of Makarenko's method—whose basis they misunderstood—that appealed to Stalin's lieutenants and led to his theories being distorted in the 1930s. Makarenko had to be tough with his youngsters because they desperately needed structure but under his toughness lay a basic trust. As a result, his students adored him and many went on to demonstrate in their own careers the effectiveness of his methods.

Makarenko's great successes as an innovative educator were during the 1920s. By the end of the decade, his ideas, which were essentially democratic, were being either rejected or distorted. At the same time, Krupskaya was forced to admit that the unified labour school she and the others at Narkompros had designed had failed to take off. "Poverty did not permit us to build workshops; there was a lack of premises, a want of equipment," she said. However, it was not only physical and organizational problems that blocked the implementation of the progressive educational ideas of the 1920s. They also fell afoul of Stalin's drive to industrialization. The child-centred experimental programs of the pedagogical humanists, which had been designed to develop creativity and individuality in Soviet school children, were not welcome to an increasingly repressive Party leadership who wanted adult workers who would do what they were told. By 1932, almost all children between the ages of eight and eleven were receiving full-time education, but it was an education that was old-fashioned, unimaginative, and heavy on military-type discipline. The needs of children were thoroughly subjugated to the needs of the State, and the humanist voices were quelled. Blonsky retreated to the Institute of Psychology, Shatsky and Lunacharsky died, and Makarenko, deprived of his young charges, turned to writing.

As for Krupskaya, I often thought of her as I drove along the Garden Boulevards in Moscow on my regular shopping expeditions, for I would pass a charming statue of her near Sretenka Gate. She is depicted as a young and graceful woman wearing a long dress and a shawl, her serious face radiant with her hopes for the future. I am told that her last years were very difficult as her influence dwindled and her cherished dreams crumbled. She continued to work on her plans for the state-run kindergarten system, but her vision of a labour-oriented polytechnical education was destroyed. In 1937, she wrote a poignant letter to the notorious A.A. Zhdanov, then a secretary to the Central Committee of the Party. "Why make it possible," she pleaded, "for those who oppose this development [of polytechnical education] so important to Marx, Engels and Lenin to say that...the Central Committee has decided to abolish labour instruction in the schools?" But the next day it did.

The 1930s were harrowing for adults and children alike. A Soviet woman I met not long ago told me what it had been like for her going to school then. Her father was an old Bolshevik, so she was able to attend a special school in Leningrad. When she entered the school in 1932, there were six or seven classes in each grade. When she left in 1941, just before the German invasion of Soviet territory, there was only one class left of her original schoolmates. The other children she had known had vanished one by one as their parents were caught up in Stalin's purges. Some were sent to boarding-schools, where more than a few starved to death, some went to relatives in the countryside, some went to Siberia with one parent in order to be near the other. She never knew exactly what happened and nobody ever said. The classes just got smaller and smaller.

The War and Its Aftermath

Whenever there is conflict in the adult world, children lose out. When that conflict is a full-scale war, then the needs of the State will take precedence over all individual needs, and not only those of children. Most of the Soviet schools that continued to operate under the devastating conditions of the Great Patriotic War did the best they could but, inevitably, the emotional life of the students was absorbed by their struggle for survival. The curriculum was a secondary concern. This was a time not for experimentation in education but for reliable and kind-hearted teachers (usually women or wounded veterans). What labour education there was was hardly of the polytechnical type recommended by the Revolutionaries. It consisted instead of boys and girls working in the fields and factories to replace the adults who had gone off to fight.

Gorbachev is an outstanding example of the successful (although in his case, unplanned) combination of work and study. Born into a peasant family near Stavropol, he was ten when Hitler's armies invaded the Soviet Union. His father fought and was wounded and the young Gorbachev lived with his grandparents. During the war years and immediately after, he had to spend almost as much time working in the fields as he did attending school. This did not prevent him from entering Moscow University at the age of nineteen, but he did so on the basis of his unusual intelligence and his status as an exemplary worker (with a Red Banner of Labour to prove it) rather than on the basis of a strong academic education.

Until the death of Stalin, most Soviet schools continued to be strait-jacketed by the rigid methods of instruction imposed during the 1930s. School uniforms had been reintroduced along with traditional teaching methods. In the late 1940s there was even a brief return in some parts of the country to segregated schooling for boys and girls. Progress in education showed up mainly in numbers—more schools, more teachers, more years of schooling for more pupils—solid achievements, it must be admitted, in a nation exhausted by war but not a manifestation of any particular State concern for the personality of the growing child or for his or her needs as an individual. From the early 1930s until the late 1950s, the social utilitarian tradition in Soviet education prevailed by a wide margin over the pedagogical humanist one. The contradictions provoked by this situation in the lives of students and their families were overwhelmed by more powerful forces associated with the war and with Stalin's terror. However, child-centred scholars continued to work quietly throughout this period, as did many teachers who loved and understood children, and who did what they could for them, often at great personal sacrifice. Most of these teachers are, alas, unknown for there is no record of their activities, except in the hearts of their students. There is one, however, for whom the Second World War was such a searing experience that he devoted the rest of his life to teaching small children with love and patience, and to writing about what he learned from them. His name is Vasily Sukhomlinsky.

The Teacher Who Loved Children: Vasily Sukhomlinsky

For twenty-nine years, Vasily Sukhomlinsky (1918-1970) was the director of a school in the small Ukrainian village of Pavlysh. He was a profoundly humane man who suffered greatly without becoming embittered. He grew up in the countryside and started teaching in rural schools when he was very young. With the advent of war he became a soldier, leaving his young wife behind in their village. When the village was occupied by the Germans she tried to help the partisans but was caught and put in prison where she gave birth to a son. Her captors threatened the life of her newborn to force her to reveal the names of partisan leaders. When she did not, they killed the baby and hanged her. The loss of his wife and his son in such circumstances was a source of deep distress to Sukhomlinsky for the rest of his life and made him particularly sensitive to the needs of children who had survived the horrors of war.

Sukhomlinsky was badly wounded at the Front (the shrapnel embedded in his chest finally killed him many years later), and since he could no longer fight he went back to teaching. Once his home district had been liberated from the Nazis, he returned to help restore the devastated local school system. He found the war had robbed many children of their childhood and he hoped to enable them to recover it in his "School of Joy", for he, too, believed that a period of play in a child's life is essential for later learning and that the imagination can never develop without it. He was also, like his predecessors Krupskaya and Makarenko, with whom he identifies in his writings, a believer in the power of education. He defined education broadly. "Every moment of life, every patch of earth is educationally important," he wrote. And he added that, so is "every person encountered by an individual in his formative years, even those encountered by chance." The task of the true educator is to make all those educational moments, places, and chance encounters, useful for the child's development as an individual and as a member of society. When he was given his own school to direct, he dedicated himself to creating within it the best possible learning environment for the village children entrusted to his care. His efforts led him to make many discoveries about what works and what does not with small children.

Reading Sukhomlinsky's books is like being in an actual classroom or out on a field-trip. I do not always agree with his conclusions, but the descriptions that he gives of his Tanyas and Danyas, Seryozhas and Kolyas are so vivid and suggestive that I am able to draw my own. His most famous work is called *To Children I Give My Heart*, a title that indicates the sentimentality that flaws his writing style. Yet, he was much too practical to be really sentimental, and reading his accounts of his years of teaching six- and seven-year-olds, it is impossible not to recognize that, when he gave his heart to these children they gave him wisdom in return.

This is what Sukhomlinsky has to say about children and work: "Work becomes a great teacher when it enters the lives of our students and gives the joy of friendship and comradeship, develops inquisitiveness and curiosity, gives birth to the excitement at the overcoming of difficulties, opens the way to ever new beauties in the surrounding world and awakes the first feeling of citizenship."

Most of Sukhomlinsky's students came from farming families so he started them off on agricultural work. He helped six-year-olds plant an apple orchard and grapevines and rejoiced with them three years later when they presented the first fruits of their labour to their families. Then he introduced them to animals. He built a bird hospital, and the younger children brought in injured birds they found in the woods and fields and learned how to care for them. Older children were given responsibility for the farm animals, lambs and calves, in order to learn the basics of animal husbandry and the satisfactions of planning and working together on a common task.

Sukhomlinsky varied the children's work in order to help them discover their gifts and inclinations. He built them a junior workshop, and introduced girls as well as boys to construction and modelling and fretwork. He strongly believed that the "source of giftedness and talent in children lies in their fingertips" and that working with their hands on a complex, difficult but not impossible task develops intellectual problem-solving skills as well as physical dexterity. This connection between the hand and the mind is an important component of Soviet educational thought, although it is seldom worked out so well in practice as it was under Sukhomlinsky's patient and dedicated supervision.

Sukhomlinsky was a pedagogical humanist; when he thought about children and work he thought first of the needs of the child. He was also a committed Soviet citizen, so the needs of the State were always before him as he planned the work education of his pupils. In his view, unless an activity has a social dimension either while it is taking place (as in joint planning and execution) or as an end-product (as a gift for Mother) it cannot be considered work. It will be only a hobby, which has its own role in a child's life but does not rank in the same category as work. Work for the whole of society has the highest value of all. Sukhomlinsky fully expected that his rural students would grow up to work on nearby State or collective farms. His task was to educate them so that they would love their work there, no matter what form it took, be proud of it and find satisfaction in it.

The School Reform of 1984

When Sukhomlinsky died in 1970, the goal of universal education for all Soviet children up until the end of the eighth class had finally been attained. However, it was to be another full decade before the ten-year general education school was the rule across the whole USSR. Thus, it was not until the early 1980s, sixty years and more after the Revolution, that the objective conditions were finally created to implement the polytechnical education envisaged by Lenin, Krupskaya, and their colleagues. The impetus for the labour orientation of the current educational reform has come from changes in both the needs of the Soviet state and the needs of Soviet children. The State needs a working population with greater technological sophistication and inventiveness than the current one to catch up to the rest of the industrial world transformed by the computer. And Soviet children need livelier, more interesting, and more relevant education if they are going to be able to make a positive response to the challenges that the twenty-first century will pose for the Soviet Union as a country, as well as to themselves as individual citizens.

After the death of Stalin, Khrushchev tried to reintroduce polytechnical labour-oriented education. However, his reforms were not well thought through and the conditions were not ripe for them. One friend of mine, who was at school during this period, recalls the useless hours she spent on an assembly line in an electric light factory. The factory manager could not figure out what to do with the raw youngsters he had been assigned, who were all thumbs. So Khrushchev's law obliged my friend to spend an extra year in school to no real purpose. The Soviet population resisted this waste of time and so, after eight years, Khrushchev's labour-oriented school reform was deemed a failure and abandoned.

But as the Soviet economy stagnated more and more under Brezhnev, State planners decided it was time to try again. When we left Moscow in 1983, school reform was in the air and, by the time I returned for a visit in September 1984, it had already been signed into law. Recognizing that it had been imposed from above, like each of the previous labour-oriented reforms, I went to the Ministry of Education to learn what it was supposed to achieve.

I was received by a ministry official in one of the typical veneered offices Soviet authorities set aside for meetings with inquisitive foreigners. Acting as a spokesman for the needs of the State—I had the impression he had not been back to a classroom since he had escaped many years before—the official confirmed that education had once again become too removed from "life". So, it was time to "combine studies with socially useful labour and include universal vocational training for students from the earliest grades".

This time the idea of labour-oriented education was more popular. A public survey taken after the draft guidelines for the reform had been published on January 3, 1984, indicated that the vast majority of people (95 per cent) saw the proposed "organic union of studies and labour as a way of overcoming negative phenomena among young people", that is, delayed civic maturity, political naïvety, and unwillingness to work when needed. For the next four months there was an intense public debate. People talked and argued vigorously, some of them with surprising frankness. Letters poured into newspapers and television stations. Even quite young children held meetings and were canvassed for their views. When the final guidelines were confirmed by the Supreme Soviet on April 12, 1984, a number of changes had been made to the original document, although on closer examination they did not prove to be substantial nor did they respond to the thoughtful comments about children's needs that had been made by such experts as Dr. Igor Kon. In an article in *Pravda* that appeared quite early in the debate, Dr. Kon stressed the importance of understanding the developmental psychology of children. He deplored the infantilism that he saw as characteristic of a certain proportion of young people in the Soviet Union and which he attributed to overprotectiveness in the school as well as in the family. He urged more room for responsible self-government by students, and a greater sensitivity on the part of teachers and the school system as a whole, to the delicate construction of self-esteem in the individual child.

If it does not address the real needs of children, can the current reform work? When I asked the official in the Ministry of Education for his opinion of the reform's chances for success, he took another sip of mineral water, and explained carefully that the reform would take two five-year plans to implement and that a lot of explanatory work remained to be done. Right away the pay and the status of teachers were to be raised, he said, salaries by as much as 30 per cent. This was a very sensible and popular way to start, at least with teachers, as one of them later told me. New courses were to be introduced slowly. And considerable time would be necessary to rewrite textbooks so that they would become livelier and more relevant. Another aspect of the reform, the addition of a year to the whole program by accommodating six-year-olds in the general school, would take two or three years to accomplish. Since all these aspects of the reform could be orchestrated from Moscow, the Ministry did not anticipate serious difficulties.

We then went on to discuss what has, in fact, proven to be the most problematic aspect of the reform, the intimate linking of an individual school and the local community. The guidelines are quite clear. Each school must be sponsored by a factory, a farm, a consumer service industry, a construction company, or whatever. Sponsors and schools are supposed to work together on a plan for providing "general labour training of a polytechnical sort to pupils in grades one through seven and beginning in grade eight to provide training in occupations". To do this sponsors are required to set up on site (or at the school) workshops for training and a permanent work and recreation camp for school children. They are required by law to allocate necessary machinery, equipment, and clothing; to pay children for their work, where appropriate; to feed them and certify them for the skills they have learned. Schools, in turn, are to provide an educational component so that vocational skills are not all that a pupil acquires. In addition, they are expected to offer more to the sponsor than a mass of raw students requiring training. Students are to "help with the landscaping" (clean up, I think that means), put on entertainments for the workers, collect scrap paper, work in the factory's day-care centre, and so on. Can such a co-operative link really be established and maintained to the mutual benefit of students and their sponsors? All past efforts at such arrangements have failed partly through a lack of energy, commitment, and imagination on the part of individual sponsors and schools. The Ministry official was sure that this new labour-oriented school reform had been so well thought through that it would be able to work where others had not. He was wrong.

Young people began to report that all they were doing in their labour classes was "kill time". They were rarely given real work, or if they were, it was menial work that they perceived as exploitive. What they wanted was to get paid for work of their own choosing as in North America. However, the paperwork for getting after-school work or a summer job, even in resort towns where their seasonal labour is welcome, is so onerous that most students are discouraged. This indicates a serious mismatch between the needs and interests of students, and the structures that have been set up to turn them into productive workers. Very soon, many people, including Gorbachev, were openly asking "Is the school reform another mistake?"

Then, on February 17, 1988, Politburo member Yegor Ligachev gave an extraordinary report to the Central Committee of the CPSU about the problems the school reform had encountered. He admitted it had bogged down, explaining that the "evolutionary nature of the reform" had come into contradiction with *perestroika*. There were no guidelines for the democratization of the school system, for example, nor had anything like enough money been allocated for the improvement of school facilities and school equipment. Furthermore, primitive vocational training had been overemphasized at the expense of a sound general education in science and technology.

To remedy the shortcomings in school management, Ligachev called for the establishment of local schoolboards made up of parents, teachers, CPSU and Komsomol members, representatives of trade unions and students' organizations, as well as people from local industries. He also called for restructuring both the Academy of Pedagogical Sciences, which has acted as a drag on the reform process since the beginning, and the educational bureaucracy. In March 1988, a State Committee for Education, chaired by Gennady Yagodin, formerly the Minister for Higher and Secondary Specialized Education, replaced the three existing ministries concerned with public education at the USSR level.

In the same speech Ligachev commented favourably on a proposal to create a new teacher's union. When this comes about, it will be an important move in defence of the needs of the child, for teachers will finally be able to exert influence on the system as a whole, not just on their own pupils. During the second half of the 1980s, by far the most interesting phenomenon in Soviet education has been the growing visibility of child-centred teachers (pedagogical humanists all) and their alignment with the most progressive elements of the CPSU against the academic establishment and the educational bureaucrats in the battle for the hearts and minds of children.

The Teacher-Innovators

I first became aware of these extraordinary teachers when I met Simon Soloveychik in the spring of 1986. I asked him about Sukhomlinsky and wondered if he had any successors. "Yes," answered Soloveychik with enthusiasm, and proceeded to count them off on his fingers: Viktor Shatalov in Donetsk, Yevgeny Ilyin in Leningrad, Sofiya Lysenkova in Moscow, Shalva Amonashvili in Georgia, I.P. Volkov in the Moscow region, Mikhail Shchetinin in the Ukraine, and more. All, he went on, were remarkable teachers with years of classroom experience who taught children, not subjects. He took Shatalov as an example.

With the 1984 reform, complete secondary-school education has become compulsory for everyone, even for those in vocational programs. This means that teachers now face the challenge of retaining the interest of every student in the class, including the 30 per cent who used to be allowed to drop out of their own accord. Soviet students cannot yet be enticed to study hard by the promise of material success in the future. Nor, in today's climate, can they be coerced. So they have to become excited about learning. Traditional teaching methods are rarely successful with uninterested children. According to Soloveychik, it took Viktor Shatalov twelve years of experimentation with restless students to find out how to reach them.

Shatalov is a math teacher. He knows many students balk at learning by exposition and rote; that some are afraid to have their mistakes corrected, that others fail to do their homework and fall behind, and still others lose their enthusiasm because they are never called on. His system is aimed at all these students. The key to it lies in the study notes he prepares for each lesson, a sheet of paper that provides each student with a template for organizing new material. These notes are devised so that students can concentrate on explanations in class knowing they have the notes to fall back on. However, they must listen to the teacher or the notes will make no sense. Shatalov separates marks and corrections. When he checks his students' notebooks, he marks them, but does not correct the mistakes. When he checks solutions to problems, he corrects mistakes but doesn't grade them. People who have watched him teaching on television (and he has appeared on prime time, right after the immensely popular 9:00 p.m. newscast "Vremya") think of their own school-days and sigh.

Neither Shatalov nor the other teacher-innovators are as radical as some educators in North America during the 1960s. They do not propose closing schools altogether, nor do they wish to get rid of the standard curriculum (although they would like to see it improved and made more flexible). They are much more practical than that. They recognize that the State needs highly qualified scientific and technical workers well trained in maths and science as well as in the use of language. But they also know that students will enjoy learning only if they are excited by the process and see its relevance. The parents of some of Shatalov's students actually claim that their sons and daughters solve algebra problems for pleasure rather than watch television.

Shatalov's method is specifically designed for mathematics, and his students have a high record of success in post-secondary education. His critics, however (and he has many, especially among the academicians), attribute his success to his personality rather than to his methods. They have tried to block the dissemination of his ideas by attacking him personally. This has also happened to other experimental teacher-innovators perceived as threatening by the establishment. Educational theorists (and not only those in the Soviet Union) seem to prefer teacher-proof pedagogics, as if that were not a contradiction in terms.

The innovators have banded together because, although they teach different subjects and come from different parts of the Soviet Union, they have a common approach. Instead of trying to pour the contents of the curriculum into their students, they believe in co-operating with them so that they will move together towards the knowledge and skills the teacher wishes to impart. Teachers call this approach the "pedagogy of co-operation", and in October 1986, several of them met in Peredelkino to hammer out an eighteen-point manifesto on the subject.

When this manifesto was published in *Uchitelskaya Gazeta*, a teachers' newpaper that is published three times a week and reaches virtually every teacher in the country, the response was overwhelming. For the next two years the newspaper featured lively debates about new ideas in education and sponsored the creation of clubs of creative pedagogy called *Eureka,* of which there are now well over five hundred in different parts of the Soviet Union. Observers have been excited by the prospect of teachers "taking a crash course in democracy by participating, in an ever broader way, in the renewal of the education system and of their own selves".

Protests sparked by *Uchitelskaya Gazeta* prevented a proposed teachers' congress from taking place in July 1987, because it was being organized by the entrenched establishment. It was postponed until January 1988, and then again until December 1988. In the meantime, the innovators issued new manifestos on behalf of children. They called for greater democratization in the whole educational system and for treating children as "personalities" with feelings to be respected. *Uchitelskaya Gazeta* ran into trouble, and its feisty editor was demoted. When the congress finally took place it received a mixed press. Both the innovators and the conservatives were able to speak out, but nothing much was resolved. In his report to the congress, Gennady Yagodin reiterated that Soviet education is "based on the Leninist principles of a uniform, labour-oriented, polytechnical school" but that structure and content have to be changed to reflect the "realities of our time". Naturally he emphasized the role of the teacher and promised an improvement in their material conditions. At the same time, he warned them against expending so many of their efforts on "extinguishing a child's inquisitiveness, liveliness and unconventionality".

A conservative school director then criticized the pedagogy of co-operation in the strongest possible terms, accusing it of "setting up the interests of society against the interests of the State". Thus the see-saw between the conservatives and the innovators goes up and down, just as it does in every other area of Soviet life, as Gorbachev struggles for reform. But the teacher-innovators know that alienated, unhappy, and overly controlled children will never make vigorous, productive adults, so they will not back off.

Teachers will always be the key to successful education in the Soviet Union. Since the time of Peter the Great, educational reforms have been imposed from above, and often for the same reason, economic necessity. Some of them have been well considered, others not. But, one way or another, it is the teachers who have had to implement them. Good teachers know what works and what doesn't; they know what children are like and what they need; and, even in the worst of times, Russia has had good teachers. This is why the pedagogical humanists are so important. Even if, as in the case of Tolstoy and Sukhomlinsky, their immediate influence is limited to the children they teach, their indirect influence on other teachers is enormous. By now hundreds of thousands of teachers have read and used their ideas.

Educating children is not like making tractors. No matter how universal the State-imposed reform, how standard the compulsory curriculum, each educational act is an individual one that involves the interaction of one particular teacher with one particular child. The gifted teacher knows that the child he or she is teaching will have to grow up to function within society, so the needs of the State must be given their due. But the same teacher will know when the demands of the State are unsuited to the developmental needs of his or her students, and will try to protect them. In that case a "reform" will be subverted. But, if the reform looks promising, then the good teacher will try to make it work.

This is a period of tremendous ferment in Soviet education, with many exciting ideas being discussed and tried out by teachers. The children of *glasnost* are having a very different experience from those who passed through the system in the Brezhnev years. In the end, for all the rhetoric, the needs of the State were almost as badly served by the school system during the late 1970s and the early 1980s as were the needs of children. However, the people who cared about children hung on and now they have a chance to be heard. What particularly impresses me about the teachers' movement is that, while it is full of passion, it is also practical and constructive, and it is aimed at producing the kind of climate in which children can learn best.

Meanwhile, as the debate rages, Soviet children continue to go to school. Millions of them file into hundreds of thousands of classrooms every morning and sit down at their desks. In Bratsk, Natasha opens her primer and reads about mothers who work in factories. In Kirghizia, Sultanmurat does sums and then goes out to help with the sheep. In Kiev, Pavlik studies the history of the CPSU and turns a lathe. And, in Murmansk, Olga works on a computer.

The schools in Murmansk are a long way from the Smolny Institute for Girls of Noble Birth. But they are not so far from the educational ideas that germinated at Smolny both before and after the Revolution. When Leningrad was known as St. Petersburg and was the elegant capital of a wide-flung empire, Murmansk was only a village on the Kola peninsula, three degrees north of the Arctic circle. But Murmansk began to grow after the arrival of Soviet power, and, as a naval base, it was vital during the Second World War. The convoys that carried supplies to our Soviet ally on the Murmansk run were a legend in my youth. My husband and I were both deeply moved as we stood on a hillside plot beside the graves of the Canadian, American, and Commonwealth sailors whose bodies had been fished from the icy waters of the Barents Sea. And we were just as moved as we looked down the hill and up the next, and the next, and saw the countless thousands of Soviet graves stretching on and out of sight.

After the war, Murmansk staggered to its feet. It is now a city of 430,000 inhabitants, and growing. It has the look and feel of a frontier town, a new frontier, the Soviet North. Soil is trucked in from the south to cover the bare rock, and new buildings shoot up every day. One of the most impressive, the best located, the best designed, and the best built, is a new Pioneer palace for the children of Murmansk.

The children we saw in Murmansk looked lively and healthy. The birth rate, we were told, was "satisfactory". Many of them stay on in Murmansk when they grow up and work in the canneries and shipyards, or go to sea in one of the factory trawlers that spend five months at a time off the coasts of North and South America. They also become teachers and policemen, scientists and construction engineers. There is plenty of work for all, the pay is higher than it is in the South, and the vacations are long.

The school we visited was an old one, as old as a building can be in a city that was bombarded into rubble during the Second World War. It is shabby and so crowded that students attend in two shifts. Outside, there is nothing to distinguish it. But inside there is a computer room. From the point of view of both the State and the child, the introduction of a course called "Fundamentals of Informatics and Computer Technology" into all schools in the USSR in September 1985 was one of the more positive aspects of the school reform. Many schools had to start teaching the course without actual computers, but not this one in Murmansk.

The teacher in charge of the computer room was tremendously enthusiastic. Although his equipment was primitive by North American standards, it was possible to see through his eyes what computers might mean to the lives of his students. He himself has never travelled far, only to Moscow where he was among the first 60,000 teachers to receive special computer training in the summer of 1985. But he has a new world in his head. He loves computers and he loves children. It is hard to tell which he loves most. What he really wants to do is to put them together.

He showed us what he had to work with: calculators, audio-visual machines, a computer corner where several keyboards were linked to a central display screen, a disk drive, and a printer. He explained that the mainframe made in Minsk was IBM compatible, and that the various other components had come from Eastern Europe, notably Bulgaria and East Germany. His students learn quickly, he said, and were in and out of the room all day. There were even a few *fanatiky*, as hackers are called in the Soviet Union. But such children are exceptional. The rest make collective decisions with their teacher as to how to get the most out of their limited equipment.

The Soviet Union has an enormous need for computers and workers skilled in their use. Faced with the technology of the future, the Soviet Union will rise or fall on how well it is able to modernize its industries (and bureaucracies) through the use of computers and related technologies. What is required, as experts now admit, is a generation of bold, inventive, competent young people who know how to work together. During the Brezhnev period, the Soviet Union fell far behind. Now, the needs of the State require that it catch up and the computer is providing an unexpected work-oriented medium to develop the personalities and abilities of Soviet children as well. In Murmansk, a happy group of youngsters and an enthusiastic, committed teacher are moving together towards the mastery of an advanced industrial culture. Their experience is labour-oriented polytechnical education at its best. If it can be replicated throughout the country, chances are that, at the beginning of the twenty-first century, the Soviet economy will finally spring to life.

CHAPTER FOURTEEN

The Young Internationalist: Unity in Diversity

I am very fond of choral music. During the years we lived in Moscow, whenever I learned there was to be a choral performance at the Conservatory, I would try to attend. The Conservatory is not far from the Canadian Embassy and easy to reach by walking along the Garden Boulevards. Once there, I would make my way through ticket-hungry music students into a crowded lobby, surrender my coat and boots to a bossy cloakroom attendant, and mount the long staircase to the second floor. If I was early, I would buy a program reeking of printer's ink and study it until the doors into the Great Hall opened, and I could enter to take my seat.

The Moscow Conservatory was built during the second half of the nineteenth century to nourish the Russian tradition in music. Designed specifically for concerts and recitals, the acoustics of its Great Hall are superb. As I waited under the gaze of Tchaikovsky and Mussorgsky, Borodin and Rimsky-Korsakov, whose plaster portraits adorned the walls around me, I could feel myself surrounded by an air of critical expectancy. Soviet concert-goers are knowledgeable and attentive, and standards are high. Once orchestra and chorus had filed onto the stage, and the conductor had raised his baton, we could be almost certain that we were in for an evening of glorious sound.

Most of the orchestras and choruses that perform at the Conservatory, or in the other concert halls of Moscow, are made up of excellent musicians who come from all over the Soviet Union. Sitting in the front row, listening to Rachmaninov's symphonic poem *Spring* or Haydn's oratorio *The Creation*, I would have an excellent view of the singers who were so absorbed in their music that I could stare at them to my heart's content. What a medley of faces! Some were easily identifiable. This soprano's triangular face and perfectly arched eyebrows could only have come from Armenia, that tenor's black hair and almond-shaped eyes, from Soviet Central Asia. Others were harder to classify. Their features were individually distinctive as if each migration, each invasion, in a thousand years of history had left a separate calling-card. Yet, under the direction of a skilled and inspired conductor, this widely varied and ethnically diverse group of singers would come together to produce a rich harmony of sound.

The national folk-dance groups we saw so often on television or at official ceremonies made a different impression. I found most of them forced and artificial, out of touch with the genuine folk traditions from which they had come. The costumes, liberally decorated with glitter and tinsel, looked as though they had been cut to a universal pattern. The gaiety of the dancers seemed feigned, a smile pasted over strenuous exercise. It was only when we went out of Moscow that we found authentic folk dances, especially in Georgia, where the fierce pride of an ancient people is passed from father to son through dance. Wearing black flaring tunics criss-crossed with silver bandoleers, old men and young boys came together and, against a background of slender gliding women in pale shimmering dresses, they rise on their bent toes and spin across the stage.

The USSR, a Multinational State

The two cultural activities I have just described reflect the fact that the Soviet Union is a multinational state. For more than sixty years, the Kremlin tried to promote the idea that the USSR was a happy family of nations, each of whom brought its own cultural distinctiveness to enrich the Union as a whole. Once, as I listened to a mixed chorus sing "The People's Anthem" from the opera *War and Peace*, composed by Sergey Prokofiev during the darkest days of the Second World War, I was taken up into this dream. But for most of this time, Soviet reality showed up in the other activities; in the bland, denatured folk dances taught to schoolchildren all over the USSR, or in the brilliant intense local art forms that had nothing to do with the rest of the country.

For the rest of us, the multinational character of the Soviet Union was long obscured by the smoke of the East-West relations, through which the USSR appeared as a monolithic state. Now, as we focus on the independence of the Baltic states, on nationalism in Moldavia and the Ukraine, on disturbances in the Caucasus and Central Asia, and on ethnic violence in Armenia and Azerbaijan, the situation looks very different. It looks, in fact, as if feelings of national (and ethnic) identity are so strong that no one, not even an ethnic Russian, feels the slightest attachment to the USSR as a whole. But it is worth remembering that the Union has existed now for more than three generations and that the hearts of children are not the sole possession of their parents. So, before we make up our minds too quickly that the whole Union is about to fly apart at the seams, we need to look at the forces for unity in the education of the Soviet child as well as at the forces that have promoted not only diversity, but thoughts of secession. These forces are not strong enough to maintain the USSR in its present form, but they will determine, to some extent, the form of any new relationship that is forged.

At the time of the census of 1979, the USSR comprised 103 recognized national and ethnic groups. Ethnic Russians predominated, with 52 per cent of the population, followed by Ukrainians with 16 per cent. With Belorussians included, over 70 per cent of the inhabitants of the USSR at that time were Slavs and the rest came from a hundred different nationalities, some large, most small.

The 1989 census has shown many changes. As a result of unequal birth rates, the number of non-Slavs, particularly in Central Asia, has increased at the expense of the Russians, although not as much as had been predicted. The rate of increase in smaller nationalities has declined. Nevertheless, each national group, no matter how small, is considered a separate member of the Soviet "family" of nations with the right to representation in the Soviet of Nationalities, one of the two chambers of the Supreme Soviet. This arrangement will continue because even a diminished Soviet Union will be a multinational state.

Officially, nationality is a form, a category into which people in the Soviet Union are sorted according to certain external characteristics. The children of *glasnost*, like generations of Soviet children before them, have been taught all through the decade of the 1980s that they live in a state whose society possesses many *national* forms for its one *socialist* content. They have been taught to recognize and respect the separate identity of each Soviet nation or nationality or people in the form of its language, geography, post-revolutionary national symbols (flag, emblem, and so forth), and non-political traditions, such as costume, folklore, dances, and sports. They have also been taught that the government of each national republic or autonomous region is modelled on the Union government in Moscow, and that it is a socialist one. Finally, they have been taught that the Communist Party of the Soviet Union is the unifying thread that ties all the nations and nationalities together into one family.

The strictly political aspect of these messages will have to be modified in the 1990s to conform with the changes that are taking place within the current borders of the USSR. Yet the idea of a "family" of nations, with all that that notion implies of fatherhood, emotional attachment, common interest, and unshakeable loyalty, remains an attractive one and I expect it will continue to be drummed into Soviet children at an early age.

Living in the Soviet Union in the early 1980s, I found this "Soviet Union as an international family" concept pushed at children everywhere I went, although how this message fitted in with the nationalistic feelings that I knew so many of these children to be encountering at home was difficult for me to assess. In those days, contradictions between what some children were learning at school and what they were learning at home were only to be expected. Given the history of the Soviet Union, it could not have been otherwise. And yet the situation was not and is not one of simple opposition between home and school or between family and State. What has happened is that over the years State policy has encouraged national pride at the same time as it has tried to diffuse it. This contradictory situation is the result of the nationalities policy that Lenin formulated at the time of the Revolution. How the children of *glasnost* resolve (or fail to resolve) the tension in their hearts between their national identity and their Soviet identity, how many of them become the "internationalists" that the State would still like them to be when they grow up, is what will eventually determine both the structure and the quality of the new relations that will have to be worked out among the many nations that now comprise the USSR. Will there be bitter conflict with all the damage that that is bound to cause? Or can there be a less painful transition in which the ideal of the tightly knit Soviet "family of nations" yields peacefully to the reality of a free association of "friends"?

Unity in Diversity

During my husband's term as ambassador to the Soviet Union, we visited almost every one of the Union republics, some of them several times. Each visit was special and full of interest, and we were reminded over and over again how distinct each republic is, even those in Soviet Central Asia whose present borders were more or less invented after the Revolution.

We would come back from these trips full of enthusiasm for the national cultures we had discovered, but in Moscow we would find it next to impossible to pursue our new-found interest. Moscow is overwhelmingly Russian, and since the formation of the Union in 1922, it has imposed its Russian self as the unifying capital of a diversified multinational state. This fact was underlined at the ceremonies we attended at the end of December 1982, celebrating the sixtieth anniversary of the Union. We watched Ukrainians tumble and dance, and listened to a haunting chorus of Georgian male singers, but not once did we hear the tributes to cultural pluralism or to the vigour of national and ethnic traditions that are such a commonplace of political speeches in Canada. Instead, the rhetoric was all about "fraternal co-operation", "the brotherhood of the workers and peasants of all nationalities", "the great Soviet family", and so on.

There are obvious contradictions between the idea of the unitary state promoted by the Communist Party of the Soviet Union centred in Moscow and the aspirations of national groups in Union republics and autonomous regions. The constitution that bound the Union together in 1922 guaranteed the right of each republic to secede, a right that was reconfirmed by subsequent constitutions. For many years, this right was treated as existing only in theory, and the likelihood of such an event taking place was considered remote. However, children have always been taught that it is there, and it is now clear that certain republics are bound to secede.

Also, for many years, there appeared to be little active racial hatred or sectarian violence in the Soviet Union, and this in spite of bitter memories left by a long history of Russian dominance, a poisonous degree of anti-Semitism that waxed and waned, and visible prejudice on the part of many Slavs against the peoples of Central Asia and other ethnic groups. Of course, this "concord" was essentially the result of State control. And yet the grief and distress so many people have felt over the ugly disturbances in Nagorno-Karabakh and, more recently, in various parts of Central Asia, as well as the rush of helpers from all over the Union to Armenia after the devastating earthquake of 1988, are genuine popular responses which can, I am convinced, be partly traced to the education of the young "internationalist" in the Soviet school. When Mikhail Gorbachev said, in his report to the XIX Party Conference in June 1988, "It is imperative to preserve the friendship and brotherhood of our peoples like the apple of one's eye.... There is simply no other way, no reasonable alternative", I am sure his words resonated in the hearts of the majority of Soviet citizens.

Education is the major means by which Soviet political authorities have tried to create true "internationalists" out of Soviet children of different ethnic backgrounds. But the way education has evolved in the Soviet Union has turned it into a double-edged sword with respect to the nationalities issue. Cutting one way, it has discouraged the formation of a separate national or ethnic

identity in students by imposing a standard curriculum throughout the USSR. Cutting another, it has encouraged the growth of
this identity by allowing that curriculum to be taught in a great
many languages other than Russian. On the one hand, history
books have presented only the Soviet version of national histories and have tended to understate, if they have referred to it at
all, the important role that religious traditions have played in the
formation of national identity. On the other hand, republics have
their own ministries of education and are increasingly encouraged
to introduce their own cultural material. There is a great emphasis throughout the Soviet Union on involving parents with their
children's education, yet compulsory education removes many
children from their home environments and has succeeded, in
some cases, in weakening family ties and cultural bonds. Children's readers in any of the Soviet languages contain Russian
literature in translation as well as stories about Lenin and Soviet heroes such as the first astronaut, Yury Gagarin. Yet, each
non-Russian reader is also rich with its own folklore and literature.

Soviet education is now faced with an enormous challenge. Is
there any way that it can reconcile unity and diversity so that these
forces reinforce each other rather than cancel each other out?
The Soviet Union is not alone in facing this challenge. A number
of other modern states are encountering growing problems in
accommodating ethnic diversity within their borders, and they,
too, are looking to their public-education systems to help resolve
their difficulties. While it is probably too late to have much
influence on the course of events in the Baltic republics, I am
convinced that as long as the USSR is federated state, and there
is any hope of restructuring it, education efforts in this direction
will continue to be made.

The Nationalities Question and Lenin's Nationalities Policy

Samarkand. What a magical name! I read the tale of Alexander
the Great and his Bactrian princess, Roxana, when I was a young
girl. Ever since, "Samarkand" has conjured up images of romance
and distant adventure. I think of silk routes, of camels and
caravanserai, of formal gardens in the desert and fountains of milk
and wine, of Mongol khans and Moghul emperors, Tamerlane

the Conqueror, Avicenna, Marco Polo and later Ulug-Beg, poets and warriors, scientists and kings. But now I have to add a dose of Soviet reality to my romantic vision. When we flew into Samarkand on an April afternoon in 1982, that reality looked bleak. Driving in from the airport, we passed blocks of modern housing crumbling at the edges and rows of untidy factories belching ugly smoke. Then we signed into a hotel of the most utilitarian sort. But, when I opened the window of our room to lean out, I could see the *Gur Emir* where the bones of Tamerlane lie under a turquoise dome. My spirits rose.

We went for a walk. Beneath the grey Soviet overlay, the magic was still there. Black-haired girls were dressed in rainbows and wore brilliants in their ears. Old men sat cross-legged in the *chaykhana* (tea-stalls) and sipped tea from delicate porcelain cups. In the bazaar, men in turbans or in black and white embroidered skull caps shouted at one another while their wives argued noisily with the vendors. The air was fragrant with all the spices of the East.

The Registan, Tamerlane's vast public square, was disappointing because its mosques and *medressehs* (Islamic colleges) are so over-restored that they no longer seem real. But not far away, the Shakh Zindeh, a jumble of tombs and mosques, pulsed with life. We joined the pilgrims who were mounting the worn stone steps to visit the Shrine of the Living King. Thirteen centuries ago, Kasim ibn-Abbas, a cousin of the prophet Muhammad, came to Samarkand to convert the people to Islam. He is buried there in an elegantly decorated tomb that was built in 1334-1335 to honour his remains. Or is he? According to legend he is actually lurking nearby, waiting for the right moment to claim his "kingdom".

Next day, wandering through the ruins of the palace of Alexander the Great on the outskirts of the city, we heard the laughter of children playing out of sight in the rubble of twenty centuries. Five small boys appeared on the top of a mound across from us and waved. Their mischievous black eyes, their close-cropped hair, and their wiry bodies reminded me of the boys I used to see near the Jaml Masjid Mosque in Old Delhi. Yet, dressed in their school uniforms with their book bags, they were unmistakably Soviet. Looking at them, I could not help but reflect

on both the similarities and the differences between them and
their distant cousins in India (Babur, the first Moghul emperor of
India, came from Samarkand). In the nineteenth century, ordinary
little boys born on either side of the Hindu Kush would have been
lucky to survive into adulthood, and if they had, they would have
spent the rest of their lives in poverty. Now, in comparison to the
average inhabitant of Northern India, the population of Soviet
Central Asia is educated and affluent. However, the personal
identity of Babur's "descendants" in Old Delhi is more deeply
steeped in Islamic tradition. For someone like myself, who has
lived in India, visiting the ancient sites of Soviet Central Asia
throws such comparisons into striking relief. Why is this region
of the USSR so Asian and yet so Soviet? I became curious to know
more about what Lenin called "the nationalities question".

At the time of the Revolution, what is now Soviet Central
Asia was an outlying region of the Russian Empire known as
Turkestan. Most of its non-Russian peoples were oppressed,
as were non-Russian peoples in the rest of the Empire (and
many ethnic Russians as well). Lenin was well aware that the
restlessness of peoples who had suffered under the Russian
imperial yoke would make them useful allies in his struggle for
power. So, in order to rally them to the Bolshevik cause, he made
national self-determination, and the restoration of the language
and cultural rights that had been flouted by the tsarist regime,
part of the revolutionary platform. Yet, as Marxists, he and his
fellow Bolsheviks dreamed of a unitary state, a communist utopia
where all the nations that had made up the former Russian Empire
would join together in proletarian solidarity. The circumstances
of the revolutionary period required that national aspirations be
supported but also held in check. How to accomplish both at the
same time lay at the core of the "nationalities question", and this
ambiguity has marked Soviet nationalities policies ever since.

After the Revolution, Lenin was faithful to the commitments
he had made to attract the support of the nationalities. Several
nations seized his promised opportunity for independence. But
only Finland, which had been part of the Russian Empire for
a century, was able to keep it. The Baltic republics (Latvia,
Lithuania, and Estonia) remained independent only as long as

both Russia and Germany were relatively weak and otherwise preoccupied. The Republic of Transcaucasia (comprising what is now Georgia, Armenia, and Azerbaijan) collapsed in 1924.

These declarations of independence were unsuccessful for a variety of reasons, not the least of which was that, because he was a Marxist, Lenin did not believe in the nation-state as a permanent entity; he saw it as a political superstructure given temporary shape by economic forces. In his view, class links would endure longer than national ties, and therefore the solidarity of the working class (proletariat) was more important than national identity. Thus, Lenin's nationalities policy was a compromise. While it provided considerable support for national self-affirmation in terms of language and culture, it gave no encouragement to political and economic institutions that might turn a nationality into a separate nation-state.

Here is what children have been taught for years in the Soviet Union today about the origins of the state. In a popular picture book by E. Permyak, Lenin is quoted as saying that "the state appears whenever a division of society into classes appears, whenever exploiters and exploited appear". Occupying the foreground of the full-page illustration that accompanies this statement is a proud and angry Russian peasant roped to the dwarfed image of a feudal lord on horseback who is dragging him into a barricaded estate in the background. Reading on, children discover that before borders (barricades) were erected by states, people shared things in common. Life was hard but it was fair. The rise of owner classes who wanted to protect their belongings was what had brought about the nation-state. The book gives no other explanation. On the contrary, the young reader is assured that, in the ideal world of the future, when a socialist economy has eliminated classes of exploiters and exploited, national borders will vanish. Once again people will share things fairly.

Later on, when children encounter the history of the Soviet Union in school, they are taught that the Union came into being because working people in the various parts of the old Russian Empire became comrades and friends during their struggle against their tsarist oppressors. This solidarity was reinforced during the Civil War, as peasants, workers, and soldiers fought against the White Army and "foreign interventionists". In this way, students are introduced to the concept of "proletarian internationalism" and are expected to accept the idea that, one day, the workers and oppressed peoples of all nations will unite in friendship and solidarity.

At some level, Lenin must have believed in this myth of origins and endings. He was certainly convinced that new attitudes and relationships would be engendered in a socialist economy when the workers themselves owned the means of production. He also believed that these changed relationships would forge such strong links among all the workers in the world that attachment to nationalism would dissipate. Apparently, he had little personal feeling for the complex emotional roots of national sentiment, and he seriously underestimated its power to endure.

Where, after more than sixty years of Union, has Lenin's nationalities policy left the five little boys I saw in Samarkand? Are they growing up Uzbek? Soviet? Both? This is where the effect of the nationalities policy on the education system can be shown to be so important. Unlike their distant cousins in India, many of whom will have little choice but to spend their boyhoods begging in the streets of Old Delhi, these boys will spend years at school. There they will study in their own language and learn about many of their own cultural traditions. I have no doubt that the boys of Samarkand will grow up Uzbek, learning and probably practising at least some of the rituals of their heritage.

However, the education system will also try to ensure that they grow up Soviet. Even though they study in the Uzbek language, they study the standard Soviet curriculum in a school that is structured in the same way as every other one in the USSR. Furthermore, they learn Russian. For some years now, there has been growing pressure to improve the teaching of Russian in schools where the local language is the medium of instruction. It has not always been properly taught, particularly in rural schools in remote areas where the teachers themselves do not know Russian very well. However, the school reform of 1984 made fluency in Russian an expectation for all students graduating from any high school in the USSR by 1990. Methods of teaching Russian are being improved so that it can be used as the *lingua franca* among the various republics and, more importantly, as the key to higher education in most areas of study as well as promotion in the structures of power.

Then there are the children's organizations. I could see by their badges that the boys were already Octobrists. Soon they would be Pioneers and eventually, although less likely than it used to be, Komsomol members. For Lenin, the Communist Party was the vanguard necessary to bring about the dictatorship of the proletariat in a country of peasants. Now the communist youth organizations are expected to lead in the formation of proletarian internationalists in a country of diverse nationalities.

All of this means that the lively little boys I saw on that April day in the ancient city of Samarkand will probably grow up to be Uzbek *and* Soviet. Whether there will be conflict or concord in their breasts between these two identities will depend a great deal on their subsequent personal histories and on the course of national, and indeed of international, events.

Language as a Force for Diversity in the USSR

For children to be able to learn to read and write in their mother tongue and to be able to study other subjects in it is, I think, the single most important contribution that Soviet education has made and continues to make to the preservation of diversity and national identity. A visit to Georgia and Armenia should put this statement in context. In each of these two Union republics, a very high percentage of school children study in their native language.

I love the lands of the Caucasus. The landscape is wild and dramatic: mountains, gorges, rushing rivers, hillsides of grapevines, sheep-studded uplands, crumbling stone villages, and some of the oldest Christian churches in the world. Georgia grows tea and citrus fruit along its semi-tropical Black Sea coast. Armenia has deep-blue highland lakes, reddish soil, and a distant view of Mount Ararat. But it is not only the beauty of the landscape that pulls me back to the lands of the Caucasus. I am also fascinated by their rich and ancient cultures and by the sturdy sense of national identity among their local peoples. And I am drawn by the legendary hospitality of the region: the Georgian wine, the Armenian cognac, the generous meals, and the eloquent toasts.

There were always toasts to peace and friendship, of course, a ritual exchange at any official Soviet meal. But then came the personal ones: "to first love" (with an admiring glance at the daughter who had accompanied us to Georgia) and "to that moment in the future, wherever one might be, when one will remember this moment". The toasts were always offered in one of the languages of the region and we would reply in English or in French.

In Armenia, we called upon the Catolicos of the Armenian church in his palace at Echmiadzin near Yerevan, which has been the seat of the Armenian church since the fourth century A.D. Romanian born, the Catolicos was a gracious and saintly man who spoke excellent French. He offered us fresh fruit from the palace garden, rosy peaches and golden pears nestled on a bed of fig leaves. He talked to us about his Canadian flock and then he made sure that we were taken to see the palace treasury. We looked at paintings, carvings and *objets d'art,* which had been sent from pious Armenians dispersed all over the world. Then we stopped before a curtained wall. The priest, who was our guide, pulled aside the draped cloth, spun the lock on the heavy metal door, slid back the bolts, and opened a large safe to reveal the gift that the Catolicos had just presented to the faithful of his church. On a marble slab the size of a tombstone, outlined in gold and decorated with precious stones, were the letters of the Armenian alphabet. Armenian is an old and cultured language and its distinctive script predates by many centuries the Cyrillic script used to write Russian. It would be impossible to express in a more graphic way the extraordinary value of the Armenian language for the preservation of Armenian identity.

In the middle of the nineteenth century, Konstantin Ushinsky wrote that the soul of a people is conserved in its native language. As far as language is concerned the Armenians have no need to worry. Almost all (97 per cent) of the Armenian children in Armenia are schooled in their own language and begin to study Russian only after they are proficient in their mother tongue. The same is true for Georgian children. In the Ukraine, 80 per cent of the schools teach in Ukrainian. This last statistic, however, does not reflect actual numbers of children involved because most Ukrainian-language schools are in the countryside. In the big city schools, in Kiev for instance, the instruction is mostly in Russian. The legal position, according to Article 121 of the Soviet Constitution, is that "all citizens of the USSR may choose their mother tongue or any other Soviet language for all purposes including their children's schooling". In the Soviet Union today, textbooks and teaching aids are published in fifty-two different languages. There is no *State* language for the whole of the USSR; equality among all Soviet languages is guaranteed by the constitution.

So what is the effect on a non-Russian child of being able to be schooled in his or her own language? It is bound to raise national consciousness in a variety of ways. The most obvious is through contact with the literary tradition that has evolved in that language. The children of Georgia study a very long poem called "The Knight in the Panther's Skin" written in the twelfth century by their great national poet, Shota Rustaveli. I read this poem in an English translation and was caught up by it, awed by the subtlety and sophistication of Rustaveli's poetic meditation on love and friendship. Perhaps the giggling dark-eyed Georgian girls whom I met in Tbilisi find the poem a little boring when they study it in class. Yet, Rustaveli's notions of chivalrous behaviour are still popular in his native land; his lines are quoted in toasts every day, and the language that he so enriched is alive and well.

The central authorities and their representatives in the republics fully approve of non-Russian children studying their own literary classics. However, national consciousness is bound to be nurtured in native-language schools in ways that are subtler and more subversive. Ethnic Russians living in areas of the Soviet Union where other languages are strong are not noted for their efforts to learn the local language. As a result many messages are transmitted in the classroom that are outside their ken. It is now quite clear that the young Lithuanian nationalists who are so active today somehow learned a more accurate version of Lithuanian history than the one that has been presented by Soviet textbooks for the last forty years.

Forces for Unity in Soviet Education

During the Christmas holidays of 1982, we took a couple of our visiting children to the New Moscow Circus. A Soviet circus provides excellent entertainment for people of all ages. The old circus in the centre of Moscow has existed for more than a century and is the traditional single-ringed European one, featuring numerous animal acts. The new one in the Lenin Hills is larger, and its tent-like shape is designed for slogans and propaganda as well as for clowns and trapeze artists. A screen circles the sloping wall just under the Big Top, and before an audience can relax and enjoy the acrobats and bears, it has to sit and watch the special messages. On this occasion, since it was the sixtieth anniversary of the formation of Union, we had several minutes of projected images from every part of the Union, carefully selected to emphasize the benefits of Soviet power. Then the lights went up on fifteen statuesque showgirls artfully arranged on a staircase, each one wearing a suggestive national costume and carrying the flag of one of the Union republics. The girls descended the staircase, gracefully waving their flags, and engaged in a slow dance on the floor of the ring. Finally they formed a circle and pointed their flags towards the centre. Up from the middle arose the sixteenth showgirl, unfurling her flag— the flag the rest of the world recognizes as the Soviet Union's—to float over all the others. Only then could we get on with the real show: the incredible Turkmenian riders in shaggy sheepskin hats, the lion-tamer from the Ukraine, the plate-spinners from Kazakhstan.

Of course, this display of images and flags struck us as pure propaganda, hard to take seriously. Yet, in its own crude way, it stood for the Soviet national dream. Throughout their school years, Soviet children are still taught that the Soviet peoples all together form a new historical community. The Union is "not a mere conglomerate...of nations who live 'under the same roof' and are unified in a single state: it has one ideology and one way of life. The Soviet people are united in perpetuity by common interests, a common goal, a common destiny, and they have in common certain spiritual features." This quotation comes from a social-studies textbook used for years by senior high-school students. New textbooks are due in 1990 that will be more sophisticated, yet I expect that the underlying vision of the Soviet Union as a new historical form will persist.

Lenin himself believed in the eventual merger of nations. Although he recognized that national barriers would take a long time to fall away, he was convinced that feeling of national identity would no longer have a *raison d'être* in a new society of friendly socialist relations and so would vanish. Soviet students have been taught this for decades. Classroom discussions on the subject concentrated not on *whether* the nations would ever merge but *when*. In the homework assignment for this section of the social-studies curriculum, students were asked to consider the following questions: "What force brings about the friendship of people and proletarian internationalism?" and "Why are communists implacable enemies of chauvinism and nationalism?"

In the final chapter of this social-studies textbook there is a resounding paragraph on the theme of *Bratstvo* or "Brotherhood": "The word 'brother' is a beautiful one" the text reads, and then goes on to say, "When we speak of fraternal relations we wish to underline that it is not just camaraderie of friendship of which we speak but relations among people that are more beautiful and more elevated than that." The text concludes, "Already today the frontiers between the republics have lost their former significance and when we travel from one end to another of our native land, who thinks of noticing how many frontiers have been crossed? National differences are slowly dying out and eventually only the names will remain as a memory of the past. United in a fraternal family humanity will then rise to its greatest strength with bold prospects for the conquest of nature." One of my Soviet friends, older now and wiser, tells me that her heart used to rise at the thought of such a "brave new world that has such people in't". Gorbachev, of course, no longer speaks of the merging of nations or the melting away of borders but the concept of many nations united in common purpose remains strong. The survival of humankind in the face of ecological and other disasters has became the rallying cry rather than the triumph of Socialism.

Another way in which the education system acts as a force for Soviet unity is by imposing uniform values through the standardized curriculum from kindergarten up. While each republic has its own ministry of education and is permitted to make some adjustments to the curriculum to fit local needs, most subjects, except language and literature, have the same content wherever they are taught. Schools that do not conduct lessons in Russian must often add extra hours to the students' study load so they can keep up with the curriculum and learn Russian as well. The Russian language itself is a force for Soviet unity, of course, not just for its role as a *lingua franca* among the nationalities but also because it is the language in which most *Soviet* concepts were originally couched. It could be said to resemble Church Slavonic as the language of the official "liturgy".

In the Soviet system of values, science and technology are highly ranked. In order to gain portable professional qualifications, children study subjects that have little room for national content. The basic languages of maths and sciences are universal ones. Sitting in on an algebra class in a junior grade, I recall noting with a start that the algebraic equations the children were working on at the blackboard were written in the Latin not the Cyrillic script. The scientific and technological education so essential for the improvement of the Soviet economy should work towards unity rather than diversity.

Finally, on a minor but significant scale, there are forces in Soviet schools that act quite directly to draw the nationalities together. One of these is the common practice of encouraging "pen pals" among different national groups. The structure of the school facilitates this in a concrete way. The fourth child in the fourth row in the fourth grade of School no. 4 in Riga, Latvia, actually has a counterpart in the fourth row in the fourth grade of School no. 4 in Kishinev, Moldavia; or Odessa, in the Ukraine; or Alma Ata, in Kazakhstan. Children are curious, so they often take advantage of such opportunities to find out about one another's lives. Frequently a whole class will write to its equivalent in another republic, exchanging information about national traditions, geography, climate, favourite games, and so on. This sometimes leads to an exchange of visits. Children from different nationalities also come together at summer camps or at sports or other types of competitions where they form enduring friendships. Most Soviet children take a genuine pride in the number of nationalities that make up the USSR, just as I used to take pride as a child in being part of the British Commonwealth of Nations. I still have a special feeling for the citizens of those nations that were coloured pink on my globe when I was growing up. When I remarked on this once to a Soviet friend she exclaimed, "How curious! When I was growing up, on *my* globe it was the nations of the Soviet Union that were coloured pink!"

Peoples of the Soviet North: A Case Study of the Soviet Nationalities Policy and Education

Most of the larger Soviet nationalities have long and complex histories and each one is as different from all the others as is, say, France from Germany. As a result, the nationalities policy, as it was developed by Lenin and his fellow Bolsheviks, has had a different impact on each one. The "dialectic" of unity and diversity has produced a situation in Lithuania that is quite distinct from that in Kirghizia, even though the educational system has the same structure in both places. The Baltic republics are historically predisposed to resent Sovietization, whereas the republics of Central Asia, having obtained some real economic benefits from their position in the Union, are not quite so negative. The smaller nationalities in the so-called autonomous republics and regions, or those who are dispersed throughout the population, have also had dissimilar experiences over the years of Soviet power. So, to assess the impact of Lenin's nationalities policy on education and children in as uncomplicated a manner as possible, I decided to look at the situation of the peoples of the Soviet North, "cousins" to our Indians and Inuit. At the time of the Revolution, these peoples were living on the natural economy; hunting, fishing, and herding reindeer. The Russians tended to consider them backward because they applied their energy and intelligence to physical and spiritual survival rather than to literacy and modern technology. Their tribal knowledge, their spirituality, and their cultural traditions were intimately bound up with their demanding way of life. Because the Soviet regime introduced new dimensions into this way of life, education and other elements of the nationalities policy have had a notable impact on succeeding generations of native children.

Initially, I found it hard to say which of the peoples of the Soviet Union were "native" and which were not. After all, almost all the nationalities living in the USSR have been there for a very long time. It was not until we visited Ulan-Ude in Buryat country, on the far side of Lake Baikal, that I began to understand the distinctions among the various forms of nationality in the Soviet Union and determine which ones could be defined as aboriginal or "native". The Buryats are a nationality (*narodnost*) not a nation (*natsiya*) in the Soviet sense of the word. They were certainly not as economically or politically developed at the time of the Revolution as were, for example, the Belorussians or the Georgians, but their strong cultural identity earned them the status of an autonomous republic within the Russian Federation.

The capital of the Buryat Autonomous Republic is Ulan-Ude. We were met at the airport and accompanied throughout our visit there by an energetic Buryat woman, one of the city administrators. She talked about her young son every time she could find an opening. She was proud to be a Buryat, she said, but her husband, whom she had met as a student in Leningrad, was an ethnic Russian. He had returned with her to Buryat country, but they had decided to send their son to a Russian-medium school to ensure maximum possibilities for his future life, a reason that educated couples often give for sending their children to Russian-medium schools in areas where Russian is not the predominant language. She went on to say that she would remind her son frequently of his Buryat heritage, but she was not going to confine him to it. It was a provocative statement and it made me think.

Ulan-Ude is surrounded by hills, meadows, and fragrant pine woods. During the summer (we were there in July), the woods are full of children who have come to the many Pioneer camps there to shore up their health against the rigours of the Siberian winter. We visited one of these, and then were taken to a remarkable open-air ethnographic museum nearby. Its director, a Buryat, showed us around with enthusiasm. We first went inside a *yurta*, the traditional round felt dwelling of the nomadic Buryat sheepherder, which can be collapsed or set up in under two hours and which is still in use in some parts of Buryat country. Then we rounded a corner, and saw, with surprise, a group of hide-covered tipis hidden among the trees. They were so similar to those I used to see in my textbooks of Canadian history that I suddenly remembered that it was from this very region near Lake Baikal that the Indians of North America are said by many experts to have migrated over the land bridge to Alaska.

One of the tipis (*choom*) had belonged to an Evenk shaman, and I examined the interior with interest. I was fascinated by the abundance of fur and the various sacred objects, and turned to the director with a host of questions. In the absence of an interpreter, we spoke the *lingua franca* of the Soviet Union. He spoke very quickly and with something of an accent so I missed some details of his explanation of shamanism, but there was no mistaking where his sympathies lay. As an educated Buryat, he was drawn to the fate of indigenous peoples everywhere. But the fact that in North America many Indians live on reservations filled him with horror. "As if," he said to us, "you had put them in a zoo."

He confirmed that Buryats do not consider themselves a "native people" in the sense in which we in North America use the term. That category is reserved for the Yakut who moved north from Lake Baikal several centuries ago, the Komi and the Karely who live farther west, and approximately twenty-six small groups who are scattered all across the Soviet North and who are known collectively as the Northern peoples (*narody severa*). Some of these *narody* are very small indeed, numbering under five hundred. Others, like the Chukchi and the Evenki, range from 14,000 to 30,000. Altogether, the native peoples including the Yakuty, the Karely and the Komi numbered about 936,000 in the 1979 census. For purposes of comparison, there are 374,000 status Indians in Canada spread over the whole country (75 per cent on reserves), 75,000 non-status Indians, 98,000 Métis (mixed-race) in the prairie provinces, and about 28,000 Inuit living in the Canadian North. In 1980, the U.S. Census Bureau listed 1,364,033 individuals in the category of "American Indian", 72 per cent more than in 1970, one third of whom live on reserves.

What the small northern peoples of the USSR have in common and what distinguishes them from an indigenous people such as the Buryats is a life-style based on what Marxist theory describes as the "natural" economy. This means most of them still live off the land, not by organizing and cultivating it, but by hunting, fishing, trapping, sealing, and following the reindeer herds. What they also have in common, judging by their folk-tales and legends, which are now frequently translated and published in attractively illustrated editions for Soviet children across the land, is a profound love of and respect for the natural world as well as the wry sense of humour so characteristic of people who live under exceptionally difficult circumstances.

When I returned to Moscow from Ulan-Ude, I questioned my Soviet acquaintances to find out what they knew about the peoples of the North. "Very little" is what they answered. Until recently, few European Russians thought about the peoples of the North when they thought about Siberia. Instead, they were apt to think, romantically, about nineteenth-century exiles, or, much more painfully, about twentieth-century prisoners. For the youthful imagination, the far-from-virtuous tales of unruly Cossacks and free-booters who went to Siberia in tsarist times in search of furs and adventure were replaced by heroic legends of Siberian megaprojects—the building of dams and railways by Komsomol members. Neither set of stories gave much of a role to the native peoples.

This lack of curiosity piqued my own and I decided to look at the native peoples more closely. Spared (though not entirely) the worst excesses of the Stalinist regime, these peoples have evolved over the last seventy years in ways that show the ambiguities and contradictions of Lenin's nationalities policy more clearly than could the post-revolutionary history of a more powerful national group.

Since my Soviet acquaintances had so little to tell me, I had to turn to books and articles to find out about the history of the native peoples of the Soviet Union. Initial contact was established between white Europeans and natives much earlier in what is now the Soviet North than it was in Canada or in the United States. Russians travelled north to the White Sea and to the Arctic Ocean as early as the eleventh century. Voyages eastward were undertaken somewhat later, but by 1581, during the reign of Ivan the Terrible, enough Russians had gone into that vast territory of *taiga* and permafrost to justify the official incorporation of Siberia into Russia. This opened the way for exploration, conquest, and settlement. The native tribes paid a regular "tribute" of fur pelts. Yakutsk, 1,800 kilometres north of Irkutsk, was founded in 1632. It is now a city of 175,000 and the capital of the Yakut Autonomous Republic. The Russians reached the Pacific in 1639.

The annexation of this enormous territory drew the native population into the orbit of what an Evenk historian calls "the historical development of the Russian people" and began to bring them out of the "primitive and squalid" material conditions in which they had been living since time immemorial. From what I have been able to learn, the early interaction between the native peoples and the Russians was not necessarily destructive to the native way of life. On the contrary, firearms made hunting easier, and the natives, in return, were able to teach the settlers a certain amount about surviving in the wilderness. While there were some skirmishes during the push eastward, there was nothing similar to the French and Indian Wars, for example, or the forcible removal, in the 1830s, of a hundred thousand Indians from the southern United States along the "Trail of Tears" to Oklahoma, no long and bitter history of treaties made and broken. Nor did the Russian Orthodox Church make a practice of sending out missionaries to convert the heathen with anything like the zeal that characterized the efforts of the churches of Western Europe and North America.

During the nineteenth century, however, the familiar pattern of corruption by trade set in. Merchants swindled native trappers, introducing them to alcohol, and to long-term indebtedness. By the time of the Revolution, eyewitnesses were describing the situation of the native peoples in many part of the North as a tragic one. Families were living in abject conditions, totally demoralized by drink and ignorance. Tribal traditions were preserved by a few shamans and elders, but most people agree that the early part of the twentieth century marked a low point in the history of the

Northern peoples. Nor did the Revolution bring an immediate improvement in their situation. In 1917, they experienced a short reprieve from the economic oppression of the tsarist regime and enjoyed a brief period of self-government through tribal councils, but the Civil War, and the struggle to establish Soviet power over the vast natural resources of Siberia, was devastating for the native inhabitants. Only after the termination of the Civil War in 1920 did Lenin's nationalities policy begin to make a difference to their future.

Education was a priority. Illiteracy among the native peoples was almost total at the time of the Revolution (because native languages were not written down, anyone who was literate would have had to be literate in Russian). The People's Commissariat for Nationalities ordered urgent steps to be taken to open primary and secondary schools for native children. The first ones were established in 1922 and they had a difficult beginning. Many parents refused to send their children to school. The teachers, who were mostly young Komsomol members, full of enthusiasm but lacking in experience, did not know the children's languages and the children knew no Russian. Sometimes months would go by before they could communicate. As for the curriculum, the teachers had to make it up as they went along. By 1929 there were 123 schools in the Soviet North, including 62 boarding-schools. And children were beginning to learn to read their own native languages because Soviet ethnographers and linguists had begun to write them down. For the school year 1932-33, there were textbooks available in fourteen native languages. Some of these languages have since been abandoned as languages of instruction because the number of children speaking them are too few. However, others have been added as alphabets have been developed for them, the latest, in 1987, being the language of the Yukaghiry.

Right from the start, one of the purposes of the nationalities policy was to train national leaders in Marxism-Leninism so that they could spread the message to their fellows. To do this, they had to be reached through their own languages and then given positions of authority. This meant that native people found themselves in the local power structure quite early in the Soviet period. They continue to play a role in the management of the territories in which they live. Many of them are also Party members and have achieved advancement this way. However, except for the tribal councils that existed for such a short time after the Revolution, there has never been any form of national representation for native peoples that has had real substance. That, of course, would have militated against the socialist "content" of the nationalities policy. The fact that a council of native peoples is now (1989) being seriously considered is most encouraging.

Another objective of the nationalities policy was to create a native intelligentsia and thus to bring the cultures of the native peoples closer to Soviet norms and standards. In theory, this was not to be done at the expense of their culture, or at least not of those portions of it (and there were many) that were not in obvious conflict with the ideals of the new Soviet state. This meant that the native culture had to be understood in order to be assessed for its ideological compatibility. Thanks to this policy, a wealth of ethnographic material was preserved that might otherwise have been lost. One native writer from the Soviet Union has observed wryly, echoing the comments of hundreds of others of his "confrères" from so-called primitive societies all over the world, "In those days...the typical Arctic family: father, mother, two children, and over there, in the corner of the hut, the researcher". With the researchers came the teachers and the others who set up the Red Chooms or cultural bases where the native peoples could mix with other nationalities who had come up to work in the North, and thus be introduced to the culture of the wider world. This is where the practice began to deviate from the theory, for while there were eventually enough educated native people to become teachers, they had often lost much of their own culture in the process. About half of the teachers working with native children today are natives, but many of them are unable to speak their native language well enough to teach it properly.

The native peoples of the Soviet North have benefited economically from Soviet policies, although not as much as was promised nor as much as has been claimed. For example, the incorporation

of the so-called natural economy into the overall Soviet economy was not without cost. Collectivizing reindeer herding in the
1930s led to the loss of 30 per cent of the reindeer, but stocks
have built up again since then. And there is something disturbing
about the fact that the native population remained stable in numbers from 1926 until 1959, in spite of the introduction of modern
medicine, child-care facilities, universal education, and other Soviet benefits. But this fact had almost nothing to do with Lenin's
nationalities policy, being related instead to the megaprojects that
brought so many willing (and unwilling) workers to the North to
exploit the regions' resources. It is now clear that both the environment and the native population were seriously damaged by
Stalin's drive to industrialization. Unfortunately, damage to the
environment continues although the native population has begun
to recover, at least in numbers. Between 1970 and 1979 there was
a 5 per cent increase and, with *glasnost*, a new consciousness of
the real concerns of native peoples has emerged.

However, all this information says little about what life was,
and is, like in the North for native children or what difference the
Soviet educational system has been able to make with respect to
children's perceptions of themselves as both Evenks, for example,
and Soviet citizens. To find out more, I turned to the personal
accounts of native writers, some of whom are now known well
beyond their small ethnic group. One of them, a Yukaghir author
named Semyon Kurilov, refers to himself as the only writer who
knows all his readers by sight. (According to the 1979 census
there are 835 Yukaghirs.) Another, Yury Rytkheu, a Chukchi,
describes growing up in the settlement of Uelen on the far tip of
the Chukotka peninsula in sight of the island of Little Diomede,
the beginning of the North American continent.

Rytkheu writes about his home, a hut or *yaranga* made of
walrus skins, his first whale hunt at the age of twelve, the intimate
involvement of the settlement in the life of the sea. One day
he drove out on a dogsled with his grandmother. "We saw
enormous whalebones," he remembers, "polished to a high gleam
by blizzards and washed white by the cold autumn rains." His
grandmother "halted the dogs, took out crumbs of reindeer meat
from a leather basket, and threw them towards the whale bones.

Here under the whale's bones lies the spirit mother who gave life to all the people of the coast. She was impregnated by this very whale who changed into a man for the purpose…she said. To this day I cannot dismiss this poetic legend about the origin of my people. It remains in the depth of my soul, filling me with a sense of mysterious community with nature, with ancient history." Rytkheu has written a haunting story based on this incident called "When the Whales Leave…" that warns about the danger of breaking away from ancient traditions.

Chukchi children today can read Rytkheu's stories in their own language. But they are not growing up in the same conditions as he did. For one thing, they live in houses with electricity and television, with all that that implies of social change and contact with the outside world. Then, like every other Soviet child, they have to go to school for many years, often in a boarding-school where they study the universal Soviet curriculum. The Chukchi family is no longer the primary source of knowledge and wisdom for the Chukchi child but has to share this function not only with other members of the tribal community (which has always been the case) but also with the Soviet state.

The formal education of the children of the Far North is the responsibility of the Ministry of Education of the Russian Federation, which is centred in Moscow. In October 1984, I interviewed the deputy director of the Department of National Schools, a lively woman from Dagestan in the North Caucasus with a touch of magenta in her hair. She told me that I was lucky to find her in Moscow because she was constantly flying all over her enormous territory. She claimed that she has flown on every type of airplane that the Soviet Union has ever produced—a fact that attests to extraordinary fortitude—and has known every kind of weather. She was full of enthusiasm for her job and has been at it for years. When I asked her how she had become involved with the education of the Northern peoples, she replied that she had trained as a teacher, taught for a few years, and then been drawn to native education because she herself was a member of a minority nationality. In Dagestan, the autonomous republic from which she comes, there are thirty distinct small nationalities, mostly mountainous tribes, each one with its own language and traditions. I accepted her statement of dedication to the preservation of national "form" but she left no room for doubt with respect to her equally strong commitment to "socialist" content.

We sat down to talk at a long table in a book-lined room at the ministry. She spread out a large map in front of me and then stood up to show me her territory. She pointed out various northern settlements where the resident population was large enough to have a school or where there was a boarding-school for the children of nomadic parents: reindeer herders, hunters, or trappers. Then she put her finger on the Chukotka Peninsula, the most distant part of her territory, twelve thousand kilometres from Moscow, ten time zones. There is where most of the Eskimosy live, she told me. There are not many of them, she went on, only fifteen hundred or so, but the children can start school in their own language. She went to the bookcase and brought me four books, an Eskimo-Russian dictionary of more than four thousand words for use in the primary school, a first reader for the preparatory class (the six-year-olds), a more advanced one with many grammatical exercises for the next class, and a story-book for general use. It has been long-standing Soviet policy, she continued, to train as many native teachers as possible for work with their own populations. A special faculty to prepare teachers for the schools of the North was established at the Herzen Pedagogical Institute in Leningrad in 1930, and has trained hundreds of native educators to advanced levels. In addition, there are now nine teachers' colleges in various parts of Siberia so that students do not have to travel so far. The Institute of Ethnography in Moscow and its associated branches in Leningrad, Akademgorodok (near Novosibirsk), and Irkutsk research the customs and traditions of the peoples of the North and have done so for many years. The Eskimo textbooks that I was shown were the fruit of collaboration between teachers and scholars, between natives and members of other Soviet nationalities.

I was given the textbooks as I left the ministry and I have had plenty of time to study them; the illustrations are very revealing. At the beginning of the first reader, the Eskimo child sets off for school amid images of the Soviet state: Moscow's Red Square and tractors. The succeeding images are seasonal ones associated with daily life at home or at school: gathering seaweed, picking berries with mother, in the house with grandmother who is embroidering a seal-skin, helping father bring in a seal, skating in winter, swimming in summer. The people in the pictures have Eskimo features, and the animals are all northern ones. Russian words and Soviet concepts are introduced slowly along with elements that are part of the school environment of *any* Soviet child: the school uniform, the kindly doctor, the friendly teacher, all positive images of the benign state. This reader, like all Soviet first-grade readers that I have seen, follows the ritual Soviet year. The First Day of School is illustrated to show children from different Soviet nationalities arriving at school with flowers. October 7, the Day of the Constitution, shows children from every republic in national costume. The day of the Revolution, November 7, features a picture of Grandfather Lenin. The next festival is New Year's Day, with Grandfather Frost, Buratino (a Russian version of Pinocchio), and an Eskimo child dressed up as a rabbit. February 23, Soviet Army Day, shows a brave Soviet soldier standing on guard. March 8, International Woman's Day, features an Eskimo Mommy and signs of spring. The first day of May, of course, is the Festival of Work, and May 9 is Victory Day, a celebration of the end of the Great Patriotic War. The images here are anti-war ones, *nyet* to the Bomb and *da* to the Dove of Peace. The school year comes to an end, and the last section of the reader is once again devoted to images of the Eskimo children's own homeland, enriched now by its connection to the rest of the Union—symbolized by the picture of a pilot bringing a gift of apples to Eskimo children from the children of Uzbekistan.

A great deal of care has gone into the making of these textbooks. The illustrations that portray the natural life of the North, the animals and the landscape (or seascape) are finely executed (although not in a native style). Most of the reading material included in the readers is made up of Eskimo folk-tales or fairy stories, supplemented by brief extracts from the works of Ushinsky and Tolstoy, as well as a few poems and stories by popular Soviet children's writers.

The overwhelming message for Eskimo children learning to read with one of these primers is that, while the corner of the earth they inhabit is beautiful and to be cherished, their lives have been much improved by the Soviet state and by the fact that they are members of the family of nations of which the Soviet Union is composed. Eskimo children exposed to these texts are expected to emerge from the second grade with some knowledge of their own language and culture but also with a positive attitude to the Soviet Union as a whole. They will also know some Russian because they have been exposed to it since the preparatory class. Eventually they will study with other Northerners or go away for post-secondary studies. Then knowledge of Russian will be essential.

The Eskimosy (Yuit, as they are actually called) are one of the smallest nationalities for whom textbooks are available. That they exist at all for so few children may well reflect the fact that the Eskimosy have relatives in North America and are more visible to the outside world than some of the other native peoples of the Soviet North. It is also obvious that they will never be sufficiently numerous to pose any kind of threat. Thus an investment in their culture suits everyone's interests.

There were 268 national schools on the map I was shown in the Ministry of Education of the Russian Federation. Textbooks and teaching materials exist for fifteen different northern native languages. Native educators from Canada are now visiting these schools regularly and coming away impressed with the respect shown the children's cultural identity. They report that Soviet native children appear to take more pride in their cultural heritage than Canadian Inuit children and they do not seem so alienated. Canadian Inuit educators, however, are uneasy at the very idea of boarding-schools. Many Soviet native children are still picked up by helicopter from the remote areas where they live with their families and flown to schools in larger settlements. There they are dressed, fed, doctored, and schooled by the State. They are returned to their parents during the winter break, if the distances are not too far, and for the long summer holiday. The experience that many young Inuit had in Canada when they went to the boarding-schools set up for them (now closed) was a bitter one, for these schools made no attempt to nourish their cultural identity. Soviet boarding-schools are supposed to honour a child's nationality, although how they manage to do that in schools where there are several nationalities is hard to imagine. And even if they do, separations from the family and from the home territory are bound to have negative effects on a child. It is not surprising that one of the things that most interests native educators from the Soviet Union when they visit the Canadian North are the locally-managed school boards that enable children to study closer to home.

Higher education poses a particular challenge to the old ways. This was underscored by a study conducted by the Institute of History, Philology, and Philosophy in Novosibirsk in 1979 on the effect of the construction of the BAM railway on the Evenk population. Among other things, this study examined the vocational interests of senior students in schools located near the construction area. A majority of the students, including the Evenks, expected to complete the full secondary-school program and to go on to further education. Few of them saw themselves as ordinary workers in the future. Nor did the Evenk students indicate much attachment to their traditional way of life. This was mentioned by only 18 per cent of the eighth- and tenth-graders. In short, the overall industrialization of the North combined with increased levels of education has changed the life expectations of young natives. Unless programs can be introduced to modernize the living conditions of those who herd reindeer, hunt, fish, and so on, these activities will become less and less popular and the young will turn away from the *taiga* to more highly skilled jobs in towns and cities, if they can get them. As we know from the Canadian experience, their traditional cultural identity will then become even more attenuated.

Nevertheless, the emphasis on native education that issued from Lenin's nationalities policy has probably preserved native consciousness better than would have been possible otherwise. And, at the same time, education has opened up possibilities for native people in the wider Soviet economy and in the power structure that would have been undreamt of before the Revolution. The Chukchi writer Rytkheu reminds us that the shaman of traditional native cultures was "a one-man academy of sciences…an intelligent and knowledgeable man" who could predict the weather and the route of the reindeer herds and give meaning to the natural flow of life and death. In his view, the scientifically educated natives who return to work with their own peoples are modern shamans. If they can combine the knowledge they have acquired in Irkutsk or Leningrad with the wisdom of their cultural traditions and use both to ensure the survival of their native communities then they will have justified Lenin's nationalities policy in a way that the State is now prepared to welcome.

Memory and National Identity

Lenin recognized that after the Revolution the peasants (who made up 80 per cent of the population of the new state) would continue to identify more strongly with nationality than with class. He accepted, therefore, that national consciousness would remain for some time even after the antagonistic classes of oppressors and oppressed had been done away with. He was prepared to respond to, and indeed to make use of, feelings of nationalism during the initial years of the new Soviet state and he demonstrated this in his nationalities policy. But he had no intention of promoting nationalism as an *ultimate* virtue because, in his utopian vision of communism as a *new* human collectivity, the nationalities would merge.

What transpired, of course, was that in the history books, Lenin's version of what should have happened replaced the truth of what actually did happen as the Union was being formed. As a result, for a very long time Soviet children have had almost no understanding of the complexities of the issues addressed by the nationalities policy. For some, there were family stories to set against the official "truth" they were taught at school. For others, however, there was nothing at all, and this was tragic because their ignorance has not only impoverished their national identity but tarnished their Soviet identity as well.

In my view, authentic national identity depends a great deal on the collective historical memory of a people, just as our personal identity depends to some degree on what we remember of our own past and what we have done with those things we would like to forget. Most of the nationalities that make up the Soviet Union are ancient ones with long histories. The Soviet Union, on the other hand, is a new multinational culture with a short one. I think it is possible to have a double identity, as a Georgian, say, and as a Soviet citizen, and to feel positively about both, but only if the individual concerned has a clear sense of the interacting history of each culture. This means *full* access to the history of Georgia prior to the Revolution, *full* access to the process by which Georgia became part of the Soviet Union, and *full* access to Soviet history from then on, with special reference to the most infamous of all Georgians, Iosif Vissarionovich Dzhugashvili, better known as Stalin. I know it is unwise to discuss nation-states in terms of individual psychology, yet I believe that just as it is essential for individuals to come to terms with the dark sides of their own personal history, so it is equally important for a nation-state such as the Soviet Union to come to terms with the horrors of its own past. The revelations that are emerging under Gorbachev are beginning the process. There will be turbulence and pain for many but the children of the 1980s deserve, and are now coming to expect, the truth.

In a passage in the second volume of her memoirs, *Hope Abandoned,* Nadezha Mandelstam, who spent the latter part of her life remembering everything that happened to her husband the poet Osip Mandelstam, to herself, and to her society during the Stalin years and after and recording it all for posterity, devotes a whole chapter to the subject of memory. "What," she asks, "can we expect to happen in a country with a disordered memory?" Because that disorder still persists, even as it diminishes, the future course of the engagement between the forces for unity and the forces for diversity in Soviet education is hard to predict. The balance between those forces that stamp a growing child with a Soviet identity and those that enable him or her to feel culturally different, and proud of it, is a delicate one. But the Canadian experience of a bilingual, multicultural federated state has shown that the richer the identities on both scales, the less likely the scales are to tip. In our provincially regulated public education system we provide French-immersion schools for English-speaking children in British Columbia and heritage-language programs for many different ethnic groups in Toronto. In doing so, we are trying to weight both sides of the scales as equally as possible. Education is certainly the most important key to balance in this sensitive area. However, what children are taught about their own cultural heritage and what they are taught about the history and institutions of the State of which they are citizens *must* be truthful and information *must* be conveyed with respect for cultural differences.

Soviet children are now reaching higher and higher levels of schooling, a source of legitimate pride for the Soviet state. Large numbers of them will, I am sure, continue to select their mother tongue as the medium for instruction. They will also continue to be encouraged to feel strong ties to their national culture. The national form, especially of the larger nationalities (I am less confident about some of the smaller ones), will be kept alive and will probably become stronger. The socialist content, however, will become more diffuse. Technology, science, the demands of both the national and the international economy, and the growing sophistication of the population as a whole will make this inevitable. What happens in the world outside the Soviet Union will also have a great impact on what happens inside it.

Along with most of my Soviet friends, I am profoundly unhappy about the violence that has erupted in the southern reaches of the Soviet Union. Murder and pillage will not resolve the problems that haunt the area and many children of different nationalities will become innocent victims. And not only the children because when "the people" become "a mob", democracy is aborted. Nevertheless, in spite of these tensions, I do not expect the Union to break up completely. Generations of association among the nationalities of the Soviet Union, including the experience of the Great Patriotic War, have soldered some real bonds which will not dissolve overnight. Besides, no matter where they grow up in the USSR today, I am convinced that *most* Soviet children are still being predisposed by education and by public upbringing to feel an emotional attachment to the larger unity that is the Soviet state. But whether the State can, or indeed should, hold on to that attachment in the face of the need for self-determination is the question of the 1990s.

It has now been nearly seventy years, more than three generations, since the formation of the Union, as the last decade of the century begins, a new curriculum is being drawn up in Moscow for the teaching of Soviet history. The first draft was still too constricted by ideology to be fair to the events that surrounded the entry of each republic into the Union. But scholars have been asked to rethink and rewrite the textbooks and to be prepared to update them every couple of years. As they do, they should bear in mind the fact that non-Russian children need to learn in school that, in the early days of Soviet power, many of their ancestors had justifiable reasons for opposing the course of events. It is true that such knowledge will increase national feeling and may engender tensions that are almost impossible to manage; yet at the same time it could actually strengthen the Soviet identity of the current generation by increasing the level of trust between non-Russian youngsters and the State.

In the Soviet Union, for much too long, manifestations of national culture like folk songs have been treated as lesser art forms while a chorus from an opera like *War and Peace* was assumed to transcend the nationalities of its singers and raise them to a higher level of culture. This is one of the reasons why the Union is in such trouble. Prokofiev is a great artist, but not necessarily a truer one than the Uzbek who composes or performs in his or her national idiom. For a family to function, each member has to be accorded the same respect. Soviet children are still being taught that the USSR is a family of nations, but Lenin's dream of socialism in national dress is no longer credible and Gorbachev is in the process of replacing it with a new dream of a federated state in which the constituent parts stay together out of choice in order to have the collective strength to confront the global problems of the twenty-first century. If he is successful, then the children of *glasnost* could grow up to become true internationalists, citizens of the whole world.

CHAPTER FIFTEEN

The Young Patriot: War and Peace

The ninth of May is Victory Day in the Soviet Union. In towns and villages throughout the whole of the USSR, old men and women, chests swollen with medals and ribbons, gather to remember the German surrender, recount their war experiences, and receive the homage of the young. In Moscow they meet in front of the Bolshoi Theatre or congregate informally along the riverside paths of Gorky Park. When two of my children came to visit me in the spring of 1983, it was to the park that we went to join the crowds paying their respects to the veterans of the bloody battles on Soviet soil that turned the tide against the Germans.

By the time we arrived, every bench along the Moscow River was occupied. Former comrades had found one another and now sat together, talking and laughing. All afternoon young people brought them flowers, tulips and narcissi mostly, and paused to listen to their stories. Four old campaigners spread a well-thumbed map on a rickety table and traced advances and retreats for anyone who cared to watch. A little later, someone produced an accordion, and two beefy veterans began to sing, their voices deep and surprisingly strong. Balding men and greying women got up from the benches and started to dance, a little stiffly at first and then with remembered grace, flashing gold-toothed smiles at the surrounding crowd.

The leaves in Gorky Park had just come out. Red tulips shone in the sunshine. The green grass glistened. The park was jammed. People lined up everywhere to ride the giant Ferris wheel, to row on one of the ponds, to buy ice-cream bars or bottles of Fanta or, if they were lucky, as many bagels as they could carry, scooped up from the baskets of white-coated *babushkas* seated here and there among the bushes. It was a good-humoured crowd having a good time, out in the park to enjoy the peace that those veterans had so painfully won for them forty years before.

We wondered, my children and I, as we strolled among them, what difference it would make once the old soldiers had all gone, when there was no one left who remembered what it really had been like during those bitter war years. Would the world be a safer place or not? Then, as we watched boys and girls come up to talk to them, we also wondered what it must be like to spend a childhood surrounded by memories of war, listening to hymns to world peace played on a military drum.

Every school-aged child in the Soviet Union today knows that Tolstoy's *War and Peace* was inspired by the War of 1812 and that it describes how the people of Russia gathered strength to turn back the French invader and transform the retreat of Napoleon's army into an ignominious rout. Every school-aged child also knows hundreds of stories that portray the Second World War (the Great Patriotic War) as yet another attack on the homeland during which the collective power of the peoples of the USSR was able to defeat and rout an even crueller invader. And so, taught by Tolstoy and by heroic tales of the Second World War, recent generations of Soviet children have grown up in the belief that war and peace are two sides of the same coin. They have learned that people have to fight to create the conditions for peace and must always be ready to fight to defend it. Never again, so the children have been taught, must a war be fought on Soviet soil, and never again must the motherland be taken by surprise. It is these two emotionally charged "never agains" that have shaped the attitudes to war and peace of all the post-war generations of children in the Soviet Union. And under the breezes of change, they still do.

The Political Life of Soviet Children

In the spring of 1981 we travelled south in search of warmth after our first long winter in Moscow. We ended up in Odessa, an old port on the Black Sea. Odessa is a gracious city of faded elegance that has given the world many artists and musicians; we explored it with interest and pleasure. But neither the beautiful nineteenth-century opera house nor the spacious promenade where Pushki` used to flirt with the ladies of the garrison could compete for my attention with the changing of the Pioneer guard.

The war memorial in Odessa is an obelisk set on a high terrace overlooking the sea. As we approached it along a tree-lined alley, we had to stop for a moment to let a small detachment of earnest youngsters goose-step past us, arms briskly swinging from side to side. We watched them march to the foot of the monument, salute their comrades on guard there, accept their rifles, and take their places. The Pioneers whom they were relieving saluted in return and then marched firmly back down the alley.

The young students left standing at attention in the chilly April breeze were barely into their teens. They were all in uniform but the girls were clearly distinguished from the boys by white woolly knee-socks and large white hair bows half-hidden beneath their forage caps. The guide who had brought us there told us proudly that she, too, had stood guard at the obelisk when she was fourteen. Her stint was short but she had never forgotten how honoured she had felt to have been chosen from among her schoolmates to perform this sacred duty.

After that, as we travelled around the Soviet Union, I often saw Pioneers on active duty; standing on guard, greeting visitors, serving as guides, appearing on the stage at Party congresses or other political events, speaking up at meetings with foreigners. In North America we are unused to seeing ten- to fourteen-year-olds so politically involved. But Soviet authorities are convinced that children learn by activity, and so political involvement is considered important here and now as well as in the future.

Politics is about the distribution of power or as Lenin said "*Kto kogo?*" (Who can do what to whom?) In the Soviet Union political power has long been in the hands of the Communist Party (the CPSU), a fact Soviet children become aware of at a very young age. Being powerless themselves, children are unusually sensitive to who has it, particularly when it affects them directly. From the time of the Revolution, the CPSU has shaped the political life of children in the Soviet Union in the hope that they might grow up loyal to the Party, respecting its role as "helmsman" guiding the political destiny of the nation. It has done this in three distinct ways: first, through the rituals of Soviet life; second, through children's collectives, particularly those associated with the Pioneer movement; and third, through the school curriculum.

Ceremonies and Celebrations: The Rituals of Political Life

In Canada, the school year has been punctuated for as long as I can remember by a number of special days that are signalled on the walls and windows of elementary-school classrooms by changing decorations. Red leaves and pumpkins represent Thanksgiving, ghosts and witches appear at Hallowe'en, snowflakes and Santa Claus at Christmas. On St. Valentine's Day little children draw red hearts and giggle. There are shamrocks for St. Patrick, bunnies for Easter, and spring flowers for Mother's Day. Our holidays are semi-religious or unabashedly sentimental. They are rarely patriotic. The only day with a clear military association is Remembrance Day in honour of Canada's war dead.

How different it is in the Soviet Union! While it is true that every year, at the end of December, schools are decorated with greenery, and costumed children receive gifts of candy and fruit from Grandfather Frost and the Snow Maiden, and that just before International Women's Day, on March 8, a girl may find on her desk a small token from an unknown admirer, all of the other important days in the school calendar, the day of the Constitution, for example, or Soviet Army Day, are heavily charged with political meaning. Teachers prepare appropriate lessons for every grade level, and auxiliary materials are available through the Communist Youth Movement that ensure that the political message of the day is underscored. The weekly edition of the class newspaper focuses on the issues the day symbolizes, and there is always a special assembly for the whole school.

In addition to major holidays, there are a number of designated days of lesser importance that may be used by a teacher or a Pioneer leader to drive home a political truth. The popular saints' days of the Russian Orthodox year and the holy days of Islam and Judaism have been replaced on the official calendar by days that celebrate the worker, the younger generation, the arts, or the military, all of which are valued by the Soviet state. Most of these days are featured in newspapers and on television, and the military-patriotic ones usually merit a special outburst of fireworks.

Not only have religious holidays been transformed into ideological ones aimed at strengthening the hold of the Communist Party over the hearts and minds of the population but new ritual days have appeared on the calendar as history has dictated (Victory Day) or as a specific need emerged. In the mid-1960s, political apathy set in so the role of ritual was intensified. Most of the days celebrating different occupations such as the truck driver or the frontier guard date from this period. So do a number of life-cycle rituals involving children, such as the ceremonial registration of the newborn (which has borrowed most of its structure, including the role of "sponsors", from Christian baptism) and the ceremony of the receipt of the internal passport at the age of sixteen, a rite of passage. There are now "ritual specialists" in each of the Union republics (usually local Party organizers or administrators) to ensure that ideologically correct and emotionally satisfying rituals are available for almost every occasion. Apparently the so-called socialist marriage rite is now chosen by the overwhelming majority of young couples over simple registration at the ZAGS office or a wedding in a church (which is not legally binding in any case). Marriage palaces are often quite splendid, and more ritual sites are being built all the time. The State's baby-naming rite, however, has been slow to gain acceptance and so, apparently, has the socialist funeral rite. Religion still touches both the beginning and the end of life, and almost every time I went into a "working" Orthodox church during a Sunday-morning service I would find one chapel full of babies being baptized and another containing two or three open caskets accompanied by family mourners.

For many a Soviet child, his or her first genuinely political experience will be a May Day parade. Carried in Mother's arms or riding on Father's shoulders, hundred of thousands of very small children take part in the annual processions that celebrate "the workers of the world" all over the Soviet Union. Pre-schoolers and little Octobrists walk close to their parents, clutching large crêpe-paper flowers and waving tiny red flags. Young Pioneers usually march separately in their school brigades. I used to watch people mill about in the streets near the Embassy as they were waiting their turn to parade through Red Square. Spontaneous or not, the crowds were enormous and the children looked as though they were having a thoroughly good time.

One child-rearing manual I consulted applauds parents for marching in parades with their pre-schoolers and advises them to take advantage of every possible opportunity to train their children to love and respect Vladimir Ilyich Lenin, as well as the Revolution, the Soviet Army, and the Motherland. "Talk to your children about the glories of the Soviet Union", parents are instructed, and "tell them how workers and peasants lived under the Tsar and how Vladimir Ilyich—friend and comrade of workers—helped them to struggle against rich men." On the three occasions I visited Lenin's tomb, many children stood outside waiting patiently with their parents. They were unusually subdued when they entered the mausoleum, and wide-eyed as they walked around the wax-like figure lying there, business-suited and half-covered by a blanket, rigid in its glass box.

Whether their parents respond with enthusiasm or repugnance to the official line on patriotism, Soviet children are bound to be affected by the pervasive nature of the political ceremonies that surround them. By the time they go to school, few children will be ignorant of the message that Lenin is the father of the nation they live in, that the CPSU is his party, and that there are three sacred traditions to be revered: the Revolution and Civil War, the Great Patriotic War, and Labour. The emotional weight of these messages will be reinforced by ritual activities all through their years at school. In such a climate it is almost impossible to remain indifferent, no matter what Soviet children think about these things when they grow up. The British Imperial World I was born into has long since ceased to exist but I still feel a special connection to all those countries that now form the Commonwealth, and my eyes mist at a royal parade.

The Political Role of the Children's Organizations

In 1924, when the children born in 1917 were ready for school, they were named Octobrists, in celebration of the October Revolution. Since that time the name ties each succeeding wave of first-graders to the Revolution. Every time they are called by this name, which is frequently during their first years at school, they receive a political message. Their teachers also remind them that Lenin loved children and that the Communist Party he founded continues to care for them. They are urged to emulate his studious childhood. Octobrists do not themselves engage in specifically political activity but they are the focus of some of the political activity of the Pioneers who guide and direct them.

At ten, little Octobrists become young Pioneers and begin to wear the triangular red Pioneer tie. Each time they put it on they are supposed to think about the unity of the three Communist Party organizations: the Pioneers, the Komsomol, and the CPSU. The Pioneer years provide Soviet children who want to be leaders with many opportunities to prove themselves, to start up the political ladder. And they will surely be watched, much as promising young athletes are watched in the sports clubs and talented performers in the music schools.

The Pioneer organization was created on May 19, 1922, four years after the formation of the Komsomol (October 29, 1918). These two dates are clearly marked on the ritual calendar of Soviet schoolchildren. The new organization borrowed much of its structure and military terminology from the Russian Boy Scout movement. The latter survived as a separate entity for a short time but disappeared in 1924. Its founding charter describes the Pioneer organization as the preparatory stage for the Komsomol. The Komsomol, which is self-supporting through membership dues, publications, and lotteries, still helps to fund Pioneer activities, as do various ministries and trade unions.

At the beginning of September, the newly elected members of a school council meet in the special room that every school sets aside for Pioneer activities. They spread out the pages of *Pionerskaya Pravda*, whose first autumn issue will contain a suggested program of political activities for the coming school year. This program is drawn up by the Central Council of the Pioneer organization in Moscow. Although each school in the country can choose how it wants to follow the program, a system of national awards favours those who hew most closely to the line. A glimpse at the annual program ("The All-Union March-route of the Young Leninists") for the school year 1984-85 will demonstrate its political tone. Since May 9, 1985, marked the fortieth anniversary of the German surrender to Soviet troops in Berlin, the program of Pioneer activities for that entire school year was focused on the Great Patriotic War. The motto for the year was "Salute, Victory!" "Let the march 'salute, victory!' become the march of memory", reads the Pioneer newspaper. "Let it teach you and your comrades a grateful attitude to those who perished in the War. Let it teach you to take care of those whom we call war veterans because we are all in debt before them in our hearts."

As I looked over this program, I tried to imagine some of the eleven- and twelve-year-olds I know in Canada sitting around at a school meeting deciding on which political activities they would pursue that year. I couldn't, because our political culture is so completely different. No one dreams of asking Canadian children to "prove your loyalty to your motherland with your studies" or to "make a reconnaissance of useful deeds". We certainly do not ask them to study English (let alone Russian) as "the language of friendship and fraternity" or to "make friends with soldiers" in any army. However, I am quite sure that most Soviet youngsters elected to the council of their school *druzhina* during that anniversary year made sure that as many Pioneers as possible completed the "routes" they had chosen. The chairman and the commissar responsible for the political organization of each *otryad* (class detachment) would have worked especially hard. An active *otryad* is known as a "right-flank" detachment, and the school that has the largest number of these detachments in the district wins a banner from the Central Council of the

Pioneer organization. Successful leaders in Pioneer councils who have helped bring banners to their schools are on their way to power. It would now appear that during the 1990s the political load of the Pioneer movement will diminish; the movement has begun to separate itself from the CPSU, if not from communist ideals. However, children growing up in the 1980s were fully exposed to the old system.

The Political-Ideological Content of the School Curriculum

When I was in a Canadian elementary school in the 1930s, I had to memorize the names of the kings and queens of England and listen to stories about the benefits of British imperial rule. I was taught how Canada was "opened up" by Europeans who stayed to build a nation. At school in France—and even in Mexico, where they went to a French lycée—my children learned nothing but French history. At the American International School in New Delhi, they learned more about the United States than they did about India. Soviet children, of course, Russians and non-Russians alike, learn about Russia.

The history taught to me as a child consisted mainly, as I remember it, of dates and certain outstanding events usually associated with royalty. It left me with a certain nostalgia for the remnants of empire but little sense of why things had happened the way they had. Soviet children are taught history in a different way. For it is in the history class that they are fitted with the narrow-angle lens that is known as the Soviet "world-view".

Soviet children study seven years of history, and in their last two years at school this history program is expanded to encompass what is known as "social studies", which until very recently was the study of Communist Party ideology in it most undiluted form. Other school subjects have a political-ideological dimension as well, such as geography, literature, and the course in grade eight called "The Fundamentals of State and Law". Since in the State's opinion only the Marxist-Leninist perspective could make sense of the events that shape human progress, it was primarily in the history class that Soviet children learned about the political roles they would be expected to play as adult citizens.

For Soviet children growing up in the 1980s, what happened in their history class was one of the clearest signs of political change. At the same time, it let them (and us) know which elements of Soviet ideology are likely to persist. What changed were the facts, particularly of the Soviet period. What did not was the "world-view", the explanatory framework into which all newly revealed facts will have to be fitted. This framework is by no means as rigid as most people think but it is just as distinctive as the Christian, say, or the Islamic world-view.

When Soviet children first go to school they concentrate on learning to read, write, and figure. What political-ideological content there is, is restricted to introducing them to Lenin and the Revolution, the Motherland, Labour, the Soviet Army, and the CPSU as objects of veneration. This is intended to develop an emotional "filter" to colour and protect the world-view "lens" they acquire through the study of history in the upper grades.

They will be ten years old (in grade four) before they encounter history as a separate subject. The textbook for this course has changed only a little during the decade, nor is it likely to look very different in the 1990s. It is Russian and Soviet history in episodic form beginning with the settlement of the Russian lands in the tenth century until the most recent Party Congress. In the various republics, other nationalities are able to incorporate some of their own pre-revolutionary history, but the accounts of the Soviet period are standard. In the 1988 edition of the textbook there were a few changes to accommodate the revelations of recent years, but basic themes remained the same.

All Soviet children are still learning about the struggle of the Russian people over the years against the foreign invader. They are following Alexandr Nevsky onto the ice in 1242 as he and his companions defeat the Teutonic Knights. Seven hundred winters later they are shivering in Leningrad under the German Blockade. Once again the invader is turned back.

And the children of *glasnost* still learn about the role of the so-called rank-and-file in historical events. Catherine the Great and the other royals are virtually ignored while teachers tell them about daily life in pre-revolutionary times. Peter the Great is the only tsar to attract attention, primarily because of his scientific interests—and his battles against foreign invaders.

Reading about the peasant revolts of Stepan Razin and Emelyan Pugachyov, and, later, about the workers' revolt of 1905, children are introduced to the concept of class. Ordinary people are one class, the class of the oppressed. The rich and the powerful are the other, the class of the oppressors. In tsarist times antagonisms between these two classes created continual tensions and struggles, which made the Revolution inevitable. Since the Revolution the task of the people has been to struggle for the creation of a new society, one which will be fair to everybody. Children are expected to complete the grade-four course feeling proud and privileged to be growing up in the Soviet Union.

As they move up from grade to grade, Soviet children meet the "laws" of social change. Studying ancient and medieval history, they see how the primitive communal societies of prehistoric times gave rise to the slave-owning orders of Greece and Rome and how struggles between slaves and their owners created tensions that set in motion the processes that eventually led to feudalism. The economic tensions created by feudal society gave rise to a new economic order called "capitalism" whose internal contradictions should eventually lead to socialism.

This method of looking at history is known as class analysis and, while it may make it easy to write exams, it creates curious distortions in the historical pictures with which we in the West are most familiar. During the past forty years, for example, Soviet students of the United States have learned more about the "annihilation" of the Native peoples and Negro slavery than they have about democracy in America. They have studied the Civil War as a "bourgeois revolution" brought about by trouble with the slaves. With respect to contemporary America, they have studied "the ongoing development of state-monopoly capitalism, the growth of multinational corporations, and the growing role of the military-industrial complex", with a continuing focus on the struggle of black and Native populations against racial discrimination and for civil rights. They have also studied the "persecution" of the Communist Party in the United States and the dominant role of anti-communism in American foreign policy.

The study of history introduces Soviet children to another concept just as integral to the Soviet world-view as class analysis—the concept of just and unjust wars. "Why does the Soviet Union have to strengthen its Armed Forces?" asks the 1984 history textbook for ten-year-olds I have been referring to. This question is repeated in the 1988 edition and the response is the same: "The Soviet Union possesses the most advanced weapons to repel the attack of any enemy…but never will our country attack another country either big or small. We live by work—not by war." A just war is, therefore, a war of defence. The Great Patriotic War was obviously a just war on the part of the Soviet people and an unjust one on the part of their German attackers. The First World War was an unjust one from every point of view. Soviet students have long been taught that "World War One was provoked by the desire of the ruling classes to redivide the world and to seize territory belonging to others". Equally unjust are wars that serve the needs of the so-called military-industrial complex in capitalist countries. Referring no doubt to Vietnam, a well-known Soviet educator wrote not so long ago that "human suffering and massive destruction caused by recent warfare in South-East Asia and elsewhere should be brought home to children's hearts and minds so that they realize that a policy of aggression, violence and oppression is contrary to man's aspirations". However, interventions on behalf of peoples struggling *against* oppression or aggression are usually depicted to children as "just" wars, wars of defence against the forces of capitalism and imperialism. Members of the Soviet Armed Forces who participate in these struggles are said to be performing their "internationalist duty". This is how the Soviet intervention in Afghanistan was initially presented to the Soviet population. The experience of Afghanistan was shattering and the Soviet Union is now withdrawing military assistance from many other parts of the world but this will not change Marxist-Leninist theory with respect to what constitutes a just war.

In the spring of 1988, history exams for senior students were abruptly cancelled. They were restored in 1989, but no longer based on a single text. Teachers are now asked to refer to the newspapers and to supplementary materials with which they have been supplied while the texts are being revised and rewritten. More importantly, they are being asked "to test the student's ability to think independently and to defend his position with sound arguments". The climate is changing so fast and events are unrolling so unexpectedly, especially in Eastern Europe, that many teachers are having difficulty coping. Classes are becoming livelier and more disputatious. One student cautiously praises Stalin's discipline. Another cries out that "all those controls were based on sheer terror. It was not rational." There is excitement in the air. But the framework of the Soviet "world-view" is still intact. Gorbachev believes in it.

Military-Patriotic Education

Anyone who lived through the Second World War will remember the Battle of Stalingrad. On February 2, 1943, following weeks of bitter fighting in wretched winter weather during which the city was virtually destroyed, Soviet troops won a decisive victory and the German retreat began back across the vast lands they had first taken and now laid waste. The Battle of Stalingrad stands in the collective memory of the Soviet people with the siege of Leningrad as one of the cardinal events of the Great Patriotic War. The war memorial on the hill called Mamayev Kurgan is the most awesome I saw anywhere in the USSR.

We visited Volgograd (as Stalingrad is now called) in the spring of 1983. Today it is a relatively prosperous industrial centre, stretching for more than sixty kilometres along the Volga River. But the soul of the city is still on the top of Mamayev Kurgan, where a gigantic statue of The Motherland brandishes for ever her defiant sword. From the bottom of the hill, on the riverside, the heroic proportions of this fierce figure in her blowing draperies are balanced by monumental sculptures of struggle and death that rise up on either side. Mounting the steps through this frozen battle (the Germans alone suffered a million and a half casualties during the battle of Stalingrad) we were accompanied by hundreds of children, older ones in school groups, younger ones with their families. We paused at the massive statue of Grief and then entered the Hall of Memory. Mournful music enveloped us as we wound our way slowly up the ramp. The children clung to the guard-rail as they climbed and gazed with wonder at the great stone arm that rises from a pool to hold aloft the eternal flame that everywhere in the USSR symbolizes the fallen. When we emerged at last at the foot of Mother Russia, we were emotionally drained. The whole complex of Mamayev Kurgan is an enormous shrine to the struggle, courage, and sacrifice of the Soviet people. No child, or adult, who visits it is likely to forget its lessons.

Among those who climbed Mamayev Kurgan with us were boys who may one day climb it again with their friends and families on their way to do their military service. If they do, then the memorial will evoke emotions in them formed by years of what the Soviets call "military-patriotic education". As they depart for their two-year commitment, the new recruits will feel, at least for a moment, that they are off to perform their sacred duty (*svyashchenny dolg*) to serve and protect the motherland.

I am old enough to have been at school during the Second World War, so I can remember what it felt like to have my patriotic sentiments aroused in a military context and to have a concept of a detestable enemy (Hitler) whom I was determined to see defeated. But Canada does not have a militaristic tradition and so, once the war was over, those sentiments dissipated. Few schoolchildren in Canada today would be able to name any Canadian military exploits. In the United States, however, during the whole of the post-war period, American children were taught about Washington and the Revolutionary War, Lincoln and the Civil War, Eisenhower and the Second World War, about their nation as a democracy and Russia as an adversary. At the same time their counterparts in the Soviet Union were learning about Lenin and the Revolution, the Great Patriotic War and the triumph of the Soviet people over the German invaders, about their country as a multinational socialist state led by the Communist Party, and about the United States as a rival to be regarded with caution.

Much of this knowledge comes, of course, from the school curriculum. In the earlier years the emphasis is more on patriotism than on militarism although I was struck by the prominence in popular history books of martial heroes such as Suvorov (1729-1800) and Kutuzov (1745-1813). General Suvorov is included because, although he was the son of a general, he started his army career as a private and so got to know the common soldier. Besides, he was a weak and sickly child who hardened himself through exercise and deliberate exposure to all kinds of weather, an excellent model for a potentially flabby generation. The image children receive of General Kutuzov owes rather more to Tolstoy than to historical fact. He is presented as a wise general and a great patriot beloved by the common people.

The GTO ("Ready for Labour and Defence") physical-education program also has a military-patriotic purpose, but children tend to pay more attention to the sports and physical-fitness standards of the GTO than they do to the military skills they are supposed to acquire or to the civil-defence lessons. In the last two years of high school, however, all students take a course of direct military preparation called *Nachalnaya Voennaya Podgotovka* (Introductory Military Training). This course became a part of the universal school curriculum in 1967.

In the first class hour, students are reminded once again about the need for strong defences against "imperialistic aggression" and their "sacred duty" as Soviet citizens to protect the motherland. Then they are taught how to use and care for weapons. They are drilled in military manoeuvres, taught orienteering and map-reading, and trained in both the theory and practice of military tactics. In a unit called "Civil Defence", students study the characteristics of the offensive weapons of the so-called imperialist states and learn how to protect themselves and others, if it is at all possible. They study decontamination methods for use with radioactivity and toxic chemicals. Although girls have long been exempted from military service, they had to take this military-preparation course all through the 1980s along with the boys and pass it in order to graduate from high school. At last, in 1989 it ceased to be obligatory for them. The response of girls to all this varies enormously, but most of my women friends expressed misgivings. Soviet authorities persist in equating the military virtues of courage, strength, endurance, and fearlessness in the face of death with manliness, and the peace-loving ones of tenderness, compassion, and conciliation with womanliness. Then they compound the situation by decrying the "feminization" of boys. Many girls feel uneasy in such an atmosphere, although there is no reason to assume that they are any less patriotic than the boys.

Before taking the introductory military course in high school, many students will already have had some elementary military experience. Although the Pioneer organization is primarily political, social, and recreational, its structure has military dimensions that accustom children to performing military activities such as marching, carrying regalia, and standing on guard, and to thinking in military terms, such as detachments, brigades, and so on. The Pioneer organization also sponsors war games known as *Zarnitsa* (Summer Lightning) that every year involve more than sixteen million children (twelve to fifteen years of age). These games are featured at many Pioneer summer camps and are designed to be exciting and fun. Two teams set out to capture each other, using various "military" strategies, and at night the children bivouac, listen to war stories, and sing beside a campfire. The military purpose of these games is unmistakable.

Zarnitsa is complemented by *Orlyonok* (Eaglet), the name given to more advanced war games played by youngsters fifteen to seventeen years of age. Students in this age-group can also join a number of paramilitary clubs organized by DOSAAF (the voluntary society for co-operation with the Armed Forces) in which they can learn to fly airplanes, operate radios, scuba-dive, parachute jump, drive motorcycles, or acquire other skills that have military uses. DOSAAF has revived the "Timurite" program for Pioneers that was popular during the Great Patriotic War. This program encourages schoolchildren to perform useful deeds on behalf of lonely people such as the widows of servicemen or war veterans.

Other out-of-school activities that encourage Soviet children to feel patriotic and ready to defend the motherland include the Clubs of Young Patriots and the Clubs of Young Pathfinders, which focus on Pioneer heroes who fought and died in the Great Patriotic War or in the Revolution and Civil War. A few years ago one of these latter clubs, researching the story of a brother and sister who had supposedly died on the barricades in Moscow during the Revolution, discovered to their surprise that the sister was still alive. They located her and interviewed her.

What she told them about her brother became a popular book called *Kuznechik* (Grasshopper). It was added to the stack of books and films that encourage patriotic emotions in the young. It is notable that these books rarely refer to military exploits beyond Soviet borders and it is highly unlikely that there will ever be a popular children's book written about Afghanistan, surely the most searing military experience of the 1980s for Soviet young people.

With so much emphasis on the military, I was surprised to discover that war toys in the Soviet Union are relatively restrained. They bear little resemblance to the widely popular G.I. Joe products found in so many North American homes. To begin with, they comprise only 3 per cent of the market (I often went into toy stores to check). On the whole, these toys are generic ones: guns, miniature soldiers, tanks, airplanes and model kits for making them, Civil War helmets and capes, and so on. Considering the expertise that goes into modern Soviet weapons systems, they are surprisingly unsophisticated. They are also as poorly made as most of the other toys on the market. Judging by my shopping trips, Canadian stores stock toys considerably more suggestive of violence.

Who Is the Enemy?

"Soviet fighting men! Strengthen combat organization and discipline! Be active participants in restructuring in the army and navy and reliable defenders of the peaceful labour of the Soviet people!" So reads one of the slogans prepared for May Day in 1989. In spite of the changed international climate, including the withdrawal of Soviet troops from Afghanistan, and new proposals on arms control, Soviet children are still being urged to maintain their guard.

And yet one cannot help but wonder who it is that Soviet children are now being asked to envisage as "the enemy". In a speech to the XIX Congress of the Komsomol in 1982, the movement's then leader, B.N. Pastukhov, said, "Cultivation of patriotism means bringing up a brave warrior, defender of the Fatherland, ruthless to its enemies. Love for the socialist fatherland is impossible without class hatred in today's world."

Fierce words indeed and, judging by the rest of the text, spoken with conviction. And yet what do they actually mean to today's child in the Soviet Union? At the time of the Revolution the class enemy was easy to identify. It was anybody who had some money or who had held power in tsarist times. During the Civil War the enemy was the White Guard and the foreign interventionists. During the Great Patriotic War the enemy was Nazi Germany. The Soviet Union is wary of most of its neighbours, and in the 1960s China was considered a threat. During the Cold War, the enemy was the United States and rather vaguer reference was made to other "imperialist" states in the capitalist world. As recently as 1985, *Pravda* could rant about "conditions in which the military threat from the forces of imperialism is growing" and demand "that military-patriotic education be improved and made more effective". And this after a twenty-year expansion of all the military-patriotic activities for children that I have just described.

Now, however, Gorbachev is talking about "a new dialectic of common interests" and welcoming "new political thinking" on the international scene with "its regard for universal values and emphasis on common sense and openness". Even the concept, so often attributed to Lenin, that the interests of the working class override all other human values, has been called into question. Another quotation from Lenin has been found to support the idea of a common humanity. What I expect to happen in the next few years is that the strictly military aspect of military-patriotic education will diminish in importance and patriotism will increasingly be associated with safeguarding the socialist values proclaimed by the present regime. Children will continue to be reminded that socialism is a more humane system than capitalism, but at the same time they will be encouraged to value international co-operation on behalf of the survival of the human species. This process has already started; it is now time to examine the other side of the coin to see what Soviet children have been learning about peace.

Education for Peace and International Understanding

Since 1983 every school in the Soviet Union has been required to start the first day of the school year with a "Peace Lesson", which it is encouraged to organize in its own way. In some schools, senior students plan lessons about peace over the summer and then teach them to first- and second-graders. They ask them what they think peace means and then tell them stories about the Great Patriotic War and its personal tragedies. War veterans are often invited into classrooms so that schoolchildren can ask them questions directly. Many schools hold a general assembly to which parents are invited so that they can listen with their children to a writer or an artist or a political personality who wishes to share his or her concerns about war and peace. From *Pionerskaya Pravda* comes the following account by a reporter who attended the peace lesson in Moscow School no. 270 on September 1, 1984.

> The children have flowers in their hands. The school radio plays "The Bells of Buchenwald" [a well-known song about the horror of the death camps, written during the 1960s]. I watched the children suddenly quieting down and the faces of parents and teachers assume a grave expression. The first lesson of the new school year—the peace lesson—starts with a minute of silence in memory of the twenty million Soviet people who sacrificed their lives for peace on earth.

> Boys and girls are listening with bated breath to Anatoly Andreevich Ananiev. His novels describe a generation that grew up into adulthood in the trenches and defended the motherland.... Ananiev talks about his trips to Latin America, about his participation in peace marches, he speaks about himself and at the same time about each of the children. "The peace lesson should awaken in you a sense of responsibility to our time, of responsibility for your destiny, for the destiny of the motherland and of mankind. There should not be another war! Should not! This is our main common duty!"

One should not be surprised that the intensification of military activity and of military-patriotic education at the end of the 1970s that accompanied the Soviet intervention in Afghanistan was followed by the creation of the peace lesson in 1983. This double emphasis on war *and* peace was characteristic of Soviet policy for so many years that, in the West, "war" almost succeeded in giving "peace" a bad name. And yet it would be wrong to dismiss the peace lesson as a piece of propaganda tainted by hypocrisy. There are many people, indeed nations, who, over the centuries, have come to the making of peace through the experience of war. The children who listened to Ananiev "with bated breath" were undoubtedly being taught to value peace even if they were not being taught how to achieve it.

The Russian word for peace is *mir. Mir* is also the Russian word for the world and all who live in it. The huge signs that one sees everywhere in the Soviet Union reading *Miru-Mir* translate as "Peace to the World". The first meaning of *mir* is peace in the sense of tranquillity, gentleness, friendship. The second meaning emerged when *mir* was used figuratively to describe the "peaceful association" of people in a village community who came together to agree about the conduct of the village's affairs. These two meanings encompass the official Soviet attitude to peace. Soviet children are taught that there can be no world peace without concord among the world's peoples but they are also taught that since most non-socialist countries are made up of "antagonistic" classes, such as capitalist owners and exploited workers, or imperialist rulers and colonized masses, world peace will be impossible until these antagonisms are resolved. The Soviet Union is a country in which (in the past students were often reminded of this, although the message is no longer convincing and will require adjustment) many nationalities live in concord. Therefore, it has a responsibility to help other countries arrive at the same condition. Only then can *mir,* in both of its senses, be established. *Miru-Mir* , therefore, is about the Soviet Union's mission to bring peace to a world torn by the strife caused by economic injustice. Those who maintain a system of antagonistic classes for their own profit or pretend that such antagonisms do not exist are the real enemies of peace.

Until very recently, messages delivered to Soviet children about peace gave more prominence to the enemies of peace and to how peace in the Soviet Union was being undermined than they did to peacemakers and to how international peace could be built. During the years we lived in Moscow, this was especially true, and it often resulted in tensions that were both painful to observe and frustrating to experience. In the early 1980s, public events involving foreigners were always tainted by official xenophobia. There have been improvements since, but as long as foreigners are restricted to the ghettos that the Soviet government has created for them, this taint will continue to spoil relations.

I will tell a characteristic story from my own experience in order to convey some idea of the climate in which, for too long, Soviet children have been expected to learn about peace and international understanding. It is not about children but it encapsulates, in the events of one afternoon, the tantalizing atmosphere in which even the most friendly public exchanges between Soviets and foreigners took place for years.

March 8, International Women's Day, is one of the most popular of the Soviet Union's ritual holidays. Its ideological messages are twofold: "Look at the fine job the Soviet Union has done with respect to the equality of women!" and "Let's express our solidarity with working women all over the world, particularly with those who have been victimized and oppressed". In reality the day is mainly celebrated by the population at large as a combination of St. Valentine's Day and Mother's Day. Nikolay, the steward at the Residence, always presented me with a small bouquet of roses, and one year the drivers at the Embassy clubbed together to buy me a piece of the pretty blue and white *gzhel* pottery I had begun to collect.

International Women's Day was also the one day in the year when I and the wives of the other ambassadors accredited to the Soviet Union had some limited contact with wives of Soviet politicians and Soviet women distinguished in their own right. This happened at a tea-dance at which the only men present were the waiters and the members of the orchestra. The first time I went, the hostess was Brezhnev's daughter, Galina, who stood at the top of the red-carpeted steps to greet us, her resemblance to her stocky father barely disguised by floating panels of peach-coloured chiffon. We shook her hand and passed through into a large hall where Soviet women smiled at us from the other side of long tables laden with food. We stood and listened to speeches about peace and international friendship, we ate and drank and smiled some more, and then, for an hour or so, we danced. We danced in pairs, we danced in groups, we danced until we dropped laughing and out of breath into the waiting chairs. I danced with Mrs. Gromyko. Mrs. Gromyko danced with the wife of the Chinese Ambassador. Galina danced with all comers. Western women in smart afternoon dresses, African women in brilliant cottons, Asian women in silks, we danced with each other and we danced with the Soviet women. A few of them we recognized; the great ballerina, Ulanova, the first woman cosmonaut, Tereshkova. But who were all the others? We never found out. In the end, when we foreigners returned to our separate embassies, laden with flowers and gifts, and the Soviet women went back to their apartments, all of us carried away memories of warmth and good feeling, but alas, not much else.

I am sure that the Soviet women who danced with us that day enjoyed being with us. Such an experience, however, will make no difference to peace and international understanding until every Soviet woman feels free to ask a foreigner home for supper. That was not the case then, and it still isn't, even though every time I return to Moscow I find the situation has improved. Unfortunately officialdom continues to limit the movements of foreigners in ways that effectively hamstring the natural emergence of mutual understanding. In my view, cultures can only truly appreciate one another as a result of an accumulation of widely differing contacts over an extended period of time. While individual friendships have often sprung up between foreigners and Soviet citizens in spite of official barriers, as I know to my profit, these relationships can never compensate for the absence of the full and free exchanges that take place among the peoples of Western Europe and North America. In the interests of peace and common human problems, the barriers will have to go. Where they are breaking down fastest in the Soviet Union today, it is often as a result of contacts among children.

Soviet children have long been told that one of the ways they can help to attain *mir* is through solidarity with children in other countries, particularly those in friendly socialist countries such as Czechoslovakia or Cuba, or in countries such as India and Ethiopia where children are known to live in especially difficult circumstances. But nowadays they can also contact children in capitalist countries. Many clubs of international friendship have been established in schools and Pioneer palaces to encourage these feelings of solidarity. Foreign residents in Moscow, who still run up against the limits of State tolerance, are legitimately skeptical about "friendship societies", yet few Soviet children would understand our skepticism. They themselves are perfectly disposed to be friendly, as I discovered on numerous occasions. One of these occasions was a visit to a club of international friendship at Moscow's Pioneer palace on a fine spring day in 1986.

As I walked across the grass to the main building of the Pioneer palace the playing-fields were covered with active children. A bearded young man met me at the door and led me to the Hall of International Friendship, where foreigners are received and clubs of international friendship congregate. The group I was to meet was in a corner of the hall talking to a wide-eyed young girl named Ekaterina who had just returned from a trip to the United States. Child diplomacy is a small but growing factor in East-West relations. Ekaterina's visit had been made in the spirit of Samantha Smith, the young American girl who wrote to Andropov about nuclear war and was then invited to visit the USSR. The Soviets have long encouraged this kind of activity for children as a form of "peace education", first within the Soviet Union, then within the socialist bloc. For many years children have been invited to Artek, the showpiece Pioneer camp on the Black Sea, from all over the world. Now Soviet schoolchildren are being allowed to spend time in the West.

While we were waiting for the children, I asked my bearded host, who as a full-time employee of the Pioneer palace— a member of its "faculty", he explained—was in charge of friendship clubs, to tell me a bit about them. He explained that the clubs are organized for three age levels. The first level (children from grades three to five, eight- to ten-year olds) is called "My Country, the USSR" and focuses on cross-national friendships within the USSR. Club members study the languages of other Soviet nationalities, learn about their cultures, and start writing to pen pals. This is the model for all peace education activity aimed at children in this age range, whether it takes place inside or outside of school. Clubs for the second age level (eleven- to thirteen-year-olds) focus on other socialist countries. Members study national languages—German, Bulgarian, Spanish, perhaps—and other cultural forms. They establish relations with official youth organizations in these countries and enter into correspondence with them. They may even have exchanges. A third level of friendship clubs exists for students in grades eight to eleven. These students, some of whom are Komsomol members, are expected to expand their circle of interest to the whole world. They study the countries whose languages they have been learning in much greater depth. It is the young people in these latter clubs who take part in the youth festivals that are such a part of the international socialist youth movement.

There are 920 clubs of International Friendship in Moscow. Among other activities, their members raise money for the Soviet Peace Fund by collecting scrap metal or newspapers for recycling. Or they may hold a "solidarity fair" on behalf of needy children in a country such as Vietnam, selling objects they have made themselves. They also go to factories and give "peace concerts". They accept donations from the workers or raise money by selling school-made souvenirs. They can send this money to the Peace Fund through any bank in the country. The Peace Fund publishes a regular catalogue of activities, listing the clubs or schools that have contributed money. Volunteers from the Peace Fund frequently go to schools or to clubs of international friendship to explain what the Peace Fund does. The Peace Fund is not the only organization that sends money abroad. Children can also send money to poor children in other countries through the Soviet Red Cross/Red Crescent society, which sponsors clubs or *kruzhki* (circles) in most schools. And now they can also send money to the Soviet Children's Fund.

While the young man was telling me all this, a small group of children began to gather around. They were about ten or eleven years of age, both girls and boys, including a boy who was physically handicapped. Two or three of the girls were shy. The smallest, however, was anything but and spoke surprisingly good English. I told them that I wanted to know what they thought about Canada and asked them to tell me the first thing that popped into their heads when they heard the word. Their initial responses had to do with nature: "big and beautiful", "nature similar to ours", "we live on the same parallel", "people who look like us", "forest and nature", "maple leaves". Then the boys talked sports.

I asked the children if they knew of any Canadian books and one them replied that she knew there was a Canadian writer who wore skirts and couldn't go to the United States. I later learned that Farley Mowat had just been in the USSR and had appeared in his kilt on Soviet television. Friendly and eager, these children were quick to spot the similarities between our two countries. But the differences were beyond them. A friendship club does not encourage children to explore differences among political cultures to the point where the ideal of international friendship can be transformed into the reality of international understanding.

UNESCO clubs currently being formed in Soviet schools taking part in UNESCO's Associated Schools Project should do this better. The Associated Schools Project, linking schools from over ninety countries, has been in existence since the 1950s. It has gained momentum in recent years. By the end of 1985, nearly two thousand schools world-wide were involved, including about forty in the USSR. The challenge for these schools is to discover innovative and imaginative ways to further the aims that UNESCO adopted in 1974 with respect to "International Understanding, Cooperation and Peace". Associated schools are expected to concentrate on four basic topics: world problems and the role of the United Nations system in solving them; human rights; other countries and cultures; man and the environment.

In March 1988, I visited one of the Soviet Union's associated schools, School no. 20 in central Moscow, in the company of a young man from the Soviet UNESCO office. He told me that because Gorbachev and his political colleagues are paying so much more attention to the United Nations, more than fifty Soviet schools are now involved in the project, with many more expected to join. That School no. 20 is a special language school (in this case English) facilitates exchanges. Indeed, as one of the senior language teachers told us, a recent delegation of American children would have been lost if the students at School no. 20 had not been able to speak at least some English. The American students came to class every day for a couple of weeks, and after they returned to their home school in the state of Washington the two schools organized a simultaneous swim meet. Results flashed back and forth via the telex at the American Embassy.

The teachers and students with whom we spoke were keen to expand the international activities of their school. They pointed with pride to the drawings, posters, and world maps that decorated their walls and stairwells. Most items were in English and celebrated various aspects of world culture. Some were specifically devoted to the principles of UNESCO. However, the teachers back-pedalled when I asked if students debated human-rights issues as recommended by UNESCO. They said they did not believe their students were sophisticated enough to deal with such complicated questions and they preferred to focus instead on cultural or environmental issues.

The lack of informed debated on the more complex issues of war and peace, such as arms control, defence, and human rights, weakened peace education in the USSR all through the 1980s. Soviet students were not allowed to study issues associated with the arms race in sufficient depth to come to an informed opinion. This is what four young Canadians discovered when they visited Moscow in June 1987. Seth Klein, Alison Carpenter, Desirée McGraw, and Maxime Faille, high-school students from Montreal, spent the school year of 1986-87 criss-crossing Canada to speak with their contemporaries about the threat posed by the continued existence of nuclear arms. They had a very successful tour, reaching 120,000 Canadian students in 162 communities. At the end of it, they went to San Francisco, and then on to Moscow, to see what teenagers in the United States and the USSR had to say.

They had a busy time in Moscow. They went to a Pioneer camp where they saw the strategy and supply room for *Zarnitsa*. Not surprisingly, they were taken aback by the military paraphernalia and by the very thought of children involved in war games. The director turned towards them to explain that "Soviet children have to learn young how to defend peace". Lesson number one of Soviet peace education: peace is something that has to be fought for. The Montrealers met some older students and heard them say that, although they did not support the arms race, nuclear parity was essential. Lesson number two: peace through strength.

When the young Canadians met a small group of eleven- to thirteen-year-olds, however, there was some sign of deviation from the old lesson plan, something that persuaded them that the wind is shifting. The meeting took place at the official "House of Friendship" on Prospekt Kalinina. The accompanying adults were persuaded to leave the children alone with the four Canadian teenagers. A young medical student stayed behind to translate. Seth described what happened next: "We wanted to get a sense of the ability these young people felt towards effecting change. First we asked political questions, 'What would they do if there was a person in government who did not support disarmament?' The answer was that that would not happen. 'But what if it did?' we asked. Then that person would be fired, was the answer. 'And if he was not?' we countered. Silence. Then the answer, 'We would demonstrate.'"

The Canadians were encouraged by this positive answer and decided to test the children's sense of political power at a more personal level. They asked them what they would do if they had a teacher who they thought was very bad. "The students got very excited and their eyes lit up," wrote Seth. The medical student, who was in her early twenties, also got excited as she translated what they had to say. In the past year they had had a bad teacher, the students had passed around a petition, and the teacher was transferred. The medical student told Seth and his friends that this would never have happened when she was at school. Seth commented that if an entire young generation could be brought up in an atmosphere of *glasnost* and *perestroika* they would experience greater freedom to act in their own interest and acquire a sense of what the exercise of this kind of power could mean for them as individuals. This experience would become, in his words, "addictive". Rather than give this freedom up, he was convinced that young people would push the process further.

"Trust, but Verify"

The children of *glasnost* have grown up surrounded by conflicting messages about war and peace, all emotionally charged. On the first day of school, they have been told that peace is good, and therefore war must be bad. But almost in the same breath, they have been told that pacifism is bad and military preparedness good. They continue to be told that the Revolution was glorious, and the Great Patriotic War was ennobled by valour and sacrifice. They have been taught that intervening on behalf of the oppressed in other countries is admirable yet they have witnessed the ambivalence and indifference with which the veterans from Afghanistan have been treated. They have been asked to draw and paint images of peace and to be friendly to children from other countries, yet they are still being taught to be on the defensive against the systems from which these children come. And now they are watching the collapse of the communist system in countries that still remain members of the military alliance that was established to defend the Eastern bloc from capitalist imperialism. It is very confusing.

What sense can Soviet children make out of all these messages? What are they thinking now about war and peace, and how will they respond if a challenge arises? If the Soviet Union is invaded, there can be little doubt that its people would fight. Whether the current generation will be disposed to intervene militarily in the affairs of other nations is now very unlikely.

Engaging an educated population in a war of aggression today is a complex task. Leaving aside the risk of accidental war (which is always a possibility in the nuclear era), there are a number of pre-conditions that would have to be met before such a war could be undertaken with a reasonable hope of success. For one thing, the population would have to be convinced that such a war was justified and that there was no other way to resolve the conflict that had been put forward as an excuse for it. For another, the same population would have to be prepared to suspend individual judgement and submit itself to orders imposed from above, as happens in the army.

Coercive authoritarian institutions such as armies and secret police have existed in Russia and other parts of the Soviet Union for centuries. These have hardly ever encouraged independent thought in adults, let alone children, and so their continued existence constitutes a real danger. The more these structures loosen up (there is now talk of turning the Soviet Army into a volunteer force) the safer we will all be. Unfortunately, the Soviet school system remains authoritarian (if not coercive) and until the teacher-innovators have made further inroads it will be difficult to render Soviet children resistant to the imposition of authority.

There is, however, a saving grace that may help to counteract the danger inherent in submissiveness. This is the degree to which Soviet society has developed a healthy attitude to children, shows respect for them, and encourages civil authorities to protect them from violence and humiliation, either at home or at school. A quotation from Anton Chekhov, frequently cited in the Soviet Union today, may help to clarify this comment.

In 1889, Chekhov wrote to his friend A.S. Suvorin about his childhood and about the painful process by which he had acquired the sense of personal freedom he had to have in order to become a mature writer. Chekhov's father had been born a serf and carried with him all his life his serf's heritage of combined harshness and servility. As a child, Chekhov was whipped, taught "to respect rank, to kiss the hands of priests, to truckle to the ideas of others". As a boy he "used his fist, tortured animals…was a hypocrite in his dealings with God and man, solely out of a realization of his own insignificance." And yet this young man managed to "squeeze the slave out of himself, drop by drop", until one fine morning he awoke to find that the blood coursing through his veins was "no longer that of a slave but of a real human being." How was this possible? The answer lies partly in the fact that, despite his despotic temper, his father valued him and, Chekhov says, bequeathed him his artistic talent. His loving mother shaped his soul.

There is no doubt in my mind that the family atmosphere and all the little interactions that take place there during a child's earliest years are what contribute most to the formation of a child's fundamental attitude to war and peace. Even very small children can sense within themselves feelings of peace or of conflict. Families provoke or reinforce these feelings. Children who are continually treated with violence are usually at war with themselves; their responses to the rest of the world are either aggression or submission. Children who are loved and tenderly cared for are more at peace with themselves; being more trustful, they are able to learn methods beyond simple aggression or submission for the resolution of conflict. For there is bound to be conflict. All children need to assert themselves in order to grow, and being assertive can be risky. Although there are no published statistics on domestic violence in the Soviet Union, I assume that it is as prevalent in the European portion of the country as it is in the rest of Europe, and probably more so in Central Asia and the Caucasus, especially with respect to women. Many Soviet children certainly witness violence at home, even if they don't personally experience it.

If the most damaging thing for a child is to be a victim of family violence, then the next most damaging thing is to be treated violently by society. In this respect Soviet society has some advantages over North America. Corporal punishment is forbidden at school and discouraged at home. This does not mean that children are not occasionally beaten, but corporal punishment has no defence in law as it has in Canada and the United States. Nor are children able to watch the glorification of violence on television or read sensational accounts of violent acts in newspapers and magazines. It is true that all Soviet children are supposed to know how to shoot before they are eighteen, but civilian access to guns is strictly controlled. Violence for its own sake is not a social value. Soviet women are strongly opposed to violence, and more and more often (as the divorce statistics show) they reject the men who practise it.

But a child's exposure to violence is not the only factor that determines his or her personal response to the issues of war and peace. There are at least three others that I consider to be important. The first I have already mentioned: it is the attitude a child develops to authority. The second is critical thinking. The third is the question of trust. Clearly, Soviet children are brought up to be susceptible to the dictates of authority. It is also abundantly clear that up until recently they have had too few opportunities to develop the capacity to think critically about the issues of war and peace. The question of trust, however, requires further elaboration.

What do I mean by "trust"? This is a question that needs to be answered on two levels. On the psychological level, trust is an attitude that has to be nurtured from earliest childhood. It is a developmental challenge underemphasized in Soviet theories of child development although it is implied by Vygotsky's assertion that an infant's social life is opened by its mother's first smile. In my view, it is crucial that small children be surrounded by loving and responsive caretakers so that they can develop a fundamental attitude of trust. Trustful children reach out for knowledge and experience. Mistrustful children resist both. On the political level, trust becomes an attitude informed by knowledge. I fully accept the Russian proverb that President Reagan liked to quote, "*Doveryay, no proveryay*" (Trust, but verify). This is where critical thinking comes in. The susceptibility of Soviet children to authority can easily combine with an uncritical acceptance of their military-patriotic education to send them off to war when they are old enough. This is what happened in Hungary (1956), Czechoslovakia (1968), and Afghanistan (1979). Young soldiers were told that these wars were "just" wars. They were ordered to go and perform their international duty, and they obeyed.

However, the role of Soviet troops in Czechoslovakia was not what the young had been told it was; as student travel began to increase among the countries of the socialist bloc, Soviet students heard a different version of the events of 1968 from some of their Czech contemporaries. According to a Soviet friend, who was a student at the time, this made a difference to her whole generation. The experience of Afghanistan has had an even greater impact on the current generation of young adults. More than a million of them served there over nine years and their direct experience has troubled the whole nation. Some informal interviews with Soviet soldiers on the outskirts of Kabul in May 1988, just prior to the beginning of the Soviet withdrawal, revealed that, while some soldiers held on to a lingering belief in the legitimacy of the Soviet response to the Afghan government's "request" for assistance, there was a great horror of war. The general attitude was probably best summed up by the comment of Private Moshnikov: "Now that I've seen war, I don't want to see it any more. I don't want to go into combat. I want there to be peace in all the world."

Young people in the Soviet Union (with the benefits of education and travel) will be more critical in future of such concepts as "internationalist duty". As many Soviet educators today are uncomfortably aware, once students discover that a teacher has lied to them, they are disinclined to believe anything else the teacher says. They may continue to do what the teacher tells them to do out of established habit, but their hearts won't be in it. And whatever they do for an authority whom they no longer respect will hardly be the kind of constructive action that is now so necessary for the solution of international problems.

"Since wars begin in the minds of men it is in the minds of men that the defences of peace must be built," states the UNESCO constitution. UNESCO's Associated Schools Project is a model of the kind of education that can provide young people with an adequate grasp of global issues. But knowledge is not enough if the question of trust is ignored. Albert Einstein once said that to build peace our "circle of compassion must expand to encompass the whole world". A mistrustful person rarely feels compassion for people beyond his or her ken. To create in children the capacity first of all to trust and then to verify is one of the most important challenges facing parents and teachers anywhere in the world. This will happen when children are treated as persons from the very beginning. For to respect children as human beings is to nourish them with love and reason, and then to set them free.

Afterword

Afterword

On our last morning in Moscow I woke up early. Slipping out of bed, I went into the deserted salon to draw back the heavy brocade curtains and let in the light of day. It was September 29, 1983. Four weeks earlier, a Soviet fighter pilot had shot down a Korean passenger plane as it strayed over military installations in the Soviet Far East. There were eleven Canadians on KAL flight 007 and it had been tense at the Embassy while telexes flew back and forth over the Atlantic and we waited to find out exactly what had happened. It was a painful time, made even more difficult by the wrench of our coming departure. As I stood at the window, I felt weighed down by the tragedy and full of concern for our Soviet friends whom we would be leaving behind so soon. Perhaps it would help to take one last look at the school across the way? I put off last-minute chores and settled myself on the window-ledge to enjoy the reassuring sight of little children on their way to school.

Three senior students, carrying briefcases and parcels, were the first to arrive. They opened the heavy school door and went in, propping it open behind them. Two teachers followed, heads bent in earnest conversation. Then the younger children appeared, flooding in from both ends of the street: the girls wearing brightly coloured windbreakers over their brown serge dresses, the uniformed boys coatless. A father leaned over to give a last piece of advice to his small, hesitant daughter; a mother steered her young son towards the door. But most of the children came to school on their own, their arms full of books or carrying satchels on their backs.

The boys stayed outside as long as they could, lingering in small groups. A couple shared a copy of *Pionerskaya Pravda*, studying what must have been the sports section. Four others amused themselves by jumping on and off the curb, pausing from time to time to help friends carry thick bundles of newspapers into the school for the weekly paper drive. The tide of chatter rose and then fell as more children moved inside. A student monitor came out to summon the remaining stragglers. A little girl in a sky-blue jacket, a big white bow on her bobbing pony-tail, came flying down the street and ducked in under the arm that was pulling the door shut. Then all was silent.

Watching these children, so ordinary, so normal, so like children I had known in other countries, I found myself looking at them with hope. But neither I, nor any other foreign observer speculating about the future of the Soviet Union in those dismal days, foresaw what is happening there now; the astonishing opening up of Soviet society under Gorbachev. These children were more fortunate than we knew. Every generation represents a new chance for its nation but this one is more likely to fulfil its promise than any other since the Revolution. If it does, then the Soviet Union will be richer—and so will the rest of us.

Four years later, in September 1987, I returned to Moscow and went into the school to talk with some of students there, to see for myself how they were getting along; to find out, if I could, what younger children were dreaming about in the era of *glasnost*. My method was one I knew to have been successfully employed in the study of children's values in Canada, the USA, and France. Fairy stories and folk-tales often turn on the granting of three magic wishes; this is such a common theme across cultures that social psychologists in the West have found it a reliable way to determine what groups of children value most. As a result, a number of studies, dating back to 1936, exist to provide a basis for comparing what Soviet and North American children of the same age find desirable.

"Do you know the *skazka* that Pushkin wrote about the poor fisherman who caught the golden fish?" I asked several classrooms of children in School no. 59. "Yes, yes, of course we do." All the hands shot up. "Well, what three wishes would *you* ask the fish to grant you in return for setting him free? Think now, anything you want."

"I wish we could keep animals at school," called out Anton. "And I want to find a dinosaur," said Kirill. "I would rather have a big car," broke in Sergei. "And I really want a video," said Nadya. Yulya wanted a talking parrot, Tanya, a bicycle. Another Sergei wished for a TV set that would show the future. But these personal and material wishes turned out to be exceptional for, more than anything else, the sixty children whose wishes I gathered that morning (they were seven to ten years of age) wished for good and loyal friends, for the health and welfare of their families, for success at school (for their classmates as well as themselves), and for peace.

I was aware that these children had just had their annual peace lesson, and that at the beginning of the school year most children are enthusiastic about studying, so perhaps their wishes would be different at some other time of the year. However, when I asked some Soviet friends to collect more wishes for me in the spring, and to do so in other parts of the country, the results turned out to be much the same. Although Ira, aged eight, wanted "to be as tall as Gulliver and as small as a gnome" and Olya wished that animals could talk, and Alyona dreamed of going to Artek, the famous Pioneer camp on the Black Sea, the majority of their wishes still related to friends, family, school success, and peace. Studies of North American children since the 1930s consistently show that a larger proportion of their wishes are for material goods, about 44 per cent of the total. Their wishes also tend to be more individualistic than those of the Soviet children who want "everyone in the class to study well" or that "Grandma and Grandpa would live for a long, long time."

Other evidence supports my conclusions that members of this generation of Soviet youngsters still value education, the natural

world, peace, family and friends more than possessions. Like
most young children, they are idealistic and patriotic but, in the
past, Soviet children's ideals have often had a hard time surviving
the realities of adult life. Now, however, it appears that their
belief in their country's vision has a chance of continuing beyond
adolescence. A poll taken in the autumn of 1987 revealed that 73
per cent of Soviet youngsters have recently developed more faith
in the feasibility of Soviet ideals. Teachers, too, have started to
report that the democratic principles that are now entering Soviet
life are producing "new children who take a lively interest in
everything that goes on around them".

A comparative study of American and Soviet teenagers conducted under the auspices of the Department of Psychiatry of
Harvard Medical School, the Center for International Studies at
MIT, and the Soviet Academy of Sciences, published in 1988,
reinforces these observations. It also points out an interesting contrast. While the Soviet youngsters are more worried about global
threats (nuclear war, the environment, and so forth) than are their
American contemporaries, they don't seem to take them as personally and are, generally speaking, considerably more optimistic
about the future. For example, 92 per cent of the Soviet sample
thought that the greatest problems facing world today could be
solved, as compared to 61 per cent of the Americans. And 71 per
cent of the Soviets thought life would be better for their children,
whereas only 50 per cent of the American teenagers had the same
expectation.

At the same time as I was collecting Soviet children's wishes in
School no. 59, Monique de Gramont, a Montreal journalist, was
using the same technique to gather the wishes of an equivalent
number of Canadian children. She went to a French-language
public school in Montreal where she discovered that, like some
of his Moscow counterparts, Mathieu wanted to travel in time.
"First of all I will go into prehistoric times. And I mustn't forget
my camera so I will have proof." Cassandre, like Olya, wanted
to talk to the animals. Ariel wished he could "fly out of the
galaxy, discover other inhabited worlds". Twenty-seven of the
Canadian children wished for world peace, nine for an end to
famine and poverty, five for the disappearance of pollution. In all

these categories, their wishes paralleled those of their age-mates in the Soviet Union.

But then the differences began. The Canadian girls had higher and more varied career aspirations than did the Soviet girls. Delphine wanted to become a pediatrician; Sophie and Barbara, international models; Ariane, a film producer. Among the Soviet girls only Marina, who wanted to be a teacher, and Margarita, who wanted to become a pianist, expressed any professional ambitions. But school, which was uppermost in the Soviet children's minds, rarely figured in the Canadian children's wishes. Nor did families and friends. And there was evidence of serious personal anxiety in the Canadian children's wishes that was quite absent from the Soviet children's, anxieties about loneliness, illness, and even death. De Gramont suggests that the natural optimism of children may be eaten away by the daily doses of disaster that are ladled out by the North American media, or, more disturbingly, by prolonged misery at home.

And if I were to catch a golden fish when I spread my net one day, what would *I* wish? The children never asked me, but I have been thinking about it. I, too, dream of world peace, but I now know too much about the human roots of violence to expect miracles. I also know, though, that the cycle that leads to both personal and public violence can be broken in childhood. So, my first wish for the Soviet children in Moscow's School no. 59, and for the Canadian children in Montreal, is that their childhoods be protected, full of love and respect, free from abuse, neglect, exploitation, and humiliation. My second wish is that all these children, Soviet and Canadian, boys and girls alike, be free to pursue their personal dreams: to travel, to have many friends, to achieve distinction in their chosen careers, and, while they are still children, to play and to have fun. And if the fish has any energy left after all that, then perhaps he might grant me my third wish, and conjure up a space bridge. Then Mathieu, Catherine, Fabrice, Ariane, and all their classmates in Montreal could sit down with Anton, Nadya, Olya, Sasha, and their Moscow friends, not just to watch passively while the twenty-first century unrolls on Sergei's magic TV set, but, all together, to make it happen.

Notes

Abbreviations

CDSP = *Current Digest of the Soviet Press;* a weekly journal of translations.
MN = *Moscow News*, the English edition of *Moskovskie novosti*.

Preface

page i

I have taken the definition of the genre, "The History of the Present", from Moshe Lewin who uses it in the preface to his perceptive book *The Gorbachev Phenomenon: A Historical Interpretation* (University of California Press, 1988). See also Geoffrey Hosking, *The Awakening of the Soviet Union* (Cambridge: Harvard University Press, 1990).

page ii

The definition of communism comes from *Political Terms: A Short Guide* compiled by Boris Putrin, trans. Valentin Kochetkov (Moscow: Novosti Press, 1982).

Introduction

Most useful general sources for Soviet context of children's lives:
Geoffrey Hosking, *A History of the Soviet Union* (Fontana, 1985).
Basile Kerblay, *Modern Soviet Society*, trans. Rupert Sawyer (Pantheon Books, 1983).
David Lane, *Soviet Economy and Society* (Oxford: Basil Blackwell, 1985)

Moshe Lewin, *The Making of the Soviet System* (New York: Pantheon Books, 1985).

Chapter 1

page 16

All quotations are from "The Tasks of the Youth Leagues", a speech delivered at the Third All-Russia Congress of the Russian Young Communist League, October 2, 1920. The English translation prepared by Progress Publishers appears in many collections of Lenin's writings, including V. I. Lenin, *On Religion* (Moscow: Progress Publishers, 1981), pp. 50–66.

page 19

The English text of Shatrov's play can be found in *Five of the Best Soviet Plays of the 1970s*, trans. M. Davidow and M. Gordeyeva (Moscow: Raduga, 1983).

page 21

The moral code of communism is quoted from Khrushchev's speech to the XXII Congress of the CPSU to be found in *The Documentary Record of the CPSU*, ed. C. Saikowski and L. Gruliow (Columbia University Press, 1962).

"The immense tasks..." from *The Basic Guidelines for School Reform* approved by the Supreme Soviet, April 12, 1984 (official translation), and a year later, in much the same tone, the CPSU committed itself to do everything necessary to shape "a harmoniously developed, socially active personality combining within itself spiritual richness, moral purity and physical perfection". *Pravda*, October 26, 1985.

page 25

Mikhail Gorbachev, *Perestroika—New Thinking for Our Country and the World* (Harper and Row, 1987).

Gorbachev's words are taken from the proceedings of the Four ₁ing Meeting of the V. I. Lenin Soviet Children's Fund, October 14, 1987 (Moscow: Prosveshchenie, 1988).

Chapter 2

page 37

Soviet authorities define *vospitanie* as the social formation of the child's values, motives and patterns of social response.

page 41

The observer was Michael Binyon, who was the correspondent for the London *Times* when we were there and the question is from his book, *Life in Russia* (New York: Pantheon Books, 1984).

page 44

Patrick Dunn's essay comes from *The History of Childhood*, ed. Lloyd de Mause (London: Souvenir Press, 1976).

Maxim Gorky's comments are from his book, *My Childhood*, trans. R. Wilks (Penguin, 1966).

Vladimir Nabokov's *Speak, Memory* (New York: G. P. Putnam's Sons, 1966) is a fascinating if idiosyncratic picture of childhood in Russia at the beginning of the century.

page 45

All quotations from Margaret Mead can be found in *Childhood in Contemporary Cultures*, ed. Margaret Mead and Martha Wolfenstein (University of Chicago Press, 1955).

All quotations from Urie Bronfenbrenner come from *Two Worlds of Childhood* (New York: Russel Sage Foundation, 1970).

The Soviet definitions of temperament, personality and character are to be found in *Doshkolnik* (pp. 45–48), one of the four volumes of *Mir detstva* (Moscow: Pedagogika, 1979), a series of books on child-rearing prepared by the Academy of Pedagogical Sciences to reflect prevailing psychological theories of child development.

page 46

The 1783 commentator was quoted by Patrick Dunn.

Leo Tolstoy, quoted in Nikolay Tolstoy, *The Tolstoys* (Coronet Books, 1985), p. 274.

page 48

Doshkolnik. *Mir detstva,* op. cit., p. 111

Yury Azarov on discipline from *A Book about Bringing up Children*, (Moscow: Progress Publishers, 1983), English translation.

page 51

Quotations used in this chapter are from *Anton Makarenko, His Life and His Work in Education*, trans. Katharine Judelson (Moscow: Progress Publishers, 1976).

page 53

The Russian and Soviet feeling for the collective is admirably described by John McLeish in *Soviet Psychology: History, Theory, Content* (London: Methuen, 1975).

page 54

On collectives, see A.V. Petrovsky, *The Collective and the Individual*, trans. Frances Longman (Moscow: Progress, 1985). See also L.I. Novikova and A. Lewin, "The Collective and the Personality of the Child", *International Review of Education*, vol. 16 (3) (1970):, 323–41.

page 59

Simon Soloveychik, "Goo-goo and the Bogeyman", trans. Eugenia Lockwood. *Soviet Psychology*, XXVI (2) (1987–88).

page 60

"It is…" from D. I. Feldshtein, in *Age-Group and Pedagogical P ;ychology*, trans. Inna P. Medow and John Crowfoot (Moscow: Progress Publishers, 1984), p. 308.

Lada Aidarova, *Child Development and Education*, trans. Lyudmilla Lezhneva (Moscow: Progress Publishers, 1982).

page 62

The discussion between Azarov and Dr. Spock is contained in the last chapter of Azarov's *A Book about Bringing up Children*, op. cit.

page 63

"A Capable Child…" is the title of an article by Lena and Boris Nikitin in *Quarterly Review of Education* 6(3) (1976): 470–79 in which they describe bringing up their seven children with very careful planning.

Chapter 3

page 72

The Family and Soviet History—the useful sources were as follows: J. Brine (ed.), *Home, School and Leisure in the Soviet Union* (George Allen and Unwin, 1980). April A. Von Frank, *Family Policy in the USSR since 1944* (Palo Alto, California: R. & E. Research Associates Inc., 1979). Gail Lapidus (ed.), *Women, Work and Family in the Soviet Union* (M. E. Sharpe Inc., 1982). Ludwig Liegle, *The Family's Role in Soviet Education* (New York: Springer, 1975).

page 73

Alexandra Kollontai's comments come from her 1918 article, "The New Morality and the Working Class", quoted by David Lane in *Politics and Society in the USSR* (Weidenfeld and Nicolson, 1970), p. 375.

page 74

"All social links..." from Nadezhda Mandelstam, *Hope Abandoned*, trans. Max Hayward (Penguin Books, 1976), p. 18.

"We have muddled..." from ibid., p. 679.

page 75

"The demographic policy..." from V. Yazykova, *Socialist Life Style and the Family*, trans. A. Lehto (Moscow: Progress Publishers, 1984), p. 173.

Viktor Perevedentsev has written numerous articles and booklets for public consumption on the topics of young families and on youth in the workplace. A useful article available in English is "The Social Maturity of School Graduates", *Soviet Education* 29(2) (1986).

page 77

Statistics and comments regarding average age of marriage from Yazykova, op. cit., p. 43.

page 78

Comments on problems in early years of marriage from E.S. Kalmykova, "Psychological Problems of the First Years of Marriage", translated in *Soviet Psychology*, XXII (3) (1984).

page 80

"*Limitchiks*"—article by Perevedentsev in *Ogonyok* 34 (1988), *CDSP* XXXIX (52).

page 81

Dyadya Vanya described by Leonid Sergeyev in *Morning Trams*, trans. Janet Butler (Moscow: Raduga, 1985).

Data regarding family budget and possessions from the *New York Times*, May 30, 1988 based on *USSR Facts and Figures* (Academic International Press, 1987), ed. John L. Scherer. Cars in 1985, 15 per 100 families from *CDSP* XL (30) (1988). Telephones from *Izvestia*, June 26, 1989. The Soviet Union ranks somewhere between the 50th and the 60th of the world's countries in terms of per capita consumption of goods and services [*MN* 34 (1988)].

page 85

Statistics from Perevedentsev and Yazykova. The former is particularly concerned about the phenomenon of fatherlessness. Reasons for divorce, Yazykova, op. cit., p. 146.

page 86

My information on the city of Moscow's department of marriage and the family came from an interview I had at City Hall with the head, A. F. Severina, and several of her colleagues.

page 87

Telefon Doveriya for adolescents, *CDSP* XL (36) (1988).

On birthrate: V. Perevedentsev, in *Semya*, 4 (1989).

page 89

Immolations in Tadzhikistan, *CDSP* XXXIX (32) (1987). Bride-price in Turkmenia, *Trud*, April 29, 1987 [*CDSP* XXXIX (21)]

Mandelstam's letter, op. cit., p. 693

page 90

Akhmatova from *Selected Poems*, ed. by Walter Arndt, trans. Robin Kemball (Ann Arbor: Ardis, 1979), p. 10

Chapter 4

Most of the material for this chapter comes from visits I made to kindergartens and schools and from interviews I had with students, parents, child-care workers, teachers, school directors and other educational authorities.

page 94

Quotations are from the *Fundamentals of Legislation of the USSR and the Union Republics on Public Education*, 1973, Section I, art. 4: "Basic Principles of Public Education in the USSR", in *Legislative Acts of the USSR*, Book 3, English text (Moscow: Progress Publishers, 1983).

page 96

In 1988 there were 17.5 million children in year round pre-school institutions (58 per cent of all children in this age group). However, many places are overcrowded and there were no spaces for 1.5 million children whose parents had requested them. (Report of USSR State Statistics Committee re 1988 Plan Fulfilment. *Pravda*, January 22, 1989 [*CDSP* XLI (4)].)

page 97

Krupskaya's kindergarten document is quoted from *Doshkolnoe vospitanie* 11(1982): 45–48, trans. Eugenia Lockwood.

Description of the pre-schooler's day is based on Kitty Weaver, *Lenin's Grandchildren: Pre-School Education in the Soviet Union* (New York: Simon and Schuster, 1971) and confirmed by my own experience fifteen years later.

page 99

Letter from a kind-hearted story-teller is quoted from A.I. Sorokina, *Didakticheskie igry v detskom sadu* (Moscow: Prosveshchenie, 1982), trans. Eugenia Lockwood.

page 102

Quote from Ada Baskina, "A Child Goes to School", *Soviet Life*, October 1986, p. 25.

page 106

The debate about lowering the age of school-entry is well described by John Dunstan in "Now They Are Six: Soviet Primary Education in Transition" in *Soviet Education in the 1980s*, ed. J. J. Tomiak (St. Martin's Press, 1983).

page 113

"It is really socially useful activity..." from Nadezhda Krupskaya, *On Labour-Oriented Education and Instruction* (Moscow: Progress Publishers, 1985), English edition.

page 114

The Pioneer movement in the school is fully described in *Kniga vozhatogo* (Moscow: Molodaya gvardiya, 1982) and is confirmed by my own experience.

page 117

Louis Menashe, "The New Wave from Russia", *New York Times Magazine*, May 5, 1985.

Roberta Markus, *Adaptation: A Case Study of Soviet Jewish Immigrant Children in Toronto* (Toronto: Permanent Press, 1979).

Chapter 5

page 128

Tsvetaeva's and Akhmatova's readings at the Polytechnical Museum are described by Ronald Hingley in *Nightingale Fever* (New York: Alfred Knopf, 1981), Chapters 7 and 15.

page 129

These concepts are further elaborated in an interview he had with Larisa Kuznetsova which she has published in her book *Femmes d'hier et d'aujourd'hui*, trans. Hélène Karlovski and Marc-Antoine Parra (Moscow: Progress Publishers, 1983), pp. 195–213.

The 1850 study is quoted from "Society and the Sexes in the Russian Past" by Dorothy Atkinson in *Women in Russia*, ed. D. Atkinson, A. Dallin and G. W. Lapidus (Stanford University Press, 1977), p. 34.

page 130

The data on the ratio of marriageable males to marriageable females was obtained from Viktor Perevedentsev.

page 133

Anton Makarenko, *The Collective Family*, trans. Robert Daglish (Anchor Books, 1967), p. 297.

page 134

The sections of Khripkova and Kolesov's book from which my quotations are taken to be found in *Soviet Education* 26 (1) (1983).

page 135

Kon's views on sex education from *Uchitelskaya Gazeta*, September 25, 1984, trans. Nina Ryan.

Course outline to be found in *Soviet Education* 29 (5 and 6) (1987).

Kon's response from "Openly about the Forbidden", *Ogonyok*, July 27, 1987, trans. Eugenia Lockwood.

page 136

Short stories with women as sexual aggressors were discussed in *Literaturnaya Gazeta*, January 1, 1985.

page 137

All quotations are taken from the text of *Etika i psikhologiya semeynoy zhizni* (Moscow: Prosveshchenie, 1984), trans. by Eugenia Lockwood, Nina Ryan and the author.

page 144

The wishes for Masha were printed in *MN* 10 (1988).

"Women want..." from a debate in *Literaturnaya Gazeta*, October 10, 1984 [translated in *CDSP* XXXVII (5) 1985], continued in *Literaturnaya Gazeta* 3 January 1, 1985.

page 146

I. Kon, "Sailing Directions in a Sea of Troubles", *Sovetskaya Rossiya*, August 31, 1984, trans. Nina Ryan.

Chapter 6

pages 150ff

Sources for history of Soviet psychology:
Alex Kozulin, *Psychology in Utopia* (MIT Press, 1984). John McLeish, *Soviet Psychology—History, Theory, Content* (London: Methuen, 1975). Jaan Valsiner, *Developmental Psychology in the Soviet Union* (Indiana University Press, 1988).

page 151

"Catching up with Davydov", *MN* 21 (1988).

pages 152ff

Books and articles by and about Vygotsky:
Alex Kozulin, "The Concept of Activity in Soviet Psychology", *American Psychologist*, March, 1986. Andrew Sutton, "Cultural Disadvantage and Vygotskii's Stages of Development", *Educational Studies* 6 (3) (1980). Stephen Toulmin, "The Mozart of Psychology", *New York Review of Books*, September 28, 1978. Lev Vygotsky, *Thought and Language*, trans. and ed. Alex Kozulin (MIT Press, 1986). Lev Vygotsky, *Mind and Society*, ed. Michael Cole, V. John Steiner, S. Scribner and E. Souberman (Harvard University Press, 1978). James V. Wertsch, *Vygotsky and the Social Formation of Mind* (Harvard University Press, 1985).

page 153

Alexandr Luria, *The Making of Mind*, ed. Michael Cole and Sheila Cole (Harvard University Press, 1970), p. 40.

page 156

Quotation from Davydov comes from his paper, "*Vozrastnye aspekty razvitiya vsestoronney i garmonichnoy lichnosti*", published in the collection *Psikhologo-pedagogicheskie problemy stanovleniya lichnosti i individualnosti v detskom vozraste* (Moscow: Akademiya Pedagogicheskikh Nauk, 1980), pp. 3–14.

Quotation from Dubrovina comes from her paper, "*Razvitie sposobnostey i formirovanie lichnosti shkolnika*", published in the above collection, pp. 156–60.

page 158

M. A. Zender and B. F. Zender, "Vygotsky's View about the Age Periodization of Child Development", *Human Development* 17 (1974): 24–40, contains translation of an article by Vygotsky on ages and stages.

Quotes from Lada Aidarova, from *Child Development and Education*, trans. Lyudmilla Lezhneva (Moscow: Progress Publishers, 1982).

Quotes from Valeriya Mukhina, from *Growing Up Human*, trans. Peter Greenwood (Moscow: Progress Publishers, 1984).

page 161

Vygotsky on play. See "Play and Its Role in the Mental Development of the Child", trans. Catherine Mulholland in *Soviet Developmental Psychology*, an anthology, ed. M. Cole (White Plains: M. E. Sharpe, 1977).

page 163

Tolstoy's comments on games are from his book, *Childhood, Boyhood, Youth*, trans. Rosemary Edmonds (Penguin, 1964), p. 37.

page 167

Definition of Praxis from Robert Heilbroner's clear and concise book *Marxism For and Against* (Norton, 1980).

Chapter 7

General Sources:

John Dunstan, *Paths to Excellence in Soviet Schools* (Windsor: NFER, 1978). Jim Riordan (ed.), *The Gifted and the Handicapped* (Routledge, 1988). Jane Knox, "The Changing Face of Soviet Defectology", *Soviet Thought*, vol. 38 (1988). Mike Lambert, "Deaf-Blind: Defying the Barriers", *Special Children*, February, 1988. Vladimir Lubovsky, "Some Urgent Problems of Soviet Work with Handicapped Children", *Soviet Education* 31 (5) (1989). Philip Stringer, "Special Education in the Soviet Union and the Child with Learning Difficulties", *AEP Journal* (Association of Educational Psychologists) 6 (4) (1984). Avril Suddaby, "A Temporary Phenomenon", *Special Children*, February 1987. Andrew Sutton, "Thoroughly Perfectible Pupils", *The Times Educational Supplement* 14 (10) (1988). Also by the same author, "The Soviet Experience", *Special Children*, February, 1987. "L. S. Vygotsky and Contemporary Defectology", *Soviet Psychology* XXI (4) (1983). See also XXVI (1)(1989).

page 175

The definition of defectology comes from V. I. Lubovsky, "Defectology: the Science of Handicapped Children", *International Review of Education* 20 (3) (1974).

page 176

Most of the information I received from Vlasova in the interview is also contained in the following two books: T.A. Vlasova and M.S. Pevzner, *O detyakh s otkloneniyami v razvitii* (Moscow: Prosveshchenie, 1973); *Obuchenie detey s zaderzhkoy psikhicheskogo razvitiya* (Moscow: Prosveshchenie, 1981), ed. T.A. Vlasova, V.I. Lubovsky and N. A. Nikishina.

page 181

Quotations from A. I. Meshcheryakov from *Awakening to Life: Forming Behaviour and the Mind in Deaf-Blind Children*, trans. Katharine Judelson (Moscow: Progress Publishers, 1974).

page 190

Zone of *next* development (Americans translate it "proximal"): "the distance between the actual developmental level as determined by independent problem solving and the level of potential development as determined through problem solving under adult guidance or in collaboration with more capable peers". L.S. Vygotsky, *Mind and Society*, ed. M. Cole et al. (Harvard University Press, 1978), p. 86.

page 193

I have supplemented Lebedinskaya's comments with information from a book she edited in 1982, *Aktualnye problemy diagnostiki zaderzhki psikhicheskogo razvitiya detey* (Moscow: Pedagogika, 1982).

page 197

For knowledge of this debate I am indebted to my friend Jeanne Sutherland, the widow of Sir Iain Sutherland who was the British Ambassador to the Soviet Union during the second half of our posting there. Lady Sutherland wrote a Master's thesis for the University of London in 1975 on special schools for talented children and has pursued her interest in the subject.

page 198

Debate about special language schools is represented by a series of articles from various newspapers translated in *CDSP* XXXIX (8) (1987).

Akademgorodok—The science competition is described by Academician Mikhail Lavrentiev in *Prospects* 5 (2) (1975).

Chapter 8

page 207

U. N. Convention on the Rights of the Child—text widely avail ible from UNICEF offices.

page 209

Constitution (Fundamental Law) of the USSR (English edition) (Moscow: Novosti Press Agency Publishing House, 1984).

page 210

References to be found in *Soviet Legislation on Children's Rights* (English text) (Moscow: Progress Publishers, 1982) and in *Legislative Acts of the USSR*, vol. 3 (English text) (Moscow: Progress Publishers, 1982).

page 213

Kidnapping—*CDSP* XL (4) (1988).

page 214

There is a good discussion of Soviet family law by Yury Luryi in *The Manitoba Law Journal* 10 (2) (1980).

page 216

Rape of Minor—see Valery Savitsky, "What to punish and how", *New Times* 8 (1989) p. 29.

page 218

Article on children's home translated by Nina Ryan.

page 220

Alexandra Kollontai, *Selected Articles and Speeches*, trans. Cynthia Carlile (Moscow: Progress Publishers, 1984).

page 222

Authority from Institute of Crime Prevention interviewed in *Neaelya*, 7, 1985 [*CDSP* XXXVII (6)].

page 223

Judges—Besides Judge Orlov, the other two "judges" were actually "people's assessors", the Soviet counterpart of American lay jurors. See article by George P. Fletcher called "In Gorbachev's Courts", *New York Review of Books*, May 18, 1989.

page 225

212,457 minors took part in commission of crime in 1989, a 14.9 per cent growth since 1988. One-third of crimes committed in groups. Thirty-six per cent of law breakers come from single-parent homes. *Izvestia*, February 30, 1990, translated in *CDSP* XLII (8).

"Barbed Wire Sky", *Ogonyok* 3 (1988), translated in *CDSP* XL, (9).

page 227

From *Komsomolskaya Pravda*, August 4–7, 1989, translated in *CDSP* XXXV (34). In 1988 there were approximately 30,000 juveniles being held in 88 educational labour colonies of whom 1,400 were girls, *CDSP* XLI (11) (1989).

Chapter 9

page 232

Nuclear accidents were at Chernobyl and near Chelyabinsk in the Urals in 1957.

page 233

History of Soviet medicine from William A. Knaus, M.D., *Inside Russian Medicine* (New York: Everest House, 1981).

page 238

Chazov's complaints about maternity homes and other comments about the poor state of the Soviet health system are from an interview with him in *Literaturnaya Gazeta*, April 29, 1989 [*CDSP* XXXIX (19)]. In 1990 Chazov was removed as minister.

page 239

Latest infant mortality rates from *Argumenty i Fakty* 45 (1989) [*CDSP* XLI (50)]. Re situation in the 1970s see Murray Feshbach and Christopher Davis, *Rising Infant Mortality in the USSR in the 1970s*—US Department of Commerce, Bureau of the Census-Series, P–95, no. 74, September 1980.

page 240

"Smoking like chimneys", *Literaturnaya Gazeta*, August 1, 1984 [*CDSP* XXVI (51) (1984)]. "Breast alcoholism", *Izvestia*, July 4, 1984. A brief drop in unhealthy newborns after Gorbachev's resolution on alcoholism in 1985 had translated itself by 1989 into a powerful upsurge, *Izvestia*, October 30, 1989 [*CDSP* XLI (44)].

page 241

Abortion—In 1988 70–80 per cent of all first pregnancies of city dwellers and 90 per cent of rural ones were ending in abortion, nearly 8 million a year. Eighty per cent of the population were using ineffective contraception and only 10 per cent of demand for contraceptives could be met. *CDSP* XL (27).

page 243

Dr. M. Studenikin, *Kniga o zdorovye detey* (Moscow: Meditsina, 1985).

page 248

A.G. Khripkova and D.V. Kolesov, "Hygiene and Sex Education of General Education School Pupils", *Soviet Education* 26 (1) (1983).

page 250

Man and human health curriculum can be found in *Soviet Education* 29 (5 and 6) (1987).

AIDS in babies, *Pravda*, January 28, 1989 [*CDSP* XLI (5)].

page 251

Overweight American children—Teenage obesity has escalated to 39 per cent since 1960 in the USA and for children 6–11, 54 per cent. Eighty-five per cent fail physical fitness tests. Reported in *Globe and Mail*, January 10, 1989.

page 253

Teeth—*Izvestia*, January 6, 1985 and February 20, 1985, translated in *CDSP* XXXVII (1 and 8) (1985).

page 254

Folk remedies. See Nancy Condee, "Russian Remedies", *The Wilson Quarterly* XII, (3) (1988): 167–71.

page 255

Mental health—Dr. Nancy Rollins, *Child Psychiatry in the Soviet Union* (Harvard University Press, 1972). See also *Soviet Neurology and Psychiatry*, a journal of translations (Armonk, N.Y.: M.E. Sharpe) for further confirmation of Soviet approaches to mental illnesses in children, e.g. XVII, (4) (1985) on epilepsy, depression and *anorexia nervosa*; XIX, (1) (1986) on family history in schizophrenia; and XX (1) (1987) on medical-genetic counselling of families of mentally retarded children.

page 258

Self-destructive behaviour, *CDSP* XL (36) (1988).

Chapter 10

Background books and articles (history and theory):
N.I. Ponomaryov, *Sport and Society*, trans. Jim Riordan (Moscow: Progress Publishers, 1981). Jim Riordan, *Sport in Soviet Society* (Cambridge University Press, 1977). Also by Riordan "Giftedness in Sport" in John Dunstan (ed.) *Soviet Education—the Gifted and the Handicapped* (Routledge, 1988). N.N. Schneidman, *The Soviet Road to Olympus, Theory and Practice of Soviet Physical Culture and Sport* (Toronto: OISE Press, 1978).

page 269

Vlasov's comments in an interview in *MN* 37 (1988).
Interview with Mukhina, *MN* 10 (1987).

page 270

Re physical education, see Jim Riordan, "School Physical Education in the Soviet Union", *Physical Education Review* 9 (2) (1986): 100–117. See also G.I. Kukushkin, *The System of Physical Education in the USSR*, trans. A. Zdornykh (Moscow: Raduga, 1983).

page 275

Vladislav Tretiak, *Tretiak: The Legend*, trans. Sam and Maria Budman (Edmonton: Plains Publishing Inc., 1987).

page 277

Re children and sports see M. Kondratyeva and V. Taborko, *Children and Sport*, trans. Christopher English (Moscow: Progress Publishers, 1979), as well as G.I. Kukushkin, op. cit.

page 289

Children's lore is admirably defined by Iona and Peter Opie in *The Lore and Language of Schoolchildren* (Oxford University Press, 1959).

page 290

M. Osorina and O.N. Grechina, "Modern Folklore Stories of Children" in *Russky folklor* XX (1981), trans. Nina Ryan.

page 296

Bruno Bettelheim, "The Importance of Play", *The Atlantic*, March 1987.

Chapter 11

page 301

Obraztsov comments about children and art are further elaborated in his book *My Profession*, trans. Doris Bradbury (Moscow: Raduga, 1985), which is well worth reading for what it has to say about the art of puppetry.

page 302

Leo Tolstoy, *What is Art?*, trans. Aylmer Maude (London: Oxford University Press, 1930).

page 305

Much of the information on children's theatre comes from Miriam Morton's descriptive but uncritical book, *The Arts and the Soviet Child* (New York: The Free Press, 1972). To my knowledge, there is no other book by an English-speaking non-Soviet writer that addresses this aspect of Soviet children's lives. Another source more up to date but in Russian is Z.Y. Korogodsky, *Vash drug, teatr* (Moscow: Znanie, 1984).

page 306

The code of conduct is quoted in Morton, op. cit., p. 77 and confirmed by my own experience.

page 308

Yevgeny Shvarts, *The Dragon*, trans. Max Hayward and Harold Shukman (Penguin, 1966).

page 309

"To talk about love..." from Korogodsky, *Vash drug, teatr*, op. cit., p. 78.

page 310

The quotes from Natalya Sats (and Shostakovich) come from her book *Novelly moey zhizni* (Moscow: Iskusstvo, 1979).

page 312

Banevich is quoted from his program notes to *The Story of Gerda and Kai*.

page 313

Re music schools. This information was published in the magazine *Soviet Union* in February 1987, which added that there were also around 1,000 children's choral groups in the Soviet Union as well as, in the Russian Federation alone, 25,000 amateur music groups involving 1,500,000 children.

page 315

In *Soviet Education* 30 (1) (1988) there is a translation of Kabalevsky's school program including an introduction by Dr. Davydov.

page 316

Nemensky's lament was published in *Literaturnaya Gazeta*, February 19, 1986, trans. Eugenia Lockwood.

page 318

The manual for pre-school teachers on teaching arts and crafts *Metodika obucheniya izobrazitel-noy deyatelnosti i konstruirovaniyu* (Moscow: Prosveshchenie, 1979).

page 319

The account of the mural disaster is from *Izvestia*, April 16, 1986 [*CDSP* XXXVIII (15)].

page 322

The discussion of aesthetic education is paraphrased from an article translated in *Soviet Education* 22 (5) (1980) entitled "Psychological Principles in the Aesthetic Development of Children and the Problem of Aesthetic Education" by Z.N. Novlyanskaya and A.A. Melik-Pashaev. This was the article that first alerted me to Nemensky.

page 326

The quotation is from Rolan Bykov's article "Before and After 'The Scarecrow' ", *Yunost* (9) (1985): 90, trans. Eugenia Lockwood.

Chapter 12

page 330

Soviet Children's Books—Almost all the books I mention are available in English translations, although some are out of print. While I have read many of these (and other) works in Russian, I thought it would be of more interest to an English-speaking reader to discuss books that are accessible to our own children as well. Most of the books are translated and printed in Moscow, but there are two exceptions which I would like to mention here, because both are worth reading: Chinghiz Aitmatov, *The White Ship*, trans. Mirra Ginsburg (New York: Crown Publishers, 1972) and Yevgeny Ryss, *Search behind the Lines,* trans. Bonnie Carey (New York: William Morrow, 1974). I am also aware that I have left many writers out of the bookcase for lack of space but would like to add three here who are well known for their translations: Boris Zakhoder, who translated *Winnie-the-Pooh* and *Mary Poppins* and himself writes high-spirited tales and poems for young children; Alexandr Volkov, who adapted *The Wizard of Oz* for Russian children; and Natalya Demurova, who translated *Alice in Wonderland*. Also I must mention Yury Koval, who was voted the most popular author of 1987 by children all across the USSR.

page 331

For Maxim Gorky on books see *On Literature* (University of Washington Press, 1973).

page 338

Korney Chukovsky, *From Two to Five*, trans. and ed. by Miriam Morton (University of California Press, 1968). See also Lydia Chukovskaya, *To the Memory of Childhood*, trans. Eliza Close (Northwestern University Press, 1989). There is a full discussion of Chukovsky and Marshak and some of the other children's poets in E. Sokol's book *Russian Poetry for Children* (Knoxville: University of Tennessee Press, 1984).

page 340

"Fish are…" trans. Alisa Lockwood.

"It served…" trans. Eugenia Lockwood.

page 354

See *Knizhny golod*, "Soviet Book Hunger", John and Carol Garrard, *Problems of Communism*, September–October 1985.

page 355

My information about the House of Children's Books (*Dom detskoy knigi*) comes from a visit I made to it in 1983 and material I received from its director later.

page 358

Lada Aidarova on learning to read is from her book, *Child Development and Education*, trans. Lyudmilla Lezhneva (Moscow: Progress Publishers, 1982).

page 361

Two excellent books describe the ideological content of the literature lesson in Soviet times: Felicity Ann O'Dell, *Socialization through Children's Literature: The Soviet Example* (Cambridge University Press, 1978). N.N. Schneidman, *Literature and Ideology in Soviet Education* (Toronto: Lexington Books, 1973).

page 362

The outline of the literature curriculum is to be found translated in *Soviet Education*, 29 (11 and 12) (1987).

page 363

Ilyin is quoted in *Komsomolskaya Pravda*, August 1986, trans. Eugenia Lockwood.

page 365

From Boris Pasternak, *Selected Poems*, trans. Jon Stallworthy and Peter France (Penguin Books, 1984) p. 154.

Chapter 13

A very full bibliography on soviet education and related topics is published regularly in the *Soviet Education Study Bulletin*. Its editorial address is: Dr. John Dunstan, c/o CREES, University of Birmingham, P.O. Box 363, Birmingham, England, B15 2TT.

page 368

What "polytechnism" means for Soviet education is that Soviet students are supposed to be taught the scientific knowledge from which industrial and agricultural technologies are derived.

page 373

Russian Roots of Soviet Education, see Nicholas Hans, *The Russian Tradition in Education* (Routledge and Kegan Paul, 1963).

page 374

Quotation in *Catherine the Great* from J. L. Black, "Citizenship Training and Moral Regeneration as the Mainstay of Russian Schools", in *Studies on Voltaire and the Eighteenth Century* (Oxford: The Voltaire Foundation, 1977).

page 375

Quotation from K. Ushinsky in *Man as the Object of Education* (Moscow: Progress Publishers, 1978).

page 376

Tolstoy—quote from a letter to S.N. Tolstaya in *Tolstoy's Letters*, Vol. II, ed. and trans. R.F. Christian (New York: Charles Scribner's Sons, 1978), p. 618.

page 377

Narkompros—see Sheila Fitzpatrick, *Education and Social Mobility in the Soviet Union 1921–1934* (Cambridge University Press, 1979).

Quotation from Stanislav Shatsky—*A Teacher's Experience*, trans. Katharine Judelson (Moscow: Progress Publishers, 1981).

page 378

Pavel Blonsky—see Alex Kozulin, *Psychology in Utopia* (MIT Press, 1984). Also A.A. Nicholskaya, "The Works of Blonsky", translated in *Soviet Education*, 23 (11) (1981).

M. G. Danilchenko, "P. P. Blonsky on the School and the Teacher", translated in *Soviet Education*, 23 (11) (1981).

page 379

Anatoly Lunacharsky, *On Education*, trans. Ruth English (Moscow: Progress Publishers, 1981).

page 380

Quotes from Nadezhda Krupskaya from *On Labour-Oriented Education and Instruction* (Moscow: Progress Publishers, 1985), p. 51.

Blonsky, quoted in Kozulin, op. cit.

page 380

On Makarenko see *Sovetskaya Kultura*, February 6, 1988. Quotes from *Anton Makarenko. His Life and His Work in Education*, trans. Katharine Judelson (Moscow: Progress Publishers, 1976).

page 381

"...fourteen- and fifteen-year-olds..." *CDSP* XXXIX (34) (1987).

page 382

"Poverty..." quoted in Kozulin, op. cit., p. 133.

"...why make it possible..." from Krupskaya, op. cit., p. 111.

page 383

Gorbachev's youth described in an article by Archie Brown in *Problems of Communism*, May–June 1985.

page 385

Quotation from Sukhomlinsky from *On Education*, trans. Katharine Judelson (Moscow: Progress, 1977).

page 386

Vasily Sukhomlinsky, *To Children I Give My Heart*, trans. Holly Smith (Moscow: Progress Publishers, 1981).

page 388

"...organic union..." from *Sovetskaya Rossiya*, March 23, 1984. The best summary of the reform in English is "Soviet Education beyond 1984: A Commentary of the Reform Guidelines" by John Dunstan in *Compare* 15 (2) (1985).

page 389

I. Kon in *Pravda*, January 16, 1984.

"General labour training" *CDSP* XXXVI (42) (1984).

School no. 59, about which I have written so often, has close links with the Ministry of Mineral Fertilizers, which helps when there are problems, and provides financial support. Children from the school do not work at any factory, but work shops are located in the school. Boys learn some professions connected with construction, like house painting and plaster work. Girls sew, and also make some simple things for a tailoring establishment.

page 390

"Students killing time" see *CDSP* XXXVII (17) (1985). See also Perevedentsev, "The Social Maturity of School Graduates", *Soviet Education*, 29 (2) (1986).

page 391

See also Soloveychik's weekly column "Junior World" in the weekly journal *New Times*.

page 392

Shatalov — see Soloveychik in "How to Teach Math", *Soviet Life*, September 1986, and in "The Teacher and the Class", *Soviet Union* 1 (1987). See also Avril Suddaby on Shatalov in *Soviet Education Study Bulletin* 3 (1) (1985), 6 (1) (1988), and 7 (1) (1989) ("Perestroika in Soviet Education"); also Jeanne Sutherland in 7 (1) (1989), "Soviet Education since 1984".

page 393

"Pedagogy of Cooperation" translated in *Soviet Education*, 30 (1) (1988). See also "The Methodology of Reform", *Soviet Education*, 31 (7) (1989).

page 394

Uchitelskaya Gazeta—see reports in *MN* 8 (1988) and 47 (1988) as well as *CDSP* XL (50) (1988).

Teachers' Congress — *Pravda*, December 21, 1988, translated in *CDSP* XL (52).

Chapter 14

page 402

With respect to the nationalities question Lenin said: "What we want is a voluntary union of nations—the kind of union that will permit no coercion to be visited by one nation upon another— the kind of union that is founded upon the most complete trust, upon a lucid awareness of fraternal unity, upon wholly voluntary consent." Quoted in *The Soviet Multinational School under Developed Socialism*, ed. F.G. Panachin, translated in *Soviet Education*, 28 (5–6) (1986): 19.

On February 25, 1986 Gorbachev reported to the XXVII Party Congress: "Our Party's tradition traceable to Lenin of being particularly circumspect and tactful in all that concerns the nationalities policy...calls at the same time for resolute struggle against national narrow-mindedness and arrogance...." (Official translation.)

page 403

A resolution of the XIX Party Conference (1988) restated the principles of unity in diversity as 1) the internationalist unity of working peoples, 2) the right to self-determination, 3) the revival and development of national cultures, 4) acceleration of progress in formerly backward national regions, 5) overcoming of discord among nationalities. (Official translation.)

page 412

"...not a mere conglomerate...of nations". This and the following quotations translated by Caroline Lussier come from the social-studies textbook for senior high-school students used during the 1980s, *Obshchestvovedenie* (Moscow: Prosveshchenie, 1981).

page 417

The attitude of Soviet native people to the idea of a reservation is now changing as they begin to agitate for growing autonomy based on "reserved" territories—see *CDSP* XLI (14) (1989).

page 419

Statistics for Canadian Native Populations come from the *Globe and Mail*, Saturday, March 21, 1987. Those for the American are from the *Wilson Quarterly* X (1) (1986), which contains a special report on American Indians.

page 418

An excellent survey of the history and situation of the peoples of the Soviet North is to be found in the Fall/Winter 1988 issue of *Inuktitut*, published by Indian and Northern Affairs, Canada. Most of my statistics come from it. See also V.N. Uvachan, *The Peoples of the North and Their Road to Socialism*, trans. S. Shcherbovich (Moscow: Progress Publishers, 1975).

page 422

Rytkheu writes about his grandmother in "People of the Long Spring", *National Geographic* 163 (2) (1983). The joke about the researcher also comes from this article.

page 426

The Soviet–Canadian Arctic Exchange Program begun in 1984 has been very successful, particularly with respect to Theme IV of the protocol, Education. See my article "Neighbours Across the Arctic" in *The Soviet Education Study Bulletin* 7 (1) (1989).

page 427

Study on Evenk youth from *BAM i narody Severa*, ed. V.I. Boiko (Novosibirsk: USSR Academy of Sciences, 1979). There are two interesting articles on educational policies related to the nationalities in *Soviet Education in the 80s* (ed. Tomiak): Nigel Grants, "Linguistic and Ethnic Minorities in the USSR; Educational Policies and Development", and Frances Cooley, "National Schools in the Yakutskaya ASSR".

page 429

Quote from Nadezhda Mandelstam from *Hope Abandoned*, trans. Max Hayward (Penguin Books, 1976), p. 191.

Chapter 15

page 436

Rituals—much of this information comes from an excellent study called *The Rites of Rulers* by Christel Lane (Cambridge University Press, 1981).

page 437

From *Doshkolnik. Mir detstva* (Moscow: Pedagogika, 1979), p. 336.

page 440ff

Marxist-Leninist world view: the fact that children of *glasnost* have been trained in it is important not because they will necessarily hold on to its basic tenets, but because many, if not most of them, will continue to look at the world in a single-minded way, rather than use the pluralistic approach that comes from a more open form of education.

page 441

Course outline for history translated in *Soviet Education*, 29 (11 and 12) (1987).

page 443

Cancelled history exams and new texts—*Izvestia*, September 4, 1988, translated in *CDSP* XL (36).

page 444

Debating students—reported by Philip Taubman, *NYT*, October 13, 1988.

page 445

American children's military-patriotic education is described by Robert Coles in *The Political Life of Children* (Atlantic, 1986), p. 254.

page 446

The textbook for the course on military training is *Voenno-patrioticheskoe vospitanie uchashchikhsya na zanyatiyakh po nachalnoy voennoy podgotovke* (Moscow: Prosveshchenie, 1984).

page 447

Zarnitsa—a 1989 movie from Gorky Studios entitled "Until First Blood" directed by V. Fokin examines critically the impact that these games have on the children who play them, indicating that they continue to be popular.

page 448

Slogan for 1989—*CDSP* XLI (15) (1989).

page 460

From Chekhov's letter to A.S. Suvorin in *Letters of Anton Chekhov*, selected and edited by Avrahm Yarmolinsky (New York: Viking Press, 1973).

page 461

See *Seeds for Peace, The Role of Pre-School Education in International Understanding and Education for Peace* (UNESCO, 1985).

page 463

Soldiers in Afghanistan—David Shipler, *NYT*, April 28, 1988.

Afterword

page 465

A study prepared for the 8th Conference of the International Association for Cross-Cultural Psychology in Istanbul (Turkey) in 1986 by Thomas A. Fournier, Monique Lortie-Lussier and Gloria L. Fellers of the University of Ottawa entitled "Canadian Children's Wishes" lists nine other studies of a similar nature.

page 467

Poll quoted in "Change of Generations", *Izvestia*, May 20, 1988, translated in *CDSP* XL (20).

"...new children..." N.N. Paltyshev, a teacher from Odessa speaking at the Teachers' Congress in December 1988 (quoted in *Izvestia*, December 22, 1988).

"American and Soviet Teenagers' Concerns about Nuclear War and the Future." Eric Chivian, M.D., J.P. Robinson, Ph.D., J.R.H. Tudge, Ph.D., N.P. Popov, D.Sc., F.G. Andreyenkov, Ph.D. *New England Journal of Medicine* 319 (1988): 407–413.

"*Si Une Fée T'Accordait Trois Voeux...*" Monique de Gramont, *Châtelaine*, January 1988 (translations mine).

Index